Here's What You Get on the CD:

he CD included with the second edition of the *MCSE: Proxy Server 2 Study Guide* contains invaluable programs and information to help you prepare for your MCSE exams. You can access and install the files on the CD through a user-friendly graphical interface by running the CLICKME.EXE file located in the root directory.

 System Requirements: 486/100MHz, 16MB RAM, 2×CD-ROM, SoundBlaster-compatible sound card, 640×480, 256-color display, Windows 95/NT 4 or later.

The Sybex CD interface is supported only by Windows 95 and Windows NT. To access the CD contents from Windows 3.x, you must use File Manager.

The Sybex MCSE Edge Tests for Proxy Server 2

Test your knowledge with *The Sybex MCSE Edge Test for Proxy Server 2*, a custom version of The Edge Tests, designed exclusively for Sybex by The Edge Group. All of the questions from your Sybex MCSE Study Guide are presented in an advanced testing engine, along with bonus questions to further aid in your studies. We've included versions of the test for Windows 3*x* systems, as well as Windows 95 and NT 4 systems. To install the Edge Test for Windows 3.1 or 3.11, run the SETUP16.EXE file located in the EDGE\PLTFRM16 folder on the CD.

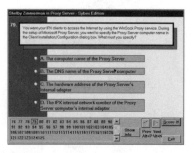

Network Press MCSE Study Guide Sampler

Preview chapters from the best-selling line of MCSE study guides from Sybex. We've also included a copy of the Adobe Acrobat Reader, which you'll need to view the various preview chapters. From the core requirements to the most popular electives, you'll see why Sybex MCSE Study Guides have become the self-study method of choice for tens of thousands seeking MCSE certification.

Microsoft Train_Cert Offline *Update and* Internet Explorer 4.0

Look to Microsoft's *Train_Cert Offline Update*, a quarterly snapshot of Microsoft's Education and Certification Web site, for all of the information you need to plot your course for MCSE certification. You'll need to run *Internet Explorer 4.0* to access all of the features of the *Train_Cert Offline* Web site, so we've included a free copy on the CD. To install *Internet Explorer 4.0*, run the SETUP.EXE file located in the MICROSFT\IE3\CD folder. To install the *Train_Cert Offline* Web site to your system, run the SETUP file located in the MICROSFT\OFFLINE folder.

 Please consult the README file located in the root directory for more detailed information on the CD contents.

MCSE: Proxy Server 2
Study Guide

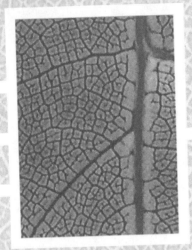

MCSE: Proxy Server 2
Study Guide

Erik Rozell
and Todd Lammle
with James Chellis

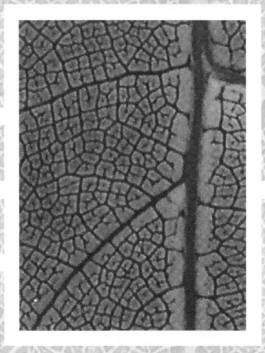

San Francisco • Paris • Düsseldorf • Soest

NETWORK PRESS®
SYBEX

Associate Publisher: Guy Hart-Davis
Contracts and Licensing Manager: Kristine Plachy
Acquisitions & Developmental Editor: Neil Edde
Editor: Shelby Zimmerman
Technical Editor: Eric Vasserman
Book Designer: Patrick Dintino
Graphic Illustrator: Andrew Benzie
Electronic Publishing Specialist: Bill Gibson
Production Coordinator: Duncan Watson
Production Assistants: Beth Moynihan and Rebecca Rider
Indexer: Nancy Guenther
Companion CD: Molly Sharp and John D. Wright
Cover Designer: Archer Design
Cover Photographer: FPG International

Library of Congress Card Number: 97-80847
ISBN: 0-7821-2194-2

Manufactured in the United States of America

10 9 8 7 6 5 4 3

November 1, 1997

Dear SYBEX Customer:

Microsoft is pleased to inform you that SYBEX is a participant in the Microsoft® Independent Courseware Vendor (ICV) program. Microsoft ICVs design, develop, and market self-paced courseware, books, and other products that support Microsoft software and the Microsoft Certified Professional (MCP) program.

To be accepted into the Microsoft ICV program, an ICV must meet set criteria. In addition, Microsoft reviews and approves each ICV training product before permission is granted to use the Microsoft Certified Professional Approved Study Guide logo on that product. This logo assures the consumer that the product has passed the following Microsoft standards:

- The course contains accurate product information.
- The course includes labs and activities during which the student can apply knowledge and skills learned from the course.
- The course teaches skills that help prepare the student to take corresponding MCP exams.

Microsoft ICVs continually develop and release new MCP Approved Study Guides. To prepare for a particular Microsoft certification exam, a student may choose one or more single, self-paced training courses or a series of training courses.

You will be pleased with the quality and effectiveness of the MCP Approved Study Guides available from SYBEX.

Sincerely,

Holly Heath
ICV Account Manager
Microsoft Training & Certification

MICROSOFT INDEPENDENT COURSEWARE VENDOR PROGRAM

Erik Rozell: To my mother Eleanor, my biggest fan and worst critic

Acknowledgments

I would like to recognize, with much appreciation, my friend and colleague, Mary Pablo, for her assistance as my pre-submission editor. Mary is an accomplished manager at a large, national firm, where she is responsible for the coordination and control of over 200 stores. Mary's vast computer experience and insight regarding people helped her convert many of my overly technical sections to text that could be understood in layman's terms. Thank you, Mary.

I also want to express gratitude to my project manager, Todd Lammle, for getting the contract to write this book and locating valuable add-in material. I first met Todd while working at Toshiba, where he introduced me to writing for Sybex. I have written chapters for his *MCSE: TCP/IP for NT Server 4 Study Guide* and he has written a few for me. Since that time, Todd and I have worked on a number of projects together and have developed a close working relationship that has ultimately resulted in this book. Thanks again Todd… and see you on the cover.

Without a network to test on, this book would have been impossible. I would like to thank Dennis Rozell for setup and maintenance of our Windows NT test lab. A fantastic and efficient network engineer, Dennis is a systems consultant with more than 23 years of experience doing integration at all levels.

Additional thanks to William Joseph Scully III (Bill) for his help developing exercises and creating implementation instructions and procedures. Bill is a network technician at NetPro Computer Services, where he handles application implementation, desktop support, and system deployment for a variety of companies. Bill's experience with user-level understanding helped make our exercises accessible and accurate.

Also, I would like to thank Eric Vasserman, who performed the technical edit for this book. Eric is an excellent engineer who has done work for Lockheed Martin Corporation, the city of Los Angeles, and NetPro Computer Services. Thanks again for the assistance, Eric.

Many thanks are due to our editors, Shelby Zimmerman and Jim Compton. Shelby and Jim edited the text in preparation for printing. They displayed seasoned skill toward addressing this book's audience. Further, I would like to thank Neil Edde. Neil's sharp intellect, dry wit, and positive attitude, combined with his limitless patience, guided the development and evolution of this project.

Thanks also to Sybex's Duncan Watson, production coordinator, Bill Gibson, electronic publishing specialist, and Andrew Benzie, illustrator, for all their work to make this book a reality.

While the following people have not directly helped with the book, they have been inspiring in the development of it:

Elias Abughazeleh: E.D.B.T.Z. (abbreviation of a proverb); Mark Bales: Don't let what you can't do get in the way of what you can; Guillermo Chapa: Every dog has its day; Norm Corison: I'm stunned (sarcasm on technology); Colin O. Cox: If it was important, don't you think I would have already heard about it?… Slacker; John Gordon: Why not… everyone else seems to have won (the lottery); Yury Furman: Faster is not good enough; Jeff Freilach: Make Sure (stock market advice); Haijin (Jim) Hu: What do you mean you have to turn it on?; Danielle Khim: One day…; Frank J. LaChapelle: Money is fun but health is number one; Peter Luk: Watch what you say; Heather Miller: We're all salespeople through the road of life; Hector Moreno: Not Me!; David Nordstrom: Do they really make hamburgers out of kangaroo meat?; Denelle L. Rozell: No problem; Stacy D. Rozell: Sanitize before you use it; Ronda Rozell: Ok. But can I keep it?; Jim Shaw: That's what they think!; Greg Silver: Full speed ahead… it will reveal all product defects; Steve Smith: It all goes somewhere…; Noel S. Stoyanoff: Sounds good to me; Ken Tcheng & Dana Bowdish: Imagine that!; Shaun Walsh: Don't sweat the small stuff… it's all small stuff; Dino Wibowo: No comment… I prefer not to prove it; George Wolder: Oceanside is better (on retirement); Phil Yee: It all ends up here.

Contents at a Glance

Table of Contents

Table of Exercises

Introduction

The Microsoft Certified Systems Engineer (MCSE) certification is *the* hottest ticket to career advancement in the computer industry today. Hundreds of thousands of corporations and organizations worldwide are choosing Windows NT for their networks. This means that there is a tremendous need for qualified personnel and consultants to help implement NT. The MCSE certification is your way to show these corporations and organizations that you have the professional abilities they need.

This book was approved by the Microsoft Corporation because it gives you the knowledge and skills you need to prepare for one of the key elective exams of the MCSE certification program: Microsoft Proxy Server 2.0 on Microsoft Windows NT. Certified by Microsoft, this book presents the information you need to acquire a solid foundation in the field of Microsoft Proxy Server, to prepare for the Windows NT Proxy Server 2.0 exam, and to take a big step toward MCSE certification.

Is This Book for You?

If you want to learn how Microsoft Windows NT Proxy Server 2.0 works, this book is for you. You'll find clear explanations of the fundamental concepts you need to grasp.

If you want to become certified as a Microsoft Certified Systems Engineer (MCSE), this book is also for you. *Microsoft Certified Professional Magazine* recently published a survey revealing that the average MCSE is earning well over $70,000 per year, while the average MCSE consultant is earning over $95,000 per year. If you want to acquire the solid background you need to pass Microsoft's most popular elective exam, move a step closer to your MCSE, and boost your career efforts, this book is for you.

What Does This Book Cover?

Think of this book as your guide to Microsoft Windows NT Proxy Server 2.0. It covers topics such as installing and configuring Proxy Sever, troubleshooting problems, selecting equipment, choosing an ISP, and much more.

How Do You Become an MCSE?

Attaining Microsoft Certified Systems Engineer (MCSE) status is a challenge. The exams cover a wide range of topics and require dedicated study and expertise. This is, however, why the MCSE certificate is so valuable. If becoming an MCSE was too easy, the market would be quickly flooded by MCSEs and the certification would become meaningless. Microsoft, keenly aware of this fact, has taken steps to ensure that the certification means its holder is truly knowledgeable and skilled.

To become an MCSE, you must pass four core requirements and two electives. For a complete description of all the MCSE core requirement options go to the Microsoft education Web site at `http://www.microsoft.com/train_Cert`.

Where Do You Take the Exams?

You may take the exams at any of more than 800 Sylvan Prometric Authorized Testing Centers around the world. For the location of a testing center near you, call (800) 755-EXAM (755-3926). Outside the United States and Canada, contact your local Sylvan Prometric Registration Center.

To register for a Microsoft Certified Professional exam:

1. Determine the number of the exam you want to take.

2. Register with the Sylvan Prometric Registration Center that is nearest to you.

3. After you receive a registration and payment confirmation letter from Sylvan Prometric, call a nearby Sylvan Prometric Testing Center to schedule your exam.

What the Microsoft NT Proxy Server 2.0 with Windows NT Exam Measures

The Windows NT Proxy Server 2.0 exam covers concepts and skills required for the support of Windows NT computers running Microsoft Proxy Server. It emphasizes standards and terminology, planning, implementation, and troubleshooting for Proxy Server.

The exam focuses on fundamental concepts relating to Windows NT Proxy Server operation. It can also be quite specific regarding Windows NT requirements and operational settings, and particular about how administrative tasks are performed in the operating system. Careful study of this book, along with hands-on experience with the operating system, will be especially helpful in preparing you for the exam.

Microsoft provides exam objectives to give you a very general overview of possible areas of coverage of the Microsoft exams. For your convenience we have added in-text objectives listings at the points in the text where specific Microsoft exam objectives are covered.

Exam objectives are subject to change at any time without prior notice and at Microsoft's sole discretion. Please visit Microsoft's Training & Certification Web site (www.microsoft.com/Train_Cert) for the most current exam objectives listing.

How Microsoft Develops the Exam Questions

Microsoft follows an exam development process consisting of eight mandatory phases. The process takes an average of seven months and contain more than 150 specific steps. The phases of Microsoft Certified Professional exam development are listed here.

Phase 1: Job analysis   Phase 1 is an analysis of all the tasks that make up the specific job function, based on tasks performed by people who are currently performing the job function. This phase also identifies the knowledge, skills, and abilities that relate specifically to the performance area to be certified.

Phase 2: Objective domain definition   The results of the job analysis provide the framework used to develop objectives. The development of objectives involves translating the job function tasks into a comprehensive set of more specific and measurable knowledge, skills, and abilities. The resulting list of objectives, or the objective domain, is the basis for the development of both the certification exams and the training materials.

Phase 3: Blueprint survey   The final objective domain is transformed into a blueprint survey in which contributors—technology professionals who are performing the applicable job function—are asked to rate each objective. Contributors may be selected from lists of past Certified Professional candidates, from appropriately skilled exam development volunteers, and from within Microsoft. Based on the contributors' input, the objectives are prioritized and weighted. The actual exam items are written according to the prioritized objectives. Contributors are queried about how they spend their time on the job, and if a contributor doesn't spend an adequate amount of time actually performing the specified job function, his or her data is eliminated from the analysis.

The blueprint survey phase helps determine which objectives to measure, as well as the appropriate number and types of items to include on the exam.

Phase 4: Item development   A pool of items is developed to measure the blueprinted objective domain. The number and types of items to be written are based on the results of the blueprint survey. During this phase, items are reviewed and revised to ensure that they are:

- Technically accurate

- Clear, unambiguous, and plausible

- Not biased for any population subgroup or culture

- Not misleading or tricky

- Testing at the correct level of Bloom's Taxonomy

- Testing for useful knowledge, not obscure or trivial facts

Items that meet these criteria are included in the initial item pool.

Phase 5: Alpha review and item revision   During this phase, a panel of technical and job function experts reviews each item for technical accuracy, then answers each item, reaching consensus on all technical issues. Once the items have been verified as technically accurate, they are edited to ensure that they are expressed in the clearest language possible.

Phase 6: Beta exam   The reviewed and edited items are collected into a beta exam pool. During the beta exam, each participant has the opportunity to respond to all the items in this beta exam pool. Based on the responses of all beta participants, Microsoft performs a statistical analysis to verify the validity of the exam items and to determine which items will be used in the certification exam. Once the analysis has been completed, the items are distributed into multiple parallel forms, or versions, of the final certification exam.

Phase 7: Item selection and cut-score setting   The results of the beta exam are analyzed to determine which items should be included in the certification exam based on many factors, including item difficulty and relevance. Generally, the desired items are those that were answered correctly by anywhere from 25 percent to 90 percent of the beta exam candidates. This helps ensure that the exam consists of a variety of difficulty levels, from somewhat easy to extremely difficult.

Also during this phase, a panel of job function experts determines the cut score (minimum passing score) for the exam. The cut score differs from exam to exam because it is based on an item-by-item determination of the percentage of candidates who answered the item correctly and who would be expected to answer the item correctly. The cut score is determined in a group session to increase the reliability among the experts.

Phase 8: Exam live   Microsoft Certified Professional exams are administered by Sylvan Prometric.

Tips for Taking Your Proxy Server 2.0 on Microsoft Windows NT Exam

Here are some general tips for taking your exam successfully:

- Arrive early at the exam center so you can relax and review your study materials, particularly tables and lists of exam-related information.

- Read the questions carefully. Don't be tempted to jump to an early conclusion. Make sure you know *exactly* what the question is asking.

- Don't leave any unanswered questions. They count against you.

- When answering multiple-choice questions you're not sure about, use a process of elimination to get rid of the obviously incorrect questions first. This will improve your odds if you need to make an educated guess.

- Because the hard questions will eat up the most time, save them for last. You can move forward and backward through the exam.

- This test has many exhibits (pictures). It can be difficult, if not impossible, to view both the questions and the exhibit simulation on the 14- and 15-inch screens usually found at the testing centers. Call around to each center and see if they have 17-inch monitors available. If they don't, perhaps you can arrange to bring in your own. Failing this, some have found it useful to quickly draw the diagram on the scratch paper provided by the testing center and use the monitor to view just the question.

- This test is often perceived as the most difficult of the Microsoft Certified Professional tests. Many participants run out of time before they are able to complete the test. If you are unsure of the answer to a question, you may want to choose one of the answers, mark the question, and go on—an unanswered question does not help you. Once your time is up, you cannot go on to another question. However, you can remain on the question you are on indefinitely when the time runs out. Therefore, when you are almost out of time, go to a question you feel you can figure out—given enough time—and work until you feel you have got it (or the night security guard boots you out!).

- This is not simply a test of your knowledge of Microsoft Proxy Server 2.0, but on how it is implemented in Windows NT.

Once you have completed an exam, you will be given immediate, online notification of your pass or fail status. You will also receive a printed Examination Score Report indicating your pass or fail status and your exam results by section. (The test administrator will give you the printed score report.) Test scores are automatically forwarded to Microsoft within five working days after you take the test. You do not need to send your score to Microsoft. If you pass the exam, you will receive confirmation from Microsoft, typically within two to four weeks.

How to Use This Book

This book can provide a solid foundation for the serious effort of preparing for the Microsoft Proxy Server 2.0 on Microsoft Windows NT exam. To best benefit from this book, you might want to use the following study method:

1. Study a chapter carefully, making sure you fully understand the information.

2. Complete all hands-on exercises in the chapter, referring to the chapter so that you understand each step you take.

3. Answer the exercise questions related to that chapter. (You will find the answers to these questions in Appendix A.)

4. Note which questions you did not understand, and study those sections of the book again.

5. Study each chapter in the same manner.

If you prefer to use this book in conjunction with classroom or online training, you have many options. Both Microsoft-authorized training and independent training are widely available. Cyberstate University offers excellent online MCSE courses across the Internet, using the SYBEX materials. Their program includes an online NT lab where you can practice some of the exercises in this book, as well as videos, software, and lectures, all centered around the SYBEX MCSE Study Guide series. You can reach Cyberstate at 1-888-GET-EDUC (888-438-3382) or www.cyberstateu.com

To learn all the material covered in this book, you will need to study regularly and with discipline. Try to set aside the same time every day to study, and select a comfortable and quiet place in which to do it. If you work hard, you will be surprised at how quickly you learn this material. Good luck.

What's on the CD?

The CD includes the *Network Press Edge Test for Proxy Server 2* exam-preparation program. This custom program, produced exclusively for Network Press by The Edge Group, gives you the opportunity to test your knowledge of the material under exam conditions. Microsoft's *Train_Cert Offline Update* provides you with authoritative information on all of Microsoft's education and certification programs, and the Network Press MCSE Sampler provides sample chapters from other MCSE Study Guides.

Contact Information

To find out more about Microsoft Education and Certification materials and programs, to register with Sylvan Prometric, or to get other useful information, check the following resources. Outside the United States or Canada, contact your local Microsoft office or Sylvan Prometric Testing Center.

- Microsoft Certified Professional Program: For information about the Microsoft Certified Professional program and exams, and to order the latest Microsoft Roadmap to Education and Certification call (800) 636-7544.

- Sylvan Prometric Testing Centers: To register to take a Microsoft Certified Professional exam at any of more than 800 Sylvan Prometric testing centers around the world, or to order this Exam Study Guide call (800) 755-EXAM.

- Microsoft Certification Development Team: To volunteer for participation in one or more exam development phases or to report a problem with an exam go to `http://www.microsoft.com/Train_Cert/mcp/examinfo/certsd.htm`. Address written correspondence to: Certification Development Team; Microsoft Education and Certification; One Microsoft Way; Redmond, WA 98052.

- Microsoft TechNet Technical Information Network: For support professionals and system administrators outside the United States and Canada, call (800) 344-2121 or your local Microsoft subsidiary.

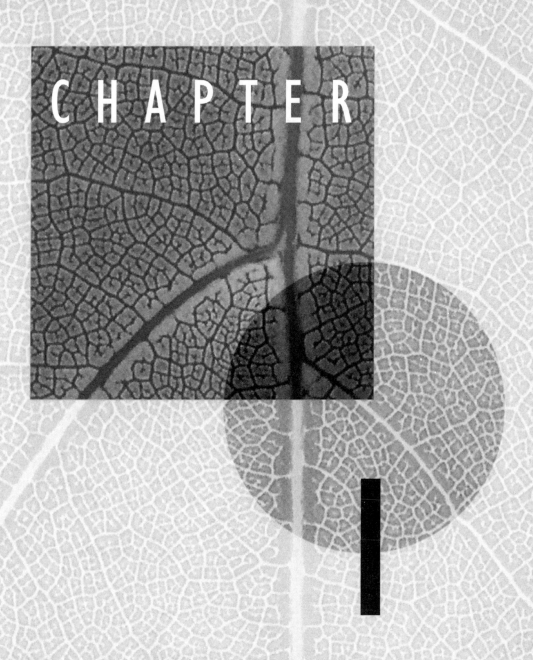

CHAPTER

1

Getting to Know
Microsoft Proxy Server 2.0

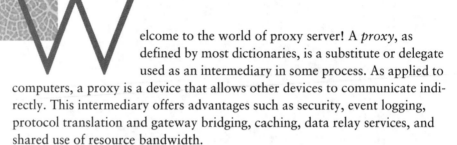

elcome to the world of proxy server! A *proxy*, as defined by most dictionaries, is a substitute or delegate used as an intermediary in some process. As applied to computers, a proxy is a device that allows other devices to communicate indirectly. This intermediary offers advantages such as security, event logging, protocol translation and gateway bridging, caching, data relay services, and shared use of resource bandwidth.

Proxy servers are commonly used to create an access point to the Internet that can be shared by all users. Because proxy servers cache data, Internet service providers such as AOL and CompuServe frequently use them to help facilitate traffic from their dial-up subscribers. Proxy servers may support anywhere from one user to as many users as the system's hardware can support. When users wish to read information from the Internet rather than requesting data directly from the object, they communicate with the proxy server that fills the request either from its cache or from the object itself. No direct communication is established between the system requesting the data and the Internet.

If you are unfamiliar with Microsoft Proxy Server, or are planning to take the certification test, keep these important objectives in mind as you work though this chapter. They are target issues of the chapter, and it should be your goal to be thoroughly familiar with them once you have completed it. After reading this chapter and completing the exercises and review questions, you should be able to:

- Define what a proxy server is

Exam objectives are subject to change at any time without prior notice and at Microsoft's sole discretion. Please visit Microsoft's Training & Certification website (www.microsoft.com/Train_Cert) for the most current exam objectives listing.

- Discuss why and in what situations you would use Microsoft Proxy Server

- Explain the organizational role of Microsoft Proxy Server

- List the features and functions of a proxy server

- Know what a firewall is and how it relates to a proxy server

What Does a Proxy Server Do?

A proxy server is a system or device that operates between a client application, such as a Web browser and a server (see Figure 1.1). It intercepts all requests sent to the server to see if it can fulfill the requests itself. If not, it forwards the request to the server. The great thing that proxy servers can provide, when configured correctly, is complete security.

FIGURE 1.1

A proxy server

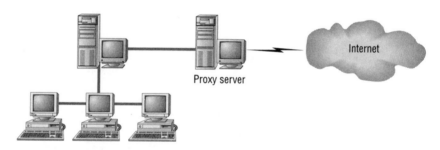

Private Network

Proxy servers have two main purposes: to improve performance and to filter requests. Improved performance is apparent to users by the reduction of wait time. Administrators notice the effect in the collective reduction of required bandwidth. And when filtering is used, proxy servers allow sites to be censored from view. Combined, the two functions enhance the capabilities and manageability of any Internet-ready network.

Proxy servers can dramatically increase performance for groups of users by caching results of all requests over a designated period of time. For instance, imagine that two users, Bill and Ted, access the World Wide Web through a proxy server. First, Bill requests a certain Web page, which we'll call Page 1.

Later, Ted requests the same page. Instead of forwarding the request to the Web server where Page 1 resides, the proxy server simply returns the Page 1 that it already retrieved for Bill. When Page 1 is stored is the cache, it is assigned a freshness stamp, which determines how long the data can be returned before it requires updating. If information changes before the server retrieves the new information, the old information will still appear. To avoid this problem, users have the option to request a refresh of cached data. Because the proxy server is often on the same network as the user, this operation is performed faster than it would be if the data were retrieved from the actual source.

Proxy servers make the request process faster and more efficient by filtering requests. For example, a company might use a proxy server to prevent its employees from accessing a specific set of Web sites, IP addresses, services, and so forth. You might be asking yourself why you would want to block internal employees from services of the Internet. The answer may range anywhere from preventing file transfers, which may introduce a virus, to restricting company data from being released without authorization. Microsoft Proxy Server has the ability to filter Internet sites, objects that are stored in the cache, and communications traffic.

Why Should You Use a Proxy Server?

There are an abundance of reasons for choosing to implement a proxy server. For most, a proxy server is used to safely add Internet capabilities to the network environment. Different proxy server products offer different services. Microsoft Proxy Server includes three core services: Web Proxy, Winsock Proxy, and Socks Proxy.

Microsoft Proxy Server provides numerous capabilities, which are described in detail throughout this book. While not all functions of a proxy server will be required by all implementations, it's important to be familiar with all material so that you will know when changes are necessary.

The Web Proxy Server supports the HTTP Secure (HTTPS), FTP Read, and Gopher protocols. These same protocols are supported by popular Web browsers such as Microsoft Internet Explorer and Netscape Navigator. Web Proxy Server also supports most system platforms.

WinSock Proxy is designed for Windows-based clients. WinSock is a standard for Windows applications to communicate via TCP/IP. WinSock applications include FTP, Telnet, and RealAudio. With the use of Microsoft Proxy Server, these applications may be run via TCP/IP or IPX/SPX.

The Socks Proxy supports the 4.3a specification of the Socks specification. The Socks 4.3a specification is a standard for applications to communicate via TCP/IP. This service was designed for UNIX- and Macintosh-based clients. Applications that use Socks Proxy are similar to those that use WinSock Proxy. Functionally, the Socks Proxy does not offer all the functions that WinSock offers. Socks Proxy lacks support for UDP protocols and can not perform high validation security authentication.

Access Authority

Microsoft Proxy Server allows you to control access of inbound and outbound connections. Access authority is designed so that you can control users on your internal network as well as those on the outside who access it. However, Proxy Server is primarily designed as an outbound service. This means that the majority of your control will be exercised on users from your network. Inbound traffic will be limited in general usage, while internal user access is specific. Typically, when a proxy server is in use, most implementations reject inbound access with the exception of publishing a Web page. These access restrictions can be by user, group, service, port, or domain.

Outbound connections control a user's ability to use certain functions on the Internet. For instance, if a user wants to run FTP, they must be granted access to the protocol by the proxy server. If no access is granted, the user will not be able to transfer files with FTP. Furthermore, access authority may be used to limit a user's ability to access certain Internet sites. For example, the proxy server may be configured to either deny or grant access to all sites with the exception of a specified list. IP addresses, host names, groups, or domains may be used to define systems that are on the exception list. This subject is discussed extensively in Chapter 7.

Inbound connections are limited based on the configuration of the proxy server. For instance, if a company does not offer any Web-based services or pages, there is no inbound traffic. Therefore, the proxy server will ignore any traffic that is sent to the Internet side of the server. On the other hand, when services are offered, connections to the server may be limited according to port and authorized user access. The only major problem with allowing inbound traffic is the potential danger of making your network insecure. Depending on how inbound traffic is managed, Internet publishing could pose a security problem. Imagine that in addition to your proxy service, you also use the server as an Internet router. Needless to say, any Internet traffic could reach your private network. Obviously, in creating a secure environment, you would want to disable as much inbound traffic as possible and have no direct connections to the Internet.

Access authority is a key function of the proxy server and an important feature for providing a secure environment for your private network. Microsoft Proxy Server is only as secure as the installer makes it. When configured properly, Microsoft Proxy Server allows Internet access to be implemented in a way that is completely secure.

Caching

The caching ability of Web proxy servers is one of the few mechanisms that is preventing the Internet from falling victim to its own success. Given the popularity of the Internet and the number of users, caching is the only thing that prevents it from overloading. By caching frequently accessed sites, information, and errors (such as dead Internet links), Microsoft Proxy Server significantly reduces total required bandwidth, which gives the appearance of a faster response time and saves employee time and connectivity expenses.

Caching is much more than merely keeping a copy of data requested from the Internet. Microsoft Proxy Server includes two caching functions that maximize available resources and minimize overhead.

Obviously, with data stored in the cache, users will experience a much higher throughput than without caching. The combined product of active and passive types of caching produces a system that meets user expectations.

When combining multiple Microsoft Proxy Servers, caching is enhanced by sharing cached material between systems. Sharing caches among proxy servers can be arranged in an array or as a chain of systems. Arrays allow multiple proxy servers to behave as one, providing load balancing, scalability, and fault tolerance. Chaining proxy servers allows for the forwarding of requests upstream to servers in a logical chain until an object is found. Chaining is more common in WAN environments, while arrays tend to be found in networks with high concentrations of users in a location.

The caching system is discussed in greater detail in Chapter 3.

Passive Caching

The first type of caching is known as passive. This function methodically stores data based on size, type of request, and utilization. Depending on the data requested, passive caching would either store data for future requests or determine that an object is not cacheable. Common types of non-cacheable data include stock and time-sensitive data, and Internet searches.

Active Caching

The second type of caching is known as active. This is an advanced method for caching data based on expected usage. For instance, suppose that Microsoft Proxy Server determined that the most commonly hit sites were www.microsoft.com and www.netscape.com. Any items that were stored in the cache would be updated without users making the request. In this advanced caching system, an algorithm is used to determine in advance which items can be updated off-line (without user intervention), which is when bandwidth utilization is low and user expectancy of an object is high.

Event Logging

Logging is an important part of securing a network and justifying utilized resources. That is why Microsoft designed logging to be flexible to any network's needs. Proxy Server enables an administrator to build a journal of sites accessed, difficulties that transpired when visiting sites, Internet usage, and so on. These logs are useful when fine tuning, troubleshooting problems, and performing cost analysis.

The log functions are available in two types of data outputs. The multi-output logs allow useful information to be manipulated according to a corporate policy. The first type of data output allows data to be placed into a text file. The frequency at which the file is written is based on a time frame. The second type of data output allows data to be directly feed to an SQL database. This is especially useful when keeping long logs of access data and determining demographics of systems' usages.

As you may have noticed in your travels, most logs consume tremendous disk space and provide more information than ever would be desirable. Microsoft Proxy Server offers two types of logs, which provide either minimal (regular) or full (verbose) data outputs. In other words, logging provides two types of data output (text file and SQL) for two types of logs (minimal and full).

Logging is discussed at length in Chapter 6 as well as in other locations throughout the book.

Integration to Windows NT

Proxy Server integrates with networking security and the administrative interface of the Windows NT Server operating system. Below are some examples of Proxy Server's integration with Windows NT. The integration is the ability to use other services that are already in place on the Windows NT Server without having to re-create them itself.

NT User Directory Services: Makes use of a single logon for network users, which does not require user accounts to be re-created for the proxy server.

Dial-Up Networking Support: Uses on-demand Windows NT autodial features for Internet connections.

Administration via Internet Service Manager: Uses a common interface with Microsoft Internet utilities such as FTP Server, Gopher Server and Web Server. This common interface also facilitates management of all servers from a single console interface.

Web Server Extension: Extends internal Web Server functionality by directly linking publishing to the Internet. This allows the proxy server to appear as a Web server (called *reverse proxy*) or redirect traffic to multiple Web servers inside the private network (called *reverse hosting*).

Integrated with NT Network System Management Services: Links directly into Performance Monitor and Event Viewer.

SNMP Compatibility: The status of any Microsoft Proxy Server on the network can be obtained with an SNMP console such as IBM's NetView or Hewlett Packard's OpenView.

Gateway and Protocol Translation

A gateway is a link between two networks that allows communication between dissimilar protocols. Although a network may consist of identical protocols (for instance, two systems both using TCP/IP), you can use a gateway to create the illusion that a mixed protocol network may exist. With no way to communicate except via the gateway, a network can be made secure. That is to say, the network is as secure as the gateway that it's using. In the case of Proxy Server, the gateway can be limited to only sending data and accepting replies.

Proxy Server has the ability to translate IP addresses to the Internet such that only the Proxy Server is required to use a live Internet address. Additionally, Proxy Server supports Internet Packet Exchange/Sequenced Packet Exchange (IPX/SPX) on the private network. This provides a low-cost way to access the Internet and an enterprise-wide connection, without having to revisit an entire company's protocol infrastructure. Because most WinSock-based applications support Proxy Server, implementation expenses and time are both minimized.

As a gateway, Microsoft Proxy Server maintains high-speed capabilities by converting only requests and address information. Connections to Internet resources are created by the proxy server itself. While maintaining access control, Proxy Server can also translate addresses on the fly and forward requests. This allows virtually all systems, regardless of platform, to utilize Internet applications (provided they utilize TCP/IP or IPX/SPX).

Security Refinements

A key feature of Proxy Server is the prevention of unauthorized access to your network from outside sources. In effect, all internal resources must communicate with the proxy server to reach the outside world (the Internet). Likewise, all external resources must converse with the proxy server to communicate with internal resources. The purpose of this is to effectively hide internal IP addresses from the Internet and provide user-level security. Additional security is provided by data encryption, which is supported by means of Secure Sockets Layer (SSL) Tunneling and Windows NT Challenge/Response authentication. Windows NT Challenge/Response Authentication is a refinement built into Windows NT that Proxy Server takes full advantage of.

The security functions provide the following:

- No direct Internet access to or from the LAN. The Proxy Server performs all processes.

- Access control governing who can access the Internet from the LAN using only specified protocols and ports.

- Site-specific lockout control.

- A mask for LAN structure, topology, addressing, and so on.

- A way to thwart aggressive Internet security probes such as IP spoofing, ISS, and SATAN.

- Firewall services that allow packet static or dynamic filtering.

Shared Bandwidth

Perhaps the most advantageous feature of a proxy server is its ability to share bandwidth. This feature often proves to be the largest cost-saving function for users. For example, a company with twenty users, each requiring Internet access, could share a single link instead of than having individual dial-up accounts, phone lines, and other related expenses. Table 1.1 shows how this feature can save you money.

T A B L E 1.1: Monthly Cost of Twenty Users Accessing the Internet

	ISDN at 56K	Phone (per user)	ISP	Internal services	Total Per User	Total Cost
With Proxy Server	$80	not applicable	$20	$50	$7.50	$150
Without Proxy Server	Not applicable	$25	$20	$10	$55	$1100

Proxy server can provide a single link to the Internet that can be shared and can effectively reduce the reoccurring costs of redundant equipment, accounts, and support. With a savings of $950, an organization could purchase faster connection technology, such as ISDN 56K for $80 a month, or a frame relay that runs at 128K or faster for a couple dollars more. (Almost any method for connecting to the Internet is faster, and cheaper via a proxy.) Considering that all users are not connected to the Internet at any one time, each user will have more bandwidth available to them than if they each had individual lines. Shared and individual bandwidth are illustrated in Figure 1.2.

Shared bandwidth is clearly a cheap, logical solution to corporate Internet access. Now, just consider if this company had 200, 500, 1000, or even 2000 users. Can you see the cost advantage?

Client/Server vs. Proxy Server

Proxy Server differs from traditional direct-connection configurations (client/server) by routing all requests through itself prior to making requests to the actual Internet site. The proxy server will either fill the request from its cache or send the request to the Internet site on behalf of the client. A comparison of a Proxy Server configuration to a client/server configuration is shown in Figure 1.3. At no time will the client actually have direct communication to an Internet resource with a proxy server.

FIGURE 1.2

Shared versus individual bandwidth

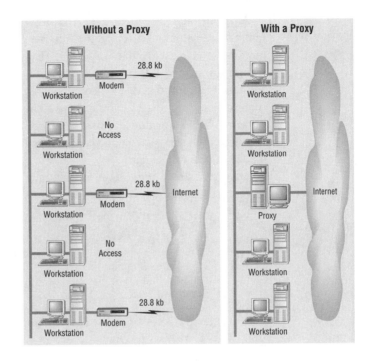

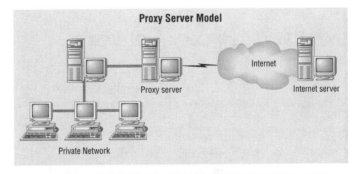

FIGURE 1.3

A proxy server configuration versus a client/server configuration

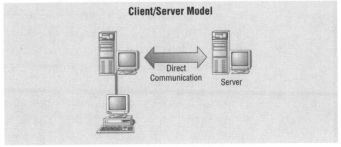

An additional process of the Proxy Server enables a client computer to make requests of an object on the Internet. An object on the Internet can be any source or target of data or service. The proxy server will perform the translation from the requesting application and protocol to the appropriate formats as required by the object requested. For instance, when an IPX client requests data, it must be translated to IP in order to be processed over the Internet. When a response is received from the Internet object, the proxy server receives the request and repackages it back to the client system that made the request.

A client/server configuration supports virtually all applications, while a Proxy server tends to be limited in function. However, Proxy Server supports the majority of IP applications, including:

- Internet Explorer, Netscape Navigator, and other Web browsers

- The RealAudio Player

- FTP batch utilities

- Applications coded in Microsoft Visual C++ or Microsoft Visual Basic with WinSock support

- Other applications that act as proxy clients

Firewalls vs. Proxy Servers

Firewall is a term derived from a part of a car. In cars, firewalls are physical barriers that divide the engine block from the passenger compartment. They are meant to protect passengers in the event of an engine fire. Firewalls in computers are logical devices that protect a private network from a public network such as the Internet. A proxy server is like a firewall, yet different in certain respects. A firewall, in a nutshell, is a computer that has routing capabilities comprised of two or more interfaces (for instance, serial ports, Ethernet, Token Ring, and so on), where IP forwarding has been disabled. One interface is connected to the Internet and the other is connected to the protected network. Various firewalls boast different services, and some include proxy services.

With a firewall in place, there are two clearly diverse networks that use the firewall system to access each other. The firewall can communicate with both the protected network and the Internet. The protected network cannot reach the Internet, and the Internet cannot reach the protected network. To reach the

Internet from the protected network, users must telnet to the firewall and access the Internet from there. Accordingly, in order to get into the protected network, users must go through the firewall first.

This setup provides excellent security against attacks from the Internet. If someone wants to make a concerted attack against the protected network, they must go through the firewall first, which makes the attack a two-step process. If someone wants to attack the protected network via a more common method, such as mail bombing or the infamous Internet Worm, they will not be able to reach the protected network.

The biggest problem with firewalls is that they greatly inhibit Internet access from the private network. This can create a reduction in Internet accessibility. Having to log into the Internet via a firewall creates a severe restriction. Programs like Netscape and Internet Explorer, which require a direct Internet connection, will not work from behind a firewall. Being unable to FTP directly to your computer will be another problem. This will require two steps: connecting from the Internet to the firewall and then connecting to the protected computer. The answer to these problems is to have a proxy server in addition to the firewall. The proxy server is constantly logged in while making requests for clients.

Without a built-in proxy function on the firewall, you would be virtually required to add a separate proxy server because Web browsers will not log into a firewall. Microsoft realizes this situation and has integrated a firewall into Microsoft Proxy Server 2.0. Due to its modular design, Microsoft Proxy Server 2.0 may be used as a stand-alone proxy server that operates in conjunction with a third-party firewall or as its own integrated solution.

Summary

This chapter provided an overview of Microsoft Proxy Server. At this point, you should know that a proxy server is a system that acts as a safeguard to Internet access. Microsoft Proxy Server is useful in securing a network against outside attack, reducing Internet connection costs, and sharing bandwidth to speed connections. Unlike typical client/server technology where workstations talk directly to host machines, the proxy server becomes a contact point that filters, caches, and permits access according to the administrator-defined configuration.

Review Questions

1. Which of the following are functions of a proxy server?

   A. Address translation

   B. Web page caching

   C. Line printer daemon

   D. Security

2. What is a proxy server?

   A. A device that configures NT Server to talk to Novell servers

   B. A system or device that operates between a client application, such as a Web browser, and a real server.

   C. A device that connects a T1 to a Frame Relay WAN link

   D. A device used to configure EGRP to Windows NT RIP

3. What are some common reasons that you might want to implement a proxy server?

   A. To connect two similar networks together

   B. To connect two dissimilar networks together

   C. To enhance security to the Internet

   D. To connect TCP/IP and IPX networks together

4. What features would you expect to find in Microsoft's Proxy Server?

   A. Access authority

   B. Event logging

   C. Integration

   D. Gateway services

   E. Protocol translation

5. Explain how shared bandwidth combines with gateway and protocol translation.

6. All proxy servers are firewalls.

   A. True

   B. False

CHAPTER

2

An Introduction to TCP/IP

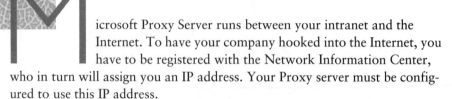

icrosoft Proxy Server runs between your intranet and the Internet. To have your company hooked into the Internet, you have to be registered with the Network Information Center, who in turn will assign you an IP address. Your Proxy server must be configured to use this IP address.

The Microsoft Proxy Server test does not cover any TCP/IP objectives. However, because you need to configure Proxy Server on your network, and must run TCP/IP on at least one Network Interface Card of the Microsoft Proxy Server, you have to know a little about TCP/IP.

In this chapter, we'll cover the basics of TCP/IP, opening with a definition of this popular pair of protocols, its beginnings, and why it's so important today. We'll progress to discover how TCP/IP fits into the Department of Defense (DOD) networking archetype and move on to explore both the DOD and the OSI (Open Systems Interconnection) reference models. We'll then zoom in for a close-up of the TCP/IP protocol suite, closing the chapter with an in-depth look at the individual protocols and utilities, including their special functions.

We'll probe further into the basics of TCP/IP and examine the supremely important subject of how accurate communication is achieved between specific networks and host systems through proper IP addressing. We'll discuss how and why that communication happens, why it doesn't when it fails, and how to configure devices on both LANs and WANs to ensure solid performance for your network.

Objectives

This chapter will give you an overview of TCP/IP. For a full understanding of networking TCP/IP with Microsoft NT, see the *MCSE: TCP/IP Study Guide* (Sybex, 1997).

If you are unfamiliar with TCP/IP, keep these important objectives in mind as you work through this chapter. They are target issues of the chapter, and it's your goal to be thoroughly familiar with them when you're done. The exercise and review section at the end of the chapter will also help you achieve this goal. You should be able to:

■ Define TCP/IP and describe its advantages on Windows NT

Exam objectives are subject to change at any time without prior notice and at Microsoft's sole discretion. Please visit Microsoft's Training & Certification website (www.microsoft.com/Train_Cert) for the most current exam objectives listing.

■ Explain the RFCs (Request for Comments) document

■ Describe how the TCP/IP protocol suite maps to a four-layer model

■ Identify and describe the protocols and utilities in the Microsoft TCP/IP protocol suite

■ Define an IP address and identify the different types of IP addresses

■ Identify both the network and host IDs in class A, B, and C addresses.

■ Identify both valid and invalid class A, B, and C addresses

■ Assign appropriate host and network IDs

■ Understand which network components require IP addresses

■ Understand common IP addressing problems

■ Define subnet and subnet masks and explain how they work

■ Outline a range of valid host IDs for multiple subnets

■ Create an effective subnet mask for a WAN comprised of many subnets

What Is TCP/IP?

TCP/IP stands for *Transmission Control Protocol/Internet Protocol.* Essentially, it is a set of two communication protocols that an application can use to package its information in order to send it across a network or networks. For readers familiar with traditional NetWare protocols, TCP is roughly comparable to SPX (Sequenced Packet Exchange), and IP approximates to IPX (Internetwork Packet Exchange).

TCP/IP also can refer to an entire collection of protocols, called a *protocol suite.* This collection includes application protocols for performing tasks such as e-mail transfer, file transfer, and terminal emulation. There are also supporting protocols that take an application's data and package it for transmission. Two examples of this type of protocol are TCP and IP. Still other protocols, such as Ethernet and Token Ring, exist for the physical transmission of data. All of these protocols are related, and are part of the TCP/IP protocol suite.

As another example, whether we realize it or not, many of us use *SMTP* (*Simple Mail Transport Protocol*). SMTP is an application protocol that enables us to communicate by e-mail. E-mail programs running on personal computers, minicomputers, UNIX workstations, and even mainframes can use the SMTP protocol to exchange e-mail.

A Brief History of TCP/IP

The period of computer history spanning the 1950s and 1960s was not a good time for networking. During this dark age of computerdom, almost all computer systems were "technocentric"—they weren't designed to connect to other systems. In that politically incorrect period of computer prejudice, hardware, operating systems, file formats, program interfaces, and other components were all designed to work only with a particular type of computer system.

The Interest in Packet-Switched WANs

In the late 1960s, the United States Department of Defense (DOD) became interested in some academic research concerning a *packet-switched WAN* (wide-area network). The basic idea was to connect multiple, geographically-dispersed networks, and allow for data, in the form of packets, to be sent to the various locations within the WAN.

The concept of *packets* can be explained like this: Imagine you have a really long letter to send—so long, it's impossible to fit it into one measly little #10 envelope. You've been given explicit instructions: You must use the #10s. So, you begin to break up the letter into smaller sections, fitting each into an individual envelope. As you address each envelope, you number them sequentially so the recipient can successfully reassemble your letter. The letter we're talking about is analogous to data that a user has created within an application and wishes to send to another user. The envelopes represent packets. In WANs, information is transported by electronically putting it into packets, which are addressed, sequenced, and then sent on their way.

The *switched* part of a packet-switched network refers to the routing of the packets to a destination. Because packets are addressed individually, they can be transmitted along different physical routes to their ultimate destination. This flexible transmission method is referred to as *packet switching*. The original reason the DOD was interested in this research was because they wanted to create a fault-tolerant WAN that could carry, command, and control information in the event of a nuclear war. Because a network of this type would have multiple, geographically-dispersed sites and data would be sent in a packet-switched manner, there would be no single point of failure in the system.

The Initial Research Issues Behind the Internet

The research arm of the DOD was an agency called the Advanced Research Projects Agency (ARPA), now called the Defense Advanced Research Projects Agency (DARPA). The mission of this group was to fund basic research that could possibly contribute to the defense effort. It was this agency that funded and managed the project to create a packet-switched WAN. The scientists and engineers that were recruited for this project came from major universities and the private firm of Bolt, Beranek, and Newman (BBN) in Cambridge, Massachusetts. The challenge they faced related to two main areas: *interconnectivity* and *interoperability*.

Interconnectivity deals with transporting information. A software protocol was needed that could package and route information between multiple sites. Out of the concept of the packet-switched WAN evolved the protocol that eventually rose to meet this need: the *Internet Protocol* (IP).

With the problem of transmission resolved, the team moved on to tackle the next issue—communication. What good was transporting information from an application on a computer *here* if the system's applications on the receiving end *there* couldn't understand it? This would be about as effective as arguing with Bavarian airport staff about your shredded luggage in Swahili—you'd be hearing each other loud and clear, but failing to communicate because you spoke different languages. As you're sure to be guessing, interoperability has to do with application-to-application communication—the interpreter rushed to the scene. Achieving interoperability was a real challenge. Applications would be running on vastly disparate hardware platforms, with equally different operating systems, file formats, terminal types, and so on. For interoperability to be a reality, a way to bridge all these differences was required.

The solution was to develop a series of standard application protocols that would enable application-to-application communication and be independent of the extensive array of computer platforms. For instance, if a mainframe-based e-mail program and a PC-based e-mail program were both using the same standard e-mail protocol, they could exchange e-mail. This would be possible despite the use of two totally different systems. This same principle was used to create standard protocols for file transfers, terminal emulation, printing, network management, and other applications.

From the ARPANET to the Internet

When the original team of researchers decided to conduct their first test of these ideas, they chose four universities for sites: the University of California at Los Angeles (UCLA), the Stanford Research Institute (SRI), the University of California at Santa Barbara (UCSB), and the University of Utah. In September of 1969, these four sites were connected using 50Kbps (kilobits per second) leased voice lines, and the resulting network was called the *Advanced Research Projects Agency Network*, or *ARPANET*.

Although the original aim of this research was military, it was soon used for other purposes. Researchers at the different sites utilized the ARPANET to log into distant sites and communicate with each other by sending files and electronic mail.

Because the funding for this research was obtained from the U.S. government, and therefore from U.S. taxpayers, the subsequent technology was considered owned by the U.S. public. And since the government hadn't classified the technology as top secret, it was considered to be in the public domain. This meant that any individual, organization, or company could receive documentation of the protocols and write programs based on them. That's exactly what happened. Other universities and research and commercial organizations soon began to use this technology to create their own networks. Some of these networks were then connected to the ARPANET.

Another factor in the rapid growth of this technology was the inclusion of the TCP/IP protocols in the Berkeley version of UNIX. The DOD folks funded two projects that lead to this. First, they had the company Bolt, Beranek, and

Newman (BBN) modify the TCP/IP protocols to work with the UNIX operating system. Then they had the University of California at Berkeley include them in their version of UNIX, called Berkeley UNIX or Berkeley Software Distribution UNIX (BSD UNIX). Things from Berkeley get around. Because 90 percent of all university science departments were using this version of UNIX, the TCP/IP protocols quickly gained wide usage, and more and more networks were created with them.

Mainframes, minicomputers, and microcomputers all became hardware platforms for TCP/IP protocols. Likewise, software environments from Digital Equipment Corporation (DEC), International Business Machines (IBM), Microsoft, and many others developed products that supported them. Over time, these networks began to connect to each other. Where there was originally only one, the ARPANET, soon there were many separate networks. Eventually, all these individual, interconnected TCP/IP networks were collectively referred to as the Internet, or more simply, the Net.

The Internet Today

Though the numbers increase with each day, the Internet connects about 40 million users worldwide. The following is a very short list of some of the networks on the Internet:

- NSFNet (National Science Foundation Network)

- SPAN (Space Physics Analysis Network)

- CARL (Colorado Alliance of Research Libraries)

- LawNet: Columbia Law School Public Information Service

- The WELL (Whole Earth 'Lectronic Link)

- E.T.Net: The National Library of Medicine

- USEnet: A very large bulletin board system made up of thousands of different conferences

We commonly use the Internet for sending e-mail. The TCP/IP protocol that relates to this function is SMTP. As mentioned earlier, this protocol allows people from all over the world, using disparate hardware and software platforms, to communicate with one another.

Another common application of the Internet is to transfer files. Someone on a Macintosh computer in Iowa can download a file from a minicomputer in Norway. This type of file transfer is accomplished, in part, by the File Transfer Protocol (FTP) running on both machines.

A third, frequently used application is *terminal emulation*, sometimes called *remote login*. TCP/IP's *Telnet* protocol allows a user to log in to a remote computer. The computer logging in acts as, or emulates, a terminal off the remote system; hence, the term terminal emulation.

Locating Information on the Internet

Surfing the Net has become so popular that, like snowboarding, it may soon be added to the Olympics. The reason for its popularity is that whether you garden to Mozart, or bungee-jump to Pearl Jam, there's something for you there. Yes, a great feature of the Internet is its astounding amount of information and other resources, like shareware and freeware. However, as answers often lead to more questions, this enormous expanse of information does often raise a few concerns for those of us staring at the screen.

Let's explore this a bit. Imagine this: There you are—just you and your computer and your mind racing with all the amazing stuff you've heard can be found on the Net. You fire up Ol' Bessie—your computer may, of course, have a different name—and the screen crackles to life. With heady anticipation, you click the Internet icon, listen for that squeal/collision modem noise, and...there it is, THE INTERNET! The Information superhighway, full of promise, can lead nowhere fast if you don't know what to do with it.

Has this been you? You know the information you are looking for. You know it's out there...but where? And what's the easiest way to get there? Fortunately, TCP/IP has application protocols that address these issues. The following are four methods of finding information on the Internet, known as *information retrieval services*:

- WAIS

- Archie

- Gopher

- World Wide Web (WWW)

WAIS

Wide Area Information Servers (WAIS) allow you to search for a specific document inside a database. WAIS is a distributed information service that offers natural-language input as well as indexed searching that lets the results of initial searches influence future searches. You can Telnet to DS.INTERNIC.NET to access a WAIS client. Log in as **wais**, without a password. WAIS searches may also be done on the World Wide Web.

Archie

A program called *Archie* was created to help users find files. Archie is essentially an indexing and search tool that works by indexing a large number of files. Periodically, participating Internet host computers will download a listing of their files to a few specified computers called *Archie servers*. The Archie server then indexes all these files.

When you are looking for a specific file, you can run the Archie client software and *query* (search through) the Archie server. The Archie server will examine its indexes and send back a description and location of the files that match your query. You can then use FTP to transfer the file or files.

Gopher

Another great Internet tool is *Gopher*. Created at the University of Minnesota, where the school mascot is a gopher, it organizes topics into a menu system and allows you to access the information on each topic listed. Through its menu system, you can see at a glance what information is available there. This menu system includes many levels of submenus, allowing you to burrow down to the exact type of information you're looking for. When you choose an item, Gopher transparently transfers you to another system on the Internet where your choice resides.

Gopher actually uses the Telnet protocol to log you into the other system. This action is hidden from users, who just see the Gopher menu interface. This means that Gopher doesn't merely tell you where your information is located, as Archie does, but also transparently takes you to it. Gopher could be characterized as a menuing tool, a search tool, and a navigation tool that sends you places.

World Wide Web

The *World Wide Web* (WWW) is a type of data service running on many computers on the Internet. These computers utilize a type of software that allows for text and graphics to have cross-links to other information. You can access a WWW server, and a particular Web page, to see a great—depending on its creator's talent—graphic display of text, pictures, icons, colors, and other elements.

To access the Web server, you use client software called a *browser program*. With a browser, you can choose an element on the Web page, which can then cross-link you to a computer animation, or play sounds, or display another Web page. Browsers can even contact another Web server located across the world. All the Web servers on the Internet are collectively referred to as the World Wide Web and can be thought of as Jungian consciousness for computers.

The most popular World Wide Web browsers are Netscape's Navigator and Microsoft's Internet Explorer.

RFCs (Request for Comments)

In life, if something is around long enough, politics will find it. Sometimes this is good. Sometimes it's absolutely necessary, as is the case when the goal is setting *standards* for TCP/IP. These standards are published in a series of documents called *Request for Comments*, or RFCs, and they describe the internal workings of the Internet.

RFCs and standards are not one and the same. Though many are actual standards, some RFCs are there for informational purposes or to describe a work in progress. Still others exist as a sort of forum, providing a place for industry input relevant to the process of updating IP standards.

The Internet's standardization process resembles that of a bill becoming a law. Similarities include the fact that there exists more than one governing body and interested party watching closely and making decisions about it. Another resemblance is that an RFC document goes through several stages, each subjecting it to examination, analysis, debate, critique, and testing on its way to becoming a standard.

First, an individual, company, or organization proposing a new protocol, improvement to an existing protocol, or even simply making comments on the state of the Internet, creates an RFC. If it deems it worthy, after at least a six-month wait, the *IESG* (Internet Engineering Steering Group) promotes the RFC to the status of *Draft Standard*, where it reenters the arena of review before finally becoming a bonafide *Internet Standard*. It is then published and assigned a permanent RFC number.

If the standard is changed or updated in any way, it gets a whole new number, so rest assured—you've got the latest model. Also handy to note: If what you're looking at *is* a revised edition, the dated version or versions are referenced on its title page. Also noteworthy, a letter that follows an RFC's number indicates the status of that RFC (for example, RFC 1390H). The following is a list of status designations for Internet protocols:

- Historic: Protocols that have either been outmoded or are no longer undergoing consideration for standardization

- Experimental: Protocols being experimented with

- Informational: Exactly what you might think

- Proposed Standard: Being analyzed for future standardization

- Draft Standard: In the home stretch—the final review period prior to becoming a standard

- Standard: An Internet protocol which has arrived and is official

There are also instructions for the treatment of Internet protocols. They are:

- Limited: Of possible use to some computer systems. Highly specialized or experimental protocols are sometimes given this designation. Historic protocols can be given this status as well.

- Elective: These protocols may possibly be implemented.

- Recommended: These should be implemented.

- Required: Protocols considered "musts." They are required to be implemented on the Internet.

Important to note is the fact that not every protocol enjoying wide usage on the Net is an Internet standard. TCP/IP's *NFS* (Network File System) is a stellar example. Developed by Sun Microsystems, the NFS is a critical TCP/IP protocol, and is therefore inextricably entwined with the Internet. This protocol, though indispensable, has not received approval from the IAG, and so cannot be given the status of Standard.

Internet Activities Board (IAB)

The *IAB* is a committee responsible for setting Internet standards and for managing the process of publishing RFCs. The IAB is in charge of two task forces: the *Internet Research Task Force* (IRTF) and the *Internet Engineering Task Force* (IETF). The IRTF is responsible for coordinating all TCP/IP-related research projects. The IETF focuses on problems on the Internet.

For more information on the Internet, try (you guessed it) the Internet. There's a memo called "Internet Official Protocol Standards," and the last time I checked, its publishing number was RFC 1800. It describes the above process much more thoroughly than space allows us here.

InterNIC Directory and Database Services

The *InterNIC Directory and Database*, provided by AT&T, is a service that furnishes us with sources of information about the Internet, including RFCs. A WHOIS server provides a white page directory of Internet users and a Gopher database provides access to Internet documents. InterNIC is a primary depository that offers many options for retrieval. Have fun!

Previously, the best way to check out RFCs, and to get up-to-date information about their sources, was to send an e-mail to rfc-info@isi.edu, including the message **help: ways_to_get_rfcs**. If you weren't looking for a specific RFC, you downloaded a file named RFC-INDEX.TXT, which offers the complete banquet of all the RFCs in the whole wide world. Today, the easiest way to go RFC hunting is to point a Web browser at www.internic.net, which will lavish you with a nice searchable interface. Still, RFCs may be obtained via FTP from these servers:

- DS.INTERNIC.NET (InterNIC Directory and Database Services)

- NIS.NSF.NET

- NISC.JVNC.NET

- FTP.ISI.EDU

- WUARCHIVE.WUSTL.EDU

- SRC.DOC.IC.AC.UK

- FTP.NCREN.NET

- FTP.SESQUI.NET

- NIS.GARR.IT

The TCP/IP Protocol Suite and the DOD Networking Model

Computers, like people, become confused and offended when protocols for proper communication aren't followed. Give one an offending command once too often and the screen just might go dark on you—complete rejection! Try that on a person, and lo an' behold... same thing happens. The TCP/IP protocol suite is essentially an integration of various communications functions governed by strict, required, and agreed-upon rules for how they are performed, implemented, and so on. The required, agreed-upon rules part refers to the standard class of protocols we talked about in our discussion of RFCs. The DOD's networking model conforms to the *International Standards Organization's (ISO)* model, which is similar in concept to the *Open Systems Interconnection (OSI)* reference model. Before we see how they all compare, let's take a look at the general concept of reference models.

Reference Models: An Overview

A *reference model* is a conceptual blueprint of how communications should take place. It addresses all the processes that are required for effective communication. These processes are divided into logical groupings called *layers*. When a communication system is designed in this manner, it's known as *layered architecture*.

Think of it like this: Imagine you and some friends want to start a company. One of the first things you'd do is sit down and think through the things that must be done, who will do them, in what order, and how they relate to each other. Ultimately, you might group these tasks into departments. Let's say you decide on having an order-taking department, an inventory department, and a shipping department. Each of your departments have their own unique tasks keeping them very busy, requiring them to focus on only their own duties.

In this scenario, departments are a metaphor for the layers in a communication system. For things to run smoothly, each department will have to trust and rely heavily on the others to do their jobs and handle their special responsibilities. In your planning sessions, you'll probably take notes to document the meeting. The entire process will then be recorded for you to discuss later, agreeing upon standards of operation that will serve as your business blueprint, or reference model, if you will.

Once your business is launched, your department heads, armed with the part of the blueprint relating to their department, will need to develop practical methods to implement the tasks assigned to them. These practical methods, or protocols, will need to be classified into a Standard Operating Procedures manual, and followed closely. The various procedures in your manual will have different reasons for having been included, as well as varying degrees of importance and implementation. If you form a partnership, or acquire another company, it will be imperative for their business protocols—their business blueprint—to match yours.

Software developers can use a reference model to understand computer communication processes and to see what types of functions need to be accomplished on any one layer. If they are developing a protocol for a certain layer, all they need to concern themselves with is their chosen layer's functions, not those of any other layer. The other functions will be handled by some other layer and protocol. The technical term for this idea is *binding*. The communication processes that are related to each other are bound, or grouped together, at a particular layer.

Advantages of Reference Models

The advantages of using a model are many. Remember, because developers know that functions they're not currently working on will be handled by another layer, they can confidently focus on just one layer's functions. This promotes specialization. Another benefit is that if changes are made to one layer, it doesn't necessarily change anything with the other layers.

Suppose an executive in your company, who's in the management layer, sends a letter. This person doesn't necessarily care if his or her company's shipping department, a different layer, changes from UPS to Federal Express, or vice-versa. All they're concerned with is the letter, and the recipient of the letter. It is someone else's job to see to its delivery. The technical phrase for this idea is *loose coupling*. Phrases you've probably heard more often go like: "It's not *my* fault—its not my department!" Or: "So-'n-So's group always messes up stuff like this—we never do!" Loose coupling provides for a *stable* protocol suite. Passing the buck doesn't.

Another big advantage is *compatibility*. If software developers adhere to the specifications outlined in the reference model, all the protocols written to conform to that model will work together. This is very good. Compatibility creates the potential for a large number of protocols to be written and used.

Physical and Logical Data Movement

The two additional concepts that need to be addressed in a reference model are the *physical movement of data*, and the *logical movement of data*.

As illustrated in Figure 2.1, the physical movement of data begins by going down the model. For example, an application creates some information. It passes it down to a communication protocol that packages it and hands it down to a transmission protocol for its actual physical transmission. The data then moves across the model, which signifies it moving across some type of physical channel—like cable, fiber, or radio frequencies and microwaves.

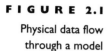

Physical data flow
through a model

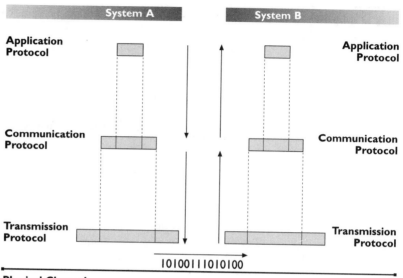

When the data reaches the destination computer, it moves up the model. Each layer at the destination only sees and deals with the data that was packaged by its counterpart on the sending side. Referring back to our analogy about the executive and the letter, the shipping department at the destination only sees the shipping packaging and the information provided by the sending side's shipping department. The destination's shipping department does not see the actual letter because peeking into mail addressed to someone else is a federal offense. The destination company's executive is the party who will open and process the letter.

The logical movement of data is another concept addressed in a reference model. From this perspective, each layer is only communicating with its counterpart layer on the other side (see Figure 2.2). Communication in the realm of humans flows best when it happens between peers—between people on the same plane in life. The more we have in common, the more similarities in our personalities, experiences, and occupations, the easier it is for us to relate to one another—for us to connect. Again, its the same with computers. This type of logical communication is called *peer-to-peer communication*. When more than one protocol is needed to successfully complete a communication process, they are grouped into a team we call a *protocol stack*. Layers in a system's protocol stack only communicate with the corresponding layers in another system's protocol stack.

FIGURE 2.2

Logical data flow between
peer layers

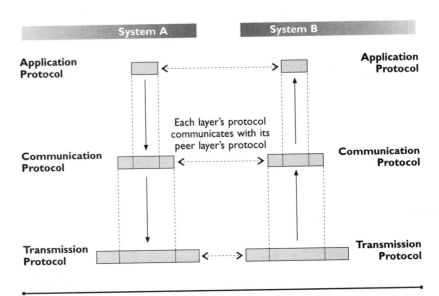

The OSI Reference Model

The International Organization for Standardization (ISO) is the Emily Post of the protocol world. Just like Ms. Post, who wrote the book setting the standards—or protocols—for human social interaction, the ISO developed the OSI reference model as the guide and precedent for an open protocol set. Defining the etiquette of communication models, it remains today the most popular means of comparison for protocol suites. The OSI reference model has seven layers:

- Application
- Presentation
- Session
- Transport
- Network
- Data Link
- Physical

Figure 2.3 shows the way these "macro-layers" fit together.

FIGURE 2.3

The macro-layers of the
OSI reference model

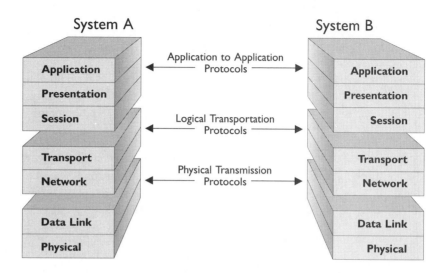

The OSI model's top three layers—Application, Presentation, and Session—deal with functions that aid applications in communicating with other applications. They specifically deal with tasks like file name formats, code sets, user interfaces, compression, encryption, and other functions relating to the exchange occurring between applications.

The Application Layer

The Application layer of the OSI model supports the components that deal with the communicating aspects of an application. Although computer applications sometimes require only desktop resources, applications may unite communicating components from more than one network application. For example, file transfers, e-mail, remote access, network management activities, client/server processes, and information location. Many network applications provide services for communication over enterprise networks, but for present and future internetworking, the need is fast developing to reach beyond their limits. For the '90s and beyond, transactions and information exchanges between organizations are broadening to require internetworking applications like the following:

- The World Wide Web: Connects countless servers (the number seems to grow with each passing day) presenting diverse formats. Most are multimedia, and include some or all of the following: graphics, text, video, and even sound. Netscape Navigator, Internet Explorer, and other browsers like Mosaic simplify both accessing and viewing Web sites.

- E-mail Gateways: E-mail gateways are versatile, and can use Simple Mail Transfer Protocol or the X.400 standard to deliver messages between different e-mail applications.

- Electronic Data Interchange (EDI): This is a composite of specialized standards and processes that facilitates the flow of tasks like accounting, shipping/receiving, and order and inventory tracking between businesses.

- Special Interest Bulletin Boards: These include the many chat rooms on the Internet where people can connect and communicate with each other either by posting messages, or typing a conversation live, in real-time. They can also share public domain software.

- Internet Navigation Utilities: Applications like Gopher and WAIS, as well as search engines like Yahoo, Excite, and Alta Vista, help users locate the resources and information they need on the Internet.

- Financial Transaction Services: These are services that target the financial community. They gather and sell information pertaining to investments, market trading, commodities, currency exchange rates, and credit data to their subscribers.

An important thing to mention here is an *application program interface* (*API*). Used jointly with application layer services, developers of protocols and programs often include APIs in the package with their products. APIs are important because they make it possible for programmers to customize applications and reap the benefits of their wares. An API is essentially a set of guidelines for user-written applications to follow when accessing the services of a software system. It's a channel into the harbor. BSD UNIX has an API called Berkeley Sockets. Microsoft changed it slightly and renamed it Windows Sockets. Indeed, things from Berkeley *do* get around!

The Presentation Layer

The Presentation layer gets its name from its purpose: It presents data to the Application layer. It's essentially a translator. A successful data transfer technique is to adapt the data into a standard format before transmission. Computers are configured to receive this generically-formatted data and then convert the data back into its native format for reading. The OSI has protocol standards that define how standard data should be formatted. Tasks like data compression, decompression, encryption, and decryption are associated with this layer.

The Abstract Syntax Representation, Revision #1 (ASN.1) is the standard data syntax used by the Presentation layer. This kind of standardization is necessary when transmitting numerical data that is represented very differently by various computer systems' architectures.

Some Presentation layer standards are involved in multimedia operations. The following serve to direct graphic and visual image presentation:

- PICT: A picture format used by Macintosh and PowerPC programs for transferring QuickDraw graphics.

- TIFF: The Tagged Image File Format is a standard graphics format for high-resolution, bitmapped images.

- JPEG: These standards are brought to us by the Joint Photographic Experts Group

Others guide movies and sound:

- MIDI: The Musical Instrument Digital Interface is used for digitized music.

- MPEG: The Motion Picture Experts Group's standard for the compression and coding of motion video for CDs is increasingly popular. It provides digital storage and bit rates up to 1.5Mbps.

- QuickTime: This is for use with Macintosh or PowerPC programs; it manages these computer's audio and video applications.

The Session Layer

The *Session layer*'s job can be likened to that of a mediator or referee. Its central concern is *dialog* control between devices, or *nodes*. It serves to organize their communication by offering three different modes—*simplex, half-duplex,* and *full-duplex*—and by splitting up a communication session into three different phases. These phases are: *connection establishment*, *data transfer*, and *connection release*. In simplex mode, communication is actually a monologue with one device transmitting and another receiving. To get a picture of this, think of the telegraph machine's form of communication: .....--..----...---..-...

When in half-duplex mode, nodes take turns transmitting and receiving—the computer equivalent of talking on a speaker phone. Some of us have experienced proper conversation etiquette being forced upon us by the unique speaker phone phenomenon of forbidden interruption. The speakerphone's mechanism dictates that you may indeed speak your mind, but you'll have to wait until the other end stops chattering first. This is how nodes communicate when in half-duplex mode.

Full-duplex's only conversational proviso is *flow control*. This mitigates the problem of possible differences in the operating speed of two nodes, where one may be transmitting faster than the other can receive. Other than that, communication between the two flows unregulated, with both sides transmitting and receiving simultaneously.

Formal communication sessions occur in three phases. In the first, the connection-establishment phase, contact is secured and devices agree upon communication parameters and the protocols they will use. Next, in the data transfer phase, these nodes engage in conversation, or dialog, and exchange information. Finally, when they're through communicating, nodes participate in a systematic release of their session.

A formal communications session is connection-oriented. In a situation where a large quantity of information is to be transmitted, rules are agreed upon by the involved nodes for the creation of checkpoints along their transfer process. These are highly necessary in case an error occurs along the way. Among other things, they afford us humans the luxury of preserving our dignity in the face of our closely watching computers. Let me explain: In the 44th minute of a 45-minute download, a loathsome error occurs...again! This is the third try, and the file-to-be-had is needed more than sunshine. Without your trusty checkpoints in place you'd have to start all over again. Potentially, this could cause the coolest of cucumbers to tantrum like a two-year-old, resulting in an extremely high degree of satisfaction on the part of his or her computer. Can't have that! Instead, we have checkpoints secured—something we call activity management—ensuring that the transmitting node only has to retransmit the data sent since the last checkpoint. Humans: 1; Computers: 0... And the crowd goes crazy!

It's important to note that in networking situations, devices send out simple, one-frame status reports that aren't sent in a formal session format. If they were, it would unnecessarily burden the network and result in lost economy. Instead, in these events, a *connectionless* approach is used, where the transmitting node simply sends off its data without establishing availability and without acknowledgment from its intended receiver. Connectionless communication can be thought of like a message in a bottle—they're short, sweet, they go where the current takes them, and they arrive at an unsecured destination.

Following are some examples of session-layer protocols and interfaces:

- Network File System (NFS): NFS was developed by Sun Microsystems and used with TCP/IP and UNIX workstations to allow transparent access to remote resources.

- SQL: The Structured Query Language developed by IBM provides users with a simpler way to define their information requirements on both local and remote systems.

- RPC: The Remote Procedure Call is a broad client/server redirection tool used for disparate service environments. Its procedures are created on clients and performed on servers.

- X Window: This is widely used by intelligent terminals for communicating with remote UNIX computers. It allows them to operate as though they were locally-attached monitors.

- ASP: Another client/server mechanism, the AppleTalk Session Protocol both establishes and maintains sessions amid AppleTalk client and server machines.

- DNA SCP: The Digital Network Architecture Session Control Protocol is a DECnet session layer protocol.

The Transport Layer

Services located in the *transport layer* both segment and reassemble data from upper-layer applications and unite it onto the same data stream. They provide end-to-end data transport services and establish a logical connection between the sending host and destination host on an internetwork. Data integrity is ensured at this layer by maintaining flow control, and also by allowing users the option of requesting reliable data transport between systems. Flow control prevents the problem of a sending host on one side of the connection over-flowing the buffers in the receiving host—an event which can result in lost data. Reliable data transport employs a connection-oriented communications session between systems, and the protocols involved ensure that the following will be achieved:

- The segments delivered are acknowledged back to the sender upon their reception.

- Any segments not acknowledged are retransmitted.

- Segments are sequenced back into their proper order upon arrival at their destination.

- A manageable data flow is maintained in order to avoid congestion, overloading, and loss of any data.

An important reason for different layers to coexist within the OSI reference model is to allow for the sharing of a transport connection by more than one application. This sharing of a transport connection is available because the transport layer's functioning happens segment by segment, and each segment is independent of the others. This allows different applications to send consecutive segments, processed on a first-come, first-served basis, that can be intended either for the same destination host or for multiple hosts.

Figure 2.4 shows how the transport layer sends the data of several applications originating from a source host to communicate with parallel applications on one or many destination host(s). The specific port number for each software application is set by software within the source machine before transmission. When it transmits a message, the source computer includes extra bits that encode the type of message, the program with which it was created, and which protocols were used. Each software application transmitting a data stream segment uses the same preordained port number. When it receives the data stream, the destination computers are empowered to sort and reunite each application's segments, providing the transport layer with all it needs to pass the data up to its upper-layer peer application.

FIGURE 2.4

Transport layer data
segments sharing a
traffic stream

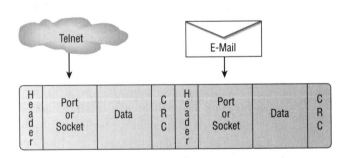

In reliable transport operation, one user first establishes a connection-oriented session with its peer system. Figure 2.5 portrays a typical connection-oriented session taking place between sending and receiving systems. In it, both hosts' application programs begin by notifying their individual operating systems that a connection is about to be initiated. The two operating systems communicate by sending messages over the network confirming that the transfer is approved and that both sides are ready for it to take place. Once the required synchronization is complete, a connection is fully established and the data transfer begins. While the information is being transferred between hosts, the two machines periodically check in with each other, communicating through their protocol software, to ensure that all is going well and the data is being received properly. The following summarize the steps in the connection-oriented session pictured in Figure 2.5:

- The first "connection agreement" segment is a request for synchronization.

- The second and third segments acknowledge the request and establish connection parameters between hosts.

- The final segment is also an acknowledgment. It notifies the destination host that the connection agreement is accepted and that the actual connection has been established. Data transfer can now begin.

F I G U R E   2.5

Establishing a connection-oriented session

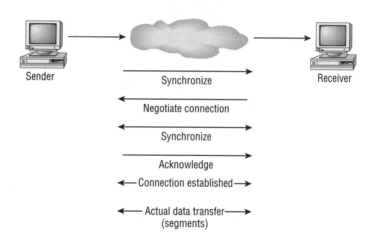

During a transfer, congestion can occur because either a chatty, high-speed computer is generating data traffic faster than the network can transfer it, or because many computers are simultaneously sending datagrams through a single gateway or destination. In the latter case, a gateway or destination can become congested even though no single source caused the problem. In either case, the problem is basically akin to a freeway bottleneck—too much traffic for too small a capacity.

When a machine receives a flood of datagrams too quickly for it to process, it stores them in. This buffering action solves the problem only if the datagrams are part of a small burst. However, if the datagram deluge continues, a device's memory will eventually be exhausted. Its flood capacity will be exceeded, and it will discard any additional datagrams that arrive. But, no worries—because of transport function, network flood control systems work quite well. Instead of dumping resources and allowing data to be lost, the transport can issue a "not ready" indicator, as shown in Figure 2.6, to the overzealous sender. This mechanism works kind of like a stoplight, signaling the sending device to stop transmitting segment traffic to its overwhelmed peer. When the peer receiver has processed the segments already in its memory reservoir, it sends out a "ready" transport indicator. When the machine waiting to transmit the rest of its datagrams receives this "go" indictor, it can then resume its transmission.

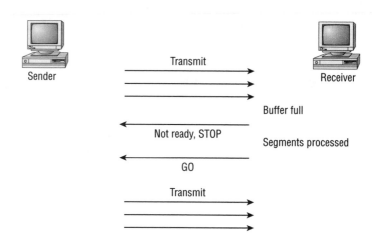

FIGURE 2.6

Transmitting segments with flow control

In fundamental, reliable, connection-oriented data transfer, datagrams are delivered to the receiving host in exactly the same sequence they're transmitted, and the transmission fails if this order is breached. Other things that will cause a failure to transmit are any data segments being lost, duplicated, or damaged along the way. The answer to the problem is to have the receiving host acknowledge receiving each and every data segment.

Data throughput would be low if the transmitting machine had to wait for an acknowledgment after sending each segment, so because there's time available after the sender transmits the data segment and before it finishes processing acknowledgments from the receiving machine, the sender uses the break to transmit more data. How many data segments the transmitting machine is allowed to send without receiving an acknowledgment for them is called a *window*.

Windowing controls how much information is transferred from one end to the other. While some protocols quantify information by observing the number of packets, TCP/IP measures it by counting the number of bytes. In Figure 2.7, we show a window size of 1 and a window size of 3. When a window size of 1 is configured, the sending machine waits for an acknowledgment for each data segment it transmits before transmitting another. Configured to a window size of 3, it's allowed to transmit three data segments before an acknowledgment is received. In our simplified example, both the sending and receiving machines are workstations. Reality is rarely that simple, and most often acknowledgments and packets will comingle as they travel over the network and pass through routers. Routing complicates things, but not to worry, we'll be covering applied routing later in the book.

FIGURE 2.7

Windowing

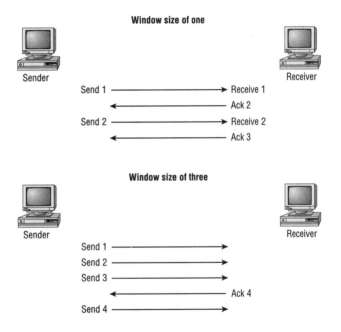

Reliable data delivery ensures the integrity of a stream of data sent from one machine to the other through a fully functional data link. It guarantees the data won't be duplicated or lost. The method that achieves this is known as *positive acknowledgment with retransmission*. This technique requires a receiving machine to communicate with the transmitting source by sending an acknowledgment message back to the sender when it receives data. The sender documents each segment it sends and waits for this acknowledgment before sending the next segment. When it sends a segment, the transmitting machine starts a timer and retransmits if it expires before an acknowledgment for the segment is returned from the receiving end.

In Figure 2.8, the sending machine transmits segments 1, 2, and 3. The receiving node acknowledges it has received them by requesting segment 4. When it receives the acknowledgment, the sender then transmits segments 4, 5, and 6. If segment 5 doesn't make it through to the destination, the receiving node acknowledges that event with a request for the segment to be resent. The sending machine will then resend the lost segment and wait for an acknowledgment, which it must receive in order to move on to the transmission of segment 7.

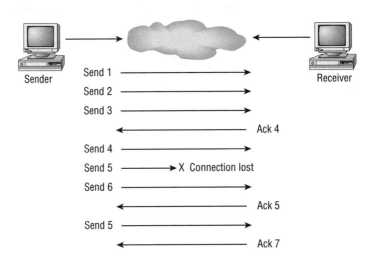

FIGURE 2.8

Transport layer reliable delivery

Network Layer

In life, there are lots of roads leading to Rome. The same holds true with the complicated cloud of networks, and the proper path through them is determined by protocols residing in layer number three—the *Network layer*. Path determination makes it possible for a router to appraise all available paths to a given destination and decide on the best one. Routers use network topology information when orienting themselves to the network and evaluating the different possible paths through it. These network "maps" can be configured by the network's administrator or obtained through dynamic processes running on the network. The Network layer's interface is connected to networks, and it's employed by the Transport layer to provide the best end-to-end packet delivery services. The job of sending packets from the source network to the destination network is the Network layer's primary function. After the router decides on the best path from point A to point B, it proceeds with switching the packet onto it—something known as *packet switching*. This is essentially forwarding the packet received by the router on one network interface, or *port*, to the port that connects to the best path through the network cloud. This will then send the packet to that particular packet's destination. We'll cover packet switching more thoroughly later on.

An internetwork must continually designate all paths of its media connections. In Figure 2.9 each line connecting routers is numbered, and those numbers are used by routers as network addresses. These addresses possess and convey important information about the path of media connections. They're used by a routing protocols to pass packets from a source onward to its destination. The Network layer creates a composite "network map"—a communication strategy system—by combining information about the sets of links into an internetwork with path determination, path switching, and route processing functions. It can also use these addresses to provide relay capability and interconnect independent networks. Consistent across the entire internetwork, layer three addresses also streamline the network's performance by preventing unnecessary broadcasts that gobble up precious bandwidth. Unnecessary broadcasts increase the network's overhead and waste capacity on links and machines that don't need to receive them. Using consistent end-to-end addressing that accurately describes the path of media connections enables the Network layer to determine the best path to a destination without encumbering the device or links on the internetwork with unnecessary broadcasts.

FIGURE 2.9

Communicating through an internetwork

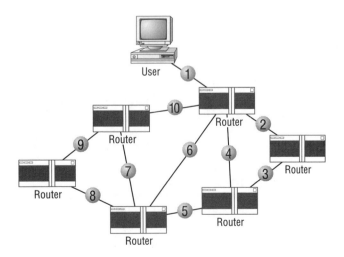

When an application on a host wants to send a packet to a destination device located on a different network, a data-link frame is received on one of the router's network interfaces. The router proceeds to decapsulate, then examine, the frame to establish what kind of network-layer data is in tow. After this is determined, the data is sent on to the appropriate network-layer process, but the frame's mission is fulfilled, and it's simply discarded.

Detailed in Figure 2.10 is the Network layer process examining the packet's header to discover which network it's destined for. It then refers to the routing table to find the connections the current network has to foreign network interfaces. After one is selected, the packet is re-encapsulated in its data link frame with the selected interface's information and queued for delivery off to the next hop in the path toward its destination. This process is repeated every time the packet switches through another router. When it finally reaches the router connected to the network that the destination host is located on, the packet is encapsulated in the destination LAN's data link frame type. It is now properly packaged and ready for delivery to the protocol stack on the destination host.

FIGURE 2.10

The Network layer process

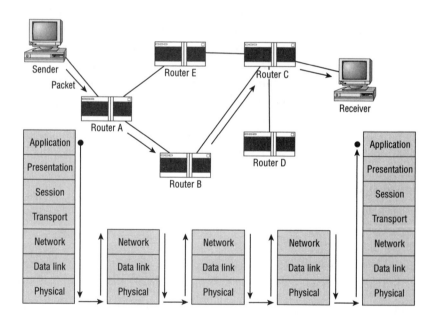

Data Link Layer

The *Data Link* layer ensures that messages are delivered to the proper device and translates messages from up above into bits for the Physical layer to transmit. It formats the message into *data frames* and adds a customized header containing the hardware destination and source address. This added information forms a sort of capsule that surrounds the original message much like engines, navigational devices, and other tools were attached to the lunar modules of the Apollo project. These various pieces of equipment were only useful during certain stages of space flight, and were stripped off the module and discarded when their designated stage was complete. Data traveling through networks is much the same. A data frame that's all packaged up and ready to go follows the format outlined in Figure 2.11. It's various elements are described here:

- The *Preamble* or *start indicator* is made up of a special bit pattern that alerts devices to the beginning of a data frame.

- The *destination address* (DA) is there for obvious reasons. The Data Link layer of every device on the network examines this to see if it matches its own address.

- The *source address* (SA) is the address of the sending device; it exists to facilitate replies to the messages.

- In *Ethernet_II frames*, the two-byte field following the source address is a type field. This field specifies the upper-layer protocol that will receive the data after data link processing is complete.

- In *802.3 frames*, the two-byte field following the source address is a length field, which indicates the number of bytes of data that follow this field and precede the Frame Check Sequence (FCS) field. Following the length field could be an 808.2 header for Logical Link Control (LLC) information. This information is needed to specify the upper layer process, because 802.3 does not have a type field.

- The *data* is the actual message, plus all the information sent down to the sending device's Data Link layer from the layers above it.

- Finally, there's the *Frame Check Sequence* (FCS) field. Its purpose corresponds to its name, and it houses the Cyclic Redundancy Checksum (CRC). An IP packet contains a bit of data called a *checksum header*, which checks whether the header information was damaged on the way from sender to receiver. CRCs work like this: The device sending the data determines a value summary for the CRC and stashes it within the frame. The device on the receiving end performs the same procedure, then checks to see if its value matches the total, or sum, of the sending node, hence the term *checksum*.

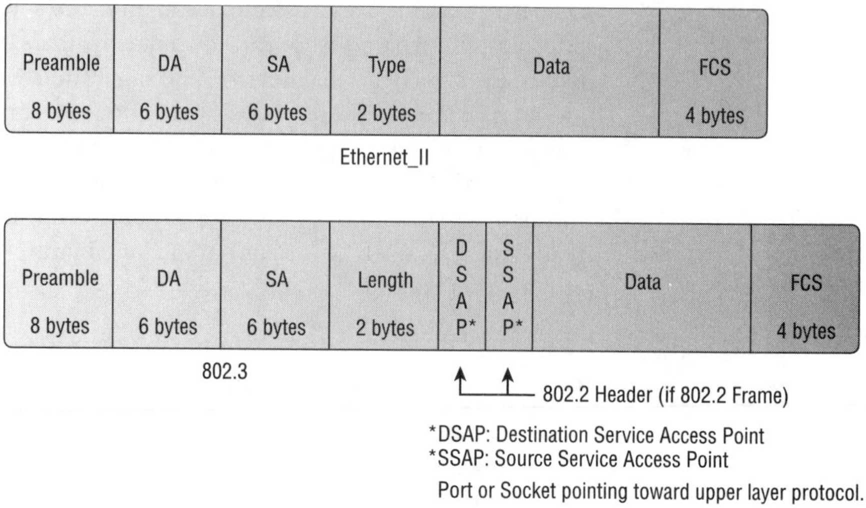

FIGURE 2.11

Ethernet_II and 802.3
frames

Preamble	DA	SA	Type	Data	FCS
8 bytes	6 bytes	6 bytes	2 bytes		4 bytes

Ethernet_II

Preamble	DA	SA	Length	D S A P*	S S A P*	Data	FCS
8 bytes	6 bytes	6 bytes	2 bytes				4 bytes

802.3

802.2 Header (if 802.2 Frame)

*DSAP: Destination Service Access Point
*SSAP: Source Service Access Point

Port or Socket pointing toward upper layer protocol.

WAN Protocols at the Data Link Layer   The typical encapsulations for synchronous serial lines at the Data Link layer are:

High Level Data Link Control (HDLC): The ISO created the HDLC standard to support both point-to-point and multi-point configurations. Unfortunately, most vendors implement HDLC in different manners, so HDLC is often not compatible between vendors.

Synchronous Data Link Control (SDLC): A protocol created by IBM to aid their mainframes in connecting remote offices. Created for use in WANs, it became extremely popular in the 1980s, as many companies were installing 327x controllers in their remote offices to communicate with the mainframe in the corporate office. SDLC defines and uses a polling media access, which means the *Primary* (front-end) asks, or polls, the *Secondaries* (327x controllers) to find out if they need to communicate with it. Secondaries cannot speak unless spoken to, nor can two Secondaries speak to each other.

X.25: The first packet switching network. This defines the specifications between a DTE and a DCE.

Link Access Procedure, Balanced (LAPB): Created for use with X.25, it defines and is capable of detecting out-of-sequence or missing frames and retransmitting, exchanging, and acknowledging frames.

Serial Line IP (SLIP): An industry standard developed in 1984 to support TCP/IP networking over low-speed serial interfaces in Berkeley UNIX. With the Windows NT RAS service, Windows NT computers can use TCP/IP and SLIP to communicate with remote hosts.

Point-to-Point Protocol (PPP): SLIP's big brother. It takes the specifications of SLIP and adds login, password, and error correction. See RFC 1661 for more information, as described by the IETF.

Integrated Services Digital Network (ISDN): Analog phone lines converted to use digital signaling. They can transmit both voice and data.

Frame Relay: This is an upgrade from X.25 to be used where LAPB is no longer used. It's the fastest of the WAN protocols listed because of its simplified framing, which has no error correction. It must use the high-quality digital facilities of the phone company and is therefore not available everywhere.

High-Speed Ethernet at the Data Link Layer   Users need bandwidth, and 10Mbps isn't good enough; they need 100Mbps—switched 100Mbps Ethernet rises to this call well. Some of the new technologies are:

100BaseFX: Ethernet over fiber at 100Mbps using 802.3 specs.

100Base4: Using 802.3 specs, 100Mbps over category 3, 4, or 5 cabling.

100BaseTX: Fast Ethernet over category 5 cabling. It's compatible with the 802.3 specifications.

100BaseVG AnyLan: IEEE movement into fast Ethernet and Token Ring, which seems to be going nowhere fast, mostly because it is *not* compatible with the 802.3 standards.

Physical Layer

The Physical layer focuses on two responsibilities: It sends bits and receives bits. Bits only come in values of 1 or 0—a Morse code with numerical value. The Physical layer communicates directly with the various types of actual communication media. Different kinds of media represent these bit values in different ways. Some use audio tones, while others employ *state transitions*— changes in voltage from high to low and low to high. Specific protocols are needed for each type of media that describes the proper bit patterns to be used, how data is encoded into media signals, and the various qualities of the physical media's attachment interface.

At the Physical layer, the interface between the Data Terminal Equipment, or DTE, and the Data Circuit-terminating Equipment, or DCE, is identified. The DCE is usually the service provider, while the DTE is the attached device. The services available to the DTE are most often accessed via a modem or Channel Service Unit/Data Service Unit (CSU/DSU).

The following Physical layer standards define this interface:

- EIA/TAI-232

- EIA/TIA-449

- V.24

- V.35

- X.21

- G.703

- EIA-530

- High-Speed Serial Interface (HSSI)

The DOD Reference Model

The DOD model is a condensed version of the OSI model. It is comprised of four instead of seven layers:

- Process/Application

- Host-to-Host

- Internet

- Network Access

Figure 2.12 shows a comparison of the four-layer DOD model and the seven-layer OSI reference model. As you can see, the two are similar in concept, but have a different number of layers with different names.

F I G U R E   2.12

The DOD model and the
OSI model

DOD Model

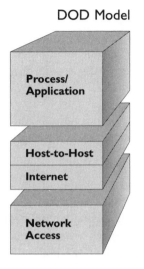

OSI Reference Model

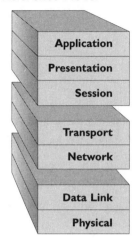

Process/Application Layer

The DOD model's layer corresponding to the OSI's top three is known as the *Process/Application layer*. A whole lot of work gets done at this layer, and in it is found a vast array of protocols that combine to integrate the various activities and duties spanning the focus of the OSI's Session, Presentation, and Application layers. We'll be looking closely at those protocols in the next part of this lesson. The Process/Application layer defines protocols for host-to-host application communication. It also controls user interface specifications.

Host-to-Host Layer

The *Host-to-Host layer* parallels the functions of OSI's Transport layer, defining protocols for setting up the level of transmission service for applications. It tackles issues like creating reliable end-to-end communication and ensuring the error-free delivery of data. It handles packet sequencing and maintains data integrity.

Internet Layer

The *Internet layer* corresponds to the Network layer, designating the protocols relating to the logical transmission of packets over the entire network. It takes care of the addressing of hosts by giving them an *IP address,* and handles the routing of packets among multiple networks. It also controls the communication flow between two applications.

Network Access Layer

At the bottom, the *Network Access layer* monitors the data exchange between the host and the network. The equivalent of the data link and physical layers of the OSI model, it oversees hardware addressing and defines protocols for the physical transmission of data.

The DOD Protocols

While the DOD model and the OSI model are truly alike in design and concept, with similar things happening in similar places, the specifications on *how* those things happen are different. This leads to a much different suite of protocols for the DOD model than those existing for the OSI model. Figure 2.13 shows the TCP/IP protocol suite and how its protocols relate to the DOD model layers.

FIGURE 2.13

The TCP/IP protocol suite

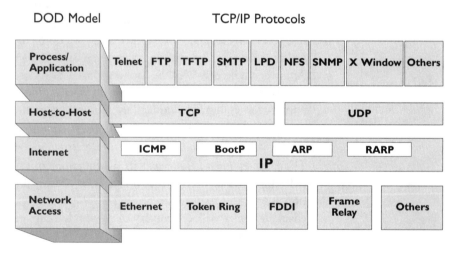

Process/Application Layer Protocols

As we explored earlier, one of the design goals of the original creators of the Internet was to have applications that could run on different computer platforms and yet, somehow, still communicate. The cavalry arrived in the form of Process/Application layer protocols, which address the ability of one application to communicate with another, regardless of hardware platform, operating system, and other features of the two hosts.

Most applications written with TCP/IP protocols can be characterized as *client/server* applications. This means that there are two major parts to the software involved and that it's probably running on two different machines.

The server part of this software duo usually runs on the machine where the data is actually residing. This machine is the Big Dog. It tends to be powerful because much of the data processing, as well as storage, is done on it. It works like this: The client software sends requests to the server software for it to fulfill. Some typical requests include searches for information, printing, e-mail stuff, application services, and file transfers.

In addition to communicating with the server, another function of client software is to provide an interface for the user. It also allows you to tinker with the data you've managed to coax from the server.

These matters in hand, we'll move along and investigate just what sort of protocols populate the DOD model's Process/Application layer.

Telnet

The chameleon of protocols, *Telnet*'s specialty is terminal emulation. It allows a user on a remote client machine, called the *Telnet client,* to access the resources of another machine, the *Telnet server*. Telnet achieves this by pulling a fast one on the Telnet server, dressing up the client machine to appear like a terminal directly attached to the local network. This projection is actually a software image, a virtual terminal that can interact with the chosen remote host. These emulated terminals are of the text-mode type and can execute refined procedures like displaying menus that give users the opportunity to choose options from them, accessing the applications on the duped server. Users begin a Telnet session by running the Telnet client software, then logging on to the Telnet server.

Telnet's capabilities are limited to running applications or peeking into what's on the server. It's a "just looking" protocol. It can't be used for file sharing functions like downloading stuff. For the actual snatching of goodies, one must employ the next protocol on the list: FTP.

FTP (File Transfer Protocol)

This is the "Grab it—Give it" protocol that affords us the luxury of transferring files. FTP can facilitate this between any two machines that are using it. But FTP is not just a protocol—it's also a program. Operating as a protocol, FTP is used by applications. As a program, it's employed by users to perform file tasks by hand. FTP also allows for access to both directories and files, and can also accomplish certain types of directory operations. FTP teams up with Telnet to transparently log you in to the FTP server, and then provides for the transfer of files.

Wow! Obviously, a tool this powerful would need to be secure—and FTP is! Accessing a host through FTP is only the first step. Users must then be subjected to an authentication login that's probably secured with passwords and user names placed there by system administrators to restrict access. (And you thought this was going to be easy!) Not to fear, you can still get in by adopting the user name "anonymous," but what you'll gain access to once in there will be limited.

Even when being employed by users manually as a program, FTP's functions are limited to listing and manipulating directories, typing file contents, and copying files between hosts. It can't execute remote files as programs.

TFTP (Trivial File Transfer Protocol)

TFTP is the stripped-down, stock version of FTP, though it's the protocol of choice if you know exactly what you want, and where it is to be found. It doesn't spoil you with the luxury of functions that FTP does. TFTP has no directory browsing abilities; it can do nothing but give and receive files. This austere little protocol also skimps in the data department, sending much smaller blocks of data than FTP. Also noteworthy is that TFTP will only open boring, public files, thereby depriving you of both the rush of having gotten away with something *and* the feeling of being special and privileged. There's no authentication as there is with FTP, so it's insecure; and few sites actually support it due to the inherent security risks.

NFS (Network File System)

Introducing...NFS! This is a jewel of a protocol specializing in file sharing. It allows two different types of file systems to interoperate. It's like this: Suppose the NFS server software is running on a NT server, and the NFS client software is running on a UNIX host. NFS allows for a portion of the RAM on the NT server to transparently store UNIX files, which can, in turn, be used by UNIX users. Even though the NT file system and the UNIX file system are unlike—they have different case sensitivity, filename lengths, security, and so on—both the UNIX users and the NT users can access that same file with their normal file systems, in their normal way.

Imagine yourself as an African back at the airport in Bavaria, heading toward the baggage claim area. With NFS in tow, you're equipped to actually retrieve your luggage, in a non-annihilated state, and get it through customs—all whilst chatting glibly in Swahili as you normally would! Additionally, the good news doesn't end there. Where Telnet, FTP, and TFTP are limited, NFS goes the extra mile. Remember that FTP cannot execute remote files as programs? NFS can! It can open a graphics application on your computer at work, and update the work you did on the one at home last night on the same program. NFS has the ability to import and export material—to manipulate applications remotely.

SMTP (Simple Mail Transfer Protocol)

Out of baggage-claim, and into the mail room.... SMTP, answering our ubiquitous call to e-mail, uses a *spooled, or queued,* method of mail delivery. Once a message has been sent to a destination, the message is spooled to a device—usually a disk. The server software at the destination posts a vigil, regularly checking this spool for messages, and upon finding them, proceeds to deliver them to their destination.

LPD (Line Printer Daemon)

This protocol is designed for printer sharing. The LPD daemon, along with the *LPR* (Line Printer) program, allows print jobs to be spooled and sent to the network's printers.

X Window

Designed for client-server operations, X Window defines a protocol for the writing of graphical, user interface–based client/server applications. The idea is to allow a program, called a client, to run on one computer and allow it to display on another computer that is running a special program called a window server.

SNMP (Simple Network Management Protocol)

Just as doctors are better equipped to maintain the health of their patients when they have the patient's history in hand, network managers are at an advantage if they possess performance histories of the network in their care. These case histories contain valuable information that enables the manager to anticipate future needs and analyze trends. By comparing the network's present condition to its past functioning patterns, managers can more easily isolate and troubleshoot problems.

SNMP is the protocol that provides for the collection and manipulation of this valuable network information. It gathers data by *polling* the devices on the network from a management station at fixed intervals, requiring them to disclose certain information. When all is well, SNMP receives something called a *baseline*—a report delimiting the operational traits of a healthy network. This handy protocol can also stand as a watchman over the network, quickly notifying managers of any sudden turn of events. These network watch-men are called *agents,* and when aberrations occur, agents send an alert called a *trap* to the management station.

The sensitivity of the agent, or threshold, can be increased or decreased by the network manager. An agent's threshold is like a pain threshold; the more sensitive it is set to be, the sooner it screams an alert. Managers use baseline reports to aid them in deciding on agent threshold settings for their networks. The more sophisticated the management station's equipment is, the clearer the picture it can provide of the network's functioning. More powerful consoles have better record-keeping ability, as well as the added benefit of being able to provide enhanced graphic interfaces that can form logical portraits of network structure.

Host-to-Host Layer Protocols

As you learned earlier, the broad goal of the Host-to-Host layer is to shield the upper layer applications from the complexities of the network. This layer says to the upper layer, "Just give me your data, with any instructions, and I'll begin the process of getting your information ready for sending." The following sections describe the two main protocols at this layer.

TCP (Transmission Control Protocol)

TCP has been around since networking's early years when WANs weren't very reliable. It was created to mitigate that problem, and reliability is TCP's strong point. It tests for errors, resends data if necessary, and reports the occurrence of errors to the upper layers if it can't manage to solve the problem itself.

This protocol takes large blocks of information from an application and breaks them down into *segments*. It numbers and sequences each segment so that the destination's TCP protocol can put the segments back into the large block the application intended. After these segments have been sent, TCP waits for acknowledgment of each one from the receiving end's TCP, retransmitting the ones not acknowledged.

Before it starts to send segments down the model, the sender's TCP protocol contacts the destination's TCP protocol in order to establish a connection. What is created is known as a *virtual circuit*. This type of communication is called *connection-oriented*. During this initial handshake, the two TCP layers also agree on the amount of information that is to be sent before the recipient TCP sends back an acknowledgment. With everything agreed upon in advance, the stage is set for reliable Application-layer communication to take place.

TCP is a full-duplex connection, reliable, accurate, jellybean-counting protocol, and establishing all these terms and conditions, in addition to following through on them to check for error, is no small task. It's very complicated, and very costly in terms of network overhead. Using TCP should be reserved for use only in situations when reliability is of utmost importance. For one thing, today's networks are much more reliable than those of yore, and therefore the added security is often a wasted effort. We'll discuss an alternative to TCP's high overhead method of transmission, UDP, next.

UDP (User Datagram Protocol)

This protocol is used in place of TCP. UDP is the scaled down economy model and is considered a *thin protocol*. Like a thin person on a park bench, it doesn't take up a lot of room—in this case, on a network. It also doesn't offer all the bells and whistles of TCP, but it does do a fabulous job of transporting stuff that doesn't require reliable delivery—and it does it using far fewer network resources.

There are some situations where it would definitely be wise to opt for UDP instead of TCP. Remember that watchdog SNMP up there at the Process/Application layer? SNMP monitors the network, sending intermittent messages and a fairly steady flow of status updates and alerts, especially when running on a large network. The cost in overhead necessary to establish, maintain, and close a TCP connection for each one of those little messages would reduce a normally healthy, efficient network to a sticky, sluggish bog in no time. Another circumstance calling for the deployment of UDP over TCP is when the matter of reliability is seen to at the Process/Application layer. NFS handles its own reliability issues, making the use of TCP both impractical and redundant.

UDP receives upper-layer blocks of information instead of streams of data like its big brother, TCP, and breaks them into segments. Also like TCP, each segment is given a number for reassembly into the intended block at the destination. However, UDP does *not* sequence the segments, and does not care in which order the segments arrive at the destination. At least it numbers them. But after that, UDP sends them off and forgets about them. It doesn't follow through, check up on, or even allow for an acknowledgment of safe arrival—complete abandonment. Because of this, it's referred to as an *unreliable* protocol. This does not mean that UDP is ineffective—only that it doesn't handle issues of reliability.

There are more things UDP doesn't do. It doesn't create a virtual circuit, and it doesn't contact the destination before delivering stuff to it. It is therefore considered a *connectionless* protocol.

Key Concepts of Host-to-Host Protocols

The following list highlights some of the key concepts that you should keep in mind regarding these two protocols.

TCP	UDP
Virtual circuit	Unsequenced
Sequenced	Unreliable
Acknowledgments	Connectionless
Reliable	Low overhead

Instructors commonly use a telephone analogy to help people understand how TCP works. Most of us understand that before you talk with someone on a phone, you must first establish a connection with that other person—wherever they may be. This is like a virtual circuit with the TCP protocol. If you were giving someone important information during your conversation, you might say, "Did you get that?" A query like that is like a TCP acknowledgment. From time to time, for various reasons, people also say, "Are you still there?" They end their conversations with a "goodbye" of some sort, putting closure on the phone call. These types of functions are done by TCP.

Alternately, using UDP is like sending a postcard. To do that, you don't need to contact the other party first. You simply write your message, address it, and mail it. This is analogous to UDP's connectionless orientation. Since the message on the postcard is probably not a matter of life or death, you don't need an acknowledgment of its receipt. Similarly, UDP does not involve acknowledgments.

Internet Layer Protocols

There are two main reasons for the Internet layer: routing, and providing a single network interface to the upper layers. None of the upper-layer protocols, and none of the ones on the lower layer, have any functions relating to routing. Routing is complex and important, and it's the job of the Internet layer to carry it out. The protocol *IP* is so integral to this layer, the very name of it is the name of the layer itself. So far, in discussing the upper layers, we've begun with a brief introduction, and left any specific treatise on their resident protocols to supporting sections. However here, IP, though only a protocol, is essentially the Internet layer. We've therefore included it in our introductory talk on the layer. The other protocols found here merely exist to support it. IP contains the Big Picture, and could be said to "see all," in that it is aware of all the interconnected networks. It can do this because all the machines on the network have a software address called an IP address.

IP looks at each packet's IP address. Then, using a routing protocol, it decides where this packet is to be sent next, choosing the best path. The Network Access layer protocols at the bottom of the model don't possess IP's enlightened scope of the entire network; they deal only with point-to-point physical links.

A second main reason for the Internet layer is to provide a single network interface to the upper-layer protocols. Without this layer, application programmers would need to write "hooks" into every one of their applications for each different Network Access protocol. This would not only be a pain in the neck, it would lead to different versions of each application—one for Ethernet, another one for Token Ring, and so on. To prevent this, IP, lord of the Internet layer, provides one single network interface for the upper-layer protocols. That accomplished, it's then the job of IP and the various Network Access protocols to get along and work together.

All network roads don't lead to Rome—they lead to IP, and all the other protocols at this layer, as well as all the upper-layer protocols, use it. Never forget that. All paths through the model go through IP. The following sections describe the protocols at the Internet layer.

IP (Internet Protocol)

Identifying devices on networks requires having the answers to these two questions: Which network is it on, and what is it's ID on that network? The first is the *software address* (the right street); the second, the *hardware address* (the right mailbox). All hosts on a network have a logical ID called an IP address. This is the software address, and it contains valuable encoded information greatly simplifying the complex task of routing.

IP takes segments from the Host-to-Host layer and fragments them into *datagrams* (packets). IP also reassembles datagrams back into segments on the receiving side. Each datagram is assigned the IP address of the sender and the IP address of the recipient. Each machine that receives a datagram makes routing decisions based upon the packet's destination IP address.

ARP (Address Resolution Protocol)

When IP has a datagram to send, it has already been informed by upper-layer protocols of the destination's IP address. However, IP must also inform a Network Access protocol, such as Ethernet, of the destination's hardware address. If IP does not know the hardware address, it uses the ARP protocol to find this information. As IP's detective, ARP interrogates the network by sending out a broadcast asking the machine with the specified IP address to reply with its hardware address. ARP is able to translate a software address, the IP address, into a hardware address—for example, the destination machine's Ethernet board address—thereby deducing its whereabouts. This hardware address is technically referred to as the *media access control (MAC) address*.

RARP (Reverse Address Resolution Protocol)

When an IP machine happens to be a diskless machine, it has no way of initially knowing its IP address. But it does know its MAC address. The RARP protocol is the psychoanalyst for these lost souls. It sends out a packet that includes its MAC address and a request to be informed of what IP address is assigned to its MAC address. A designated machine, called a *RARP server*, responds with the answer, and the identity crisis is over. Like a good analyst, RARP uses the information it does know about it, the machine's MAC address, to learn its IP address and complete the machines ID portrait.

BootP

BootP stands for *Boot Program*. When a diskless workstation is powered on, it broadcasts a BootP request on the network. A BootP server hears the request and looks up the client's MAC address in its BootP file. If it finds an appropriate entry, it responds by telling the machine its IP address and the file—usually via the TFTP protocol—that it should boot from.

BootP is used by a diskless machine to learn the following:

- Its IP address

- The IP address of a server machine

- The name of a file that is to be loaded into memory and executed at boot-up

ICMP (Internet Control Message Protocol)

ICMP is a management protocol and messaging service provider for IP. Its messages are carried as IP datagrams. *RFC 1256, ICMP Router Discovery Messages* is an annex to ICMP, affording hosts extended capability in discovering routes to gateways. Periodically, router advertisements are announced over the network reporting IP addresses for its network interfaces. Hosts listen for these network infomercials to acquire route information. A *router solicitation* is a request for immediate advertisements, and may be sent by a host when it starts up. The following are some common events and messages that ICMP relates to:

Destination unreachable: If a router cannot send an IP datagram any further, it uses ICMP to send a message back to the sender advising it of the situation.

Buffer full: If a router's memory buffer for receiving incoming datagrams is full, it will use ICMP to send out this message.

Hops: Each IP datagram is allotted a certain number of routers that it may go through, called *hops*. If it reaches its limit of hops before arriving at its destination, the last router to receive that datagram throws it away. The executioner router then uses ICMP to send an obituary message informing the sending machine of the demise of its datagram. This is network population control.

Network Access Layer Protocols

Programmers for the DOD model didn't define protocols for this layer; instead, their focus began at the Internet layer. In fact, this is exactly the quality that allows this model to be implemented on almost any hardware platform. Obviously, this is one of the reasons why the Internet protocol suite is so popular. Every protocol listed here relates to the physical transmission of data. The following are the Network Access layer's main duties:

- Receiving an IP datagram and *framing* it into a stream of bits—ones and zeros—for physical transmission. (The information at this layer is called a *frame*.) An example of a protocol that works at this level is *CSMA/CD*, or *Carrier Sense, Multiple Access with Collision Detect*. Again, purpose equals name. It checks the cable to see if there's already another PC transmitting (Carrier Sense), allows all computers to share the same bandwidth (Multiple Access), and detects and retransmits collisions. Essentially, it's Network Access layer highway patrol.

- Specifying the MAC address. Even though the Internet layer determines the destination MAC address (the hardware address), the Network Access protocols actually place that MAC address in the MAC frame.

- Ensuring that the stream of bits making up the frame have been accurately received by calculating a CRC (Cyclic Redundancy Checksum) jellybean count.

- Specifying the access methods to the physical network, such as *Contention-based for Ethernet* (first come, first served), *Token-passing* (wait for token before transmitting) for Token Ring, *FDDI*, and *Polling* (wait to be asked) for IBM mainframes.

- Specifying the physical media, the connectors, electrical signaling, and timing rules.

Some of the technologies used to implement the Network Access layer are:

- LAN-oriented protocols:

  - Ethernet (thick coaxial cable, thin coaxial cable, twisted-pair cable)

  - Token Ring

  - ARCnet

- WAN-oriented protocols:

  - Point-to-Point Protocol (PPP)

  - X.25

  - Frame Relay

What Is IP Addressing?

One of the most important topics in any discussion of TCP/IP is *IP addressing*. An IP address is a numeric identifier assigned to each machine on an IP network. It designates the location of the device it's assigned to on the network. As mentioned earlier, this type of address is a software address, not a hardware address, which is hard-coded in the machine or network interface card.

The Hierarchical IP Addressing Scheme

An IP address is made up of 32 bits of information. These 32 bits are divided into four sections containing one byte each. These sections are referred to as *octets*. There are three methods for depicting an IP address:

- Dotted-decimal, as in 130.57.30.56

- Binary, as in 10000010.00111001.00011110.00111000

- Hexidecimal, as in 82 39 1E 38

All of these examples represent the same IP address.

The 32-bit IP address is a structured or hierarchical address, as opposed to a flat or nonhierarchical one. Although either type of addressing scheme could have been used, the hierarchical variety was chosen, and for a very good reason.

A good example of a flat addressing scheme is a social security number. There's no partitioning to it, meaning that each segment isn't allocated to numerically represent a certain area or characteristic of the individual it's assigned to. If this method had been used for IP addressing, every machine on the Internet would have needed a totally unique address, just as each social security number is unique. The good news about this scheme is that it can handle a large number of addresses, namely 4.2 billion (a 32-bit address space with two possible values for each position—either 0 or 1—giving you 2^{32}, which equals 4.2 billion). The bad news, and the reason for it being passed over, relates to routing. With every address totally unique, all routers on the Internet would need to store the address of each and every machine on the Internet. It would be fair to say that this would make efficient routing impossible even if a fraction of the possible addresses were used.

The solution to this dilemma is to use a two-level, hierarchical addressing scheme that's structured by class, rank, grade, and so on. An example of this type is a telephone number. The first section of a telephone number, the area code, designates a very large area, followed by the prefix, narrowing the scope to a local calling area. The final segment, the customer number, zooms in on the specific connection. It's similar with IP addresses. Rather than the entire 32 bits being treated as a unique identifier as in flat addressing, a part of the address is designated as the *network address*, and the other part as a *node address*, giving it a layered, hierarchical structure.

The network address uniquely identifies each network. Every machine on the same network shares that network address as part of its IP address. In the IP address 130.57.30.56, for example, the 130.57 is the network address.

The node address is assigned to, and uniquely identifies, each machine on a network. This part of the address must be unique because it identifies a particular machine—an individual, as opposed to a network, which is a group. This number can also be referred to as a *host address*. In the sample IP address 130.57.30.56, the .30.56 is the node address.

The designers of the Internet decided to create classes of networks based on network size. For the small number of networks possessing a very large number of nodes, they created the rank *Class A network*. At the other extreme is the *Class C network*, reserved for the numerous networks with a small number of nodes. The class distinction for networks in between very large and very small is predictably called a *Class B network*. How one would subdivide an IP address into a network and node address is determined by the class designation of one's network. Table 2.1 provides us with a summary of the three classes of networks, which will be described in more detail in the following sections.

T A B L E 2.1   Summary of the Three Classes of Networks

Class	Format	Leading bit pattern	Decimal range of first byte of the Network address	Maximum networks	Maximum nodes per network
A	Net.Node.Node.Node	0	1–127	127	16,777,216
B	Net.Net.Node.Node	10	128–191	16,384	65,534
C	Net.Net.Net.Node	110	192–223	2,097,152	254

To ensure efficient routing, Internet designers defined a mandate for the leading bits section of the address for each different network class. For example, since a router knows that a Class A network address always starts with a 0, it might be able to speed a packet on its way after reading only the first bit of its address. Figure 2.14 illustrates how the leading bits of a network address are defined.

F I G U R E 2.14

Leading bits of a network address

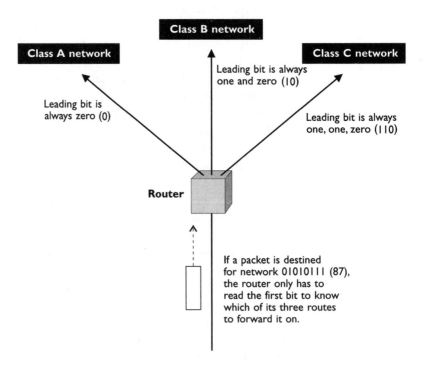

Some IP addresses are reserved for special purposes, and shouldn't be assigned to nodes by network administrators. Table 2.2 lists the members of this exclusive little club, along with their reason for inclusion.

TABLE 2.2	Address	Function
Reserved IP Addresses	Network address of all zeros	Interpreted to mean "this network"
	Network address of all ones	Interpreted to mean "all networks"
	Network 127	Reserved for loopback tests. Designates the local node and allows that node to send a test packet to itself without generating network traffic.
	Node address of all zeros	Interpreted to mean "this node"
	Node address of all ones	Interpreted to mean "all nodes" on the specified network; for example, 128.2.255.255 means "all nodes" on network 128.2 (Class B address)
	Entire IP address set to all zeros	Used by the RIP protocol to designate the default route
	Entire IP address set to all ones (same as 255.255.255.255)	Broadcast to all nodes on the current network; sometimes called an "all ones broadcast"

Class A Networks

In a Class A network, the first byte is assigned to the network address, and the three remaining bytes are used for the node addresses. The Class A format is:

Network.Node.Node.Node

For example, in the IP address 49.22.102.70, 49 is the network address, and 22.102.70 is the node address. Every machine on this particular network would have the distinctive network address of 49.

With the length of a Class A network address being a byte, and with the first bit of that byte reserved, seven remain for manipulation. That means that the maximum number of Class A networks that could be created would be 128. Why? Because each of the seven bit positions can either be a 0 or a 1, thus 2^7 or 128. To complicate things further, it was also decided that the network address of all zeros (0000 0000) would be reserved (see Table 2.2). This means the actual number of usable Class A network addresses is 128 minus 1, or 127.

Take a peek and see this for yourself in the decimal-to-binary chart shown in Table 2.3. Start at binary 0 and view the first bit (the leftmost bit). Continue down through the chart until the first bit turns into the digit 1. See that? Sure enough, the decimal range of a Class A network is 0 through 127. Since the "Much Ado about Nothing" Address (all zeros) is one of those special, reserved-club members, the range of network addresses for a Class A network is 1 through 127. Eventually, we'll see that another Class A number is in that club—number 127. This little revelation technically brings the total down to 126. But for the exam, remember 127.

TABLE 2.3

Decimal-to-Binary Chart

Decimal	Binary	Decimal	Binary	Decimal	Binary
0	0000 0000	18	0001 0010	36	0010 0100
1	0000 0001	19	0001 0011	37	0010 0101
2	0000 0010	20	0001 0100	38	0010 0110
3	0000 0011	21	0001 0101	39	0010 0111
4	0000 0100	22	0001 0110	40	0010 1000
5	0000 0101	23	0001 0111	41	0010 1001
6	0000 0110	24	0001 1000	42	0010 1010
7	0000 0111	25	0001 1001	43	0010 1011
8	0000 1000	26	0001 1010	44	0010 1100
9	0000 1001	27	0001 1011	45	0010 1101
10	0000 1010	28	0001 1100	46	0010 1110
11	0000 1011	29	0001 1101	47	0010 1111
12	0000 1100	30	0001 1110	48	0011 0000
13	0000 1101	31	0001 1111	49	0011 0001
14	0000 1110	32	0010 0000	50	0011 0010
15	0000 1111	33	0010 0001	51	0011 0011
16	0001 0000	34	0010 0010	52	0011 0100

T A B L E 2.3 *(cont.)*
Decimal-to-Binary Chart

Decimal	Binary	Decimal	Binary	Decimal	Binary
17	0001 0001	35	0010 0011	53	0011 0101
54	0011 0110	78	0100 1110	102	0110 0110
55	0011 0111	79	0100 1111	103	0110 0111
56	0011 1000	80	0101 0000	104	0110 1000
57	0011 1001	81	0101 0001	105	0110 1001
58	0011 1010	82	0101 0010	106	0110 1010
59	0011 1011	83	0101 0011	107	0110 1011
60	0011 1100	84	0101 0100	108	0110 1100
61	0011 1101	85	0101 0101	109	0110 1101
62	0011 1110	86	0101 0110	110	0110 1110
63	0011 1111	87	0101 0111	111	0110 1111
64	0100 0000	88	0101 1000	112	0111 0000
65	0100 0001	89	0101 1001	113	0111 0001
66	0100 0010	90	0101 1010	114	0111 0010
67	0100 0011	91	0101 1011	115	0111 0011
68	0100 0100	92	0101 1100	116	0111 0100
69	0100 0101	93	0101 1101	117	0111 0101
70	0100 0110	94	0101 1110	118	0111 0110
71	0100 0111	95	0101 1111	119	0111 0111
72	0100 1000	96	0110 0000	120	0111 1000
73	0100 1001	97	0110 0001	121	0111 1001
74	0100 1010	98	0110 0010	122	0111 1010

T A B L E 2.3 *(cont.)* Decimal-to-Binary Chart	Decimal	Binary	Decimal	Binary	Decimal	Binary
	75	0100 1011	99	0110 0011	123	0111 1011
	76	0100 1100	100	0110 0100	124	0111 1100
	77	0100 1101	101	0110 0101	125	0111 1101
	126	0111 1110	150	1001 0110	174	1010 1110
	127	0111 1111	151	1001 0111	175	1010 1111
	128	1000 0000	152	1001 1000	176	1011 0000
	129	1000 0001	153	1001 1001	177	1011 0001
	130	1000 0010	154	1001 1010	178	1011 0010
	131	1000 0011	155	1001 1011	179	1011 0011
	132	1000 0100	156	1001 1100	180	1011 0100
	133	1000 0101	157	1001 1101	181	1011 0101
	134	1000 0110	158	1001 1110	182	1011 0110
	135	1000 0111	159	1001 1111	183	1011 0111
	136	1000 1000	160	1010 0000	184	1011 1000
	137	1000 1001	161	1010 0001	185	1011 1001
	138	1000 1010	162	1010 0010	186	1011 1010
	139	1000 1011	163	1010 0011	187	1011 1011
	140	1000 1100	164	1010 0100	188	1011 1100
	141	1000 1101	165	1010 0101	189	1011 1101
	142	1000 1110	166	1010 0110	190	1011 1110
	143	1000 1111	167	1010 0111	191	1011 1111
	144	1001 0000	168	1010 1000	192	1100 0000

	Decimal	Binary	Decimal	Binary	Decimal	Binary
TABLE 2.3 (cont.) Decimal-to-Binary Chart	145	1001 0001	169	1010 1001	193	1100 0001
	146	1001 0010	170	1010 1010	194	1100 0010
	147	1001 0011	171	1010 1011	195	1100 0011
	148	1001 0100	172	1010 1100	196	1100 0100
	149	1001 0101	173	1010 1101	197	1100 0101
	198	1100 0110	217	1101 1001	237	1110 1101
	199	1100 0111	218	1101 1010	238	1110 1110
	200	1100 1000	219	1101 1011	239	1110 1111
	201	1100 1001	220	1101 1100	240	1111 0000
	202	1100 1010	221	1101 1101	241	1111 0001
	203	1100 1011	222	1101 1110	242	1111 0010
	204	1100 1100	223	1101 1111	243	1111 0011
	205	1100 1101	224	1110 0000	244	1111 0100
	206	1100 1110	225	1110 0001	245	1111 0101
	207	1100 1111	226	1110 0010	246	1111 0110
	208	1101 0000	227	1110 0011	247	1111 0111
	209	1101 0001	228	1110 0100	248	1111 1000
	210	1101 0010	229	1110 0101	249	1111 1001
	211	1101 0011	230	1110 0110	250	1111 1010
	212	1101 0100	231	1110 0111	251	1111 1011
	213	1101 0101	232	1110 1000	252	1111 1100
	214	1101 0110	233	1110 1001	253	1111 1101

TABLE 2.3 (cont.)	Decimal	Binary	Decimal	Binary	Decimal	Binary
Decimal-to-Binary Chart	215	1101 0111	234	1110 1010	254	1111 1110
	216	1101 1000	235	1110 1011	255	1111 1111
	201	1100 1001	236	1110 1100		

Each Class A network has three bytes (24 bit positions) for the node address of a machine. That means there are 2^{24}—or 16,777,216—unique combinations, and therefore precisely that many unique node addresses possible for each Class A network. If math just isn't your thing, I'll explain—again, using the jellybean. Say you packed 24 of those tasty little critters in your briefcase for a snack. Considering you only have 24, and therefore no intention of sharing, you divide your beans (bits), into three equal mouthfuls (bytes), readying them for lightening quick consumption. While divvying them up, you notice how pretty they are, and get totally side-tracked—now absorbed instead in arranging them in various patterns and recording each grouping until you exhaust all possible unique combinations. Counting all your sequence entries, you make the important discovery that when one possesses 24 jellybeans, there are 16,777,214 possible unique combinations in which one can arrange them—or, 2^{24}. Try this next time you're bedridden, or just unspeakably bored.

Because addresses with the two patterns of all zeros and all ones are reserved, the actual maximum usable number of nodes per a Class A network is 2^{24} minus 2, which equals 16,777,214.

Class B Networks

In a Class B network, the first two bytes are assigned to the network address, and the remaining two bytes are used for node addresses. The format is:

Network.Network.Node.Node

For example, in the IP address 130.57.30.56, the network address is 130.57, and the node address is 30.56.

With the network address being two bytes, there would be 2^{16} unique combinations. But the Internet designers decided that all Class B networks should start with the binary digits 1 and 0. This leaves 14 bit positions to manipulate, and therefore 2^{14} or 16,384 unique Class B networks.

If you take another peek at the decimal-to-binary chart in Table 2.3, you will see that the first two bits of the first byte are 1 0 from decimal 128 up to 191. Therefore, if you're still confused, even after a jellybean session, remember that you can always easily recognize a Class B network by looking at its first byte—even though there are 16,384 different Class B networks! All you have to do is look at that address. If the first byte is in the range of decimal 128 to 191, it is a Class B network.

A Class B network has two bytes to use for node addresses. This is 2^{16} minus the two patterns in the reserved-exclusive club (all zeros and all ones), for a total of 65,534 possible node addresses for each Class B network.

Class C Networks

The first three bytes of a Class C network are dedicated to the network portion of the address, with only one measly byte remaining for the node address. The format is:

Network.Network.Network.Node

In the example IP address 198.21.74.102, the network address is 198.21.74, and the node address is 102.

In a Class C network, the first *three* bit positions are always the binary 110. The calculation is such: Three bytes, or 24 bits, minus three reserved positions, leaves 21 positions. There are therefore 2^{21} or 2,097,152 possible Class C networks.

Referring again to that decimal-to-binary chart in Table 2.3, you will see that the lead bit pattern of 110 starts at decimal 192 and runs through 223. Remembering our handy, non-calculatory, easy-recognition method, this means that although there are a total of 2,097,152 Class C networks possible, you can always spot a Class C address if the first byte is between 192 and 223.

Each unique Class C network has one byte to use for node addresses. This leads to 2^8 or 256, minus the two special club patterns of all 0s and all 1s, for a total of 254 node addresses for each Class C network.

Additional Classes of Networks

Another class of network is Class D. This range of addresses is used for *multicast packets*. The range of numbers is from 224.0.0.0 to 239.255.255.255.

A *multicast transmission* is used when a host wants to broadcast to multiple destinations. Hosts do this when attempting to learn of all the routers on their network. Using the ICMP protocol, it sends out a *router discovery packet*. This packet is addressed to 224.0.0.2, fingering it as a multicast packet to all the routers on its network.

There is also a Class E range of numbers starting at 240.0.0.0 and running to 255.255.255.255. These numbers are reserved for future use.

Unless you revel in chaos, and desire to add stress to your life, neither Class D nor E addresses should be assigned to nodes on your network.

Who Assigns Network Addresses?

If your network will be connected to the Internet, you must be proper and petition the official Internet authorities for the assignment of a network address. An official Internet organization called the Network Information Center (NIC) can assist you in this process. For further information, contact:

Network Solutions InterNIC Registration Services
505 Huntmar Park Drive
Herndon, VA 22070

You may also obtain help by sending e-mail to:

`hostmaster@internic.net`

If your network will not be connected to the Internet, you are free to assign any network address you wish.

For the most part, you are now able to obtain valid IP addresses from your Internet Service Provider (ISP). The NIC would prefer for you to do it that way, as it cuts down on the work they need to do.

Subnetting a Network

If an organization is large and has a whole bunch of computers, or if its computers are geographically dispersed, it makes good clean sense to divide its colossal network into smaller ones connected together by routers. The benefits to doings things this way include:

- Reduced network traffic. We all appreciate less traffic of any kind! So do networks. Without trusty routers, packet traffic could grind the entire network down to near standstill. With them, most traffic will stay on the local network—only packets destined for other networks will pass through the router.

- Optimized network performance, a bonus of reduced network traffic.

- Simplified management. It's easier to identify and isolate network problems in a group of smaller networks connected together than within one gigantic one.

- Facilitates spanning large geographical distances. Because WAN links are considerably slower and more expensive than LAN links, having a single large network spanning long distances can create problems in every arena listed above. Connecting multiple smaller networks makes the system more efficient.

All this is well and good, but if an organization with multiple networks has been assigned only one network address by the NIC, that organization has a problem. As the saying goes, "Where there is no vision, the people perish." The original designers of the IP protocol envisioned a teensy Internet with only mere tens of networks and hundreds of hosts. Their addressing scheme used a network address for each physical network.

As you can imagine, this scheme and the unforeseen growth of the Internet created a few problems. To name one, a single network address can be used to refer to multiple physical networks. An organization can request individual network addresses for each one of its physical networks. If these were granted, there wouldn't be enough to go around for everyone.

Another problem relates to routers. If each router on the Internet needed to know about each existing physical network, routing tables would be impossibly huge. There would be an overwhelming amount of administrative overhead to maintain those tables, and the resulting physical overhead on the routers would be massive (CPU cycles, memory, disk space, and so on).

An additional consequence is that because routers exchange routing information with each other, a terrific overabundance of network traffic would result. Figure 2.15 illustrates some of these problems.

FIGURE 2.15

Liabilities to having individual network addresses for each physical network

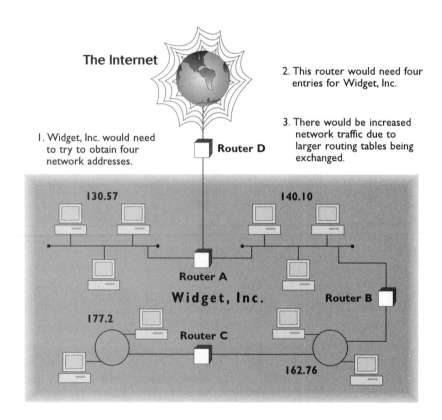

Although there's more than one way to approach this tangle, the principal solution is the one that we'll be covering in this book...subnetting.

What is subnetting? Subnetting is a dandy TCP/IP software feature that allows for dividing a single IP network into smaller, logical subnetworks. This trick is achieved by using the host portion of an IP address to create something called a subnet address.

Implementing Subnetting

As you know, the IP addressing scheme used for subnets is referred to as subnetting. Before you implement subnetting, you need to determine your current requirements and plan for future requirements. Follow these guidelines:

1. Determine the number of required network IDs.

   - One for each subnet

   - One for each WAN connection

2. Determine the number of required host IDs per subnet.

- One for each TCP/IP host

- One for each router interface

3. Based on the above requirement, create:

- One subnet mask for your entire network

- A unique subnet ID for each physical segment

- A range of host IDs for each subnet

Subnetting is network procreation. It's the act of creating little subnetworks from a single, large, parent network. An organization with a single network address can have a subnet address for each individual physical network. Each subnet is still part of the shared network address, but it also has an additional identifier denoting its individual subnetwork number. This identifier is called a subnet address. Take a parent who has two kids. The children inherit the same last name as their parent. People make further distinctions when referring to someone's individual children like, "Kelly, the Jones's oldest, who moved into their guest house; and Jamie, the Jones's youngest, who now has Kelly's old room." (They may make other kinds of distinctions too, but we won't talk about those here.) Those further distinctions are like subnet addresses for people.

This practice solves several addressing problems. First, if an organization has several physical networks but only one IP network address, it can handle the situation by creating subnets. Next, because subnetting allows many physical networks to be grouped together, fewer entries in a routing table are required, notably reducing network overhead. Finally, these things combine to collectively yield greatly enhanced network efficiency.

Information Hiding

As an example, suppose that the Internet refers to Widget, Inc. only by its single network address, 130.57. Suppose as well that Widget Inc. has several divisions, each dealing with something different. Since Widget's network administrators have implemented subnetting, when packets come into its network, the Widget routers use the subnet addresses to route the packets to the correct internal subnet. Thus, the complexity of Widget, Inc.'s network can be hidden from the rest of the Internet. This is called *information hiding*.

Information hiding also benefits the routers inside the Widget network. Without subnets, each Widget router would need to know the address of each machine on the entire Widget network—a bleak situation creating additional overhead and poor routing performance. But alas, because of the subnet scheme, which alleviates the need for each router to know about every machine on the entire Widget network, their routers need only two types of information:

■ The addresses of each machine on subnets to which it is attached

■ The other subnet addresses

How to Implement Subnetting

Subnetting is implemented by assigning a subnet address to each machine on a given physical network. For example, in Figure 2.16, each machine on Subnet 1 has a subnet address of 1. Next, we'll take a look at how a subnet address is incorporated into the rest of the IP address.

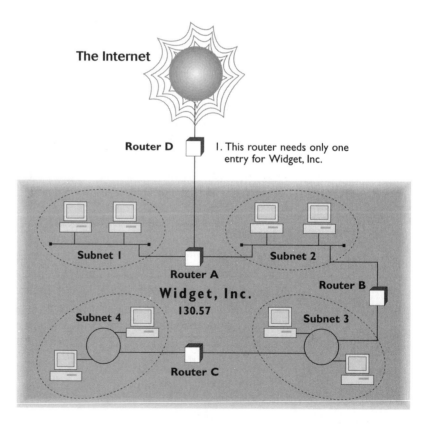

FIGURE 2.16

The use of subnets

The network portion of an IP address can't be altered. Every machine on a particular network must share the same network address. In Figure 2.17, you can see that all of Widget, Inc.'s machines have a network address of 130.57. That principle is constant. In subnetting, it's the host address that's manipulated. The subnet address scheme takes a part of the host address and redesignates it as a subnet address. In essence, it's filching good jellybeans, and replacing them with fake ones. Bit positions are stolen from the host address to be used for the subnet identifier. Figure 2.17 shows how an IP address can be given a subnet address.

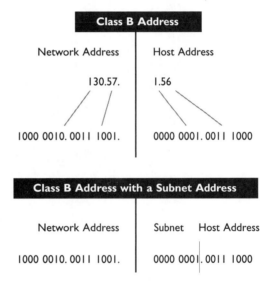

Since the Widget, Inc. network is of the Class B variety, the first two bytes refer to the network address and are shared by all machines on the network—regardless of their particular subnet. Here, every machine's address on the subnet must have its third byte read 0000 0001. The fourth byte, the host address, is the unique number—the portion we'd mess around with when subnetting. Figure 2.18 illustrates how a network address and a subnet address can be used. The same concepts and practices apply to each subnet created in the network.

F I G U R E 2.18

A network address and a
subnet address

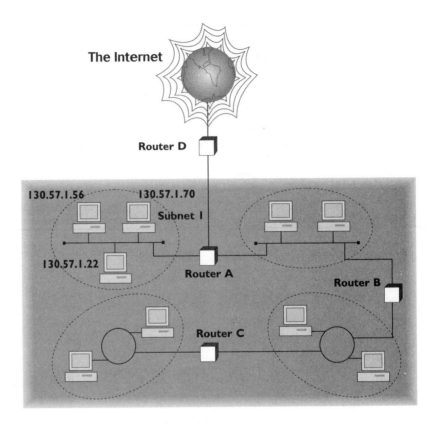

Subnet Masks

For the subnet address scheme to work, every machine on the network must know what part of the host address will be used as the subnet address. This is accomplished by assigning each machine a *subnet mask*.

The network administrator creates a 32-bit subnet mask comprised of ones and zeros. The ones in the subnet mask represent the positions that refer to the network or subnet addresses. The zeros represent the positions that refer to the host part of the address. These concepts are illustrated in Figure 2.19.

In our Widget, Inc. example, the first two bytes of the subnet mask are ones because Widget's network address is a Class B address formatted Net.Net.Node.Node. The third byte, normally assigned as part of the host address, is now used to represent the subnet address. Hence, those bit positions are represented with ones in the subnet mask. The fourth byte is the only part in our example that represents the unique host address.

F I G U R E 2.19

A subnet mask

Subnet Mask Code

1s = Positions representing network or subnet addresses
0s = Positions representing the host address

Subnet Mask for Widget, Inc.

1111 1111. 1111 1111. 1111 1111. 0000 0000

| Network Address Positions | Subnet Positions | Host Positions |

The subnet mask can also be denoted using the decimal equivalents of the binary patterns. The binary pattern of 1111 1111 is the same as decimal 255 (see the decimal-to-binary chart in Table 2.3). Consequently, the subnet mask in our example can be denoted in two ways, as shown in Figure 2.20.

F I G U R E 2.20

Subnet mask depiction

Subnet Mask in Binary: 1111 1111. 1111 1111. 1111 1111. 0000 0000

Subnet Mask in Decimal: 255 . 255 . 255 . 0

(The spaces in the above example are only for illustrative purposes. The subnet mask in decimal would actually appear as 255.255.255.0.)

All networks don't need to have subnets, and therefore don't need to use subnet masks. In this event, they are said to have a default subnet mask. This is basically the same as saying they don't have a subnet address. The default subnet masks for the different classes of networks are shown in Table 2.4.

T A B L E 2.4

Default Subnet Masks

Class	Format	Default Subnet Mask
A	Net.Node.Node.Node	255.0.0.0
B	Net.Net.Node.Node	255.255.0.0
C	Net.Net.Net.Node	255.255.255.0

Once the network administrator has created the subnet mask and assigned it to each machine, the IP software views its IP address through the subnet mask to determine its subnet address. The word mask carries the implied meaning of a lens because the IP software looks at its IP address through the lens of its subnet mask to see its subnet address. An illustration of an IP address being viewed through a subnet mask is shown in Figure 2.21.

FIGURE 2.21

An IP address viewed through a subnet mask

Subnet Mask Code

1s = Positions representing network or subnet addresses
0s = Positions representing the host address

Positions relating to the subnet address.

Subnet Mask: 1111 1111. 1111 1111. 1111 1111. 0000 0000

IP address of a machine on subnet 1: 1000 0010. 0011 1001. 0000 0001. 0011 1000
(Decimal: 130.57.1.56)

Bits relating to the subnet address.

In this example, the IP software learns through the subnet mask that, instead of being part of the host address, the third byte of its IP address is now going to be used as a subnet address. IP then looks at the bit positions in its IP address that correspond to the mask, which are 0000 0001.

The final step is for the subnet bit values to be matched up with the binary numbering convention and converted to decimal. The binary numbering convention is shown in Figure 2.22.

FIGURE 2.22

Binary numbering convention

Binary Numbering Convention

Position / Value: ◄— (continued) 128 64 32 16 8 4 2 1

Binary Example: 0 0 0 1 0 0 1 0

Decimal Equivalent: 16 + 2 = 18

In the Widget, Inc. example, the binary-to-decimal conversion is simple, as illustrated in Figure 2.23.

FIGURE 2.23

Binary-to-decimal conversion

Binary Numbering Convention

	128	64	32	16	8	4	2	1
Position / Value: ← (continued)								

Widget third byte: 0 0 0 0 0 0 0 1

Decimal Equivalent: 0 + 1 = 1

Subnet Address: 1

By using the entire third byte of a Class B address as the subnet address, it is easy to set and determine the subnet address. For example, if Widget, Inc. wants to have a Subnet 6, the third byte of all machines on that subnet will be 0000 0110. The binary-to-decimal conversion for this subnet mask is shown in Figure 2.24.

FIGURE 2.24

Setting a subnet

Binary Numbering Convention

Position / Value: ← (continued) 128 64 32 16 8 4 2 1

Binary Example: 0 0 0 0 0 1 1 0

Decimal Equivalent: 4 + 2 = 6

Subnet Address: 6

Using the entire third byte of a Class B network address for the subnet allows for a fair number of available subnet addresses. One byte dedicated to the subnet provides eight bit positions. Each position can be either a one or a zero, so the calculation is 2^8, or 256. But because you cannot use the two patterns of all zeros and all ones, you must subtract two, for a total of 254. Thus, our Widget, Inc. company can have up to 254 total subnetworks, each with 254 hosts.

Although the official IP specification limits the use of zero as a subnet address, some products do permit this usage. The Novell TCP/IP implementation for NetWare 4 and the Novell MultiProtocol Router (MPR) software are examples of products that do permit zero as a subnet address. This allows one additional subnet number. For example, if the subnet mask was 8 bits, rather than $2^8 = 256 - 2 = 254$, it would be $256 - 1 = 255$.

WARNING Allowing a subnet address of zero increases the number of subnet numbers by one. However, you should not use a subnet of zero (all zeros) unless all the software on your network recognizes this convention.

The formulas for calculating the maximum number of subnets and the maximum number of hosts per subnet are:

$$2^{\text{(number of masked bits in subnet mask)}} - 2 = \text{maximum number of subnets}$$

$$2^{\text{(number of unmasked bits in subnet mask)}} - 2 = \text{maximum number of hosts per subnet}$$

In the formulas, *masked* refers to bit positions of 1, and *unmasked* refers to positions of 0. Figure 2.25 shows an example of how these formulas can be applied.

FIGURE 2.25

Subnet and node formulas

		Network	Subnet	
			Masked	Unmasked

Network Address: 161.11 (class B)

Subnet Mask: 1111 1111. 1111 1111. | 1110 0000. 0000 0000

Decimal: 255 . 255 . | 224 . 0

The downside to using an entire byte of a node address as your subnet address is that you reduce the possible number of node addresses on each subnet. As explained earlier, without a subnet, a Class B address has 65,534 unique combinations of ones and zeros that can be used for node addresses.

If you use an entire byte of the node address for a subnet, you then have only one byte for the host addresses, leaving only 254 possible host addresses. If any of your subnets will be populated with more than 254 machines, you have a problem on your hands. To solve it, you would then need to shorten the subnet mask, thereby lengthening the host address, which benefits you with more potential host addresses. A side-effect of this solution is that it causes the reduction of the number of possible subnets. Time to prioritize!

Figure 2.26 shows an example of using a smaller subnet address. A company called Acme, Inc. expects to need a maximum of 14 subnets. In this case, Acme does not need to take an entire byte from the host address for the subnet address. To get its 14 different subnet addresses, it only needs to snatch 4 bits from the host address ($2^4 - 2 = 14$). The host portion of the address has 12 usable bits remaining ($2^{12} - 2 = 4094$). Each of Acme's 14 subnets could then potentially have a total of 4094 host addresses, or 4094 machines on each subnet.

The IPCONFIG Utility

The IPCONFIG utility can be used to verify the TCP/IP configuration parameters on a host, including the IP address, subnet mask, and default gateway. This is useful in determining whether the configuration is initialized or if a duplicate IP address is configured.

If a configuration has been initialized, the configured IP address, subnet mask, and default gateway appear. If a duplicate address is configured, the IP address appears configured, but the subnet mask appears as 0.0.0.0.

If you're using Windows 95, use the WINIPCFG utility

Let's move on to installing, configuring, and testing TCP/IP on your NT 4.0 workstation or server.

To complete these exercises, you'll need at least one computer with Microsoft Windows NT Workstation or Microsoft Windows NT Server installed.

F I G U R E 2.26

Using four bits of the host address for a subnet address

Acme, Inc.

Network Address:	132.8 (Class B; net.net.host.host)
Example IP Address:	1000 0100. 0000 1000. 0001 0010. 0011 1100
Decimal:	132 . 8 . 18 . 60

Subnet Mask Code

1s = Positions representing network or subnet addresses

0s = Positions representing the host address

Subnet Mask:

Binary:	1111 1111. 1111 1111. 1111 0000. 0000 0000
Decimal:	255 . 255 . 240 . 0

(The decimal 240 is equal to the binary 1111 0000.
Refer to Table 34.3: Decimal to Binary Chart.)

Positions relating to the subnet address.

Subnet Mask: 1111 1111. 1111 1111. 1111 0000. 0000 0000

IP address of a Acme machine: 1000 0100. 0000 1000. 0001 0010. 0011 1100
(Decimal: 132.8.18.60)

Bits relating to the subnet address.

Binary to Decimal Conversion for Subnet Address

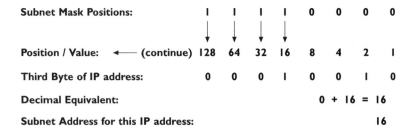

Subnet Mask Positions:	1	1	1	1	0	0	0	0
	↓	↓	↓	↓				
Position / Value: ←— (continue)	128	64	32	16	8	4	2	1
Third Byte of IP address:	0	0	0	1	0	0	1	0
Decimal Equivalent:						0 + 16 = 16		
Subnet Address for this IP address:							16	

In Exercises 2.1 through 2.5 you'll install, configure, and test the TCP/IP transport.

EXERCISE 2.1

Installing TCP/IP

1. From the Start menu, point to Settings, and then click Control Panel. The Control Panel appears.

2. Double-click Network. The Network dialog box appears.

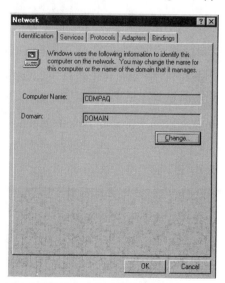

EXERCISE 2.1 (CONTINUED FROM PREVIOUS PAGE)

3. Click the Protocols tab.

4. Click Add. The Select Network Protocol dialog box appears.

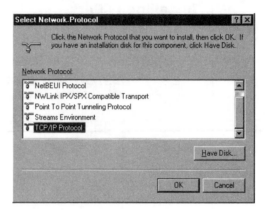

5. Select TCP/IP Protocol, and then click OK.

6. Type the path to the distribution files.

7. Click Continue.

8. The needed files will be copied to your hard drive.

9. Click Close. The Microsoft TCP/IP Properties dialog box appears.

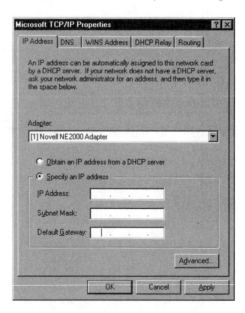

EXERCISE 2.1 (CONTINUED FROM PREVIOUS PAGE)

10. Click OK.

11. Click OK in the Network dialog box. A Network Settings Change box will appear, prompting you to restart your computer.

12. Click Yes.

13. The computer will now restart.

EXERCISE 2.2

Configuring TCP/IP

1. Go to Start, Settings, Control Panel. Then double-click Network.

2. Click the Protocol tab.

3. Double-click TCP/IP Protocol. The Microsoft TCP/IP Properties dialog box appears.

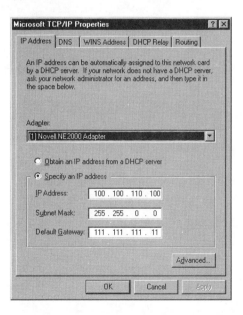

4. Type your IP Address, Subnet Mask, and Default Gateway; and click OK. A Network Settings Change dialog box appears indicating the computer needs to be restarted to initialize the new configuration.

5. Click No.

If you click Yes, the following exercise will not work.

EXERCISE 2.3

Testing the TCP/IP Configuration

1. At a command prompt, type **ipconfig**, and then press Enter. Notice the response is an empty table.

```
Command Prompt                                                    _ □ X
Microsoft(R) Windows NT(TM)
(C) Copyright 1985-1996 Microsoft Corp.

C:\>ipconfig

Windows NT IP Configuration

Ethernet adapter NdisWan5:

        IP Address. . . . . . . . . : 0.0.0.0
        Subnet Mask . . . . . . . . : 0.0.0.0
        Default Gateway . . . . . . :

C:\>
```

2. Restart your computer.

3. After rebooting and logging on as an administrator, open a command prompt.

4. Type **ipconfig**. Notice that the IP Address, Subnet Mask, and Default Gateway Configuration values are displayed.

5. Ping the loopback address by typing **ping 127.0.0.1**. You should receive four replies.

6. Ping the IP address of your workstation to verify that it was configured correctly. Type **Ping ip_address** (where *ip_address* is the ip_address of your workstaiton); then press Enter. You should receive four replies.

7. Ping the address of your default gateway. You should receive four replies.

EXERCISE 2.4

Determining the Effects of Duplicate IP Addresses

1. Configure a duplicate IP address by going to the Microsoft TCP/IP Properties box.

2. In the IP Address box, type the IP Address of someone else on your network.

3. Click OK at the TCP/IP Properties box. The Network Dialog box appears.

4. Click OK at the Network dialog box.

5. Go to Event Viewer to see the error.

6. Click Start ➢ Programs ➢ Administrative Tools, and then click Event Viewer.

7. After noticing the address conflict, close the Event Viewer.

8. Access the Microsoft TCP/IP Properties box.

9. Type your original IP address, and click OK.

10. Open a command prompt, and type **ipconfig**.

11. Verify that your address is correct.

EXERCISE 2.5

Determining the Effects of an Invalid Subnet Mask

1. Modify the subnet mask by going to the Microsoft TCP/IP Properties box.

2. In the Subnet Mask box, type an incorrect subnet mask for your network.

3. Click OK.

4. Click OK at the Network dialog box.

5. Open a command prompt, and type **ipconfig**.

6. Ping your default gateway and notice the error.

EXERCISE 2.5 (CONTINUED FROM PREVIOUS PAGE)

7. Ping a host on your network. (This may or may not work, depending on your IP address and the IP address of the destination host.)

8. Convert your computer's IP address and the IP address of your default gateway to binary format, and then AND them to the subnet mask to determine why the subnet mask is invalid.

9. Restore your subnet mask to its correct value.

Microsoft Network Monitor

The *Microsoft Network Monitor* simplifies the task of troubleshooting complex network problems by monitoring and capturing network traffic for analysis. Network Monitor configures the network adapter card to capture all incoming and outgoing packets.

You can define the capture filters so that only specific frames are saved for analysis. Filters can be defined based on source and destination MAC addresses, source and destination protocol addresses, and pattern matches. Once a packet has been captured, *display filtering* can be used to further analyze the problem. Once a packet has been captured and filtered, Network Monitor interprets the binary trace data into readable terms.

The default version that comes with NT Server can only capture data whose source or destination is the server. No other computers or servers on your segment can be monitored. However, the full version of Network Monitor is available with Microsoft Systems Management System (SMS).

EXERCISE 2.6

Installing the Network Monitor on Your Server

1. Go to the Control Panel and double-click Network.

2. Click the Services tab.

3. Click Add.

4. Click Network Monitor Tools and Agents, then click OK.

5. Type the path to the distribution files.

6. Click Close, then Yes to reboot your computer.

The Capture Process

Network Monitor uses many windows for displaying different data. One of
the primary windows is the Capture window. When this window has the
focus, the toolbar will show you options to start, pause, stop, and view captured data. On the Capture menu, click Start to start a capture. While the capture process is running, the statistical information will be displayed in the
capture window.

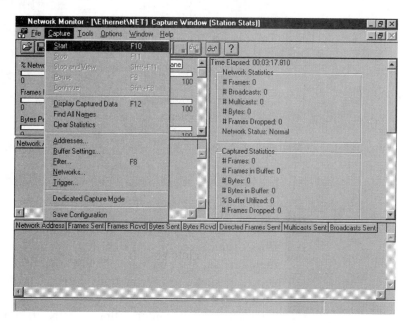

Stopping the Capture

After you have generated the network traffic you are analyzing, from the Capture menu, click Stop to stop the capture. You can then create another capture
or display the current capture data. You can also click Stop and View from
the Capture menu to stop a capture and immediately open it for viewing.

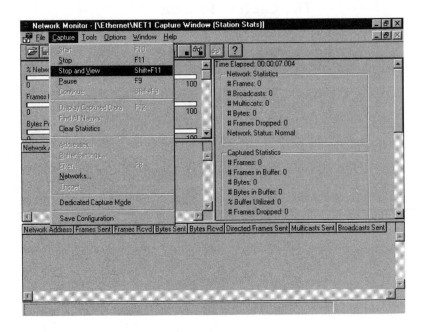

Viewing the Data

When opening a capture to view it, a Summary window appears showing each frame capture. The Summary window contains a frame number, time of frame reception, source and destination addresses, highest protocol layer used in the frame, and a description of the frame.

For more detailed information on a specific frame, on the Window menu, click Zoom. In Zoom view you get two additional windows, the Detail frame and Hexadecimal frame. The Detail frame shows the protocol information in detail. The Hexadecimal frame shows the raw bytes in the frame.

Summary

In this chapter we covered the basics of TCP/IP, opening with a definition of this popular pair of protocols, its beginnings, and why it's so important today. We progressed to discover how TCP/IP fits into the DOD networking archetype, and moved on to explore both the DOD and the OSI reference models. We then zoomed in for a close-up of the TCP/IP protocol suite, then an in-depth look at the individual protocols and utilities, including their special functions.

We probed further into the basics of TCP/IP and examined the supremely important subject of how accurate communication is achieved between specific networks and host systems through proper IP addressing. We then discussed how and why that communication happens, why it doesn't when it fails, and how to configure devices on both LANs and WANs to ensure solid performance for your network.

Review Questions

1. What is TCP/IP?

   A. A collection of packets sent through the Internet

   B. A collection of packages for use on the Internet

   C. A suite of protocols that provide routing and addressing in WANs, and connectivity to a variety of hosts

   D. A freeware program

2. What are the layers in the DOD four-layer model used by TCP/IP?

   A. Process/Application

   B. Session

   C. Network Access

   D. Internet

   E. Host-to-Host

   F. Transport

3. What core TCP/IP protocols are provided with Microsoft TCP/IP?

   A. TCP

   B. UDP

   C. DUP

   D. ICMP

    E. PI

    F. IP

    G. PAR

    H. ARP

    I. CTP

4. What parameters are required for a TCP/IP host to communicate in a WAN?

    A. IP address

    B. Subnet mask

    C. Zip code

    D. Default gateway

    E. Login name

5. It's Monday morning. Just as you arrive at your desk, your boss calls you into his office and says he read about TCP/IP in a Microsoft magazine over the weekend. Because he now knows that all Microsoft products are fabulous, he's set on someone implementing MS TCP/IP at all twelve branch office sites. He says that because of your quality work over the past few months, you're his first choice. However, before he names you the project's leader, he wants you to give him a complete explanation of TCP/IP, and how it will meet his networking needs. Can you? Try it.

6. To get a jump on the competition, you need to find some information on a new, highly efficient protocol being developed. Where would you find this information? How would you access it, and through which server? If you have access to the Internet, try this as an exercise on your computer.

7. Your boss tells you she spent lunch at the gym, where she overheard a great way to look up information on the Internet. She tells you that it organizes subjects into a menu system, and allows you to access the information on each topic listed. She's frustrated because she can't remember what it's called—can you?

8. You are the Senior Communication Technician for a small computer store. The sales staff is complaining that they cannot deliver or receive mail on their TCP/IP computers. All other applications on the network seem to work OK. The location of the problem is likely to be on *which layer* of the DOD model?

9. The IS department is planning to implement TCP/IP. Your manager, who knows and understands the OSI reference model, asks you, "What are the layers in the four-layer model used by the DOD for TCP/IP, and how does each layer relate to the OSI reference model?" What do you tell him?

10. You are the network administrator for a large accounting office. They have seven offices, all connected. You get a call from a remote office complaining that their workstations cannot connect to the network. After talking with them for a few minutes, it appears that network connectivity is down at all seven offices. What layer of the DOD model is likely at fault?

11. You want to collect the TCP/IP frames that are received by your Windows NT Server computer, and then save the data in a file to analyze later. Which utility should you use?

A. NETSTAT.EXE

B. Performance Monitor

C. NBTSTAT.EXE

D. Network Monitor

12. You need to determine whether the configuration is initialized or a duplicate IP address is configured on your NT workstation. Which utility should you use?

    A. ARP.EXE

    B. NBSTAT.EXE

    C. NETSTAT.EXE

    D. IPCONFIG.EXE

    E. PING.EXE

13. You have four NT Server computers and you want to find out which computers send the most traffic to each server. What should you do to find out?

    A. Use Performance Monitor on each server.

    B. Use Network Monitor on each server.

    C. Use NETSTAT.EXE on each server.

    D. Use NBTSTAT.EXE on each server.

    E. Use ROUTE.EXE on each server that is functioning as a router.

14. You have a network ID of 131.107.0.0 and you need to divide it into multiple subnets. You need 600 host IDs for each subnet, with the largest amount of subnets available. Which subnet mask should you assign?

    A. 255.255.224.0

    B. 255.255.240.0

    C. 255.255.248.0

    D. 255.255.252.0

15. You have a network ID of 131.107.0.0 with eight subnets. You need to allow the largest possible number of host IDs per subnet. Which subnet mask should you assign?

A. 255.255.224.0

B. 255.255.240.0

C. 255.255.248.0

D. 255.255.252.0

16. You have a network ID of 217.170.55.0 and you need to divide it into multiple subnets. You need 25 host IDs for each subnet with the largest amount of subnets available. Which subnet mask should you assign?

A. 255.255.255.192

B. 255.255.255.224

C. 255.255.255.240

D. 255.255.255.248

17. You have a Class A network address with 60 subnets. You need to add 40 new subnets in the next two years and still allow for the largest possible number of host IDs per subnet. Which subnet mask should you assign?

A. 255240.0.0

B. 255.248.0.0

C. 255.252.0.0

D. 255.254.0.0

18. You want to capture and view packets that are received by your Windows NT computer. Which utility should you use?

A. NETSTAT.EXE

B. Performance Monitor

C. IPCONFIG.EXE

D. Network Monitor

19. You have a Class B network, and you plan to break it up into seven subnets. One subnet will be connected to the Internet, but you want all computers to have access to the Internet. How should you assign the subnet mask for the networks?

    A. By using a default subnet mask

    B. By creating a custom subnet mask

    C. By assigning a subnet mask of 0.0.0.0

    D. By assigning a subnet mask that has the IP address of the router

20. You need to come up with a TCP/IP addressing scheme for your company. How many host IDs must you allow for when you define the subnet mask for the network?

    A. One for each subnet

    B. One for each router interface

    C. One for each WAN connection

    D. One for each network adapter installed on each host

21. You are using DHCP on your network. You want all clients from all subnets to access your proxy server by name. You use DHCP to give the WINS address to all clients. What other option must you give to the clients before they will be able to browse across subnets?

    A. Option 28: Broadcast address

    B. Option 47: NetBIOS scope ID

    C. Option 46: WINS/NBT node type

    D. Option 51: Lease time

CHAPTER

3

Proxy Server's Structural Design

Before you can strive to build something great, you must first begin with an idea. That idea is converted into words, and those words are compiled into blueprints. This chapter gives a bird's-eye view into the structural architecture of Microsoft's Proxy Server. Before you continue, keep in mind that many of the functions discussed in this chapter are used not only to define Microsoft's Proxy Server implementation, but also to help you determine your expectations of other manufactures' proxy products.

By the end of this chapter, you will be able to:

- Describe Microsoft Proxy Server's structural design

- Discuss the Web Proxy service elements

- Give an overview of the WinSock Proxy service

- Define the Socks Proxy service

- Explain what a cache is as it applies to Microsoft's Proxy Server

- Understand how Web Proxy, WinSock Proxy, and Socks Proxy work together as a suite

Proxy Services

The first thing you might expect to encounter is a service that is self-contained and that acts as a single process. Well, so much for your expectations. Microsoft Proxy is a suite of services that is comprised of Web, WinSock, and Socks Proxy services (see Figure 3.1). The Web Proxy service is designed to support CERN-compatible applications, while the WinSock service supports applications using Windows Sockets. (As if you couldn't have guessed by the name!) The Socks Proxy supports systems that utilize non-Windows Sockets (UNIX and Macintosh platforms). While not all applications use these classes of compatibility, the majority of utilities required for Internet access do. In instances where an application is not WinSock-, Socks-, or CERN-compatible, an upgraded or substitute product is generally available.

FIGURE 3.1

Microsoft Proxy Server services

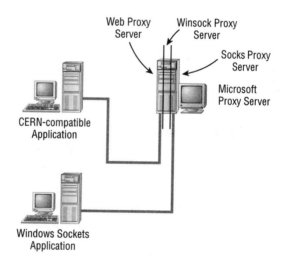

Before we discuss the Web Proxy service, let's first recall what a proxy server is and what it does. It's a system that acts on behalf of another system to provide security and access for the client or protected network. When a proxy server is implemented correctly, a network can be made completely secure.

The proxy server also helps the growth of the Internet beyond what TCP/IP version 4 is able to do. It does this by allowing more systems on the Internet than there are address spaces available. At the same time, it preserves private addresses and supports organizations whose structures are built around incompatible protocols such as IPX.

Like firewalls, routers, and bridges, a proxy is configured on a device with two network interfaces. Of the two network interfaces, one is connected directly to the private network while the other interface is connected to the public Internet. The interfaces can be of any type that permits protocol bindings. On a LAN, for example, Ethernet, Token Ring, or ArcNet commonly are bound to TCP/IP, IPX, NetBEUI, and so on. An Internet connection might utilize a modem/ISDN (serial port) or network interface (Ethernet, Token Ring, ArcNet, and so on) that connects to a router that is, in turn, connected to the Internet. In effect, the proxy server is performing specific routing functions that give it the ability to function as a gateway system separating the public and private networks. A table known as the Local Address Table (LAT) is used to determine which networks are connected to the private network. In many cases, multiple proxy servers are implemented to facilitate higher amounts of traffic.

When reading this chapter, keep in mind that we are discussing three proxy services: Web, WinSock (WSP), and Socks.

Local Address Table

The Local Address Table (LAT) is used to determine which networks are located on the private network. During Proxy Server installation, a first-run LAT table is interactively created. The LAT lists addresses in pairs such that a range is created. The range may determine a group of computers or a single system. For example, 134.57.14.x to 134.57.16.x will exclude all addresses that are on the 134.57.14.x, 134.57.15.x, and 134.57.16.x networks.

The default LAT includes addresses known as *private IP addresses*. These addresses are listed in the local routing table. Because of the way in which the NT Server's routing table is read, it is possible that the default installation may not contain all of your organization's addresses. Addresses not listed should be added manually. Also, it is possible for addresses that are not a part of your network to be included as local addresses. These addresses should be removed or the range edited to include only those addresses that are part of the internal network.

NOTE   Private IP addresses can not be routed across the Internet.

The LAT is maintained centrally at the proxy server. Proxy clients will automatically download and receive LAT updates at regular intervals. The LAT is central to defining the private and public networks. Working with the LAT to define public and private networks is discussed in further detail in Chapter 4.

Web Proxy Service

The first component of the Proxy Server is the Web Proxy service. This service is generally used directly with applications such as Internet Explorer, Netscape Navigator, Point Cast Network, and other CERN-compatible applications. This service offers the following:

- Hypertext Transfer Protocol (HTTP) support and object caching

- File Transfer Protocol (FTP) support and object caching

- Gopher protocol support

- Disk caching

- IP address aggregation (using a single address for multiple computers)

- IP address translation

- CERN-proxy compatibility

- SSL (HTTPS and SNEWS) tunneling (data encryption)

- Integrated, user-level security providing encrypted logon for browsers, which supports Windows NT Challenge/Response authentication

- Support for most operating systems, including UNIX, Windows NT Server, Windows NT Workstation, Windows 95, Windows for Workgroups, Windows 3.1, and Macintosh systems

- Masks LAN structure, topology, addressing, and so on

- Logging of Internet requests from clients

- Management of multiple servers through a single common GUI interface

- No direct Internet access to the LAN or vice versa. The Proxy Server performs all operations

CERN Compatibility

Computer technology has evolved over time. Take UNIX, for example. Originally, UNIX was an operating system that was compiled of little disjointed utilities. UNIX was one of the first operating systems to add TCP/IP. It eventually gave its foundation to DOS. Another example is TCP/IP. It owes its existence to the Department of Defense, which built the protocol as a means to support a wide area network that would be difficult to destroy in a war. TCP/IP was, and is, the select protocol of UNIX. Applications such as File Transfer Protocol (FTP), the World Wide Web (WWW), and Gopher formed around the client/server architecture. As communications matured and the GUI interface (developed in the 1970s by Xerox) was advanced in conjunction with the World Wide Web, GUI made its introduction as text that was downloaded and converted to graphic pages. The text-based format that these compiled pages used became known as Hypertext Transport Protocol (HTTP). HTTP is a protocol that allows pictures to be integrated with text to form graphic screens.

You may be asking yourself why you need to know about CERN and the related material. The answer is simple: Knowledge is power. The more you know about the origin and development of a technology, the better your use and understanding of its operation and functions. Knowledge of a product's origin and development will help you better understand its functions.

Hypertext Transport Protocol was designed by a company in Switzerland, the European Laboratory for Particle Physics (Conseil Europeen pour la Recherché Nucleair, or CERN). They needed a better communications system, so they created CERN to meet their initial communications requirements. As support for proxy-aware applications was added to their programming libraries, World Wide Web users expanded on the library additions and the CERN-proxy protocol became a *de facto* industry standard. CERN compatibility is one of the primary standards HTTP proxies are designed upon.

Today, the CERN-proxy protocol is still used. For example, Microsoft's Web Proxy service is fully compatible with this protocol.

All requests to the proxy server are sent in HTTP format, which includes Web, FTP, and Gopher inquiries. If, for example, you were transferring a file with FTP, your communications to the proxy server would be in HTTP format. The majority of HTTP instructions are based around two commands: get and post. These commands act similarly to the read and write commands in most system activities. The get command is used to request that information from a Uniform Resource Locator (URL) be sent to a server resource specified in the URL designation. Simply put, get asks a system to deliver a specified piece of information. And post is used to send information that contains a URL and data. Commonly, post is used to respond to questionnaires on the Internet; for instance, subscribing to a service that asks for a credit card number, mailing address, birth date, or other information.

It is probably easiest to think of get and post as a conversation with an automated receptionist. Telephone directory information (411) in some places uses this automated receptionist system. An automated voice asks, "What city please?" Once you respond, it then asks, "What listing?" Then, once you have verbally posted this information to the recorder, the operator replies by delivering the requested information just as get and post would deliver a requested URL.

The Web Proxy in Action

As mentioned earlier, all requests from a proxy-configured browser to the Web Proxy Server component, including Web, FTP, and Gopher requests, are sent in HTTP format. The requests issued from the browser are sent with the get command to designate the specific protocol (FTP, HTTP, and so on) along with the URL. In order to receive a document from a site, a system then requests information in a format such as this:

```
protocol://host.organization.type/directory/filename.ext
```

Table 3.1 explains the components of the URL structure. Where items are required, designations have been made to note this. However, in some strange instances, some special applications may violate there rules. If ever in doubt, use Table 3.1 to find the basic information.

	Type	Description
TABLE 3.1 The URL Structure	Protocol (Required)	HTTP, FTP, Gopher, and many others
	Host (Optional)	The name of the system you are connecting to. Generally, the initial system that responds to your request is configured by the DNS to respond without the host name or one such as Web or FTP. This is the most common configuration, which typically is set such that the DNS refers to multiple aliases and IP addresses. This also has the benefit of allowing an organization to have multiple Web servers for different pages and services, multiple FTP servers as required, and so on. The inverse is also true—all services may also be contained on a single machine referenced by different names.
	Organization (Required)	This is the company or organization from which you are requesting information. Examples of some organization names include Sybex, Microsoft, and Earthlink.
	Type (Required)	The type of organization that you are connecting to is specified here. This could be .COM, .NET, .ORG, .GOV, or a country code such as .UK.
	Directory (Optional)	In order to maintain a hierarchical structure, organizations often use directories, which specify the different functions of their site. In Windows NT and UNIX this directory may be linked to a different system. Windows NT supports this function as a virtual directory while UNIX may have the link either configured as a symbolic link or as a Network Filing System (NFS) mounted volume.
	file name (Optional)	This is the name of the document that you are requesting. These names do not follow DOS naming conventions and are not limited to eight characters as with some operating systems. Generally, if a file name is not specified, most Internet servers will deliver a default document.

	Type	Description
TABLE 3.1 (cont.) The URL Structure	Ext (Optional)	This is the extension of the document or resource that you are requesting. In the case of HTML (designed for HTTP), the documents are commonly labeled as .HTP or .HTTP. As with the file name, the extension has no character number requirement. When an extension is not specified, some Web browsers will guess at what the file type is depending on the protocol used. Although it would appear that the associated file must have a type defined, the extension may be completely different from what is commonly expected. An example is Microsoft's DEFAULT.ASP file.

With the information in Table 3.1 in mind, let us examine a request for an HTML document called MCSEINTRO2.PL from a directory called CGI-BIN on a system designated only as Web in a company called Sybex (see Figure 3.2).

FIGURE 3.2

Web Proxy in action

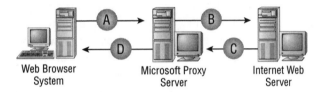

1. The Web browser sends a request to the proxy server using HTTP.

2. Proxy Server then:

   A. Reads the request upon receipt.

   B. Determines that HTTP is the requested protocol.

   C. Resolves WWW.SYBEX.COM to an IP address.

   D. Sends an HTTP request to get MCSEINTRO2.PL from the CGI-BIN directory.

3. Sybex's Web server then:

   A. Reviews the request upon receipt.

   B. Locates MCSEINTRO2.PL in the CGI-BIN directory.

   C. Sends the MCSEINTRO2.PL file to the proxy server using HTTP.

4. The proxy server relays the received information back to the requesting Web browser.

5. The browser receives, compiles, and displays the MCSEINTRO2.PL file.

Because the proxy server is making all external communications, only HTTP is used to communicate between it and a proxy client. In contrast, a system that is not using a proxy server must communicate in the protocol of the connection that is being requested. For example, to FTP a file, a direct connection will use FTP, not HTTP. In either case, the corresponding protocol will be used with the destination site. The distinction is that the communication used between a proxy server and a client is exclusively HTTP.

Systems that are not configured as proxy clients actually request information in a manner that is identical to the way proxy servers request information. When a request is made to a site, the browser reviews the requested URL and then separates the protocol (HTTP) and the host (www.sybex.com) from the URL. After the host is resolved to an IP address, the browser simply issues a get command for the requested file. In this case, the command would be GET/CGI-BIN/MCSEINTRO2.PL. Information is then returned directly to the non-proxy client system or to the proxy server, which then returns the information to the client.

Web Proxy Components

As you have already learned, all communications to the proxy server from the client are established via HTTP. With this in mind, it is no wonder that most proxy server implementations require the ability to identify the protocol used by IP applications. This extra degree of recognition helps add extra features such as request authentication, protocol conversions, and caching of retrieved materials. These added features comprise the supplementary benefits of enhanced security, improved Internet response time, access control, and decreased usage on an Internet connection.

Operating as an extension of Microsoft Internet Information Server (IIS) version 3.0 or greater on the Windows NT Server 4.0 platform, Proxy Server fully integrates into NT's in-place management utilities. Proxy Server's Web component adds two primary elements: Proxy Server ISAPI filter and Proxy Server ISAPI application.

At first glance, these components seem cryptic. However, if we decode the ISAPI acronym to Internet Server Application Programming Interface, we can see that Microsoft has implemented a simple system that is integrated into IIS as a dynamic link library (DLL) add-on. The DLL add-on provides filtering and application extensions. The primary Web components fit into the DOD model shown in Figure 3.3.

FIGURE 3.3

Web Proxy services in the DOD model

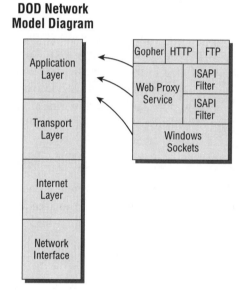

DOD Network
Model Diagram

Just in case you don't recall what an API is, it's an interface through which a program accesses certain functions that yield uniform results. This has the benefit of reduced programming code for shorter application development time. For example, when a program is opened in Windows, it use the Windows API to draw the boards around its utility for pull-down menus, colors, handle sizes, and so on.

Because all communications between the proxy server and the client are sent via HTTP, the service must be installed and running to process requests on the proxy server. This configuration helps provide an efficient and low overhead communication method that works seamlessly with the Web Proxy service DLL through the ISAPI interface.

Internet Server API Filters

The Internet Server API (ISAPI) filter component is a principal module of the two main components of the Web Proxy service. The proxy server utilizes the ISAPI filter for each HTTP request received. This action is taken regardless of the protocol for which information is requested. The ISAPI filter provides the benefit of determining which protocol service to issue to the destination, while permitting monitoring, logging, modification, redirection, and authentication of data from the Internet resource.

The ISAPI filter is accessed dynamically by the Web service. When the filter is applied, an algorithm is used to migrate through the filter's DLL entry point during request and response periods. Calls to the DLL are most notable for management information.

In case you were wondering, an entry point is the location within the API where input is placed to receive an expected response. For example, an entry point for a Windowing API may, hypothetically, apply some set of coordinate numbers, such as 3, 3, 25, 25, to create a 3×3 unit window located at a position on the screen designated by the coordinates 25, 25.

Now that we are up to our eyeballs in programming lingo, let's take a look at how this stuff really applies to us. First, we should note that the ISAPI filter is loaded from the W3PROXY.DLL and that the main purpose of this filter is to determine if a request is in the CERN-proxy or the standard HTTP format. This is important so that the proper request is delivered to the destination server for the client. Next, if a CERN-proxy request is detected, the Proxy ISAPI filter adds instructions to the request to route the response to the Proxy ISAPI application (W3PROXY.DLL). The Web service then relays the request to the Proxy ISAPI application for processing. The filtering process is simple because the CERN-proxy request contains a URL with the protocol and domain name. It is very easy to distinguish between the two. Finally, if the request is standard HTTP, then the ISAPI filter adds no additional instructions to the request, and processing within the Web server continues as normal. A request that does not contain a protocol and a domain name is standard HTTP. That is to say, HTTP is the default protocol.

Internet Server API Applications

The ISAPI application is the second principal module of the two main components of the Web Proxy service. The ISAPI application is commonly used with Internet applications that involve databases or other data links. In fact, it maintains the ability to create dynamic HTML and integrate Web applications.

The distinct difference between the ISAPI filter and the application is that the application is only activated if it is specifically called and the filter is activated by an algorithm that scans constantly for request type and management information. Also, the ISAPI application does not create a new process for each request.

The ISAPI Application in Action   As previously stated, the ISAPI application does not create a new process for each call. For operations related to Web requests, the ISAPI application performs the following steps:

1. Checks client authentication

2. Checks the domain filter

3. Checks the request against the current and valid resource cache

4. If the request is not found in the cache, acquires the requested resource, which is then added to the cache based on relevance

When a valid request is made to a site (see the example in the *Web Proxy in Action* section), the proxy reviews the requested URL and then extracts the protocol (FTP, HTTP, Gopher) and the host with the domain. Calls are then made directly to the corresponding Windows Sockets APIs for HTTP requests.

The ISAPI application offers client authentication, a domain check filter, status checking for caching, log information, and retrieval information regarding an Internet object.

HTTP Requests

HTTP protocol requests are processed asynchronously once the domain name has been resolved. In this process, the proxy server takes the following steps:

1. Resolves the host and/or domain name to an IP address

2. Opens a session to the Internet site or object

3. Issues a request to the Internet site or object

4. Receives a response header from remote site

5. Sends response data to the proxy client

6. Stores the response data in cache, as appropriate

The Web Proxy service may require a relatively long period of time to process a request. In addition, when the computer running Proxy Server's Web Proxy service is servicing many clients, many simultaneous requests may be forwarded to the Proxy Server ISAPI application.

When a request is being serviced, performance can be noticeably slower relative to the Web server's processing time. Performance may also appear more degraded as multiple clients issue multiple requests to the ISAPI application at the same time. This is the point where the Proxy Server's equipment will determine its response time, processing capabilities, and user capacity.

Keep-Alives

An important function of the ISAPI application is its ability to keep a connection active while the proxy server relays data to the client. This ability to hold connections open is referred to as *keep-alive*. The major performance increase with this feature is demonstrated when a subsequent request to a Web page is issued (if the request is made before the keep-alive times out).

Because Web browsers must establish a connection for each request, having the proxy server keep the connection open decreases the response time to a system. Think of this process in terms of having your secretary make a telephone call for you. You relay the data to your secretary. And, for a time, your secretary still will be on the phone with the person on the other end. (They are probably talking about how they can become MCSEs.) Suppose you forgot to tell your secretary to tell the person on the other end of the phone that you're playing golf on Saturday. If you remember this while the contact is still on the phone, you would simply ask the secretary to relay the message. This means that a second call does not have to be placed.

Remember that secure sites, such as FTP, require a log in. That means that access would be considerably slower if you had to repeat the login process each time you wanted to FTP files.

WinSock Proxy (WSP) Service

The first component of Microsoft Proxy Server, the Web service, provides extensive coverage for Web, FTP, and Gopher services. However, the TCP/IP protocol suite would be incomplete without additional services to support other applications that were not based on a Web browser. The second component of the proxy server is the WinSock Proxy (WSP) service. This service is generally used with applications that use the Windows Socket API. This service offers the following support:

- Transparent operation for applications using WinSock

- Windows Sockets compatible with pre-configured support for common protocols such as RealAudio, NetShow, and IRC

- Support of connectionless UDP protocols

- A gateway for IPX to IP

- IP Address translation

- IP address aggregation (using a single address for multiple computers)

- Control of inbound access by port number, protocol, and user or group

- Control of outbound access by port number, protocol, and user or group

- Logging of Internet access requests

- Windows NT Challenge/Response authentication, regardless of application support

- SSL (HTTPS and SNEWS) tunneling

- Masks LAN structure, topology, addressing, and so on

- No direct Internet access to the LAN or vice versa, (Proxy Server performs all processes)

- Site-specific lockout control by domain name, IP address, and subnet mask

- Obstruction of public (Internet) users from gaining access to private secured network

- Integration and administration through the Internet Services Manager

- Support for Microsoft Windows-based client computers

As you can see, Microsoft WinSock's Proxy service supports a wide array of applications. As you continue to read through this section, additional details will be presented along the way to provide you with complete information about the service, including an understanding of sockets, IP addressing, ports, and so forth.

What Are Sockets?

Sockets are a standard implementation of APIs to support an array of TCP/IP applications. That is to say, they are a common set of access rules and calls that IP programs can make. Through the use of sockets, there is no need for a programmer to rewrite items that the operating system should already support.

The basic sockets API allows a program to open an outbound communications channel for a client, then accept an inbound response from a server. Essentially, sockets allow data to be sent and received, and then close the channels upon completion.

Sockets originated in design from BSD (Berkeley Source Distribution) UNIX. The idea of providing a simple and standard programming interface is common in technologies such as Microsoft's NDIS, Novell's ODI, and so forth. Although these are all different applications, they support the same idea. Today, we still see sockets in UNIX, NetWare, and Windows. The Microsoft implementation of sockets is a specially modified port of the UNIX version known as WinSock.

Think about plugging a telephone into a standard RJ11 jack that relays to a telephone system or service box. When you plug the phone into that jack, you do not concern yourself with redoing the wiring, electronics, or other aspects besides the phone. Well, the same is true for socket programs—they just plug in.

A port, when referring to programming, is the recompilation between operating platforms of a piece of code. Do not confuse this with a TCP/IP port, which is for application addressing. We'll discuss TCP/IP ports later in this section.

Windows Sockets is an evolved API. Initially, WinSock provided support only in 16-bit compilations (Win16), which revolved around earlier versions of Windows. As 32-bit applications developed, Microsoft introduced a 32-bit version (Win32). As Microsoft developed and revised Windows Sockets, they included support for protocols in addition to TCP/IP. Some implementations of WinSock support IPX/SPX and NetBEUI.

TCP and UDP

TCP/IP is a protocol suite that involves support for two types of connections: one that is passive, called UDP (Universal Datagram Protocol), and the other that is active, called TCP (Transmission Control Protocol). Each type of connection is used for a different function. A passive connection is low in overhead and great for broadcast information. However, the technology is considered unreliable. An active connection is high in overhead, but secure and reliable. For example, if you listened to music over the Internet, chances are you would be listening to a broadcast, which is sent passively. This is done in a way that allows a listener to receive music without the notes jumbled and out of order. If a piece of data is lost, typically it is not a concern for this type of application. On the other hand, suppose that you required a secure connection. In this case, you would not want information sent to everyone, so you would most likely use TCP.

UDP is a connectionless-based technology. It can be thought of like the postal service or like a television station. In either case, the sender is never in direct contact with the receiver. This type of delivery service can either be multi-point or point-to-point. Point-to-point is a network configuration where one system sends information to another directly. A multi-point connection is similar, but rather than sending to a single system, multiples systems are involved.

In contrast, TCP is a connection-based technology that complements UDP. TCP, like a telephone call, behaves in a stream-oriented manner. When you want to talk to someone, the call must be placed and activated before communication can begin. Also, if the phone call is disconnected, it must be placed again before you can continue talking. Obviously, the connection is point-to-point and is delivered over an established connection.

The majority of TCP/IP applications are connection-based. These applications include, but are not limited to, HTTP, Gopher, and FTP. UDP applications include TFTP, BOOTP, RealAudio, and others. Refer to the section on addresses and ports for additional examples of both UDP and TCP.

Addresses and Ports

As an open-structured application programming interface, WinSock establishes communications by using an address and a port. The address is a typical TCP/IP 32-bit number. This number uniquely identifies a host system to a client on the Internet. For example, if we were to type **ping 206.100.29.83**, only one system on the Internet would reply.

The port number is a secondary address that is used internally for TCP/IP to route application traffic. For example, a message sent to an IP address that references port 21 is accessing an FTP application. A list of common TCP/IP application ports is listed in Table 3.2. For a more complete list, refer to the Services file in the WINNT\SYSTEM32\DRIVERS\ETC directory on the Windows NT Server.

T A B L E 3.2 TCP/IP Services, Ports, and Protocols	Service	Port/Protocol and Utility
	ECHO	7/TCP
	ECHO	7/UDP
	FTP-DATA	20/TCP
	FTP	21/TCP
	TELNET	23/TCP
	SMTP	25/TCP mail
	NAME	42/TCP nameserver
	NAME	42/UDP nameserver
	WHOIS	32/TCP nicname # usually to sri-nic
	DOMAIN	53/TCP nameserver # name-domain server
	DOMAIN	53/UDP nameserver
	NAMESERVER	53/TCP domain # name-domain server
	NAMESERVER	53/UDP domain

	Service	Port/Protocol and Utility
TABLE 3.2 (cont.) TCP/IP Services, Ports, and Protocols	BOOTP	67/UDP # boot program server
	TFTP	69/UDP
	FINGER	79/TCP
	POP	109/TCP post office
	POP2	109/TCP # post office
	POP3	110/TCP post office
	NNTP	119/TCP USENET # network news transfer
	NTP	123/UDP NTPD NTP # network time protocol
	NBNAME	137/UDP
	NBSESSION	139/TCP
	NEWS	144/TCP news
	SGMP	153/UDP SGMP
	UUCP	540/TCP UUCPD # UUCP daemon
	NFS	2049/UDP # SUN NFS

As you can see in Table 3.2, WinSock specifies a system by its IP address and a program by its port number. Note that some ports are listed twice: one entry for TCP and another for UDP.

A number of TCP/IP applications use the connectionless UDP protocol. UDP does not guarantee reliability or sequencing of packets, and it does not support resizing of packets. However, UDP applications do not require such support. Because UDP offers higher performance than TCP, it is useful for real time applications such as audio and video. UDP applications include the audio and video plug-ins RealAudio and VDOLive. Many UDP applications do not require even that all packets be received. That, of course, is up to the application using UDP.

When all elements of TCP/IP are pulled together with networking topology and an application, they form a complete communication mechanism capable of all network functions and abilities (see Figure 3.4). Your network topology provides a physical transport, the driver stack provides a data link, IP provides a routable soft-based protocol, TCP/UDP provides a network control protocol of the stack, and so forth. As the upper layers of the stack are approached, sockets and port come into play to support applications in this configuration.

FIGURE 3.4

TCP/IP communication with sockets

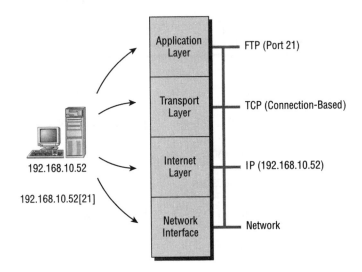

Server-to-Client Communications

Communication between two systems occurs between two IP addresses, each with an application providing a port number. A connection to a client is established by performing the following steps:

1. Establish a connection socket with either TCP or UDP.

2. Link the IP address and the port to the socket (see Table 3.2).

3. Enable an access path for the inbound IP address and port.

4. The server finalizes the connection, sets an alternate socket to the connection, and then returns to monitoring the original socket for additional connections.

5. The server exchanges data with the client.

Client-to-Server Communications

When a client opens a connection to a server the following steps are used:

1. A connection socket with either TCP or UDP is established.

2. The IP address and port are linked to the socket (see Table 3.2).

3. The connection is finalized to the port, and the IP address is specified. The port registered defines the service.

4. The client exchanges data with the server.

The procedures for communication between a client and server are almost identical to the communication between a server and a client, with the exception of exchanging ports after establishing communication on the server. In either scenario, UDP requires that the client and server each set a UDP socket, then link the socket to an IP address and port. Once this phase is satisfied, both may begin exchanging data. Note that because the protocol is connectionless, a UDP client can communicate with multiple servers at once on a single socket.

WinSock Proxy Server Service

The WSP service is a complex suite of programs that are responsible for protocol conversion as well as management of connections requested by clients. Built for Windows NT Server 4.0 with Service Pack 3 or better, Microsoft's Proxy Server is a stand-alone process built on IIS 3.0. Because security to access the server is optional, Microsoft Proxy Server is network-platform independent. This component of the WinSock Proxy is the mechanism that establishes and transfers data between Internet resources.

WinSock Proxy Client Support

We have learned that a Windows Sockets Proxy is simply a proxy server for clients running WinSock applications. We then learned how the Windows Sockets are used to create connections on the Internet between the client and server. This, as you should recall, is done through the proxy server in such a way that the starting program communicates with the proxy gateway and then the host system. Now we are going to examine the programming support behind WinSock Proxy.

At the top of our supported applications and APIs list is version 1.1 of WinSock. The proxy server can run virtually all Windows Socket programs written for version 1.1. And Microsoft Proxy Server can execute all applications locally as well as remotely. However, this is not the case with Windows Sockets version 2.0 APIs. These do not support applications that are run remotely.

WSP Client DLLs

There are two DLLs that can be installed on a client system. Each is specific for 16-bit or 32-bit Windows-based applications. Each DLL serves as a replacement for the default non-proxy WinSock DLL. To fit seamlessly, the DLL files are named to match the DLLs they are replacing. The replacement DLLs are:

- WINSOCK.DLL: 16-bit Windows-based application can be installed on Windows 3.1, Windows for Workgroups, or Windows 95.

- WSOCK32.DLL: 32-bit Windows-based application can be installed on Windows NT and Windows 95.

The DLLs seize WinSock API calls from applications on the client computer. This allows the request to be either processed locally or passed to the Windows Sockets Proxy Server. In some instances, the proxy client may pass the API request in modified form back to the original Windows Socket DLL. This situation would occur depending on the API and the socket status. On the other hand, the DLL may choose to send the request to the Windows Proxy Server.

When communicating on the private network, the WSP client DLL passes WinSock API calls to both the new and original WinSock DLL files. This allows conventional Windows Sockets communications to proceed normally as if no proxy server were installed. Furthermore, this convention allows a third-party TCP/IP stack to maintain operations even if it is not perfectly equal to Microsoft's specifications for Windows Sockets. The WSP call process is shown in Figure 3.5.

WinSock Proxy Control Channel

WinSock Proxy Server (WSP) uses a data flow process called a *control channel*. The WSP control channel manages remote WinSock messages. To keep things efficient and overhead low, the control channel's use should be kept to a minimum. Also, it is more advantageous to utilize programs that are designed with fewer Windows Sockets APIs that require special processing at the client computer. The control channel is established with the Windows client initialized with WINSOCK.DLL. Based on UDP, the channel uses a proprietary notification system, which helps facilitate the shortcomings of the connectionless protocol. The data communications of the WSP control channel are illustrated in Figure 3.6.

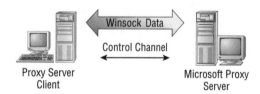

The WSP control channel is designed to do the following:

- Deliver the LAT to the client. This is the table that determines whether or not a destination is on a local network.

- Establish TCP connections from the client to the WSP server. This channel is used to build the virtual connection while attempting to connect with a remote application. Note that the channel is only used at this time. Once the connection is set, sending data over the channel will be discontinued.

- Furnish UDP communications (not connections) to and from the WSP client and/or with the WSP server. This happens when the UDP socket is linked to each instance when a new remote peer sends data to the internal application. To facilitate numerous remote applications conversing with the WinSock program, port-mapping data is sent to the client DLL each time a new remote peer sends information. Once a session has been established, known communications do not need the control channel.

- Record requests to and/or from the WSP client and WSP server. Requests such as Name Resolution (via DNS) and other remote WinSock database requests are processed by passing the client request to the WSP service using the control channel, and then forwarding the response back to the client DLL through the control channel.

The WSP DLL works as follows:

1. The WSP DLL is initialized when the first WinSock connection is attempted.

2. A control channel with the WinSock Proxy Server is established and then designated as active through the channel.

3. The Local Address Table (LAT) is copied from the server to determine which networks are on the Internet and which are local.

After the client system has received a copy of the LAT, the WSP DLL then determines if the application is trying to communicate with a local computer or one that resides on the Internet.

For connection attempts and Windows Sockets APIs destined for a local computer, the WSP DLL forwards the API calls to the now renamed WinSock DLL for processing. When a WinSock API call does not specify a destination, the proxy will forward it to the standard WinSock DLL as a local request. The fact that the default is sent to the local system provides a higher degree of security and reliability. It is far safer to refer requests back to the local network than to forward them on to the Internet. Also, because there is no indication as to whether a request should be remoted, it is more reliable to try the request locally first.

DNS name resolutions and other similar requests utilize WSP components jointly. The proxy server using the control channel sends the request remotely to the gateway computer. The request is then processed on the Internet.

The design of the WinSock Proxy demands extra processing by the client when opening a connection to an Internet resource. After the connection is established, the default WinSock DLL (16-bit or 32-bit) can be used for reading and writing a socket or file with no additional changes from the client's proxy DLL.

The control channel on both the WinSock Proxy Server and client systems utilize UDP on port 1745. The original Proxy Server 1.0 operated identically to 2.0 in this respect, except that it utilized port 9321.

TCP/IP on the Private Network

When clients on a network are configured with TCP/IP as a transport protocol, they have the ability to communicate either with local or remote resources. As the client makes resource calls and the WSP client DLL is initialized, a copy of the LAT is delivered to it via the control channel. As discussed earlier, the LAT is used to determine which destinations are located on the private network. From this point forward, any new connection attempts will be directed and processed by the WSP DLL. When directed locally, connection requests are passed directly to the WinSock DLL that originally was installed with the protocol stack. No additional processing or modifications are made to local requests. Again, if the WinSock API call does not specify a destination or it is indeterminate as to whether a connection is local or remote, the proxy server will first forward it as a local request to the standard WinSock DLL. The request defaulting to the local system provides a higher degree of security and reliability.

In some instances, your network may have multiple servers on the private network monitoring the same port simultaneously. This is a common occurrence with most mail systems as well as with FTP and intranet Web servers. This creates a problem because the multiple servers will conflict with each other while trying to create a connection on the port. To avoid this, an IP address is required on the proxy server for each service utilizing a common port. Therefore, if you have two FTP servers, both monitoring port 21, you will need two addresses assigned to the Internet interface of the proxy server. As you may recall, an IP address and port designate a socket. In order to specify which system is the destination, each set of systems that are the same require separate IP addresses.

IPX on the Private Network

Since the majority of NetWare LAN installations utilize IPX/SPX, it is no wonder that Microsoft developed their proxy server as a protocol gateway with the ability to convert IPX/SPX to TCP/IP. Microsoft's Proxy Server can be transparently integrated into a NetWare environment where clients need not be reconfigured to use the additional services, TCP/IP, or additional re-directors.

When a LAN is configured as described above, WinSock TCP/IP connection requests are immediately redirected to the Internet. No routing information is sent to the client when the WSP DLL is initialized. This makes perfect sense in that if the client does not have TCP/IP, clearly it must talk to the proxy or protocol gateway in order to communicate with any of these types of resources.

Overall, there are a minimal number of differences between IPX/SPX and TCP/IP when used with a proxy server. With the exception of determining which network a request should be sent to, the two protocols operate about the same. As a WinSock application requests a connection to an Internet resource, data is processed by the WSP DLL, which converts addresses and formatting as applicable to IPX/SPX.

Even with IPX, a control channel is still used to communicate with the proxy server. Under TCP/IP, the control channel is established via UDP. However, in the absence of TCP/IP, the control channel is established via IPX. Also, remember that if you are intending to use IPX in your environment, it must be running on both the client and the server.

Socks Proxy Service

The Socks Proxy service is designed to support Windows, UNIX, and Macintosh platforms. Because the majority of Windows-based TCP/IP applications support WinSock, you are less likely to find many applications using this service on this platform. However, for UNIX and Macintosh systems, the majority of applications are written to the 4.3a specification, which is supported.

The major drawback of the Socks Proxy is that it only supports connection- or TCP-based applications. Connectionless or UDP applications will not function without modification. Telnet, FTP, and Gopher are some examples of applications that will utilize this service. Others, such as TFTP, which is UDP based, will not function. Remember that although the protocol that you are working with is designed for either UDP or TCP, generally, TCP applications are more highly regarded for general use. UDP, while low in overhead, does not offer the security or reliability of TCP.

When working with UNIX and Macintosh systems, they generally can be configured so that they enjoy support that is equal to the support their Windows-based counterparts have. The Web browser on either platform can be configured for the Web Proxy, while the majority of other applications can use the Socks service. The difference, of course, is that the UNIX and Macintosh systems cannot communicate with the Internet or beyond the proxy server using UDP.

The Socks Proxy in Action

The Socks Proxy operates based on two operations: connect and bind. To make a connection to an Internet application, a client sends a connect request. The connect request contains the Socks protocol version number, Socks command code, destination IP address, destination TCP port number, user ID, and null field.

The destination Socks server that the client attempts to communicate with will reply to a given request after processing. The reply will either grant or reject access, or fail. Assuming that access is granted, the client can begin immediately transferring data. However, if the request is rejected or fails, the connection to the server will be disconnected at once. The reply message may or may not contain reasons for the failure.

The Socks service allows an application to be linked to another application with a bind operation. The bind operation functions by setting link information based on the TCP header. Typically, the TCP header includes the source and destination systems' IP addresses and port numbers.

Putting It All Together

Microsoft Proxy Server contains a suite of services comprised of a Web, Socks, and WinSock Proxy service (WSP). By themselves, no component does everything. However, they work together to support almost all Internet applications.

When a client is configured to use the entire proxy server, the Web browser makes use of the Web Proxy service and all WinSock applications of the WinSock Proxy service. When combined, generally all Internet services are covered. However, do not be fooled into thinking that all services are completely covered. For example, the Ping utility uses ICMP rather than TCP or UDP to send data. This means that the Ping utility does not work. Ping, as a utility, acts more as an exception than a rule. An application generally does not function on ICMP.

When the private network is configured with TCP/IP, the Local Address Table is set to include the proxy server's internal IP address as not being on the local network. In effect, this demands that all access between client and server utilize the proxy server rather than connect directly. However, if IPX/SPX is the only protocol on the network, this step is implemented by default and does not have to be set.

HTTP and Gopher requests collaborate in the following way:

1. The Web browser sends a request to the proxy server.

2. The WSP client DLL redirects the TCP connection request.

3. The WSP client DLL checks the destination IP address against the Local Address Table and determines if the request needs to be remoted.

4. The WSP client DLL builds a connection to the WSP service, which in turn establishes a connection from the WSP service through Internet Information Server to the Proxy ISAPI components. Remember that you may have multiple proxy servers. This means that the WSP service and the Proxy ISAPI components may be separate from each other. This is excellent for load balancing, which we will discuss in Chapter 9.

5. Client requests are sent to the WSP. In this step, the WSP provides Windows NT Challenge/Response authentication and support for both IPX/SPX and TCP/IP on the private network.

6. From this point, the WSP service relays the request to the proxy components. Through the Proxy ISAPI application, caching is activated.

7. Assuming the request cannot be filled from the cache, the Proxy ISAPI application requests the Internet resource.

With IPX/SPX, the only option is to send all requests as remote. The reason for this is that there are no local IP services because there is no IP on the network.

As you can see, both proxy services work together so that services are fulfilled jointly. However, these services also can be utilized individually. As single components, the proxy servers are less powerful than when combined.

Cache Design

One of the most important functions of a proxy server is its ability to cache data. Some time ago, the founder of 3-COM and inventor of Ethernet, Bob Metcaff, predicted that the Internet would suffer a failure that would bottleneck the system and destroy it. About a year after announcing the prediction, Metcaff wrote out his prediction on a piece of paper and ate it. (Quite literally eating his own words!) In truth, Metcaff was right on target. He just overlooked cache as the factor that would prevent this catastrophe from occurring.

The information in this section only applies to the Web Proxy service.

Caching is so effective that when logs are activated, it is often presumed that there is an error on the server. This assumption is made because no log entries are made when certain Internet resources are accessed. This assumed error was found to be a factor of caching. Clients that made requests to certain Internet resources were not being logged because the clients were reading from the proxy server's cache rather than the actual site.

Caching is clearly an effective method for increasing speed and decreasing network utilization. However, not every object or item accessed on the Internet is cached because the cache is not merely a copy of everything requested from the Internet. There is a method to all the caching madness. An algorithm is applied to determine if a object is cacheable or not. We will discuss this algorithm later.

By this time you may be asking yourself why we don't cache everything. Well, the answer is quite simple. Suppose that you wanted to access a secured site where passwords are required or information is volatile (for example, a site with stock quotes). If these items were cached, you could never get the most current copy of the site you are accessing. In order for an Internet resource to be cached, it must abide by the following guidelines:

- Access to the Internet resource must be established via FTP or HTTP.

- Access to the Internet resource must be via the get request.

- The URL line cannot contain any "?keywords" as in Internet searches.

- The object must not be SSL encrypted or protected.

- The Expires HTTP header field must contain a later date than the date in the Date header field. (It would be ineffective to cache old information.)

- The HTTP header may not contain Pragma: no-cache, Set-Cookie, or WWW-Authenticate.

- The HTTP result code must be 200 (success), 403 (forbidden request), or 404 (URL not found).

The rules listed above are intended to keep the Internet safe and secure. However, there is nothing in the HTTP 1.0 header that prevents or restricts a server from caching a resource. Typically, an Internet site will only want to notify a proxy server not to cache the object by setting the Expires header to the present date and time. This will allow a server to post new information without the concern of outdated or insecure data being cached.

Cookies

Aside from being a fattening dessert, a *cookie* is a commonly used method for either delivering information from a custom Web page or authorizing or tracking a connection in a way that is insecure. Although the HTTP header may also contain cookies, with the exception of the SetCookie header, they typically are ignored. After a cookie is set, all transactions that follow can be cached. That, of course, presumes that the Expires header does not indicate that the delivered data is not out of date.

Caching Types

The two types of caches that are implemented on Microsoft Proxy Server are passive and active. Each type of cache has its own distinctive use and applications.

Passive Caching

Passive caching is the most basic mode of caching (see Figure 3.7). The Web Proxy Server provides on-demand access as requested to items held in its data store. Essentially, the proxy server acts as a go-between in the operation of Internet requests. If it is within the ability of the proxy server to return the request without connecting to the Internet resource, it will do so. Otherwise, the resource will be contacted; and if it meets the criteria for material that can be cached, it is added to the passive store.

FIGURE 3.7

The passive caching process

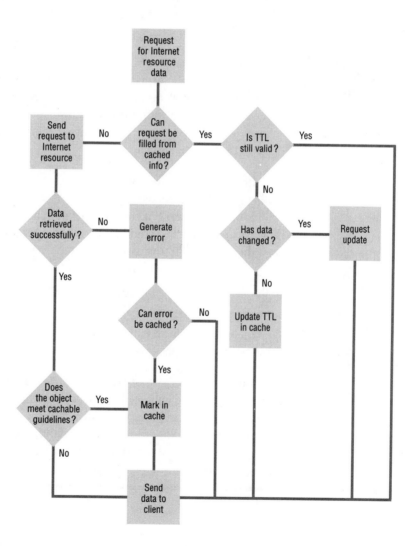

Materials stored in the cache are granted a certain shelf life (called TTL or Time to Live). TTL is like the expiration date stamp on dairy products in the supermarket. After the expiration date passes, objects become questionable and usually should be thrown away. While the information is fresh, any request for that information will be served directly from the cache. This makes the transfer of information extremely fast because no traffic is generated to the actual resource over what is typically a slow link. After the TTL has expired, the information is dropped from the cache. Not until the information is requested again will the proxy server connect to the Internet resource to obtain the information again and assign a new TTL to that data.

TTL is used in most network communication to limit the range that a broadcast or packet of information travels. As with a proxy server, once a TTL has expired, a network message is dropped. This prevents a network from becoming overrun with traffic. Often when using commands such as Ping over a slow link, you must use a –i to specify a longer TTL duration than what is set as the default.

Although TTL is the primary method used to determine if a cached item is still valid, other factors are involved that can drop an object from the cache. Think of it this way: If a container of milk hasn't reached its expiration date, but has turned green, would you still drink it? Okay, maybe you would, but you shouldn't! With the assumption that the information (or the milk) went bad, a browser's manual override will force a proxy server to retrieve fresh information.

With Microsoft Internet Explorer, an object can be refreshed manually by pressing the F5 key.

At this stage, the size of your disk cache can be a factor. For instance, suppose that you only allocated 50 megabytes for data and aside from normal viewing, every client in the company is exploring a host of different sites. With the cache at its maximum storage threshold, objects will be dropped according to their age, popularity, and size. An increase to the cache will better serve the users because there will be a longer periods of time when the object can still be requested.

Active Caching

To improve the speed of the proxy server, Microsoft implemented active caching. This technology works on the crystal ball principle. It predicts an expected request and generates that request for a subset of objects. This type of caching is formulated based on the following three items:

TTL A shorter TTL generally means fresher data. However, this comes at the expense of having data retrieved more slowly. The longer a TTL can be assigned, the faster data will appear to be retrieved.

Popularity Commonly accessed sites such as www.netscape.com (the busiest Web site in the world) or www.microsoft.com are foreseen and cached before such a request is placed by the proxy server or used by the clients. The popularity is determined by the number of hits to a site.

Server Load Caching can be more actively sought after when the server is encountering low use. This means that the server will not attempt to update its active cache when it has actual requests to fulfill.

As you can see, Microsoft Proxy Server's active caching almost has the ability to read your mind. Well, not really, but it does provide an excellent performance boost to a client request when combined with the passive cache.

Caching Array Routing Protocol

When operating in an array configuration, Microsoft Proxy Server 2.0 enhances the caching by sharing data between proxy servers. This algorithm is known as the *caching array routing protocol* or CARP.

CARP was designed to provide two main benefits. First, because CARP is deterministic when resolving a request path, there is no query messaging between proxy servers that is typically associated with conventional Internet Cache Protocol (ICP) networks. ICP is a process that creates heavier congestion as the number of servers increases. Second, CARP eliminates the redundancy that occurs on an array of proxy servers.

The design of CARP is a hashing algorithm such that the process does not require each system to be queried for cache data content. This algorithm is deterministic and therefore is predictable. This protocol is only used in the communication between two or more proxy servers configured in an array. CARP is designed such that it promotes efficiency and speed.

The hashing algorithm operates by assigning a value to each proxy server according to certain system and request conditions. Every time the same conditions occur, the same result will be produced. The server with the highest value is always selected first. If it is not available, the proxy server with the next highest value is selected.

In simplified terms, CARP works as follows:

1. The current proxy server retrieves a list of array members and computes hash values.

2. The proxy server gets the URL to route upstream and computes a hash of the URL.

3. The hash computations are combined. The hash combination algorithm takes into account a load factor assigned to each proxy as well as that server's ability to take on additional requests.

4. The proxy server with the highest value is selected and forwards the URL request.

5. Other URL values are computed to achieve load balancing.

Summary

In this chapter we covered the architecture and structural design of Microsoft Proxy Server. The two components of Proxy Server are the Web and WinSock services. Combined, these two components provide virtually full support for the entire TCP/IP protocol suite as implemented by Microsoft in the Windows environment.

The Web Proxy service is comprised of two sub-components: the ISAPI filter and ISAPI application. The ISAPI filter is used to determine which requests are bound for remote destinations, the protocol to be used, and so forth. The ISAPI application is used with coded pages that are linked to a form or a database. The Web Proxy service is platform independent.

The WinSock Proxy service provides Windows Sockets support to applications operating in the Windows environment. The service uses two WinSock DLL files for support of both 16-bit and 32-bit applications. Depending on the operating system, one or both of the DLLs may be used. The WinSock Proxy supports both TCP/IP and IPX/SPX Windows clients.

Microsoft Proxy Server is complemented with an advanced caching system that provides passive and active caching. Passive caching operates by determining which Internet resources may be stored, then assigning a TTL to them. When additional clients request data, they will read the cached item if they are available. This allows faster access to commonly accessed data. Active caching is based on determining which items stored in the cache are popular and in need of an update. As an object's TTL expires, that object may be automatically updated with fresh data, depending on how it was utilized during its life. Active caching provides increased throughput by performing updates only when bandwidth use is low.

Review Questions

1. Explain what CERN compatibility is, where it comes from, and how it applies to Microsoft Proxy Server.

2. Explain ISAPI and describe the difference between the Proxy Server ISAPI filter and the ISAPA application.

3. How is a specific application identified on a system through the Internet?

4. Briefly explain how a WinSock Proxy client works and operates with TCP/IP. How about with IPX/SPX?

5. Explain how Microsoft Proxy Server's caching system works.

6. Which would you want to cache via Microsoft Proxy Server?

   A. Stock market information

   B. Text and graphics home page data

   C. Internet e-mail pages

   D. Internet information searches

   E. Large FTP data files from beta releases

7. What are the two types of caches used in Microsoft Proxy Server?

    A. Active caching

    B. General caching

    C. Passive caching

    D. Smart caching

    E. Advanced caching

8. What are the names of the Windows Sockets Dynamic Link Libraries?

    A. WinSock.DLL

    B. WSP.DLL

    C. Wsock16.DLL

    D. WinSock.SYS

    E. Wsock32.DLL

9. Which operating systems use both a 16-bit and 32-bit WinSock DLL?

    A. Windows NT

    B. Windows 3.1

    C. Windows for Workgroups

    D. Windows 95

    E. Macintosh

10. Which of the following are not connectionless-based applications?

    A. RealAudio

    B. Gopher

    C. IRC

    D. NETSHOW

    E. FTP

CHAPTER

4

Installing Proxy Server

A word of warning learned from experience: Always cover yourself when you make systems changes. Before you get your hands dirty installing Proxy Server, be sure that you have a system backup and that no users are accessing the system during the reboot.

This chapter covers the hardware and software requirements for Microsoft Proxy Server. By the time you've finished reading this chapter, you should be able to:

- Understand Proxy Server's physical hardware requirements

Exam objectives are subject to change at any time without prior notice and at Microsoft's sole discretion. Please visit Microsoft's Training & Certification website (www.microsoft.com/Train_Cert) for the most current exam objectives listing.

- Detail prerequisite software that must be installed prior to Proxy Server

- Prepare Windows NT for Proxy Server installation

- Describe what events take place during installation

- Explain installation options

- Configure client workstations

- Back out of an installation

Remember that each of the items listed here is central to your success on the MCSE exam. You should have no hesitation when asked about information on the list.

Hardware and Software Prerequisites

It is not unusual for a software manufacture to specify that a program has the ability to run on a particular system without first taking into account the program's actual usefulness. Software manufacturers often do this because they have the view that there are minimum settings as well as recommended ones. They make the assumption that as computer equipment ages, it will be replaced with newer, faster equipment.

For example, Windows 95 can run on four megabytes of RAM. However, with this much RAM the system probably would not be useful for applications such as advanced word processing or publishing. On the other hand, this system may be satisfactory for training users to play solitaire or use a mouse.

Like all other applications, Microsoft Proxy Server includes a list of minimum equipment as well as a list of recommended equipment.

Microsoft ✓ *Exam* *Objective*	**Plan an Internet site or an intranet site for stand-alone servers, single-domain environments, and multiple-domain environments. Tasks include:**
	• Choosing appropriate connectivity methods
	• Choosing services
	• Using Microsoft Proxy Server in an intranet that has no access to the Internet
	• Choosing hardware

Minimum Requirements

The minimum requirement for Microsoft Proxy Server to operate is a bare system that has the ability to run Windows NT Server 4.0. This system should have 24 megabytes of RAM if it has an Intel processor (486 or better), and 32 megabytes if it has a RISC-based system. Proxy Server's program files will consume approximately 10 megabytes. Assuming that caching will be used, you will need an additional 100 megabytes plus 0.5 megabytes per user on an NTFS-formatted volume. If you are upgrading from a previous installation of Microsoft Proxy Server 1.0 that had its cache on a FAT-formatted drive, you must convert the drive to NTFS first. Note that five megabytes is the smallest cache that can be created. (Most companies have adequate systems to meet these needs.)

Microsoft ✓ ***Exam*** ***Objective***	**Choose the location, size, and type of caching for the Web Proxy service.**

As for software, Microsoft Proxy Server requires that Windows NT Server 4.0 be installed along with Internet Information Server (IIS) version 3.0 (with service pack 3 or later). All other required software components are configurable items, such as TCP/IP, that exist with Windows NT 4.0 and IIS.

We will talk more about configuration as we progress through the chapter.

Microsoft ✓ ***Exam*** ***Objective***	**Configure Windows NT to support Microsoft Proxy Server.**

Suggested Equipment

Now the real issues come out. In order for Proxy Server to add any value, the system it's on should be at least a Pentium class system with 32 megabytes of RAM and a reasonably quick hard drive for any 56k or faster connection.

At this point, you may be asking yourself, "Why are these system requirements suggested? What difference does system hardware make?" Well, suppose that you are running a server and decide that because it is only used to support printing, the company could benefit from adding Proxy Server for Internet access. You would begin the installation by adding IIS 2.0, then upgrade to IIS 3.0 with service pack 3. (Keep in mind that IIS 3.0 is generally added as an upgrade while installing service pack 3.) While this initially would have little impact on performance, as your system grows and its use increases (and believe me, it always does), the ability of the system to maintain processes will decrease. This means that the number of print jobs the system can handle will diminish, as will the number of proxy requests it can support. To compensate, the system may swap to the hard disk or delay some programs. This will then affect the Proxy Server cache performance. If the system has a slower hard drive, given the extra overhead of swapping to the hard drive, the system will appear to move like a snail inching its way though a salt factory. So, the bottom line is that only in a laboratory environment are the minimum settings adequate. To actually work and be useful, it is necessary to have a system that is better than what the minimum requirements call for.

Microsoft ✔ ***Exam Objective***   **Identify the licensing requirements for a given Proxy Server site.**

Microsoft's licensing agreement is subject to change and is presented during installation of the Proxy Server product. In summary, Microsoft Proxy Server requires that you own a single license per server installation. The server is required to run both Windows NT Server and Internet Information Server. Microsoft does not require client access licenses to use either Microsoft Proxy Server or Microsoft Internet Information Server. Microsoft Proxy Server may not be rented, leased, or lent. However, it may be sold with the understanding that no copies will be kept in any format. Also, Microsoft Proxy Server may not be disassembled, decompiled, or have its engineering reversed. Also, Microsoft requires that all testing and benchmarking results be submitted to them for written approval prior to release to any third party.

In addition to the minimum requirements and NT Server 4.0 and IIS 3.0 with the latest service pack, you should add any hot fixes posted on Microsoft's FTP site at `ftp.microsoft.com`. Issues that are corrected but not compiled into the current service pack are typically located here. For example, a hot fix was used to correct a hole in Microsoft's TCP/IP implementation that allowed port 139 to be exploited. The bug allowed an out of bound (OOB) message to be sent to a computer, which crashed the operating system. Windows NT Server, Workstation, Windows 95, and Windows for Workgroups were all vulnerable. This vulnerability was amplified by systems on the Internet that attacked networks with inadequate protection. Fortunately, if you did not have the hot fix and someone was destructive enough to attack your system with Proxy Server 2.0 in place, only the proxy server would have been at risk.

Installation

Microsoft Proxy Server provides an easy-to-use and simple installation procedure. For many software packages, the installation is the most importance part in determining program operation. If the installation is performed incorrectly, the program will run less effectively. However, this is not the case with Microsoft Proxy Server. It maintains a flexibility that allows an administrator to make changes to any and all components after installation.

Preinstallation

Prior to installing Microsoft Proxy Server, you should verify that the following minimum requirements have been met:

- The server has at least two network adapters. One network adapter (Ethernet, Token Ring, ArcNet, and so on) is required to connect to the local private network. The second adapter is used to connect to the Internet. For dialup connections to the Internet, you can use a modem or ISDN port, or a LAN topology used in conjunction with a router. LAN topologies are commonly used with point-to-point (T1, T2, OC1, and so on) and frame relay connections.

- You are logged-in with an account that has administrator-level security (or an equivalent level of security).

- If caching will be enabled, a partition must exist that has been formatted with NTFS or changed to NTFS with the Windows NT Convert utility.

- TCP/IP must be installed and configured to communicate on the Internet. The Internet service provider (ISP) generally provides the IP address. Depending on the type of service that is provided by the ISP, often a DNS server and other configuration information are supplied. Also, either TCP/IP or IPX/SPX must be bound to the local LAN adapter to support clients. Since Proxy Server will resolve names for clients, Proxy Server must have a DNS server defined in its TCP/IP configuration.

- Service pack 3 (or later) for Windows NT 4.0 must be installed.

■ Internet Information Server must be installed and configured. Note that installing service pack 3 will upgrade a previous version to the required version 3.0 (or later). If service pack 3 had been installed prior to Internet Information Server, you will have to reapply the service pack.

Do not assign a default gateway on Proxy Server. Doing so will create multiple network paths that don't exist. This will slow down the operation of your system because timeouts on the invalid paths will take place.

We recommend verifying your knowledge and configuration by following the scenario in Exercise 4.1.

To install a network adapter, open the Control Panel and double-click the Network icon. Then click the Adapter tab and select Add.

EXERCISE 4.1

Installing Windows NT, Current Service Packs, and two NICs

The Rodeo Peace Corporation, a small bomb and land mine company based in Beverly Hills, California, has hired you to develop a cost-efficient plan for gaining access to the Internet. The company is looking for an easy-to-manage system that will integrate seamlessly with their Windows NT and UNIX network. Management has determined that Internet access needs to be made available to the 10 designers, five mechanical engineers, and six marketing employees in the firm (all manufacturing is performed in the Middle East).

After reviewing several of the options you've presented them with, including direct access, management has decided to implement Microsoft Proxy Server. While a direct connection could be a problem with their rivals, the Pacoima International Peace Foundation, the security of Microsoft Proxy Server makes it a secure way to link to the public Internet.

EXERCISE 4.1 (CONTINUED FROM PREVIOUS PAGE)

The Rodeo Peace Corporation's internal network utilizes TCP/IP with the following information:

- IP Address: 192.168.10.x

- Subnet mask: 255.255.255.0

Internet access is established through a local carrier on a T1 line. Until an IP address has been permanently assigned, you have been requested to use 172.16.5.x as the Internet range. Note that if you are trying this exercise live on the Internet, use the IP information supplied by your ISP.

If your manager so requests, you may choose to implement a test lab before implementing this configuration on the actual Internet. If you plan to do this, please consult with your manager for IP addresses prior to installation.

Once you purchase a server with two Ethernet adapters, You should install Windows NT Server 4.0 with the current service pack, and configure the two network adapters.

You must install NT Server 4.0 with TCP/IP and IIS 3.0 or greater. To install Windows NT:

1. Boot the CD-ROM or the disks.

2. Format the hard drives as NTFS.

3. Choose to install IIS. By default, TCP/IP will be selected as the protocol. At this time, it is not necessary to install any additional services such as WINS, DHCP, DNS, and so forth.

Next you should configure the second network adapter. The default installation of Windows NT Server 4.0 will not detect a second network adapter. To install a second network adapter:

1. Open the Control Panel and select Network.

2. Click the Adapter tab and select Add.

3. Select your network card from the list shown, or click Have Disk and supply the driver.

EXERCISE 4.1 (CONTINUED FROM PREVIOUS PAGE)

4. Click on and specify a TCP/IP Internet address. (In this example, you would use 192.168.10.5.)

5. Shut down and reboot.

6. Using FTP or a Web browser, connect to Microsoft's Web page and download the current service pack. Also check for any available hot fixes for the service pack.

7. Next you will need to install the service pack. From Windows NT Explorer, double-click the service pack file you downloaded.

8. Follow the directions on the screen. When the service pack has been installed, IIS will be upgraded to 3.0.

Microsoft has changed the location of these files a few times. The best way to locate them is to point your browser to www.microsoft.com, click Download Free Software in the lower portion of the page, and go to Support Drivers, then Patches, and then Service Packs.

Microsoft ✓ *Exam* *Objective*

Choose a secure access strategy for various situations. Access includes outbound access by users to the Internet and inbound access to your Web site. Considerations include:

- Translating addresses from the internal network to the Local Address Table (LAT)
- Controlling anonymous access
- Controlling access by known users and groups
- Setting protocol permissions
- Auditing protocol access
- Setting Microsoft Windows NT® security parameters

Installation

Now that you have verified that you have everything you need to run Proxy Server, you can proceed with the installation.

If you happen to make a mistake during the installation, Proxy Server has the ability to reconfigure after installation, which makes the process very forgiving.

To install Microsoft Proxy Server:

1. Insert the CD-ROM and either run Setup from the root directory or copy the CD-ROM's contents to a server and run the Setup from there. Copying the CD-ROM's contents (from a networked system with a CD-ROM) commonly is done when a server does not have a CD-ROM drive.

2. When the End User License Agreement (EULA) appears, click Yes to continue.

3. In the Microsoft Proxy Server Setup welcome screen, click Continue.

4. Enter the CD key in the CD Key box. The CD key can be found on the back of the CD-ROM case. Then click OK.

5. The product ID appears. Write down the number for your records. (This is critical if your company runs some type of software auditing program.) Then click OK.

6. The Setup program then searches for installed components. If any previously installed version of Proxy Server is detected, the Setup program will notify you and allow you to upgrade.

7. Once the Setup program is done searching the system, it will display the default installation folder, C:\MSP. If you would like Proxy Server to be installed elsewhere, click Change Folder and enter a new destination. To continue, click the Installation Options button.

8. The Microsoft Proxy Server Installation Options screen is displayed. At this point, you may choose components from the Options area. The default installation includes all components.

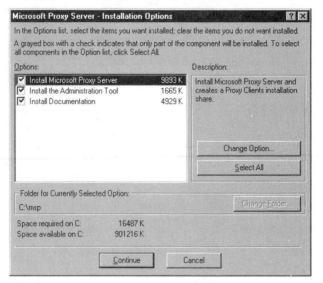

9. With the Install Microsoft Proxy Server option selected, click the Change Option button. Determine which clients will be supported and make the appropriate selections. By default, all clients are installed.

10. Click OK twice and select the Enable Caching checkbox in the Microsoft Proxy Server Cache Drives dialog screen. You may select any local drive listed on the server. You generally will choose the location based on space availability. Or you may select a drive that is separate from the location of the Windows NT swap file for better performance. An NTFS-formatted volume is required.

11. After selecting a drive, enter the cache capacity in the Maximum Size (MB) box and select the Set button to apply the settings. The setting must be a minimum of 5MB. However, it is recommended that you supply at least 100MB with .5MB for each Web Proxy Server client. So a system with 99 users should reserve 150MB (149.5 rounded up) for caching. When you're done, click OK to continue. If you have difficulty understanding any of the caching options, click the Help button.

Create a LAT.

12. The Local Address Table Configuration screen is displayed. The LAT is used to determine which IP addresses are on your private address as well as which ones should not be used on the Internet. Click Construct Table to create the LAT.

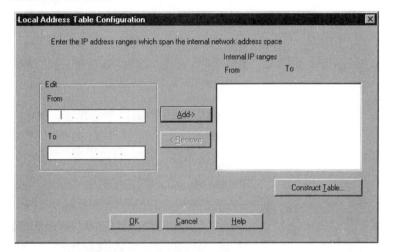

13. After the Construct Local Address Table dialog box appears, you can add the range of IP addresses local to your server by selecting the Add the Private Ranges checkbox.

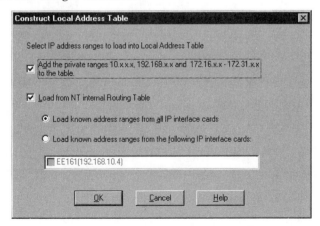

14. If you are not able to determine which IP addresses to add to the table or which IP addresses are bound to which network interface card, you should select Load Known Address Ranges from All IP Interface Cards. Ideally, you should only add those addresses associated with the internal network. Select Load Known Address Ranges from the Following IP Interface Cards if you want to select only those addresses connected to the private network. When you are done, click OK.

15. A Setup Message box will appear warning you that some of the IP addresses on your private network may actually be on the Internet and suggesting that you manually edit the LAT. Click OK.

16. The Local Address Table Configuration screen will appear again, but this time it will have a list of IP addresses in the Internal IP Ranges section. Check the list to make sure it matches what is on your private network. If necessary, add additional address pairs by typing the IP range in the From and To Edit pull-down menus. Typing the same address in both From and To will add a single address. To add addresses you've entered in the To and From boxes, click the Add button. To delete an address, select it in the Internal IP Ranges section and click the Remove button. When you are done making adjustments to the IP addresses, click OK.

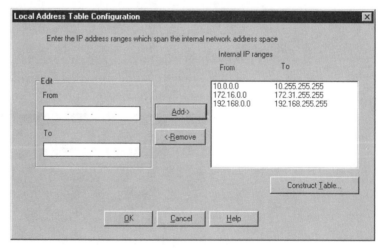

17. The Client Installation/Configuration screen appears. Define the Win-Sock Proxy client configurations that are installed by this server. To do this, select Computer Name, IP Address, or Manual. When selecting Computer Name, note that the correct entry is in the dialog box. The client Setup program will be placed in a share called MSPCLNT by the Proxy Server Setup program. When working with IPX clients, you should specify the computer name (NetBIOS) rather than the host name. Configure the Web Proxy client by specifying the name of the proxy and the port to be used by the client. This is done by checking the Automatically Configure Web Browser During Client Setup box. As with the WinSock Proxy client, note that the correct system name entry is shown in the dialog box. Usually the port will remain as port 80. When a client system is configured from the MSPCLNT share, the Setup program will automatically attempt to set Internet Explorer or Netscape Navigator browsers to use the specified server. Optionally, you may configure the Web browser to configure itself through a URL or a script. Depending on your expertise, you may find writing your own JavaScript for this process to be more effective that using the default. Click OK to continue.

Write JavaScript to configure a Web browser.

18. Set the access control for the WinSock Proxy and Web Proxy services. By default, both are enabled. Enabling access control requires an administrator to define explicit user access. Each user must be either added to a group or directly assigned rights for services. Clearing the box corresponding to access control next to each service will disable access control, allowing all users to bypass security and access the proxy services. The access control options may be changed after installation. Click OK to continue when done.

19. The Setup program copies numerous files, and then the Setup Information dialog box appears notifying the installer about packet filtering security. Click OK to continue.

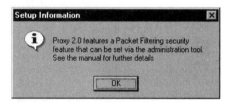

20. The Setup program will update the system. When complete, the program will notify the installer. Click OK to continue.

21. The installation is now complete. At this point you should have a fully functional proxy server that is capable of supporting users. Depending on your environment and equipment, additional configuration may be required.

Installing Proxy Documentation

Because Microsoft provides Proxy Server documentation in electronic form only, you may find it useful to install it for viewing or printing without the program. The documentation contains useful notes regarding the installation. To install the documentation without installing the actual service, follow steps 1 through 6 in the *Installation* section of this chapter. When the Installation Options dialog box discussed in step 7 is displayed, clear all boxes except the Install Documentation box. Then click the Continue button.

Because the Proxy Server documentation is in HTML format, you may use any Web browser that supports frames to view or print the documentation. An example of a browser that supports frames is Internet Explorer 3.01. Optionally, you may choose to export parts of the documentation by using the save function and selecting a data type. Most browsers also support cut and paste functions.

Once the installation is complete, you may open the documentation by selecting Start ➤ Programs ➤ Microsoft Internet Server ➤ Proxy Server Documentation (see Figure 4.1).

FIGURE 4.1

Opening Proxy Server documentation

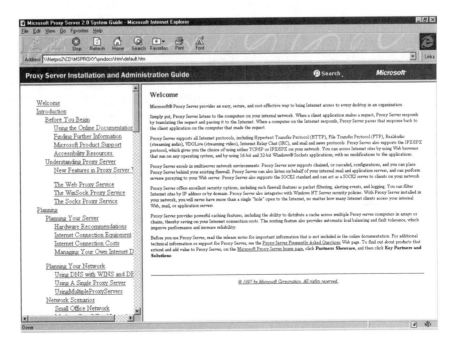

For advanced users who do not want to install any Proxy Server components but do want to read the documentation, you may bypass installing the documentation by using a Web browser and opening DEFAULT.HTM in the PRXDOCS\HTM folder of the CD-ROM. Not installing the documentation will save hard drive space. The DEFAULT.HTM file is the table of contents of the Proxy Server documentation. With some older browsers, you may experience problems with relative directories. In these cases, you will have to add the documents to an existing Web server.

What Gets Installed

During the installation, multiple changes occur on Windows NT Server. Although there are many changes that take place, only three are essential for you to know:

- The Web, WinSock, and Socks Proxy components are installed as additional services on NT Server and are integrated directly into the Internet Service Manager.

- System customization occurs with the addition of Proxy Server Performance Meter counters, HTML documentation placement, cache configuration settings, and the Local Address Table.

- A shared directory called MSPCLNT is created that contains the Microsoft Proxy Client software. This directory contains a client configuration file that is generated during the Proxy Server setup. Executing *SERVER*\MSPCLNT\SETUP (where *SERVER* is the name of the Proxy Server system) configures clients.

During installation, the Setup utility forces all existing active Web services to be shut down. This is useful knowledge for during setup if you are intending to install Microsoft Proxy during the day and are required to keep the Web services active during operation hours. The Proxy Server should be installed and configured when no services are required from the server.

As an administrator, it is useful to note that the MSPCLNT share points to the MSP\CLIENTS directory. In some rare instances, it may be necessary to add components to this directory or add a sub-directory. An example would be adding a Web browser or another Internet tool to the MSPCLNT share so users could access a single install point for all Internet services.

Exercise 4.2 provides an excellent overview and demonstrates how Microsoft Proxy Server should be set up on a system that meets all requirements.

EXERCISE 4.2

Installing Microsoft Proxy Server

Building on the scenario in Exercise 4.1, we will now install Microsoft Proxy Server. Verify installation requirements. Note and correct any problems shown in the Event Viewer prior to installation. Also, check that the system you have installed is complete with all required software and hardware.

To install Microsoft Proxy Server:

1. Insert the CD-ROM and run Setup from the root directory or the share containing Microsoft Proxy Server.

2. After the Welcome screen appears, click Continue and enter the CD Key in the space provided.

3. The product ID will appear. Click OK to continue.

4. The Setup program will display the default installation folder. Click Installation Options. Verify that all options are selected. Click OK to continue.

5. Select Choose Cache Drive. Select drive C.

6. Enter the cache capacity in the Cache Size (MB) box, then select Set. Since you have 21 users, you should allocate 111 megabytes. Click OK to continue.

7. The Local Address Table Configuration screen is displayed. Select Load from NT Internal Routing Table and select the network adapter connected to the intranet. Click OK to continue.

> **EXERCISE 4.2 (CONTINUED FROM PREVIOUS PAGE)**
>
> **8.** The Client Configuration screen appears. Click OK to accept the defaults.
>
> **9.** The Access Control screen appears. Verify that both boxes for the Web Proxy and WinSock Proxy services are checked and click OK to continue.
>
> **10.** Setup copies all necessary files. A message will appear notifying you about packet security. Click OK to continue.
>
> **11.** A dialog box appears notifying you that setup is complete. Click OK to exit the installation.

Microsoft WinSock Client Configuration

Before a user can access the proxy server, their system must first be configured as a client. The term *client* is used in the same context as it is in client/server architecture. For instance, a network client system will request data from a server, and based on the clients permissions at the server, they will be either granted or denied access to the requested data. With Proxy Server, the relationships with subordinate workstations are the same. In order to use the server, a workstation must be a client. The WinSock support programs are located in the WSP\CLIENTS directory on the Microsoft Proxy Server. This directory can be accessed by connecting to its network share name, WSPCLNT. The WSPCLNT share allows read-only access.

Microsoft ✓ *Exam* *Objective*	**Use the Proxy Server client Setup program to configure client computers.**

When executed, the WinSock Client Setup program will configure a supported workstation to use Microsoft Proxy Server. The WSP Client Setup screen will appear as shown in Figure 4.2.

After clicking OK in the Welcome screen, Setup will look for a previously installed client. If one is found, a screen like the one shown in Figure 4.3 will appear.

Select the directory in which you would like the Proxy client files to be installed. Depending on which options were selected by the administrator, the workstation's Web browser will be updated to use the Proxy Server as well (see Figure 4.4).

FIGURE 4.4

Microsoft Proxy Client
directory

As the Setup program continues, MSPLAT.TXT (Microsoft Proxy LAT) is copied to the workstation. This is the file that was generated during setup when you defined local versus remote networks; it is updated on a regular basis by the Proxy Server. The update duration for the LAT file is a preset interval. Before a connection is attempted, the client system will check the destination address against the LAT file to determine if the proxy service will be required for communication. Because the client checks the LAT file, only connections to the external networks will be established through the proxy server, unless otherwise specified by the client. Obviously, if a client can make a direct connection (on the local network), security is not an issue and an increased efficiency can be achieved by bypassing the proxy server. The Setup program copies client-related files. When it's done, you'll see the screen shown in Figure 4.5.

FIGURE 4.5

The Microsoft Proxy
Client Setup completion
screen

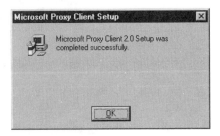

After the client installation is complete, you will notice several changes to the client computer:

- The LAT (MSPLAT.TXT) is copied to the C:\MSPCLNT directory.

- The proxy configuration file (MSPCLNT.INI) is copied to the C:\MSPCLNT directory.

- The WinSock DLL that ships with your operating system will be replaced by a modified one for use with Proxy Server.

- A program group will appear, allowing for setup or removal of the Proxy client.

- An icon for the WSP Client will appear in the Control Panel.

An alternate method for Windows-based clients to install the proxy client software is to go to http://proxyserver/MSProxy and select Install from the displayed page shown in Figure 4.6. To practice installing Proxy Server clients, follow the steps in Exercise 4.3.

FIGURE 4.6

Microsoft Proxy Web-based client setup

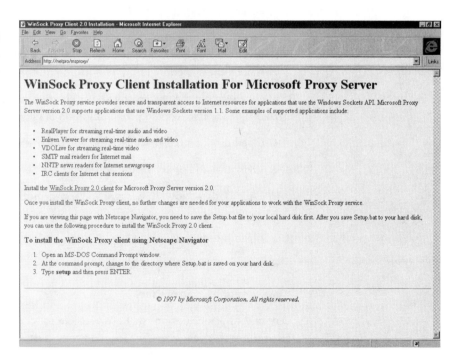

EXERCISE 4.3

Installing Microsoft Proxy Server Clients

Now that you have a functional proxy server, you must configure your clients to operate with it. This installation for Microsoft's Proxy client is simple and straightforward. Regardless of the system, the entire process should take less than five minutes.

1. Install a Proxy client from the share created during the server setup. From a client workstation, connect to \\PROXY_SERVER\MSPCLNT and run Setup.

2. The Welcome screen appears. Select OK to install.

3. Check that C:\MSPCLNT is the directory in which the client is being installed. Click Install Proxy Client.

4. The Client Setup program will copy files. When the process is complete, a dialog box will appear notifying the installer. Click OK and reboot the system.

Before breaking out the champagne and celebrating your success, you should check things out first. To verify the installation of Microsoft Proxy Client:

1. Open the Control Panel and double-click the WSP Client.

2. Verify that the proxy server appears in the Server Name box.

3. Click Update Now. A message will appear notifying you of the success.

4. Click OK. A message will appear prompting you to reboot.

5. Select Don't Restart Windows Now.

6. Close the Control Panel.

To note the various options that are available to an administrator beyond the user interface, the data files for the Proxy client may be reviewed.

> **EXERCISE 4.3 (CONTINUED FROM PREVIOUS PAGE)**
>
> Next, view the WinSock Proxy configuration files:
>
> 1. Using Notepad, open the MSPCLNT.INI file located in C:\MSPCLNT. Note the various settings that were configured automatically during the installation process. While you may change these settings directly, when possible, you should use the provided administration interface.
>
> 2. From within Notepad, open the MSPLAT.TXT file located in C:\MSPCLNT. Note that the addresses shown reflect the fact that your entire network is local.
>
> 3. Close both files and exit Notepad.

Microsoft ✓ ***Exam Objective*** | **Change settings in MSPCLNT.INI.**

Advanced Windows Sockets Configurations

Under normal conditions, most WinSock-based applications should operate without any additional configuration. However, in certain instances a situation may arise that requires you to make special modifications. These modifications are for handling WinSock client requests, and they may be set in either of two locations:

MSPCLNT.INI   This is the global client configuration file. Located in the WinSock Proxy Client installation directory, this file is updated regularly from the proxy server, overwriting the previous file. This file is useful for updating multiple systems at once from the proxy server because the file is frequently downloaded. However, you should not use this file at the workstation as it will be overwritten periodically.

WSPCFG.INI   This file operates in the same manner as the MSPCLNT.INI file, and it is located in a specific client application directory. The key benefit to using this file is that it is static and is not overwritten by the proxy server. This file is useful when fine tuning a single system on your network.

Each of these two files allows you to control a global or application-specific configuration. The global configuration setting is stored by adding a section called [Common Configuration] to the client configuration file. The setting in the [Common Configuration] section will be used for all WinSock applications that do not have application-specific settings. Application-specific settings are configured per WinSock application configuration and are stored in the configuration file according to their name. For example, Microsoft Exchange will have a section called [EXCHNG32]. As you can see, the section name corresponds to the EXCHNG32.EXE executable file. If this section includes any customized entries, then the program will follow those customized settings. For instance, adding Disable=1 in the [ENCHNG32] section would disable the Exchange client from operating with the WinSock Proxy service.

When working with Exchange, note that the Exchange server can be a client of the proxy server. Due to the control function between the proxy server and the client, RPC port 135 may be required depending on the type of Exchange client that is accessing the server. The RPC ports that are used for subsequent connections are 1024 through 5000. You will find further details on this in Microsoft's knowledge base when looking up Exchange's interactions with firewalls. Also, if multiple Exchange servers are accepting mail from the Internet, each server must be linked to its own address at the proxy server. The Exchange server will be required to have the WinSock Proxy client installed and an entry in the WSPCFG.INI file where a section is added for the Internet Mail connector. An entry such as the following appears:

```
[msexcimc]
ServerBindTcpPorts=25
Persistent=1
KillOldSession=1
```

Also, you should create a second WSPCFG.INI file that contains entries needed for the Exchange Store (STORE.EXE). This addition will facilitate other ports. STORE.EXE sets POP mail on port 110, NNTP on port 119, and IMAP4 on port 143. This second WSPCFG file should be placed in the directory where STORE.EXE is located.

```
[Store]
ServerBindTcpPorts=110,119,143
Persistent=1
KillOldSession=1
```

Finally, you should verify that your DNS MX records refer to the Proxy Server computer and not to the Exchange Server computer. This is primarily due to the fact that the MX record is different from a regular GetHostByName call. You must configure network TCP/IP properties, using the Control Panel, to use DNS for the Exchange Server computer. The WinSock Proxy client application will automatically redirect the DNS MX request. When completed, stop and start the Exchange services or reboot the Exchange Server computer for the new settings to take effect. These actions will allow you to contact the Exchange Server by connecting to the Proxy Server computer's external IP address using SMTP, NNTP, or POP. When an internal DNS server is available on your network, you should use DHCP to configure the internal server. In this manner, both internal and external DNS servers can resolve names on your internal network and on the Internet.

Prior to performing any WinSock Proxy Client services, the WinSock Proxy Client application will search for the Disable entry under the [Common Configuration] section of the MSPCLNT.INI file. If the Disable entry is set to 1, the WinSock Proxy service is disabled. Otherwise, the WinSock Proxy client application looks for a WSPCFG.INI file in a client WinSock application directory. If this file exists in the WinSock application directory, the file is parsed for a section that contains the name of the executable file for the WinSock application in brackets. In the previous example, we used [EXCHNG32] for EXCHNG32.EXE. If a section is not found, the WinSock Proxy client application scans for the [Common Configuration] section. If this section also doesn't exist, it looks for the same sections in the MSPCLNT.INI file. Using this search order, only the first section found will be used to apply the application-specific configuration settings.

In each custom configuration section, the following setting may be applied:

- Entry: A description of the custom setting.

- Disable: This setting is used to disable the WinSock Proxy service for all WinSock Proxy client applications when the value is set to 1. In the [Common Configuration] section of the MSPCLNT.INI file, this setting overrides any other settings.

- NameResolution: Used to set name resolution to either local or redirected. By default, all dot-convention names are resolved through a redirected channel. To force name resolution as local, set this value to L; otherwise, for redirect, use R.

- LocalBindTcpPorts: Designates a TCP port, list, or range that is bound locally.

- LocalBindUdpPorts: Designates a UDP port, list, or range that is bound locally.

- RemoteBindTcpPorts: Designates a TCP port, list, or range that is bound remotely.

- RemoteBindUdpPorts: Designates a UDP port, list, or range that is bound remotely.

- ServerBindTcpPorts: Designates a TCP port, list, or range used by a server application. An *accept operation* on these ports is intended to serve clients both locally and on the Internet. The port must be available both on the client computer and the Proxy Server computer in order to function.

- ProxyBindIp: Designates an IP address or list that is used when binding with a corresponding port. Used by multiple servers that use the same port and need to bind to different ports on the Proxy Server computer. The syntax of the entry is: `ProxyBindIp=[port]` : `[IP address], [port]` : `[IP address]`. The port numbers apply to both TCP and UDP ports.

- KillOldSession: This setting is used to handle open session connection. When the value is set to 1, this setting is used to notify a proxy server that if a session from an old instance of an application is still open, that session should be terminated before the application is granted a new session. This keeps proxy users from having to restart an application that did not close out an old session. While internally the proxy server can also perform this same function, there is a 10 minute timeout for an old session to be discovered. And unless the application was restarted in conjunction with the proxy server closing the port, the application would still have a problem because the port that you need to connect on will already be in use.

- Persistent: This setting is used to keep a session active when a service is stopped or restarted. When the value is set to 1, this entry can be used to maintain a specific server state on the Proxy Server. The client sends a keep-alive message to the server periodically during an active session. If the server is not responding, the client tries to restore the state of the bound and listening sockets upon server restart.

- ForceProxy: Used to designate the use of a specific Proxy Server for a specific WinSocks application. The syntax of the entry is `Force-Proxy=[tag]` : `[entry]`, where tag equals i for an IP address, x for an IPX address, or n for a name. Entry is the address of the name. If the n flag is used, the WinSock Proxy service works over IP only.

- ForceCredentials: Used when running a Windows NT service or server application as a WinSock Proxy client application. When the value is set to 1, it forces the use of alternate user authentication credentials stored locally on the computer running the Windows NT service. The user credentials are stored on the client computer using the CREDTOOL.EXE application that is provided with Proxy Server. User credentials must reference a user account that can be authenticated by Proxy Server, either local to Proxy Server or in a domain trusted by Proxy Server. The user account is normally set not to expire; otherwise, user credentials need to be renewed each time the account expires.

- NameResolutionForLocalHost: Used to specify how the LocalHost computer name is resolved. This entry aids WinSocks applications that rely on the IP addresses that the local host computer resolves to. Such applications call `gethostbyname("LocalHost")` to find their local IP address and send it to an Internet server. When this option is set to L (the default), `gethostbyname()` returns the IP addresses of the local host computer. When this option is set to P, `gethostbyname()` returns the IP addresses of the Proxy Server computer. When this option is set to E, `gethostbyname()` returns only the external IP addresses of the Proxy Server computer (those IP addresses that are not in the LAT).

Together, these setting can be combined to designate WinSock communication parameters. The following is an example for an application named WNSCKAPP:

```
[WnSckApp]
Disable=0
NameResolution=L
LocalBindTcpPorts=5555
LocalBindUdpPorts=5000-5022, 5200-5280
RemoteBindTcpPorts=23
RemoteBindUdpPorts=4000-4050
ServerBindTcpPorts=100-300
ProxyBindIp=80:192.168.10.15, 82:192.168.0.0
KillOldSession=1
Persistent=1
ForceProxy=i:192.168.5.5
ForceCredentials=1
NameResolutionForLocalHost=L
```

There is no provision for client applications that require connections both on the internal network and on the Internet. A port can appear in only one of the entries, either as Local, Remote (redirected), or Server (redirected). For such applications, connections for the internal network are directed through Proxy Server as well.

While many WinSock applications such as RealAudio offer the ability to work directly with a proxy server, you should not use anything other than the Microsoft Proxy Server client.

LAT Files

Microsoft ✓ *Exam Objective*   **Create a LAT.**

As mentioned earlier, the LAT files are used to determine whether or not a network is local. This is done to achieve flexibility in utilizing a proxy server, based on its location. There are two types of LAT file services: those stored manually and those stored automatically. Note that the LAT files are regular text files that may be modified with any text editor, as shown in Figure 4.7.

FIGURE 4.7

Editing the Proxy LAT file

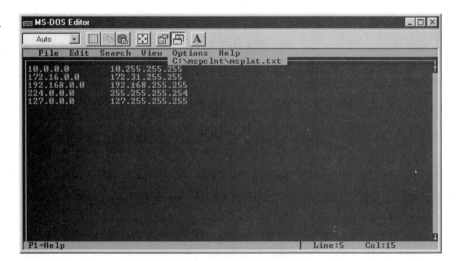

Only the WinSock Proxy service uses the LAT. All other proxy services will always assume that a resource is remote unless otherwise specified.

Automatically Updating the LAT

The MSPLAT.TXT file is delivered automatically to clients on a periodic basis. On occasion, it is necessary to debug or try theoretical situations where this table must be modified. Because it is not for all users to have this file modified and then replicated, Microsoft allows this file to be modified on a per system basis. Modifications to the MSPLAT.TXT file are temporary because the automatic update overwrites any changes. Any temporary changes will have to be added back in manually. This ensures that each client is current with the network architecture without being modified individually.

Manually Updating the LAT

Because the MSPLAT.TXT file is updated frequently, the changes made to the file are temporary. The updated changes may be updated again for each scenario where users require modifications or permanent additions. With flexibility in mind, Microsoft has engineered a file mechanism called LOCALLAT.TXT to store permanent LAT information. This file is stored in the WSPCLNT directory and must be created manually. It is typically best to just copy the MSPLAT.TXT file to the LOCALLAT.TXT file and make changes accordingly. You should try to avoid too much overlap of identical information. The local LAT file is useful for custom configuring users on hidden networks to use the proxy server. Note that the LOCALLAT.TXT file is only used by the WinSock Proxy service.

Private Addresses in the LAT

As you have probably noticed, there are a number of entries that appear in the LAT. These addresses are based on your local, private network's address as well as addresses that are reserved as private. Table 4.1 shows the various private address ranges as they apply to the each address class. Note that your network should be included in the LAT as shown on the last line.

TABLE 4.1	**Address Class**	**Starting Range**	**Ending Range**
Addresses in the LAT	A	10.0.0.0	10.255.255.255
	B	172.16.0.0	172.32.255.255
	C	192.168.0.0	192.168.255.255
	Your Network	First Network Address	Last Network Address

The addresses that appear in Table 4.1 are not routable on the Internet. This means that no Internet resource will have an IP address in this range. These addresses are only used in private networks that perform address translation or use a proxy server. These addresses are useful when configuring a network that will never be directly connected to the Internet. The address range that you choose will depend on the size of your company. An organization with 10 people should use a Class C network, while an organization with 90,000 people should use a Class A network. Note that all Class A addresses have already been assigned. And with the exception of 10.x.x.x on the private address list, no other address should be used (in conjunction with the Internet or a proxy intermediary). Using an address that is already active on the Internet will result in faulty communications when trying to contact the actual site that owns the address.

Bypassing Proxy Client Services

In many situations, users within an organization will require more than one Internet connection. If you are asking yourself, "Why would users have more than one access point to the Internet?" you're not alone. However, consider the applications that field users or those who take their laptops home with them will require. Internet access for home as well as the office can be essential. As installed, the WinSock Proxy client will not support any dialup or other Internet connection. In fact, all TCP/IP-based applications will fail because the Proxy Server will not be available.

The WinSock Proxy client can easily be disabled, allowing additional Internet connections to be used. To disengage the WinSock Proxy client, use the following procedure:

1. From the WinSock Proxy client, open the Control Panel and Select WSP Client.

2. Clear the Enable WinSock Proxy Client checkbox.

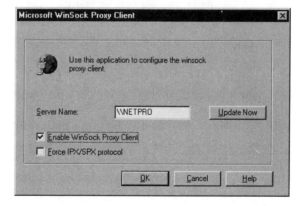

3. Click OK to accept the changes.

4. Restart the system.

The WinSock Proxy client can be re-enabled by following the same procedure and clearing the checkbox in step 1.

Supported Web Browsers

Microsoft Proxy Server supports any Web browser that supports the CERN-proxy standard. Although there are standards for communication with a proxy server, this is not the case for all browser applications. Microsoft Proxy Server configures to work with Microsoft Internet Explorer and Netscape Navigator. However, an automatic configuration would not happen when either adding a browser after the WSP client configuration or switching to a secondary ISP. Also, due to the nature of programming, this information tends to change slightly from version to version and is intended only as an overview for configuring a Web browser for proxy support. All operating systems including Windows, UNIX, and Macintosh use the same or similar formats for configuring Web-browser support. In general, all operating systems will support HTTP, FTP, and Gopher protocols via the Web Proxy service. When reviewing the configuration information here, remember that it pertains to the browser program regardless of the operating system, but that there are exceptions. For instance, UNIX clients may use the Socks Proxy, which in based on the Socks 4.3a standard. In this standard, name resolution is specified; however, Web browsers do not support this feature. They must be configured such that name resolution of Internet addresses is available on the client computer. In short, if you are running a Web browser as a Socks client on a non-Windows client platform, you need to provide a DNS proxy server to your clients for name resolution. The DNS proxy server resolves names by forwarding client requests to a server on the Internet. In determining which proxy service you are configuring your client to operate with, remember that they will work only with the service that they are configured to work with. That means that a request designated from a Socks client will not revert to a Web client request if the request is not configured in that manner (regardless of how the LAT is configured). Aside from the Web Proxy, only the Socks Proxy has platform independence. (WinSock is limited to Microsoft Windows platforms only.)

All systems that are not using IPX with the WinSock client (in other words, systems other than Windows 95 and NT with IPX) must have TCP/IP installed to operate with a browser. For example, if you had a UNIX system, it must be configured with TCP/IP, which uses the correct addressing scheme of your network. Then, and only then, can you configure the operating system's Web browser. There is no need to remove other protocols such as AppleTalk from Macintosh systems. You must have TCP/IP installed except for WinSock clients running IPX.

Microsoft ✓ **Exam** **Objective**

Configure Proxy Server and Proxy Server client computers to use the Proxy Server services. Configurations include:

- Microsoft Internet Explorer client computers
- Netscape Navigator client computers
- Macintosh® client computers
- UNIX client computers
- Client computers on an IPX-only network

Microsoft Internet Explorer

For each version of Internet Explorer there is a different procedure for configuring proxy support. In general, the configuration items include HTTP, Security (secure sockets layer protocol), FTP, Gopher, and Socks (firewall bypass software). Each of these items requires the host name or IP address of the proxy server and the port number to which data should be sent. Because users tend to use only a single proxy server, Microsoft includes a checkbox to use the same proxy server for all settings and ports. Also, the configuration of Internet Explorer offers an Exclude list of specific hosts, separated by a semicolon. By default, there are no names in the Exclude list. Optionally, you may choose not to use the proxy server for local (intranet) addresses by clicking the checkbox. Only HTTP, Secure (HTTP), FTP, and Gopher protocols are supported by Microsoft Web Proxy Server, although the other proxy clients can be enabled indirectly.

For Windows NT and Windows 95, you can use the following procedure to configure the client workstation:

1. From the Start Menu, select Settings ➤ Open Control Panel ➤ Internet. Or, from the Explorer desktop, use the right mouse button to click the Internet icon on the desktop screen.

2. The Internet Properties screen will appear. Select the Connection tab and click the Connect Through a Proxy Server checkbox. Then click the Settings button to define the proxy server to the client.

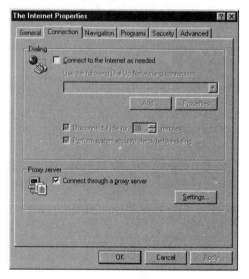

3. In the Proxy Settings dialog box enter the IP address or host name of the Microsoft Proxy Server for each class of services: HTTP, Secure, FTP, Gopher, and Socks. Also, for each entry, be sure to include the port number of each service. All services may use the same port on a system.

In such cases, place a check mark in the Use the Same Proxy Server for Addresses Beginning With checkbox.

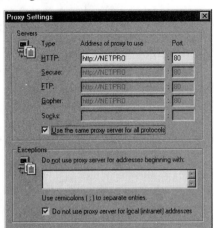

4. While the LAT file from the server defines a list of exclusions, you may opt to include other names or domain names that are on your intranet. To disable proxy server, click the Do Not Use Proxy Server for Local (Intranet) Addresses checkbox.

5. Once the settings have been added, click OK twice. This will save your settings to the Internet Explorer Properties area.

For complete and accurate information for your version of Internet Explorer, consult Internet Explorer's online documentation.

Netscape Navigator

Netscape Navigator is currently available in a number of versions. As with Internet Explorer, the proxy configuration of Netscape will depend on the version. Generally, the configuration items include HTTP, Security (secure sockets layer protocol), FTP, Gopher, WAIS (Wide Area Information Service), and Socks (firewall bypass software). Each of these items requires the host name or IP address of the proxy server and the port number to which data should be sent. By default, Socks is set to port 1080. Like Internet Explorer, Netscape features an Exclude list for domains that do not require proxy services. Only HTTP, Secure (HTTP), FTP, and Gopher protocols are supported by Microsoft Web Proxy Server, although the other proxy clients can be enabled indirectly.

Although there are several versions of Netscape Navigator available, we will discuss two of Netscape's more popular and current versions: Netscape Navigator 4.*x* and Netscape Navigator 3.*x*.

1. For version 4.*x*, start Netscape Navigator and select Preferences from the Edit pull-down menu.

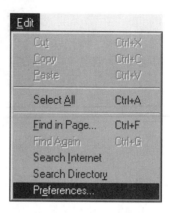

2. The Preferences screen with a structure tree on the left side will be displayed. Locate Advanced and click the plus sign, then click Proxies.

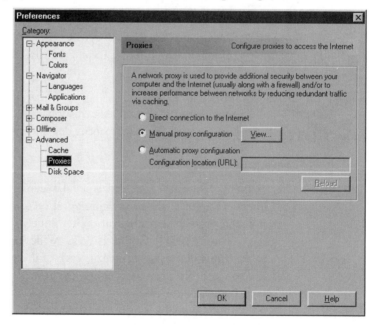

For version 3.*x*:

1. Start Netscape Navigator and select Network Preferences from the Options pull-down menu.

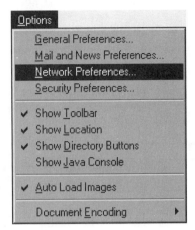

2. Click the Connections tab located at the top of the dialog box.

3. Three options should now be available: Direct Connections to the Internet (No Proxies), Manual Proxy, and Automatic Proxy Configuration. By default, Direct Connections to the Internet is selected. When a proxy server contains a configuration file expressly written for your system, you may choose Automatic Proxy Configuration, type in the URL containing the configuration, and click Reload. However, because we are not configuring such a file, we will focus on the manual proxy configuration. Click Manual Proxy, and then click View. The Manual Proxy Configuration box will appear.

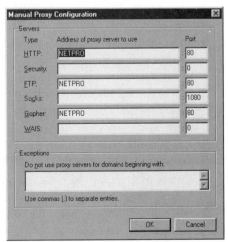

4. Enter the IP address or host name of the Microsoft Proxy Server for each class of services: HTTP, Security, FTP, Socks, Gopher, and WAIS. Also, for each entry, be sure to include the port number of each service. There may be different IP addresses listed because multiple servers may be used.

5. Define which systems you want to bypass the proxy server by typing the domain name or the beginning of the site name in the box labeled Do Not Use Proxy Servers for Domains Beginning With.

6. Once the settings have been added, select OK twice. This will save your settings to Netscape's Properties area.

For complete, accurate information for your version of Netscape Navigator, consult Netscape's online documentation.

You may have noticed that Internet Explorer and Netscape Navigator have comparable configuration setups. This is because programmers can only design a program so many different ways when it is intended to perform a set function or task. This applies to all proxy servers as well. After reading this book and gaining an understanding of the functions of Microsoft Proxy Server, you should be able to work with other proxy servers with few problems.

Automatically Configuring a Web Browser

Microsoft Proxy Server enables an administrator to create a configuration file to automatically configure a client every time a Web browser is opened. The configuration file is a JavaScript file that is downloaded to a client each time the browser is opened. The JavaScript file resides on the proxy server and improves overall performance by keeping the browser up to date with current configuration settings, allowing faster retrieval of Web pages and a lower proxy server array load for browsers that support automatic configuration. Under normal operating conditions, the script will run each time a URL request is generated by the user. The script will then off-load some of the routing work performed by members of the Proxy Server array.

The key feature of this script is that it allows an array of proxy servers to be automatically set at a client. As a URL is requested, a predetermined path is always used to request the same information. All reconfigurations are performed without having to individually modify each client. Microsoft Internet Explorer 3.02 (or newer) and Netscape Navigator 2.0 (or newer) can utilize this feature.

The JavaScript is generated automatically during installation, based on the options set in the Advanced Client Configuration dialog box. Or you may design your own configuration file in JavaScript and place it on your Web server. When a Web browser looks for the configuration script, the Web server will intercept the request and return the custom script to the browser. In short, the script is downloaded; then, when it's executed it provides a hash routing algorithm that specifies which proxy server to use.

The routing performance benefits from the automatic configuration file only apply if the Web Proxy client browser points directly to a Proxy Server array.

Automatic configuration can be enabled on a supporting Web browser by typing **http://*servername*/Array.dll?Get.Routing.Script** in the URL dialog box. This is the URL that is automatically generated during installation. Note that a substitute script may be configured and used in place of the default script. Client browsers that do not support automatic configuration must be configured manually.

Netscape Navigator is reasonably straightforward when it comes to configuring the automatic URL. For version 3.*x*, you will find the configuration on the Proxy tab in Network Configuration under the Options pull-down menu. For version 4.*x*, you can find the configuration under Proxies in the Preferences dialog box under the Edit pull-down menu. In either case, you will notice that there is an Automatic Proxy Configuration option under the Manual Proxy Configuration option.

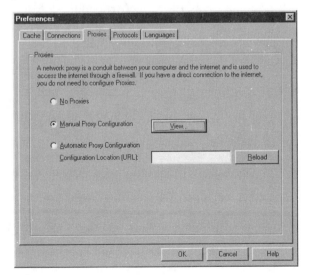

With Microsoft Internet Explorer, however, the automatic configuration options are not with the proxy configuration settings. The automatic settings can be found in the Advanced tab of the Options dialog box. You must click the Automatic Configuration button to view its settings.

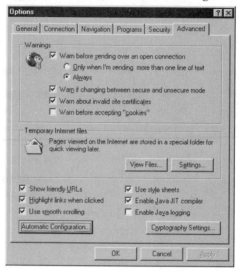

Both Internet Explorer and Netscape Navigator use virtually the same configuration settings in the Automatic Configuration dialog box. When the box initially appears, it will simply list a URL line. You may either enter the script automatically created during Proxy Server's installation, which is **http://*servername*/Array.dll?Get.Routing.Script,** or a separate custom script that you created. To test the configuration, click the Refresh button for Internet Explorer or the Reload button for Netscape Navigator.

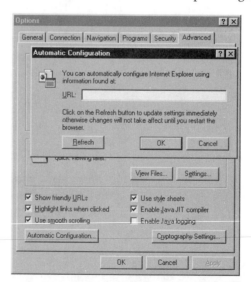

Backing Out of an Installation

Whether it's because you really screwed up or you installed Microsoft Proxy Server incorrectly on your computer, there is a procedure for removing all or selected components of Proxy Server, or for simply replacing missing or corrupted files and settings.

1. Insert the Proxy Server CD-ROM, or from a copy placed on the network, run the Setup program.

2. The Setup program will check for installed components. Once the installed files are found, an option screen will appear prompting you to select one of the following buttons depending on what you want to do:

   ■ **Add/Remove** adds or removes a specific component. Follow the instructions as they apply to your current installation.

   ■ **Reinstall** reinstalls Proxy Server. Then follow the onscreen instructions.

   ■ **Remove All** removes all of Proxy Server's components. When prompted for confirmation, select Yes.

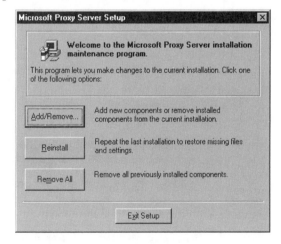

3. You will be prompted to confirm your action in the Uninstall Microsoft Proxy Server dialog box.

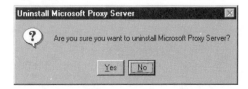

4. The Setup program will stop the Web service, then remove some entries. You will be prompted to delete the cache and related log files. If you are planning to reinstall Proxy Server, keep the cache; otherwise, remove it. Click OK to continue.

5. The Setup program will finish removing files and restart the Web service. When complete, you will see the Microsoft Proxy Server Setup dialog box. Click OK.

6. Once complete, take steps as applicable to update clients with changes. For example, if you removed Proxy Server, all clients should be set such that they no longer make calls to that server.

A faster way to perform an uninstall is to select Start ➢ Programs ➢ Uninstall in the Proxy Server folder.

In order to meet the changing demands of an administrator's position, it is necessary to know all aspects of a product, including its removal. We recommend enriching your experience with Microsoft Proxy Server by performing the actions outlined in Exercise 4.4.

EXERCISE 4.4

Removing Microsoft Proxy Server

1. Run the Setup utility.

2. Select Remove All Components from the Options dialog box.

3. Repeat the steps in Exercise 4.2.

Summary

Microsoft Proxy Server is an add-on component that integrates with Windows NT and Internet Information Server. This chapter marked the introduction to the hands-on experience of installing Proxy Server. Before the product can be installed, certain hardware and software requirements must be met. Because most systems meet the minimum hardware requirements, this is generally not a problem. It is recommended that you use a system that has at least a Pentium processor with 32 megabytes of RAM and a reasonably quick hard drive (at least 500 megabytes) with any 56k or faster connection. Microsoft Proxy Server also requires Windows NT Server 4.0 with the latest service pack. When installed, the service pack will automatically update the installed copy of IIS to meet the requirements. It is recommended that you install Windows NT with two network adapters and IIS before attempting to install Proxy Server. Once this is done, you may add the latest service pack from Microsoft's Web page and install Proxy Server.

Remember that the minimum recommendation is intended for the product to run efficiently, not just run. You can use the minimal NT requirements if you aren't concerned with efficiency.

During installation, a number of changes are made to the system. First, services in the IIS Manager are stopped for a brief period so the proxy component can be added. Because the services can be stopped, there is no need to reboot the system. A share called MSCLNT that contains the WinSock support files for Windows-based clients is created. Clients that connect to this share and execute the Setup program will become clients of the proxy server. Once a client is configured, it may fully utilize the proxy server. The Web-based clients may be configured either automatically or manually depending on the configuration of the workstation and the Web browser application.

An administrator may easily back out of an installation by running the proxy server Setup program again and selecting Remove All. Clients also have the option to uninstall the client components or temporarily disable them as needed.

Review Questions

1. Your company has given you a 386SX-25 system with 12 megabytes of RAM, a 200 megabyte hard drive, and a 14.4k modem. Your boss has read that Microsoft Proxy Server only requires what that operating system has in order to operate. He would like to spend as little as possible on a proxy server for 35 people. Explain why this server is inadequate for the company's needs, what hardware the company should have, and why.

2. You have an internal network with Web and FTP servers that do not require security or protection. Currently, all systems on the network use a proxy server. Explain how you can disable the proxy services just for local systems.

3. What is the name of the share for installing Microsoft Proxy Server?

4. What port does HTTP require on a proxy server?

5. You are going to install Proxy Server for 21 people. How much hard disk storage should your server have available for the proxy cache?

   A. 100MB

   B. 121MB

   C. 110MB

   D. 111MB

   E. 11MB

6. What is the name of the Setup program used to install Microsoft Proxy Server?

   A. SETUP

   B. INSTALL

   c. INSTPRXY

   D. CONFIG

   E. ADDSERV

7. What are the names of the two LAT files?

   A. MSPLAT.TXT

   B. LOCALLAT.TXT

   c. HOSTS.

   D. LMHOSTS.

   E. SERVICES.

8. What does LAT stand for?

   A. Local Area Table

   B. Local Address Table

   c. Lite Address Traffic

   D. Long Attribute Type

   E. Logical Address Table

9. What program is used to remove Microsoft Proxy Server?

   A. SETUP.EXE

   B. REMOVE.EXE

   c. CLEARPXY.EXE

   D. INSTALL.EXE

   E. DELPROXY.COM

10. You install Proxy Server on your local network, which has the following configuration:

Internal adapter	192.168.101.165	255.255.255.0
External adapter	172.16.10.2	255.255.255.0
Router	172.16.10.1	255.255.255.0

How should you configure the default gateway on the Proxy Server?

A. Internal: 172.16.10.1   External: 172.16.10.1

B. Internal: None   External: 172.16.10.1

C. Internal: 172.16.10.2   External: 172.16.10.1

D. Internal: None   External: 192.168.101.165

E. Internal: Blank   External: Blank

11. You need your Proxy Server to access the Internet through RAS, and all users on your local network use the Proxy Server to reach the Internet. Your network configuration is as follows:

Internal adapter:	192.168.101.165 to 255.255.255.0
RAS adapter	172.16.10.3 to 255.255.255.0

What range of IP addresses should you include in your LAT?

A. 172.16.10.0 to 172.16.10 255

B. 172.16.10.3 to 172.16.10.3

C. 192.168.101.0 to 192.168.101.255

D. 192.168.101.0 to 192.168.101.255 and 172.16.10.3 to 172.16.10.3

12. You have an NT Server with two NIC cards that you want to install Proxy Server on. The internal network adapter has the IP address of 10.1.1.100 255.255.255.224 and the external adapter has an address of 192.168.10.10 255.255.255.0. Which two addresses must you add to the LAT?

A. 10.1.1.121

B. 10.1.1.100

C. 192.168.10.255

D. 192.168.10.10

13. What services can you use on your network if you have MAC, UNIX, and Windows computers?

A. Only the Web Proxy

B. Only the WinSock Proxy

C. Only Socks Proxy

D. Both Web Proxy and Socks Proxy , but not WinSock Proxy

E. Web Proxy, Socks Proxy, and WinSock Proxy

F. None of the above

14. You proxy server is configured as follows:

Internal adapter   172.16.10.169 255.255.255.192

External adapter   172.16.10.2 255.255.255.0

What IP address range should you include in the LAT?

A. 172.16.10.2

B. 172.16.10.2 to 172.16.100.255

C. 192.168.10.1 to 192.168.10.255

D. 192.168.10.128 to 192.168.10.191

15. Your Proxy Server is configured as follows:

Internal adapter	192.168.10.6 255.255.255.0
Internal adapter	192.168.20.3 255.255.255.0
External adapter	172.16.10.3 255.255.255.0

What IP address ranges should you include in the LAT?

A. 192.168.10.0 to 192.168.10. 255 and 192.168.20.0 to 192.168.20.255

B. 192.168.1.0 to 192.168.255.0 and 192.168.20.3 to 192.168.20 3

C. 172.16.10.0 to 172.16.10.255

D. 172.16.10.3 to 172.16.10.3

16. Your network has a Proxy Server, but uses an Internet DNS server for name resolution. The DNS server has an IP address of 192.168.10.20. What must you do for clients to be able to use a Web Proxy service to access the Internet?

A. Specify the address of the DNS server on the Proxy Server.

B. Include the DNS server address in the LAT.

C. Specify the DNS server IP address in all client configurations.

D. Make the DNS server the default gateway.

17. You want to install Microsoft Proxy Server on a system with two hard drives. Drive C is a FAT file system and is 2.3GB in size. Drive D is an NTFS and is only 300MB. The NT OS is installed on drive C, and during the installation of Proxy Server you want to add a 150MB disk cache on drive C, but drive C is dimmed and drive D is the only one available. What do you need to do to allow the cache to reside on drive C?

A. Run CHKDSK.

B. Add another drive.

C. Convert drive C to NTFS.

D. Make the FAT partition smaller.

CHAPTER

5

Fundamentals of Microsoft
Internet Information Server

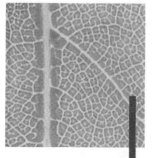

n order to install and operate Microsoft's Proxy Server, you must first have a solid understanding of Microsoft's Internet Information Server. But before you can understand something, you've got to know what it is. So here goes—exactly what *is* Internet Information Server?

Windows NT 4.0 introduced the Microsoft Internet Information Server, which is really both a network file server and an application server that allows you to publish information on the Internet or on an intranet. IIS transmits information using Hypertext Transfer Protocol (HTTP). File Transfer Protocol (FTP), which allows users to transfer files between their site and yours, can also be configured for the server. Gopher services that use menus to link to other computers and services, and to locate documents can also be configured. But recently it's been superseded by HTTP.

If you are familiar with IIS, you may not need to review this chapter.

Since IIS version 3.0 is required to run Microsoft Proxy Server, this chapter's main purpose is to show you how to install, upgrade, and maintain the Internet Information Server. In it, we'll also present IIS's internal set of tools designed and used for the configuration of Microsoft's Proxy Server. In the sections that follow, we'll explore the following topics in detail:

- Installing Internet Information Server

Exam objectives are subject to change at any time without prior notice and at Microsoft's sole discretion. Please visit Microsoft's Training & Certification website (www.microsoft.com/Train_Cert) for the most current exam objectives listing.

- Configuring Internet Information Server

- Internet services

- Upgrading Internet Information Server

Installing IIS

Okay—so how do you get things up and running? Well first, know that Proxy Server won't even begin to install unless IIS is already in place. Plus, Proxy Server 2.0 requires, at minimum, IIS version 3.0 in order to be installed, but you should always install the latest service packs anyway. They're available through the Internet at www.microsoft.com.

We've included some exercises to give you experience installing the Internet Information Server and configuring the protocols. From the Control Panel select Network and then the Services tab to install the following items:

- **Internet Service Manager**: Installs the administration program for managing services

- **World Wide Web Service**: Creates a Web publishing server

- **Gopher Service**: Creates a Gopher publishing server

- **FTP Service**: Creates a File Transfer Protocol (FTP) publishing server

- **ODBC Drivers and Administration**: Installs Open Database Connectivity (ODBC) drivers

Before installing the Microsoft Internet Information Server, you need to close all open applications—even the Control Panel window—or you're likely to get an open file error message. Also, if you intend to install the Gopher service, it's a good idea to declare an Internet domain name in the TCP/IP configuration (under the DNS tab). If you don't define an Internet domain name, you'll be notified to set one during the installation to ensure that Gopher operates properly.

Exercise 5.1 will take you though the steps for installing Microsoft's Internet Information Server 2.0, which is included on the Windows NT 4.0 CD. We will upgrade to version 3, since it is required to run Microsoft Proxy Server 2.0, and then install IIS version 4.

EXERCISE 5.1

Installing Microsoft's Internet Information Server

1. Click your right mouse button on Network Neighborhood, and then choose Properties.

2. Click the Services tab.

---

3. Select Add. You will be presented with a list of services.

4. Select Internet Information Server v2.0. (When installing Microsoft NT Version 4.0 Server, the Install Internet Information Server icon appears by default on the desktop. You can double-click the icon as shown below.)

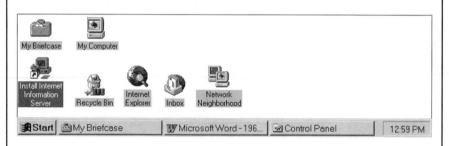

5. Type in the path to the Distribution files. A Welcome screen will appear notifying you to close all background applications. Close all other programs and then click OK.

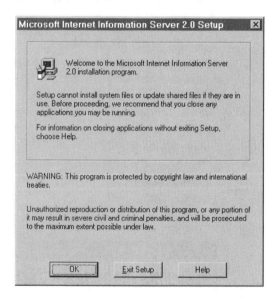

6. You'll be given a menu listing all the service components. Click the adjacent box to select each desired component. Note that there's one extra item—Help and Sample Files. Select this option if you want to install online Help and sample HyperText Markup Language (HTML) files. Then click OK to continue.

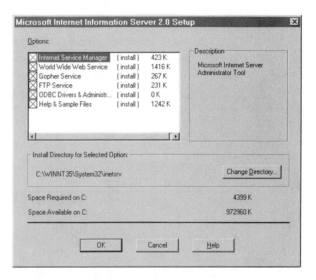

7. A list of directories is presented for the locations of World Wide Web, FTP, and Gopher publishing.

EXERCISE 5.1 (CONTINUED FROM PREVIOUS PAGE)

8. This is the path of the home (root) directory for each service you're installing. It's your option to accept the default directory and place all files to be published in that directory. By default, and unless configured otherwise, the files in that directory, plus all subdirectories, will be available to clients. If you have existing files to be published, as in HTML files, type the fully qualified path to them or relocate the files to the new home directory, making adjustments where necessary in the documents to reflect the directory change. Note that the Setup program doesn't allow network shares to be specified as root publishing directories. If your files are stored on a network share, you'll need to use Internet Service Manager to configure your publishing directories after Setup is completed.

9. Click OK to continue.

10. You'll then be asked if it's OK to create directories. Choose Yes.

11. If you're installing the Gopher service and haven't declared an Internet Domain Name, you will receive a warning at this point. Click OK.

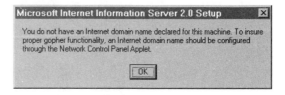

12. Also, if you're configuring your system with FTP, you may receive the following warning regarding the anonymous user account: "Your computer's guest account is enabled for network access." This means that any user can access the FTP service, regardless of whether they've been granted access to do so. Do you want to disable the guest access to the FTP service on this computer? This question is an individual judgment call. Do you want anonymous access? This is also your decision.

The final phase in configuring the installation involves the *ODBC (Open Database Connectivity)* drivers. ODBC allows the Internet utilities to interface with a database—usually via *SQL Server.*

In the Install Drivers dialog box, you'll be prompted to select SQL Server. Then select OK to complete the installation.

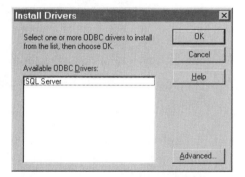

You'll need to provide access to set up the ODBC drivers and data sources by using the ODBC *applet* icon in the Windows NT Control Panel. If you have an application running that uses ODBC, you may see an error message telling you that one or more components are in use. If so, close all applications and services—in this case the ones that use ODBC. You have the option of entering the Advanced section of the SQL dialog box to gain access to how the selected drivers are installed, managed, and translated.

In the Advanced Installation Options dialog box, you'll choose whether you want to perform a version check, install the driver manager, or look manually at each module's version by clicking on the Versions button. This will reveal the currently installed version of the Microsoft Code Page Translator, the ODBC Driver Manager, and SQL Server. Click OK to complete the installation.

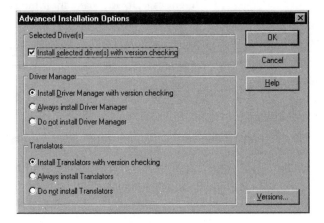

But maybe you don't need a certain service, and you're running low on disk space. If you want to remove a Microsoft Internet Information Server component after installation is complete, you'll need to use the procedure in Exercise 5.2.

EXERCISE 5.2

Removing the Microsoft Internet Information Server Component

1. Choose Start ➤ Programs, then choose Microsoft Internet Server (Common).

2. Run the Internet Information Server Setup.

3. A Welcome screen will appear notifying you to close all background applications. Close all other programs and then click OK.

4. A menu will appear, asking you if you would like to Add/Remove Components, Repeat Last Install, or Remove All. If you add components, the instructions are the same as in the last exercise. If you select to remove all components or repeat the last installation, you will be prompted for confirmation before continuing.

Configuring IIS with the Internet Service Manager

All of the services that you've installed for the Microsoft Internet Information Server can be managed by the Internet Services Manager, located in the Microsoft Internet Server (Common). This program is designed to assist you in the configuration and enhancement of your internetwork services. By using a single program to manage Internet services, you're able to manage all Internet services running on any Windows NT system in your network in a streamlined manner.

Control View Formats

Internet Service Manager enables administrators to manage any Internet Information Server sites from a single location anywhere on the Internet. Depending on the number of systems running internetwork services, you can choose from three different view formats found in Microsoft Internet Service Manager's View menu: Report View, Servers View, and Services View.

Report View

This selection provides an alphabetical listing of all selected computers. A host's name may appear more than once since each installed service is shown on a separate line. While in the Report View, you may sort by any column simply by clicking the header. This view tends to be most useful when you're managing one or two systems running Internet Server. The default view is shown in Figure 5.1.

FIGURE 5.1

IIS Manager's Report View

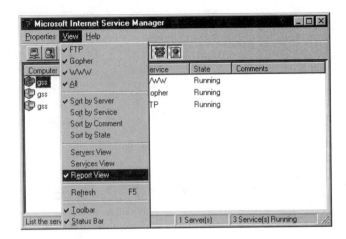

Servers View

This view, shown in Figure 5.2, is ideal for larger installations of Internet Information Server. It's the computer name of all systems running any of the Peer Web services. Click the plus symbol next to a server name to display which services that server is running. You can also double-click the server name. Double-click a service name to see its property sheets. This display is an easy-to-view tree which displays the services as traffic lights—Red (stopped), Yellow (paused), and Green (running).

FIGURE 5.2

IIS Manager's
Servers View

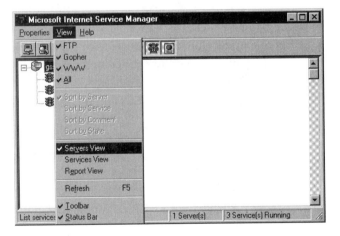

Services View

This is the most efficient way to determine where a particular service is running. All systems running a service such as FTP will be listed under that grouping. Click the plus symbol next to a service name to see which servers are running that service, or double-click the service (shown in Figure 5.3). Double-click the computer name under a service to see the property sheets for the service running on that computer.

FIGURE 5.3

IIS Manager's Services View

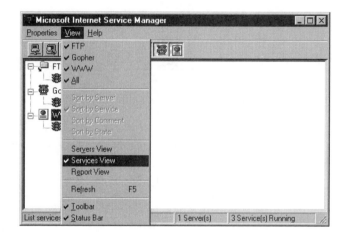

Control View Functions

No matter which view you choose, you'll be able to perform similar functions. The main reason behind changing views is to refine and assist the management process. You'll notice that the all functions are included in the button bar, and that they're identical to those in the pull-down menus. The three functions performed in the Manager are Connecting to a Server, Services Control, and Service Configuration.

Connect to Server

The Connect to Server function, as shown in Figure 5.4, can be selected through either the Connect button, or the pull-down menu under Properties. This function is used to enable you to attach to the server you wish to manage. Use the Find All Servers button or pull-down option to locate systems dynamically.

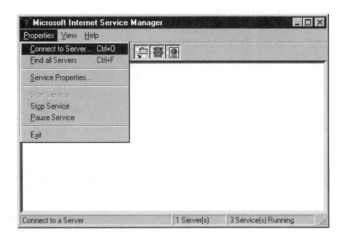

Services Control

The Services Control function, shown in Figure 5.5, provides the ability to stop, start, or pause a service. Ordinarily, this type of function is done through the Server Manager or Control Panel. However, for many users, this activity is difficult and cumbersome. Because of this, improvements were in order, and you can now simply use either the button bar or the pull-down menu.

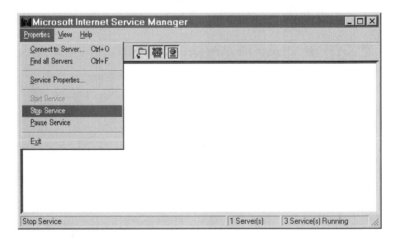

Service Configuration

The Service Configuration function (see Figure 5.6) is only accessible by double-clicking the leaf item in the displayed tree. There is no button bar or pull-down menu for this one. When you double-click the desired item, you'll access a setup page. The page is very similar to other service pages. They only vary slightly from service to service.

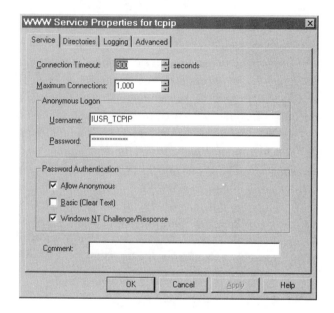

FIGURE 5.6

IIS Manager Service Configuration

Internet Services

Unlike Windows NT 3.5*x*, the services are configured with a new anonymous account created by Setup, rather than by defaulting to the guest account. The new account name is called IUSR_*systemname*. It uses a randomly-generated password and the privilege to log on locally. When Peer Web services are installed on domain controllers, this account is added to the domain database automatically. After setup has completed installation, you can change the username and password for the account from the Service Property sheet inside the Internet Service Manager. The new username and password must match the same username and password in the Windows NT User Manager. The Web, FTP, and Gopher services use the IUSR_*systemname* user account by default when anonymous access is allowed (not Guest). Rights for this account can be configured like all others through User Manager. File permissions can be set on NTFS drives for IUSR_ *systemname* with Windows NT Explorer. The configuration for each service is discussed in the following sections.

FTP Service

As we mentioned earlier, FTP is the protocol used to transfer files between two computers on a network that uses TCP/IP. To use FTP to transfer files between two computers, both computers must support their respective FTP roles. One needs to be a client and the other a server. The FTP client issues command to the server, such as commands to download files, upload files, create directories on the server, and change directories on the server.

Under Microsoft Windows NT 4.0, FTP management is performed through the Internet Service Manager. As With Windows NT 3.5*x*, you can use any FTP client, including most Web browsers, to connect to the FTP server. To see the configuration of a host system with the FTP service, double-click the server from the Service View (see Figure 5.7). You'll then be presented with the property sheets, including Service, Messaging, Directories, Logging, and Advanced.

Service Property Sheet

Typically, this first property sheet in the FTP property screen should not be changed. It allows you to set connection time-out values (measured in seconds) for hosts to initially connect to the FTP service. If you have extremely slow lines and your users have a hard time connecting, you can make this time-out longer. This property sheet also lets you set the maximum FTP connections to your server—the default setting is 1000. The Service screen also lets you set an anonymous connection name, which is set to IUSR_*systemname* by default.

Messaging Property Sheet

Shown in Figure 5.8, the FTP Messages property sheet provides a Welcome message (logging on), an Exit message (logging off), and a Maximum connections message (limit of users logged on).

FIGURE 5.7

FTP Manager Service

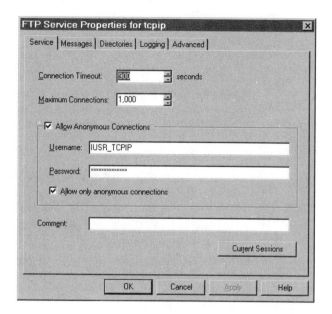

FIGURE 5.8

FTP Manager Messages

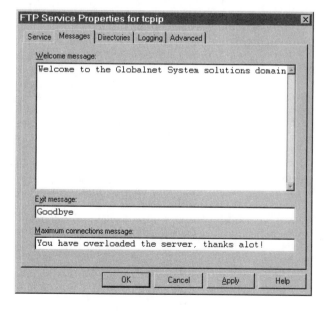

Directories Property Sheet

This sheet offers the configuration of directories, whether they be UNIX or DOS—a feature not fully offered by Windows 3.5x. By default, all files and subdirectories will be available, if placed in the home directory. The home directory is the location where you should place all FTP materials. Although there can be only one home directory, you can choose to add and create virtual directories, as shown in Figure 5.9.

FIGURE 5.9

FTP Manager Directories screen

Virtual directories aren't visible to users, and can only be seen if the client machine knows the alias of the virtual directory. These directories are commonly used to distribute files that aren't open to the public, but still use anonymous names and passwords. With both home and virtual directories, you can designate the data storage area on another system. The input fields for a username and password in the Add or Edit dialog box are no longer grayed out if the directory is on an alternate system. Keep in mind that when you use the network, you must provide a valid ID and password for the server that you're attaching the FTP service to. Errors will be displayed and reported on each entry line on the directory sheet. The point at which you add directories (home or virtual) is also the point at which you'll designate read and write access. As with 3.5x, security will be limited according to the anonymous account's file permissions. Finally, due to limitations that some browsers impose—that the FTP listing be styled in UNIX format—you may choose your directory listing system as UNIX or MS-DOS. This is a global setting for all directories.

Special Directories   These directories can be used within the home directories to control the root directory displayed to FTP users. These directories must be physical subdirectories—they can't be specified by using virtual directories.

Username Directories   These are directories within the home directory with names that match a particular username. If a user logs on with a username that has a matching directory in the home directory, that directory is used as the root. FTP username directories aren't created by default during setup.

Anonymous Directory   This is also a directory within the home directory. If a user logs on using the password **Anonymous**, the directory name Anonymous is used as the root.

Annotated Directories   Each directory can contain a file that can be used to summarize the information that the directory contains and automatically provide access to remote browsers. This is done by creating a file called ~FTPSVC~.CKM in the FTP directory. Most of the time, you'll want to make this a hidden file so that directory listings don't display it. From an FTP client, you would type **Site ckm** at the command prompt, or use the Registry Editor to enable annotated directories by adding the following value:

```
HKEY_LOCAL_MACHINE\SYSTEM\CurrentControlSet\Services
\MSFTPSVC\Parameters

AnnotateDirectories REG_DWORDRange: 0 or 1Default = 0 (directory
annotation is off).
```

This Registry entry doesn't appear by default in the Registry, so you must add an entry if you want to change its default value. If Directory Annotation is enabled on your FTP service, Web browsers may display error messages when browsing your FTP directories. You can eliminate such errors by limiting each annotation file to one line, or by disabling Directory Annotation.

Logging Property Sheet

This sheet, shown in Figure 5.10, allows you to enable FTP service logging, which allows you to keep track of all FTP activity to your NT FTP server.

F I G U R E 5.10

FTP Manager Logging

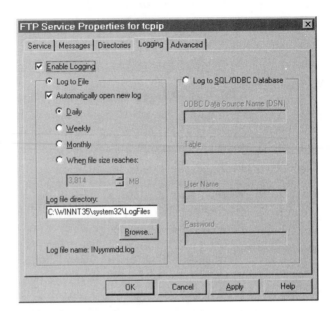

It can be enabled by checking the Enable Logging box. You may either send the logs to file or to an SQL/ODBC database. If you elect to send it to file, you may specify the location where you'd like the log files placed. Also, you have the option to open a new log daily (Inyymmdd.log), weekly (Inyymmww.log), monthly (Inyymm.log), or when the file reaches a designated size (INETSRVn.log). The filenames for the log vary according to the trigger you use, as shown in each set of parentheses ending with a .LOG extension. If you decide to send the information to an SQL/ODBC database, you must provide an ODBC data source name, the Table, and a username and password along with it.

Advanced Property Sheet

As shown in Figure 5.11, this sheet limits access to the FTP server in two ways: source systems and network utilization.

FIGURE 5.11

FTP Manager Advanced
Properties sheet

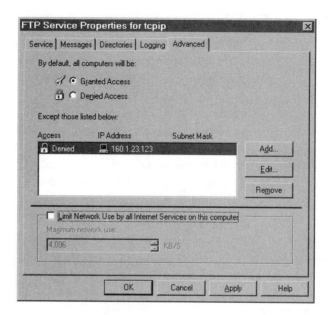

FIGURE 5.11

FTP Manager Advanced
Properties sheet

The functions presented here were offered in a limited manner, at best, in Windows NT 3.5x.

By default, all systems are granted access. If you want to limit access, you have three options. First, you can grant access to all computers with the exclusion of those you add as single computers, or a certain group of computers. Second, you can deny access to all computers, with the exception of those you add as single computers or a group of computers. When adding a single computer, use the button with the three dots to look up a host name from DNS (if registered) to get that system's IP address. When adding a group of computers, this option (host name lookup) isn't available. However, you now have the option to specify a subnet mask. The last way the Advanced sheet allows you to limit access to the FTP server is by setting a maximum network utilization in terms of kilobytes per second. This is done by clicking the box next to the Limit Network Use by All Internet Services on this computer dialog box. As you have probably figured out, this option affects all Internet services: Web, FTP, and Gopher.

Gopher Service

We talked about Gopher in Chapter 2, and although it's not shiny and new to TCP/IP, support for it is a new feature to Windows NT 4.0. To refresh your memory, a Gopher service is a function you can use to create links to other computers or services, annotate your files and directories, and create custom menus. The implementation that is included with Windows NT is full-featured, including something called Gopher Plus Selector Strings. This allows the server to return additional information to the client, like administrator name, modification date, and MIME type. From the Internet Service Manager, all configuration functions are the same as those for FTP, with the exception that there isn't an option to specify messages, or an option to specify read/write access from the Directories sheet (see Figure 5.12).

FIGURE 5.12

Gopher Manager
Service tab

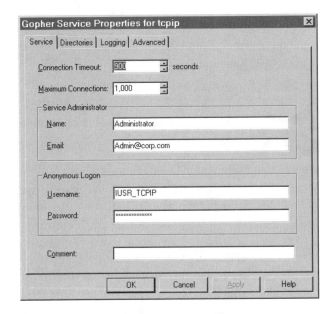

- All Gopher files should be placed in the Gopher home directory (\INETSRV\ GOPHROOT) by default. This makes browsing the Gopher directories a breeze for clients. Tag files can be created to enable links to other computers or services, to annotate your files and directories, and to create custom menus.

To enable Wide Area Information Search (WAIS) index searching, you must change the following entry in the Windows NT Registry from 0 (disabled) to 1(enabled): HKEY_LOCAL_MACHINE\SYSTEM\CurrentControlSet\Services\ GopherSVC\CheckForWAISDB

Gopher Tag Files

Tag files allow you to jazz up the standard Gopher display sent to clients with additional material, and also allows you to provide links to other systems. Tag files are responsible for all the information about a file that's sent to a client. This information must include the name of the file to be displayed for the client. Typically, tag files contain a display name, host name, and port number. If you're utilizing Gopher Plus, you can add more information to each tag file, such as the server administrator's name and e-mail address, the file's creation date, and the last modification date. In order to use these features, you must first create the file, and then store it on the Gopher server. The tags for your Gopher site can be created with the gdsset utility. For syntax information on this utility, type **gdsset** by itself on a command line. You'll then be presented with the following information:

```
Usage: gdsset [-crl] [-g<GopherItemType>] [-f <FriendlyName>][-s
<Selector>] [-h<HostName>] [-p<PortNumber>]-D<Directory> -d
<filename> [-a <AdminName>] [-e <AdminEmail>]-c change (edit/
create) the existing tag information(Default is to create a new
tag information)-r read and dump the tag information on consoled
specifies that given file is actually a directory-g specifies
Gopher object type.
```

Gopher Object Type

The Gopher Object Type is a single character—usually a digit from 0 to 9. The default type is 9 for binary. See the following Gopher type codes for complete details (valid when -r not used):

-f *<FriendlyName>*	specifies Friendly Name for object (valid when -r not used)
-l	specifies that link information is to be set for write (valid when -r not used)

-s *<Selector>*	specifies the selector for link (valid when -l is used)
-h *<HostName>*	specifies the Host for link (valid when -l is used)
-p *<PortNumber>*	specifies the Port number for link (valid when -l is used)
-a *<AdminName>*	specifies the Administrator Name, defaults to the service administrator's name in the Service dialog box of the Microsoft Internet Service Manager
-e *<AdminEmail>*	specifies the Administrator Email, defaults to the service administrator's e-mail name in the Service dialog box of the Microsoft Internet Service Manager

Note that this command line automatically sets the hidden file attribute on the tag files you create. Typical use of the command is as follows:

```
gdsset -c -g# -f description of file -a administrator's name -e
e-mail
```

The remainder of the command options are typically for supporting advanced features, such as providing links to other hosts. Also, this command can be used in *batch mode*, or *nested batch mode* with the for command. Refer to online help for more details on performing this action. After the information has been set for a file, you can quickly determine its accuracy by using the gdsset -r filename command.

Gopher Type Codes

The following is a list of all the possible type codes for Gopher. Again, if not specified, the default is 9 for binary. These codes are used following -g in the gdsset command.

0	A file, usually a flat text file
1	A Gopher directory
2	A CSO phone book server
3	An error
4	A Macintosh file in Binhex format
5	An MS-DOS binary archive

6	A UNIX UUencoded file
7	An index-search server
8	A Telnet session
9	A binary file
c	A calendar or calendar of events
g	A graphic interchange file (GIF) graphic
h	An HTML World Wide Web hypertext page
I	An in-line text that is not an item
I	Another kind of image file
m	A BSD format mbox file
P	A PDF document
T	A TN3270 mainframe session
:	A bitmap image (use Gopher Plus information for type of image)

Tag files are hidden files. Use the `attrib` command, Explorer, or File Manager to set the hidden attribute for tag files. On drives formatted with a FAT file system, the tag filename uses the same name as the file it describes, with .GTG as the file extension appended to the 8.3 naming convention. The name then becomes 8.3.3. For example, if the content filename is SAMPLE.TXT, the tag filename would be SAMPLE.TXT.GTG. The tag files on FAT can be edited with most ASCII text editors. On drives formatted using NTFS, :GTG is appended to the filename instead of .GTG. In this case, if the content filename is SAMPLETXT, then the tag filename would be SAMPLE.TXT:GTG.

Unlike FAT files, NTFS tag files can't be edited by most text editors because they're stored in an alternate data stream. If a tag file is stored on an NTFS volume, you must first manually move the tag file before you move the corresponding data files. When you move the tag file you'll have to modify the hidden attribute both before and after the move. Again, hiding and unhiding files is done through the `attrib` command, File Manager, and Explorer.

World Wide Web Service

Windows NT 4.0 adds Web services to its suite of TCP/IP applications. Now you can create and design your own intranet or Internet Web page quickly and easily. Traditionally, this service has been performed by UNIX-based hosts or Windows NT systems utilizing third-party vendor software. The software is generally costly, and in many cases, more than just a bit of a challenge to configure.

In 4.0, the configuration method is the same whether you'll be using your system on the Internet or on an intranet. The only major differences from one implementation to the next deal with how security is configured. With Windows NT workstation, just as sharing files doesn't make your workstation a dedicated file server, publishing Web pages doesn't make your workstation a dedicated Internet server. If you need a dedicated Internet server with advanced administration capabilities, and the ability to respond to a multitude of simultaneous connections, you should use Microsoft Internet Information Server. It's included with Windows NT Server Version 4.0.

Web pages are constructed in HTML (hypertext markup language), which includes both hypertext and hyperlinks. This is the standard document form Web browsers support. HTML enables a Web page to make connections and reference other Web pages both locally and on foreign hosts, even if they're part of an entirely different network. Although you can create these files in practically any text editor, it's generally a good idea to use a product such as Internet Assistant for Word (free from Microsoft), Netscape Navigator's Editor, or another HTML-specific editor. Doing so will ensure proper formatting and reduce debugging time, and will allow you to link to any SQL/ODBC database. This support can be added by setting up the ODBC drivers and data sources using the ODBC applet in the Windows NT Control Panel. During installation, if you have an application running that uses ODBC, you might receive an error message telling you that one or more components are in use. If this happens, before continuing, close all applications and services that use ODBC. When setting up peer Web services, you'll find that most Internet browsers, such as Internet Explorer (ships with NT 4.0), structures its addressing sequence in URL format. URL syntax is a specific sequence of protocol, domain name, and path to the requested information. Configuring the Web Service sheets can be achieved through the Internet Service Manager. Most configuration functions are the same as FTP's, with some exceptions. First, there's no option to specify messages, because it's done by the HTML Web page.

Microsoft ✓ **Exam Objective**

Official Microsoft Exam Objective: Configure server authentication. Authentication options include:

- Anonymous logon
- Basic authentication
- Microsoft Windows NT Challenge/Response authentication

Web Service Sheet

The configuration is the same as FTP's with the exception that password authentication is done at three levels (see Figure 5.13):

- Allow Anonymous

- Basic (Clear Text)

- Windows NT Challenge/Response

FIGURE 5.13

Web Manager Service tab

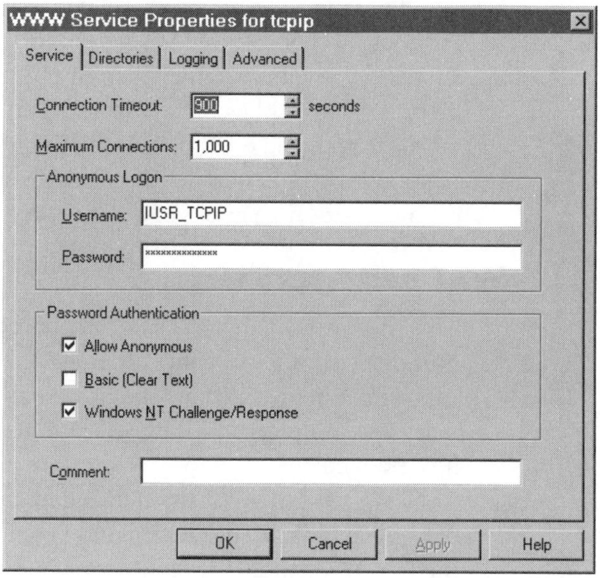

Anonymous Access

The anonymous configuration is the most common on the Internet, and is generally used to allow the public to see your Web page. When this is the only configured password authentication option, the user will be logged in as the anonymous account regardless of name or password.

But even when you use anonymous access, all activity on a system running Internet Information Server determines permissions by user name. Associating a user name with every action is fundamental to Windows NT security.

Basic or Clear Text

Basic, or clear text, is a simple level of password protection. As with FTP, passwords are sent unencrypted and therefore may be viewed with a packet analyzer. Depending on your needs, this can be a drag. By Default, the basic option isn't enabled, but basic authentication can be encoded when used in conjunction with *Secure Sockets Layer (SSL),* which ensures usernames and passwords are encrypted before transmission. All browsers support basic authentication.

Windows NT Challenge/Response

Windows NT Challenge/Response is a system by which the service will honor requests by clients to send user account information using the Windows NT Challenge/Response authentication protocol. This protocol uses a one-way algorithm—a mathematical formula that can't be reversed—to prevent passwords from being transmitted. The Windows NT Challenge/Response authentication process is started automatically when an access denied error is encountered on an anonymous client request.

Web Directories Sheet

This sheet is primarily the same in concept as FTP's configuration sheet, however there are a few distinct differences. First, notice that by default, this sheet lists both a home directory and a virtual directory named scripts. This provides a secure place to locate your scripts files, as well as creates a public Web home directory.

Next, you can select the enable default document to select a specific Web page, in HTML, to be delivered to your Web browser when it's not even specified to do so. Simply type the name of the default document in the designated dialog box. You can also enable directory browsing on the directory sheet shown in Figure 5.14. Directory browsing allows a user to be presented with a hypertext listing of directories and files so they can navigate freely through your directory structure.

FIGURE 5.14

Web Manager
Directories Properties
sheet

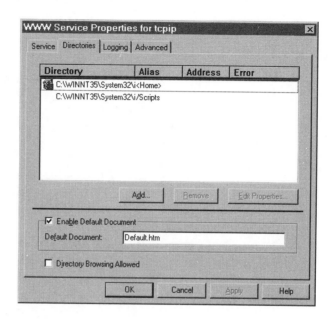

You can choose Edit Properties to add or modify directory entries. You have the same Virtual Directory options as with FTP. This allows you to add directories outside the home directory, including those that reside on other hosts. See the FTP Directory Properties sheet (shown in Figure 5.15) for complete details on doing this. Also, as with FTP, virtual directories won't appear in Web directory listings; you must create explicit links in HTML files for the user, or the user must know the URL in order to access virtual directories. You can also virtualize a server by clicking on the box next to Virtual Server. This will allow you to specify an IP address for the entry. Finally, as with FTP, the Web service uses access control. It must match any existing NTFS rights to work. These rights include Read, Execute, and Require Secure SSL Channel. Read should be selected for information directories, but it's not a good idea to use this option for directories containing programs. Execute allows clients to run any programs in a given directory. This box is selected by default for the directory created for programs. Put all your scripts and executable files into this directory. Do not select this box for directories containing static content. Select the Require secure SSL channel (Not Installed) box if using Secure Sockets Layer (SSL) security to encrypt data transmissions. This must be installed with the key manager in order to work.

FIGURE 5.15

The FTP Directory
Properties sheet

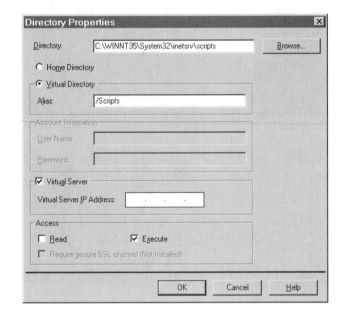

Key Manager

The Key Manager is used to create a Secure Socket Layer security encryption implementation. The Key Manager may be launched by selecting Start ➤ Programs ➤ Microsoft Internet Server (Common). Key Manager is a central tool that can be used to manage all security keys on any NT-based system with Microsoft's Peer Web Services. You can connect to a remote system by choosing the Servers pull-down menu, or by using the toolbar.

The Secure Sockets Layer protocol provides communications privacy over networks by using a combination of public key cryptography and bulk data encryption for data privacy. By using this protocol, clients and servers can communicate in a way that prevents eavesdropping, tampering, or message forgery.

Internet Explorer encrypts data such as Hypertext Markup Language (HTML) form with private information by using you server's public key. The encrypted form is sent to the server. The data is then decrypted by the server, which uses it's private key. The data can be decrypted only with the private key, held by the server.

Creating New Keys

Key Manager is used to generate the key pair and activate the generated key. A key is not active until you send the certificate request file generated by Key Manager to your certificate authority.

To create a new key, select Create New Key in the Key pull-down. Fill in the information in this dialog box, then click OK to create two files. The first file is a key file containing a key pair. The second file is a certificate request file. When your request is processed, the provider will return a certificate to you. Figure 5.16 shows the Create New Key and Certificate Request dialog box.

FIGURE 5.16

The Create New Key and Certificate Request dialog box

The information that you need to enter in the New Key dialog box is:

Key Name: A descriptive name for the key you are creating

Password: Specifies a password to encrypt the private key

Bits: Generates a key pair—by default 1024 bits long. Options are 1024, 512 or 768 bits

Organization: Your company name

Organizational Unit: The division or department within your company; for example, Sales

Common Name: The domain name of the server; for example, www.company.com

Country: Two-letter ISO Country designation; for example, US, FR, AU, UK, and so on

State/Province: The full, non-abbreviated name of your state or province

Locality: The full name of the city where your company is located

Request File: The name of the request file that'll be created or accepted by default. Accepting default automatically copies the Key Name you have designated, and attaches a .REQ extension to it to create the request filename. For example, if you have typed security in the Key Name box, the default request filename will become SECURITY.REQ.

WARNING Do not use commas in any field. Commas are interpreted as the end of that field and will generate an invalid request without even giving you so much as a warning!

When you've filled in all the information, click OK. Retype your password when prompted, and click OK again. Your key will appear in the Key Manager window under the computer name. Once completed, you'll need to contact VeriSign's Web site at www.verisign.com to get details on how to get a certificate to activate your key. The key generated by Key Manager isn't valid for use on the Internet until you obtain a valid key certificate for it from the proper key authorities. Until you do so, the key can't be used as shown in the New Key Information screen in Figure 5.17, and will lie dormant on its host computer.

Once you have your key, you should then select the Key Graphic, and use the Key pull-down menu to select Install Certificate. This will validate the key and give you a date range during which the key is usable. A summary for the key appears in the lower-right corner of the screen, and reflects the information that you gave when you created the key. When installing the key, you'll

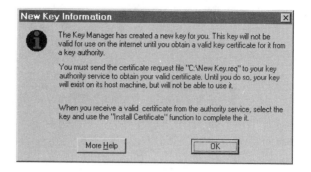

be prompted to select or type in the IP address of the server to which you want to apply the Secure Sockets Layer key. Your choices are None, Default, or you can specify or select an address.

Applying Your Certificate to Your Server

After you complete your certificate request, you will receive a signed certificate from the certification authority. Consult your certification authority for complete details. It will look something like this:

```
-----BEGIN CERTIFICATE-----

JIEBSDSCEXoCHQEwLQMJSoZILvoNVQECSQAwcSETMRkOAMUTBhMuVrM

mIoAnBdNVBAoTF1JTQSBEYXRhIFN1Y3VyaXR5LCBJbmMuMRwwGgYDVQ

QLExNQZXJzb25hIEN1cnRpZm1jYXR1MSQwIgYDVQQDExtPcGVuIE1hc

mt1dCBUZXN0IFN1cnZ1ciAxMTAwHhcNOTUwNzE5MjAyNzMwWhcNOTYw

NTEOMjAyOTEwWjBzMQswCQYDVQQGEwJVUzEgMB4GA1UEChMXU1NBBIER

hdGEgU2VjdXJpdHksIE1uYy4xHDAaBgNVBAsTE1B1cnNvbmEgQ2VydG

1maWNhdGUxJDAiBgNVBAMTGO9wZW4gTWFya2V0IFR1c3QgU2VydmVyI

DExMDBcMA0GCSqGSIb3DQEBAQUAA0sAMEgCQQDU/71rgR6vkVNX40BA

q1poGdSmGkD1iN3sEPfSTGxNJXY58XH3JoZ4nrF7mIfvpghNi1taYim

vhbBPNqYe4yLPAgMBAAEwDQYJKoZIhvcNAQECBQADQQBqyCpws9EaAj

KKAefuNP+z+8NY8khckgyHN2LLpfhv+iP8m+bF66HNDU1Fz8ZrVOu3W

QapgLPV90kIskNKXX3a

------END CERTIFICATE-----
```

Beautiful, isn't it? Copy and save the text to a file, using a tool such as Notepad, and give it a name you can remember—something like CERTIF.TXT. Then use Key Manager to install your signed certificate on the server. Exercise 5.3 will lead you through the steps.

EXERCISE 5.3

Installing a Certificate

1. Select Programs ➢ Microsoft Internet Server (Common) ➢ Key Manager.

2. Choose Key ➢ Create New Key.

3. Fill in your information in the dialog box, then choose OK.

If you don't specify an IP address while installing your certificate, the same certificate will be applied to all virtual servers created on the system. If you're hosting multiple sites on a single server, you can specify that the certificate only be used for a given IP address by adding the specific IP address, for example: 160.191.82.54.

Your final step to completing the setup is to commit to the changes. You can do this by either exiting the program, or using the pull-down menu. Then choose Yes in the Key Manager dialog box shown in Figure 5.18.

FIGURE 5.18

Select Yes in the Key Manager dialog box to commit to the changes.

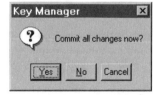

IIS Versions 3 and 4

To install Microsoft Proxy Server 2.0, you need to have IIS version 3.0 or greater installed. The configuration of IIS version 2.0 and 3.0 are the same, so below we just show how to upgrade to 3.0. The test does not cover IIS installation or the differences between versions.

We will also install IIS version 4 beta from the Internet.

Upgrading to IIS Version 3.0

We installed and configured the IIS version 2 server, so now let's upgrade to version 3. You can do this in two ways. If you have the Microsoft service pack 2 CD, IIS version 3 can be installed from this. Also, you can pull down the files for free from the Microsoft Web site. To install from the CD:

1. Insert the service pack 2 CD into your server.

2. Open the CD and it will automatically open Microsoft Internet Explorer.

3. Arrow down about a half page and it will say Internet Information Server 3.0 on the left side.

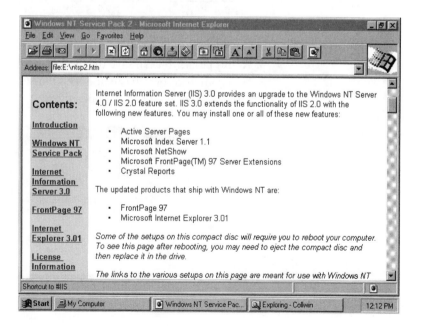

4. Click Internet Information Server 3.0. This is actually a shortcut to the IIS files.

5. Arrow down almost all the way to the bottom of the page, and click Install IE 3.01.

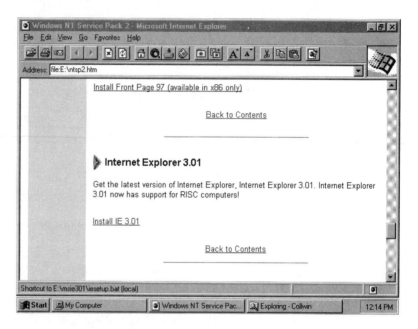

6. At this point, you can save the file to your desktop, or anywhere else on your computer, or you can just open the file, and it will start upgrading your installation of IIS. Let's just open the file.

7. Click Yes to start the IIS 3 installation. It will extract the files needed for the installation.

8. Click I Agree on the license agreement form. It will continue to copy files and then ask you to restart your computer.

9. Choose Yes.

Installing IIS Version 4

If you're going to install IIS version 4, you need to delete any previous version of IIS on your machine first. So, basically, it's not an upgrade, but a fresh installation. Let's take a look at how we can install version 4. But first, make sure you have service pack 3 installed, and then download the appropriate IIS version 4 files from the Microsoft Web site.

Go to the Microsoft Web site and either order the CD for IIS version 4, or download the installation files. On a 28.8 modem this will take around 4 hours! The download options are shown in Figure 5.19. If you're on your NT Server, you can download and install at the same time. In this example, we will choose Download Only, then click next.

FIGURE 5.19

The Download Options page for IIS 4.0

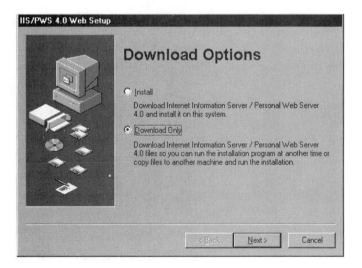

I. Choose your Language and CPU/Operating Type, then click Next.

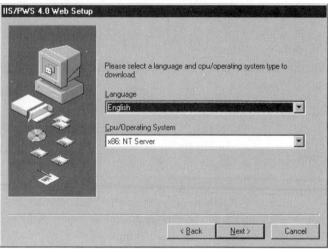

2. Select the installation option you prefer, then click Next. Remember, if you choose Minimum, you can't choose Typical Installation later.

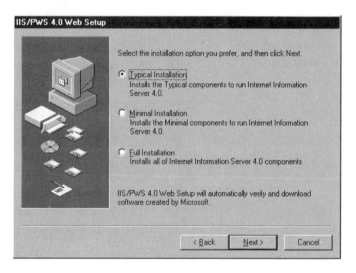

3. If you have a 28.8 modem, you should choose Minimum at this point; but if you want the full installation, start the download at night, and it should be done by the time you get to work in the morning!

4. Choose a path in the Save in Folder text box, then click Next.

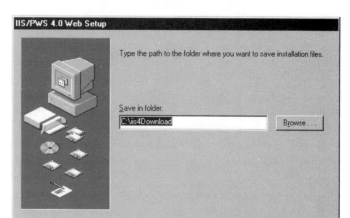

5. The installation will now go to the Microsoft Web site and download the necessary files.

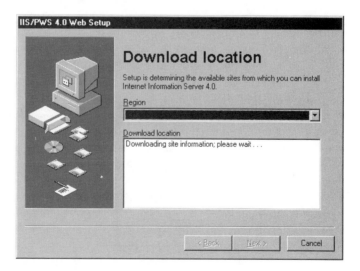

6. Choose a site to download the files.

7. When complete, go to the download directory, (by default it is C:\IIS4DOWNLOAD) and click Setup. First, make sure you have service pack 3 installed. You should see a setup welcome screen.

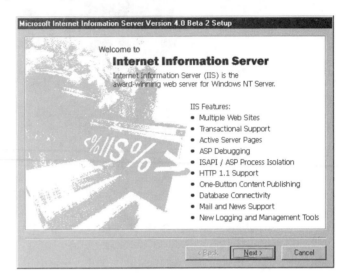

8. Click Next.

9. Click Accept on the Microsoft License agreement, then click Next.

10. Choose the Installation option you would like: Minimum, Typical, or Custom.

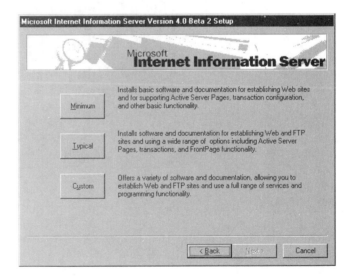

11. We're going to choose Minimum because those are the files we pulled from the Microsoft site.

12. Click Next to accept the default directories for Web, FTP, and application files.

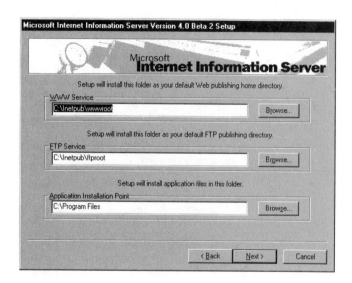

13. Setup will then copy the files. This takes several minutes.

14. When finished, you get a nice "Thank You from Microsoft" note. Click Finish.

15. Restart your computer for the new setting to take effect.

Summary

In this chapter, we introduced the Microsoft Internet Information Server as both a network file and an application server. Internet Information Server (IIS) allows you to publish information on the Internet or on an intranet. We learned that the IIS transmits information using Hypertext Transfer Protocol (HTTP). We also saw how File Transfer Protocol (FTP) and Gopher services can also be configured for the server. In this chapter, we explained the design principles and architecture behind the Internet Information Server.

Review Questions

1. Under Microsoft Windows NT 4.0, FTP management is performed through what?

   A. DOS prompt

   B. Internet Service Manager

   C. Key Manager

   D. Web Manager

2. The FTP Manager Advanced tab limits access to the FTP server in which two ways?

   A. Login

   B. Source systems

   C. Network utilization

   D. Password

3. The FTP Manager Messages tab offers which options?

   A. Welcome message (logging on)

   B. Exit message (logging off)

   C. Error message

   D. Maximum connections message (limit of users logged on)

4. Under the FTP Manager Services tab, the maximum connections defaults to?

   A. 500

   B. 20

   C. 200

   D. 1000

5. Under the FTP Manager Services tab, the default connection timeout is?

  A. 10 minutes

  B. 5 minutes

  C. 15 minutes

  D. 25 minutes

6. Web pages are constructed in?

  A. HTML

  B. Web

  C. URL

  D. HTTP

7. The World Wide Web (WWW) is?

  A. A graphical, easy-to-navigate interface for looking at documents on the Internet

  B. Shareware

  C. Freeware

  D. HTTP documents

8. Hyperlinks are?

  A. Shortcuts on Web documents to aid in connecting to other pages, downloading files, etc.

  B. Directories in the Web server

  C. Fast Internet connections

  D. FTP servers

9. A Uniform Resource Locator (URL) is?

   A. The standard naming convention on the Internet

   B. An HTTP document

   C. A Web server

   D. Shortcuts on Web documents to aid in connecting to other pages

10. Web password authentication is done at what three levels?

   A. Allow Anonymous

   B. Basic (Clear Text)

   C. Windows NT Challenge/Response

   D. Disable Anonymous

CHAPTER

6

Internet Service
Manager and Proxy Server

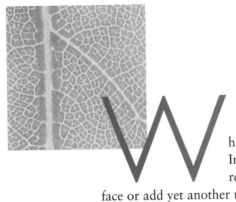

hat is the ideal solution to a not-so-ideal problem? Internet access management is such a problem. It may require that you, the administrator, learn a new interface or add yet another utility to every desktop in the system's management organization. In this chapter, we will discuss the ideal solution to Internet access management by presenting an overview of the controls provided by Microsoft's Internet Service Manager as they apply to Proxy Server.

The material we cover in this chapter is quite straightforward. You should have no problem with the concepts and descriptions presented here, whether you are a beginner or an expert. By the end of this chapter, you will be armed with all you need to know about:

- Internet Service Manager administration

Exam objectives are subject to change at any time without prior notice and at Microsoft's sole discretion. Please visit Microsoft's Training & Certification website (www.microsoft.com/Train_Cert) for the most current exam objectives listing.

- Configuring the Web Proxy service with IIS
- Configuring the WinSock Proxy service with IIS
- Configuring the Socks Proxy service with IIS

The focus of this chapter is on where the various controls are located and how to use them. The functions you'll configure here are in many cases quite complex, and you'll find more detailed information about them in other chapters, as noted throughout.

Internet Service Manager Administration

The previous chapter gave a full overview of the Internet Service Manager provided with Internet Information Server. At this point, you should be familiar with the following:

- The services controlled from the interface

- How the service works as a management tool on different systems

- The general abilities of the IIS interface

To manage Microsoft's Proxy Server with IIS, simply click Internet Service Manager from the Microsoft Internet Server folder, located in Programs on the Start menu. Once the management screen appears (see Figure 6.1), you may select any of the services listed to begin configuring it.

F I G U R E 6.1

Microsoft Internet
Service Manager

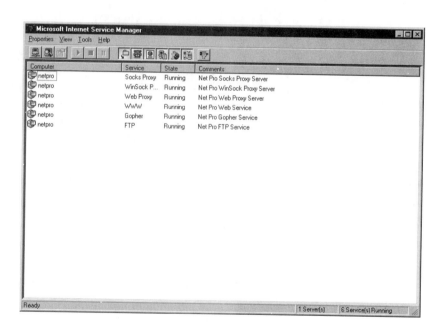

If you are using a version of IIS older than version 2.0, it is highly recommended that you upgrade to the most current version. On its Web site, Microsoft provides Windows NT service packs that contain upgrades and new pieces of software designed to fix various problems that may occur within a particular NT version. Service pack 3, for instance, includes IIS 3.0. You should also check for more recent "hot-fixes" on the Web site.

Microsoft Proxy Server 2.0 will integrate with all versions of IIS starting with 3.0 and greater. As of this writing, Microsoft Proxy Server requires that you install to a server and not the personal Web services that you would find on a workstation. Through IIS version 4.0, no major problems with the integration of Proxy Server have been noted.

Microsoft ✓ ***Exam Objective***

Given a scenario, decide which user interface to use to perform administrative tasks.

As you work through this chapter, you should note the functions and uses of each service and their respective tabs. As we progress, you will see that there are certain situations to which each service tab applies. For instance, suppose that you wanted to publish Web pages. You would use the Publishing tab on the Web Proxy service described in this chapter. Also, you will want to apply security, which we discuss in Chapter 7. Figure 6.2 reflects the services as they relate to IIS. As you can see, once the Proxy Server services have been installed, they appear as part of IIS itself.

FIGURE 6.2

Microsoft Proxy Server integrates seamlessly into IIS.

```
IIS
 |---WWW
 |---FTP
 |---GOPHER
 |---OTHER IIS ADD-ONS
 |---WEB PROXY SERVICE
 |---WINSOCK PROXY SERVICE
 |---SOCKS PROXY SERVICE
```

Having full knowledge of the user interface is important so you have a basic knowledge to be able to do the exercises in the book.

| *Microsoft* ✓ *Exam* *Objective* | **Configure the various Proxy Server services.** |

Setting Up the Web Proxy Service

Microsoft's Web Proxy service is configured from the Internet Service Manager. From the main IIS management screen, select the Web Proxy service icon. From here, you have the option of selecting which aspect of the service to control.

The control parameters are grouped into six sections, each of which has a tab on the Web Proxy Service Properties window: Service, Permissions, Caching, Logging, Routing, and Publishing. A number of the controls affect the other proxy services. The controls that span multiple services are the Shared Services and Configuration, both located on the Service tab. To avoid repeating information, these configuration items are discussed in a later section of this chapter. The relationship of the Web Proxy service controls is reflected in Figure 6.3.

Viewing and Configuring Web Proxy Service Information

The Service tab is used to view and configure general Web Proxy service information. The administrator's view of this tab is reflected in Figure 6.4.

From this tab, an administrator can perform the following tasks:

Review the product version   The first item displayed reflects the version of Proxy Server that you have installed. This information is more important for troubleshooting than anything else. As service packs and updates are released, the version number can be used to track the revision and the build.

View the product ID   You can also view the product that was installed to a particular system. This is useful for maintaining legitimate licensing and for support when determining which media were used during installation.

```
WEB PROXY SERVICE
├── Service Tab
│    ├── Version
│    ├── Product ID
│    ├── Comment
│    ├── [SHARED SERVICES]
│    ├── [CONFIGURATION]
│    └── Current Sessions
│
├── Permissions Tab
│    └── Enable
│         ├── Edit -> Select Users
│         ├── Copy To -> Select Other Protocol
│         └── Remove From
│
├── Caching Tab
│    └── Enable
│         ├── Cache Expiration Policy
│         │    └── Frequency of Update
│         │         └── Enable Active Caching
│         │              └── Frequency of Prefetch
│         ├── Cache Size
│         │    └── Size / Location
│         └── Advanced
│              ├── Limit Size
│              ├── Return Expired at % of TTL
│              ├── Enable HTTP Caching
│              │    └── TTL Settings
│              ├── Enable FTP Caching
│              │    └── TTL Settings
│              └── Cache Filters
│                   ├── Add
│                   ├── Edit
│                   └── Remove
│
├── Routing Tab
│    ├── Heading Alias
│    ├── Up Stream Routing
│    │    ├── Direct Connect
│    │    └── Web Proxy
│    │         └── Modify
│    └── Backup Route
│         ├── Direct Connect
│         └── Web Proxy
│              └── Modify
│
├── Publishing Tab
│    └── Enable
│         ├── Discard All
│         ├── Send to Web Server
│         ├── Send to Another Server
│         └── Exception
│
└── Logging Tab
     ├── Verbose / Regular
     ├── Text File
     │    ├── Frequency / Size of Log
     │    └── File Location
     └── SQL Database
          ├── Data Source Name
          ├── Table
          ├── UserName
          └── Password
```

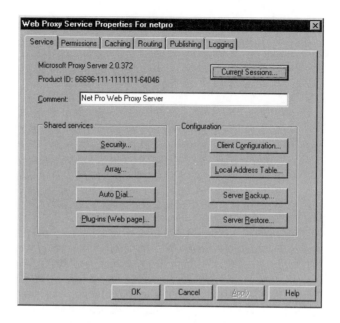

Define the server's functionality by placing a comment   The comment you enter here will appear in the Internet Services Management tool's list of proxy servers, so you will typically use it to identify each server uniquely by name. Any text typed in the Comment box will appear in the manager.

**Microsoft
Exam
Objective**

Monitor current sessions.

Display the current sessions   This option allows an administrator to determine which users are currently connected to the Web Proxy Server. The displayed information includes the connected user's name, the time they connected to the server, and the duration of the connection. At times, it is useful to see which connections are in use. For example, this function can be used to determine whether a system can be taken off-line, and also to see which users are being selfish with connections, possibly by leaving their system on the Internet even when they're not using the connection. The connection screen, shown in Figure 6.5, simply allows you to view this information; you cannot control the connections.

FIGURE 6.5

Displaying current
sessions

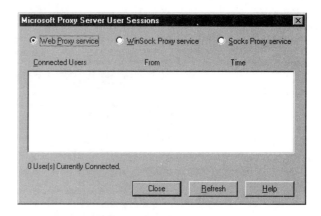

Access the shared services This is a group of services that are shared among all three proxy services. The services include security, array controls, auto dialing, and Web page plug-ins. (The Web page plug-ins do not apply to the Socks service.) See the *Configuring the Shared Services* section later in this chapter for details.

Access the common configuration controls Similar to the shared services, the common configuration controls are used among all three proxy services. These configuration items include client configuration, local address table settings, and server backup and restoration. (The Socks service does not use client configuration settings.) See *The Shared Configuration Controls* later in this chapter for details.

Assigning Web Proxy User Permissions

Setting up access control—establishing which users and groups have access to which Web resources on the proxy server—is one of the most important tasks an administrator can perform. Chapter 7 provides a complete discussion of proxy server access control. As discussed there, establishing user permissions is the most basic form of security a network can implement.

From the Web Proxy Permissions tab, an administrator can assign users rights to access the Internet Web pages, as shown in Figure 6.6. To give you some hands-on experience working with permissions, Exercise 6.1 shows the steps for setting up user access rights.

FIGURE 6.6

The Web Proxy
Permissions tab

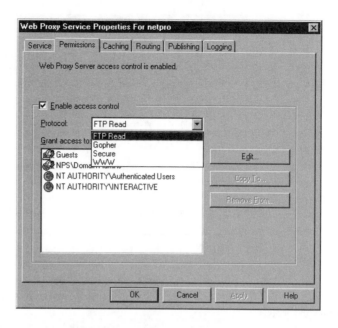

FIGURE 6.6

The Web Proxy Permissions tab

EXERCISE 6.1

Setting Up User Permissions

To set up user access rights, use the controls on the Permissions tab in the following order:

1. **Enable Access Control**. Selecting this option changes the proxy server from an open system, in which anyone can use any Web service, to one in which only specific users and groups are allowed access to specific services.

2. After enabling access control, use this pull-down box to select the protocol for which you'll grant access to the users and groups you specify in step 3. The protocols include:

   - **WWW**. Enables HTTP communication with a Web browser such as Netscape Navigator or Internet Explorer.

   - **Secure**. Enables SSL connections via HTTPS (a secure version of HTTP).

   - **Gopher**. Permits access to links and files on Gopher servers.

   - **FTP Read**. Allows users to download files from FTP sites.

EXERCISE 6.1 (CONTINUED FROM PREVIOUS PAGE)

3. **Grant Access To**. Initially empty, this list box displays the users and groups to which access to the selected Internet protocol has been authorized. To add users or modify their access rights, select the Edit button. This displays a standard Windows NT user add/edit window, in which you select users and groups from a domain list, as shown in Figure 6.7.

4. **Remove From**. This option simply deletes users or groups from the list.

5. **Copy To**. This option copies user permissions between protocols.

FIGURE 6.7

Adding users and groups to be granted permissions

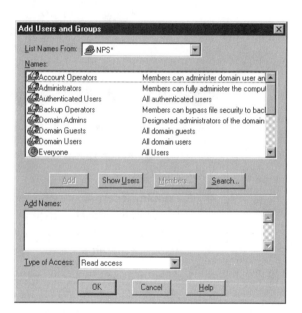

Grant or restrict access to the Internet for selected outbound users and groups who use the various Proxy Server services to access the Internet.

Microsoft
Exam
Objective

Choose a secure access strategy for various situations. Access includes outbound access by users to the Internet and inbound access to your Web site. Considerations include:

- Translating addresses from the internal network to the Local Address Table (LAT)
- Controlling anonymous access
- Controlling access by known users and groups
- Setting protocol permissions
- Auditing protocol access
- Setting Microsoft Windows NT® security parameters

Proxy server management works on the basis of separating services but allowing rights to be granted or revoked to all at one time. To set up permissions for more than one service (protocol), you'll need to repeat steps 2 and 3 above or use the Copy To function.

When initially setting up permissions, it's a good idea to create your groups in User Manager and then assign the groups' rights in Internet Service Manager. As users are created, you will be able to give them access to the proxy server without actually having to configure anything beyond adding each user to a group.

Microsoft
Exam
Objective

Configure server authentication. Authentication options include:

- Anonymous logon
- Basic authentication
- Microsoft Windows NT Challenge/Response authentication

When the Enable box is cleared, users are logged into the proxy server anonymously. This means that any user on the network can access the proxy server. Leaving the permissions disabled is useful in situations where users are all trusted not to abuse the service. Allowing the service to maintain open access potentially creates security-related issues.

However, there are a few methods you can use to control anonymous access. The most common is to manipulate the access to the local service so control is cached according to a specified user (usually IUSR_*systemname*).

Remember that you also control anonymous access by disabling the function—that is, by checking the Enable Access Control box—and then granting specific access rights to the username "anonymous," using the procedure just shown.

Customizing and Fine Tuning Web Proxy Caching

Aside from the relay functions of the proxy server, the ability to configure caching is perhaps the most important part of the service. Recall that you may configure a cache as either *active* or *passive*. Passive caching simply means recording data as it is requested. Active caching, on the other hand, is updating frequently when accessed periodically. The Caching tab enables an administrator to customize and fine tune performance.

Microsoft
Exam
Objective

Configure active caching and passive caching.

A cache stores information locally, so it can be accessed more quickly than from its original resource. This means less time and network traffic. Cache memory is commonly used in computers to load data quickly from RAM. It is not something to be stingy with. Allocate generously.

Clicking the Enable Caching checkbox allows the Proxy Server to store information requested by a client and later respond quickly to an identical request to the same resource. To determine how long the cache remains in effect, Microsoft Proxy Server allows administrators to define a Cache Expiration Policy. To set the expiration time, you select to receive either more updates, fewer Internet requests, or a balance between the two. Select the first option for more update checks if the information you're caching is so time-critical that you would rather slow down the system to check for updates than give the user outdated information. This tends to slow things down a bit since the proxy server will check for changes more often. Selecting fewer Internet requests reduces traffic significantly and sets the cached object's Time to Live (TTL) period to the maximum duration as defined in the Advanced section of the tab. Figure 6.8 shows the Caching tab.

FIGURE 6.8

Configuring the Web
Proxy cache

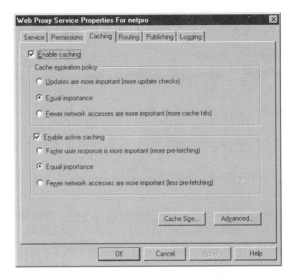

When the Enable Caching box is cleared, no caching occurs and there is no reduction of network traffic. The cache expiration policy can mean greater efficiency to the system. Be aware, however, that it may also respond to clients with obsolete data. Many Web sites do not change very often, but for other sites such as those with volatile information, this can be a serious issue.

You enable active caching by clicking the corresponding checkbox. Active caching is a technique designed to save time and traffic. It's typically used so that the updates are made while system utilization is low. When users request updates, they may never see the actual data directly from the resource; rather, they may just receive the cached object. Active caching can be adjusted for more *pre-fetching*, less pre-fetching, or a balance. Pre-fetching is when the server requests and caches data before a user makes a request for it. Note that the TTL on actively cached objects is reset only when a client requests data, not when the request was last updated. For more information on caching design, refer to Chapter 3.

To apply what we have learned about caching, let's pretend your company network (proxy server) is highly utilized during business hours, but not during all other hours. A good application of caching would be to configure the passive cache for more hits, while setting the active cache for more pre-fetching. In this configuration, users during the day will use less bandwidth since they will be receiving more data from the cache; and while network utilization is low in non-business hours, the proxy server can actively request updates to objects stored in the cache.

Choose the location, size, and type of caching for the Web Proxy service.

The cache size can also be configured from this page. Selecting Change Cache Size displays the Cache Drives window, shown in Figure 6.9, where you can adjust the number of reserved megabytes. It is a bad idea to allocate a small size, since objects are dropped from the cache as it reaches its capacity according to the objects' popularity for request from clients. While setting the cache size, you must also define the drive location of the cache. As the window warns, *an NTFS partition must be used for caching.* Typically, the best performance is obtained by selecting a drive that the main proxy system and Windows NT operating system are not installed on. That is, you should select not just a different partition, but a different physical drive. Note that caching is allowed only on local drives, and defining alternate drives on RAID-striped systems has no benefit beyond selecting the drive for free disk space. When multiple drives are available, using multiple caches often adds speed. When using a RAID-striped storage system, the cache is automatically spread across multiple physical drives.

FIGURE 6.9

Setting the cache size and location

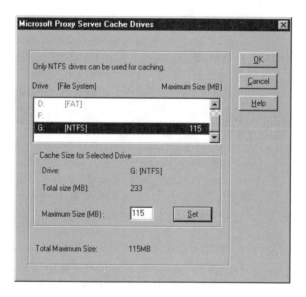

You can further fine-tune the cache by clicking the Advanced button on the main Caching tab. This displays the Advanced Cache Policy window, shown in Figure 6.10, where you can define the size of cached objects to use expired objects to fill requests when a site is unavailable, and filter which types of resources are cached. The options include the following:

Limit Size of Cached Objects To   Select this checkbox and then define the number of megabytes to be reserved for a given object. Any object that exceeds this specified size will not be cached.

Returned Expired Objects For Up To   Check this box to return a cached Web page, even though the TTL has expired, when the original site is unavailable. When you choose this option, you also set the percentage of the TTL period for which the outdated information will be available. For example, if the TTL is 1440 minutes (24 hours) and you set this option at 50 percent, users will be able to get a cached page for 12 hours after expiration if the original site is unavailable. Note that while this has the advantage of providing data when an object cannot be accessed, it can also provide a false impression if the data retrieved is now different from what is at the site. The return percentage must be greater that zero percent for the function to have any meaning.

Object Time To Live (TTL)   Set this according to type (HTTP or FTP) by selecting the appropriate checkboxes. When HTTP caching is enabled, you can set the TTL to an unlimited time by selecting TTL = 0. Only when the ISP or the Web page itself defines an expiration date will an object ever expire. Alternately, you can define the TTL as a percent of an object's age if the source provides the time the object was last modified. Both a Maximum and Minimum TLL in minutes must be set. When FTP caching is enabled, the TTL can be set by a flat period of time defined in minutes. Setting the Minimum TTL and the Maximum TTL to 0 will force the proxy server to issue a GET-if-Modified-Since HTTP header for client Web browser requests.

Cache Filters   This button displays a screen where you can specify which sites or pages should be cached. You configure the cache filter by selecting Add, Edit, or Remove for any entry or object. This allows you to define which objects are stored in the cache. Entries may include only the URL (to allow or disable caching for an entire site), or an entire URL with object path or wildcard (*). Note that when making an entire site cacheable, you are, in fact, only caching those items which are accessed. You will not cache objects on a site that users do not request. Objects can be set as always being cached or never being cached. Sample entries are shown below:

- `www.sybex.com/books` Caches the books directory on the Sybex Web site.

- `www.sybex.com/books*` Caches the books directory and all its subdirectories on the Sybex Web site.

- `*.sybex.com/books` Caches the books directory on all systems (WWW, FTP, and so on) in the Sybex domain.

- `*.sybex.com/books*` Caches the books directory and all its subdirectories on all systems (WWW, FTP, and so on) in the Sybex domain.

FIGURE 6.10

The Advanced Cache Policy window

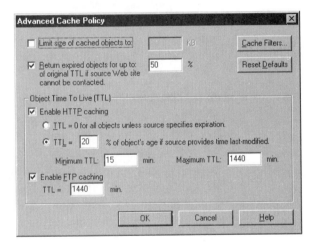

Routing Proxy Requests

The Routing tab, shown in Figure 6.11, is the primary interface for working with multiple proxy servers. Here you can define upstream routing, backup routing, and routing within an array. As explained further in Chapter 9, multiple proxy servers can be chained together or made to operate in an array configuration.

Microsoft ✓ Exam Objective	**Choose a strategy to balance Internet access across multiple Proxy Server computers. Strategies include:** • Using DNS • Using arrays • Using Cache Array Routing Protocol (CARP)

When configured in an array, multiple proxy servers operate as a single system. This provides load balancing, fault tolerance, and enhanced performance. This configuration is most often used in networks where a large concentration of users are in a single location. For more distributed networks, chaining proxy servers is a common practice. This allows caching between WAN links and between proxy servers.

Each proxy server must define itself according to an HTTP Alias. This is the name that is appended to the proxy request so that it may be returned to the correct server. Typically, the alias is the same as the name of the system where the proxy server resides. Once this has been configured, you may define upstream routing. This may be a direct connection to the Internet or a Web proxy or array, as shown in Figure 6.11.

FIGURE 6.11

Routing among proxy servers

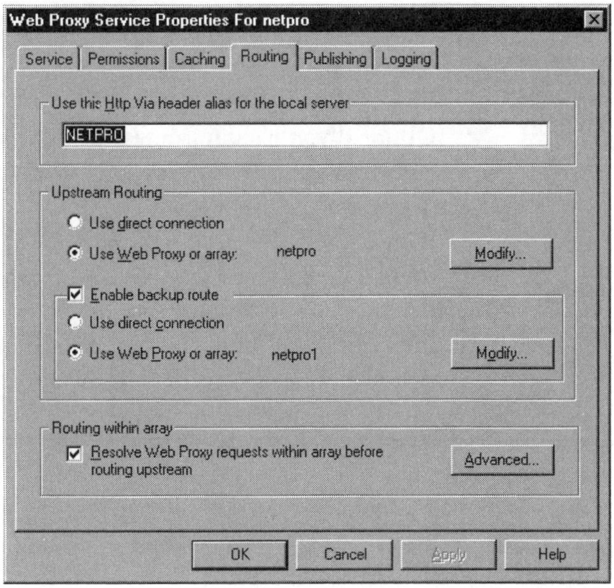

A direct connection would be applicable if the server was linked either directly to the Internet or via a dial-up connection. Otherwise, you'll select Use Web Proxy or Array and use the Modify button to select an upstream Web Proxy Server. Supply the host name and port number for the upstream server as shown in Figure 6.12. With the Auto-Poll Upstream Proxy for Array Configuration box checked, the array will automatically set itself. This setting should be accurate, assuming that the upstream server is also a Microsoft product. If a user name and password are required, check the Use Credentials to Communicate with Upstream Proxy checkbox. You may select either to send the credentials as basic/clear text or as NT Challenge/Response encrypted.

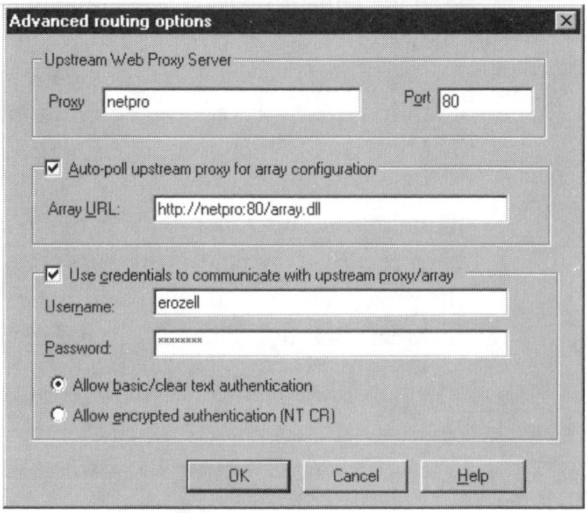

FIGURE 6.12

Use the Advanced Routing Options window to select a proxy server located upstream

Optionally, a backup route may be defined by checking the corresponding checkbox. The rules of operation are identical to those for defining a primary upstream routing path.

If an array has been configured (see Chapter 9) you may optionally attempt to resolve Web requests within the array prior to routing them upstream. To enable this, check the corresponding box on the main Routing tab in the Web Proxy Configuration dialog box. Selecting the Advanced button allows an array to be defined according to the appropriate IP address, as shown in Figure 6.13. (The Advanced button is shown in Figure 6.11.)

Routing options are discussed in further detail in Chapter 9, *Multiple Proxy Servers and Internet Access*.

FIGURE 6.13

Advanced Array routing options

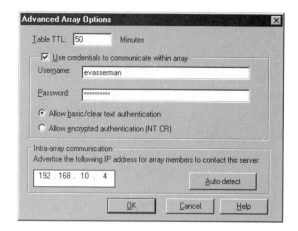

Publishing Web Pages

On the Publishing tab, you can check the Enable Web Publishing box to allow Web content to be published to the Internet. By default, this option is disabled. However, checking this box will enable users to publish Web pages through the proxy server. This function allows port 80 connections to pass. Similar to the way in which Web Proxy clients communicate with the proxy server, Internet clients talk directly to the proxy server as if it were the actual Web server. Recall that if multiple servers are running, multiple addresses may be required. The Publishing tab is shown in Figure 6.14.

FIGURE 6.14

Web Proxy Publishing

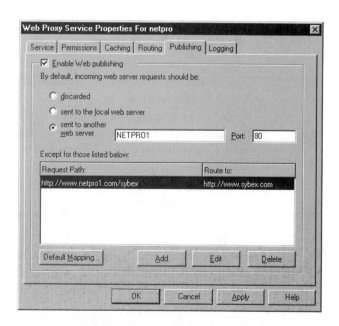

When this function is enabled, requests from the Internet can be discarded, sent to the local Web server, or sent to another Web server as a default filter for incoming requests. By adding a specific URL to an exception list, you can route valid requests to an alternate server other than the default. For example, suppose that all requests to www.netpro.com should be rejected. However, those that access www.netpro.com/field_info should be routed to the internal corporate Web page. Setting the exception for /FIELD_INFO will allow those external users who have been informed and authorized to access the site to connect, while others will assume that there is nothing to see. Obviously, if you do not want to accept packets, you should discard them. If you want to use the proxy server as a Web server as well, you should select Send to the Local Web Server. Otherwise, if you want to redirect Web requests to another Web server, you should select Send to Another Web Server. In our example with netpro, we were redirecting requests to another server that was not the proxy server. As you can see, the Web publishing feature allows both reverse hosting and proxying.

The *reverse proxying* feature enables inbound requests to be routed to an internal server. That server may exist on the private network, which may use a private IP address. Inbound requests may be cached at the proxy server.

The *reverse hosting* feature allows multiple Web servers to be represented at the proxy server. When requests are received, they can then be routed according to the URL request. Inbound requests may be cached at the proxy server.

The Web Publishing function of Microsoft Proxy Server is discussed in further detail in Chapter 7, *Controlling Access*.

Logging Web Proxy Activities

An important part of securing the Proxy Server is maintaining a log file of Internet resources accessed. This allows an administrator to view how the Proxy Server has been used. For example, suppose that many users were complaining about slow Internet access. While this could be attributed to many factors, including some that are server-related, it is possible to see whether certain users are monopolizing the server. In such cases, it may be desirable to either increase bandwidth to meet demand, or separate users to different proxy servers. Or suppose managers suspect that some employees are spending company time on sites that aren't work-related or visiting obviously inappropriate sites. A log will document who is abusing their Web privileges and possibly lead to further action. In short, the logging options allow you to audit Internet access. Figure 6.15 summarizes the controls from this tab available to an administrator.

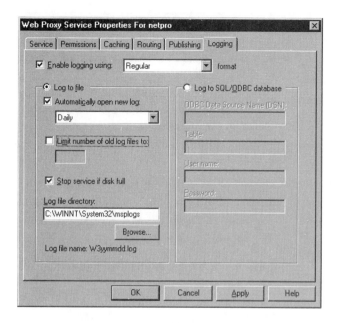

**Microsoft
Exam
Objective**

Configure auditing.

The Web Proxy Server has powerful logging features that enable you to
log all activities. Depending on the level of control that an organization
wants to impose on their users, log files can be either recorded to a text file
or an SQL/ODBC database. This flexibility allows an administrator to use
practically any management tool or custom database to record and analyze
data. Regardless of the data output format, each log file entry contains a
client's name, the protocol type (TCP or UDP), the protocol, the size of
requested objects, and the time and date of a request. When data is collected
into an SQL format, companies can compile statistical data which managers
use to track employee performance.

> **NOTE** Structured Query Language (SQL) is a platform-independent programming lan-
> guage that can be used to interface with a database program. Open Database
> Connectivity (ODBC) is a connection technology that allows communication
> to a driver, which then communicates with a database.

Microsoft ✓ **Exam Objective**

Configure Proxy Server to log errors when they occur.

Check the Enable Logging box on the Logging tab page to turn on logging. You then have the option of performing *regular* or *verbose* logging. Regular logging provides a simplified subset of the data provided by the verbose option. This is often more desirable in situations where storage space is at a premium. The target data is based on server, client, connection, and object information.

Regular logging includes the following information:

- Client machine and user names

- Destination name and port

- Log date and time

- Object name and source

- Protocol name

- Result code

- Service name

Verbose logging maintains a list of all possible information access on the Internet. This includes all items listed in Regular logging, plus the following information:

- Authentication status

- Bytes sent and received

- Client agent and platform

- Destination address

- Object MIME

- Operation

- Processing time

- Proxy name

- Referring server name

- Transport

If you choose to log data to a text file, you need to make further selections. For example, you can select Automatically Open New Log to create a new text file on a periodic basis (Daily, Weekly, or Monthly). Under this option, the log files are automatically named according to the duration. For example, if Daily logging were selected, the file would be named W3*yymmdd*.log (W3W*yymmw*.log for weekly, and W3M*yymm*.log for monthly). To prevent storage from becoming overrun with log files, you can also instruct the server here to keep only the most current logs, and specify the number to keep. If, for example, you need a daily report that is turned in once a week, you would keep five logs on a daily basis. That is to say, the one that you are working on in addition to five that are stored on the hard drive. If you need time for days off or illness, an administrator should keep enough logs so that information is still available when they return. Also, to ensure that existing logs are kept, there is also an option to stop the service if the disk is detected as full. (The packet filter log will stop all services if the disk is full.) Note that the log file will be saved to the directory you specify on this screen.

Since the log files (if they are not SQL/ODBC) are text-based, an administrator may choose to e-mail logs to a designated account. This can be done using Windows NT's scheduling abilities and a product such as Exchange. Essentially, the AT command is used in conjunction with Exchange's command-line mail utility, MAPISEND (from the Exchange Resource Kit). The command-line tools included with Microsoft Exchange work in the same manner as UNIX's SEND-MAIL utility.

When Log to SQL/ODBC Database is selected, products such as Sybase, Oracle, Microsoft SQL Server, Microsoft FoxPro, and many other SQL/ODBC programs may be used to manage data. As logs are stored, they are kept in a single file in which each logged event is stored as a record.

In order to use SQL/ODBC, you need to define the following information:

ODBC Data Source Name (DSN) Designates the Proxy Server. This is a logical name that is used by ODBC to reference the driver and related information used to access data. This related information may include the name of the system where the database is kept.

Table Defines the database within the SQL program. Note that this is the entry that specifies where the logs will be stored.

User Name Used to log into the SQL database. This is typical of most secure database programs.

Password Used in association with the user name to log into a secure database program. In general, most databases use identical security program entry points, and so programs such as Proxy Server can interface with the database without being concerned with the security requirements of the program.

Understanding how to set up SQL logging is essential to working with Proxy Server.

In order to communicate directly with an SQL or ODBC database, a driver must be installed. You can observe the installed drivers by looking in the Control Panel of either a Windows NT or Windows 95 system by clicking the 32-bit ODBC icon.

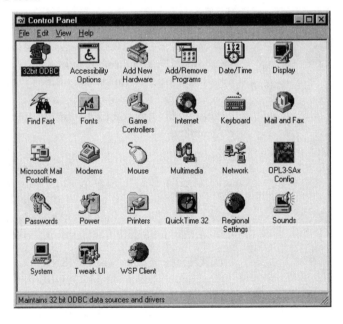

After installing the driver associated with a given database, you must define a unique system DSN (Data Source Name) for database logging. Optionally, you can use the default Proxy Server DSN, Proxy Server SQL. The DSN specified must be identical to the SQL Server or Microsoft Access database DSN specification used for logging. Note that there are user DSN settings, system DSN settings, and file DSN settings. When working with Microsoft products, remember the following:

- Microsoft SQL Server allows the DSN configuration to be set according to the server name, network address, and network library parameters. While both the default network address and network library parameters may be used, a unique system name must be specified.

- Microsoft Access is designed such that the system DSN is the file name of the database. For instance, if you are logging into a Microsoft Access database named PRXYINFO.MDB, the system DSN is PRXYINFO.

- A user's ODBC is on a user-level basis and is visible only to the current user on the local system. For this reason, these are not commonly associated with server-level logging programs. On the other hand, system DSNs are visible to all users on a system, including services.

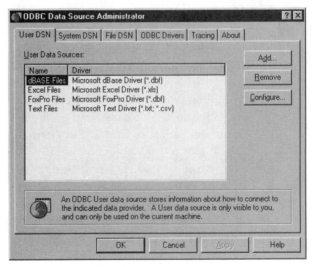

File DSNs are used for users who all have the same driver installed. Commonly, users will see this type of DSN when working within a workgroup. These data sources need not be dedicated to a user or local computer.

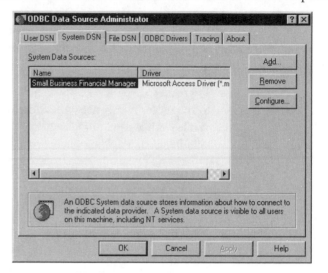

It is highly recommended that you review ODBC options prior to configuring your SQL database with Proxy Server. If you are already experienced in working with a database, this is typically not an issue; however, for those who are not, this information may help your understanding.

Certain Proxy Server events are also logged to the Windows NT event log. This logging is automatic and occurs in the event of program errors, certain user authentication errors, and internal problems. For example, suppose that the Proxy Server cannot connect to the ISP, or that it does not start up. These errors will be logged directly into the NT event log. An administrator may view these errors through the event viewer. Internal errors and such are discussed in Chapter 12.

Note that some administrators will also want to use the auditing features from Users Manager for Domains. However, this tends to be less useful in Proxy Activities since it only logs successes and failures of a limited number of items, as shown in the diagram below.

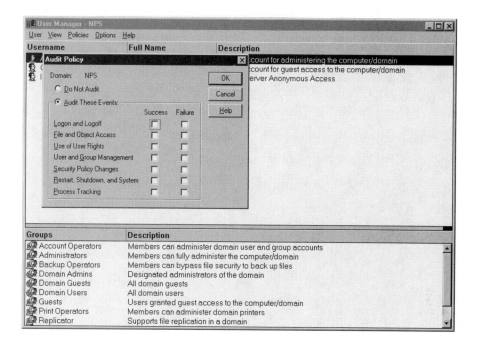

Setting Up the WinSock Proxy Service

Like the Web Proxy service, the WinSock Proxy service is configured from the Internet Service Manager. From the main management screen, select the WinSock Proxy service icon. From here, you have the option of selecting which aspect of the service to control. The control parameters are broken down into four sections: Service, Protocols, Permissions, and Logging.

A number of the controls affect the other proxy services. The controls that span multiple services are the Shared Services and Configuration, located on the Service tab. To avoid repeating information, these configuration items are discussed later in this chapter. Figure 6.16 shows the hierarchy of the WinSock Proxy service controls.

FIGURE 6.16

Options configured
through the WinSock
Proxy service window

```
WINSOCK PROXY SERVICE
├---Service Tab
│    ├---Version
│    ├---Product ID
│    ├---Comment
│    ├---[SHARED SERVICES]
│    ├---[CONFIGURATION]
│    └---Current Sessions
│
├---Protocols Tab
│    ├---Add  -> Protocol Definition
│    ├---Edit -> Protocol Definition
│    ├---Remove
│    ├---Save
│    └---Load
│
├---Permissions Tab
│    ├---Enable
│    └---Edit -> Select Users
│              ├----Copy To -> Select Other Protocol
│              └----Remove From
│
└----Logging Tab
     ├---Verbose / Regular
     ├---Text File
     │    ├---Frequency / Size of Log
     │    └---File Location
     └---SQL Database
          ├---Data Source Name
          ├---Table
          ├---UserName
          └---Password
```

Viewing and Configuring WinSock Proxy Service Information

The Service tab is used to view and configure general WinSock Proxy service information. From this tab, an administrator performs the same basic functions as with the Web Proxy service. Figure 6.17 shows this tab.

From the Services tab, an administrator can perform the following tasks:

Review the product version   Near the top of the window you see the version number of the Proxy Server you have installed. This information is more important for troubleshooting than for anything else. As service packs and update occur, the version number can be used to track the revision and the build.

FIGURE 6.17

The WinSock Proxy
service tab

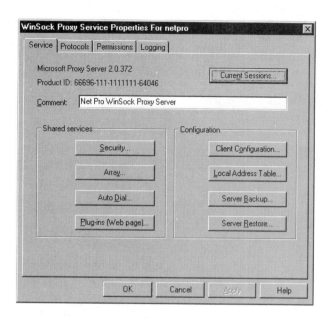

View the product ID You can also view the product that was installed to a particular system. This is useful for maintaining legitimate licensing and for support when determining which medium was used during installation: Internet download, floppy disk, CD-ROM, and so on.

Define the server's functionality by placing a comment The comment you enter here will appear in the Internet Services Management tool's list of proxy servers, so you will typically use it to identify each server uniquely by name. However, any text typed in the Comment box will appear in the IIS Manager main screen.

Display the current sessions This option allows an administrator to determine which users are currently connected to the Winsock Proxy Server. The displayed information includes the connected user's name, the time connected to the server, and the duration of the connection. At times, it is useful to see which connections are in use. For example, it can be used to determine whether a system can be taken off-line, and also to see which users are being selfish with connections, possibly by leaving their system on the Internet even when they're not using the connection. The connection screen, shown in Figure 6.18, simply allows you to view this information; you cannot control the connections.

FIGURE 6.18

Displaying current
sessions

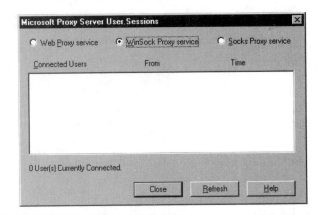

Access the shared services This is a group of services that are shared among all three proxy services. The services include security, array controls, auto-dialing, and Web page plug-ins. (The Web page plug-ins do not apply to the Socks service.) See *Configuring the Shared Proxy Services* section later in this chapter for details.

Access the common configuration controls Like the shared services, the common configuration controls are used among all three proxy services. They include client configuration, local address table settings, and server backup and restoration. (The Socks service does not use client configuration settings.) See *The Shared Configuration Controls* later in this chapter for details.

Adding, Modifying, or Removing Winsock Protocol Entries

The WinSock Proxy Server works with virtually all WinSock applications (protocols). Typically, each of these services uses a port defined by convention for that application. For instance, FTP uses TCP on port 21. These applications and their port assignments can be found in the SERVICES file; and you can view, add, remove, or modify them using the Protocols tab. By default, the more common WinSock applications are included in the default installation of Microsoft Proxy Server. Figure 6.19 shows what you will find in a default installation.

Each supported WinSock protocol defines a port, type (TCP or UDP), and the direction of the request (inbound or outbound). From the Protocols tab, you may add, modify, or remove entries. For example, to keep users from using a certain service you may want to remove the protocol definition from the WinSock Protocols list. The reason that you may want to remove the definition is that you may have users with unlimited access and you want to block anyone from using a specific service.

FIGURE 6.19

Viewing the default
WinSock Proxy protocols

FIGURE 6.19

Viewing the default
WinSock Proxy protocols

New or unlisted protocols that operate on TCP or UDP can easily be added to the WinSock Proxy Server. Exercise 6.2 will take you through the steps.

EXERCISE 6.2

Adding Protocols to the WinSock Proxy Service

1. Verify that the protocol to be added does not already exist in the supported list, then click Add. The Protocol Definition dialog box will appear as shown below.

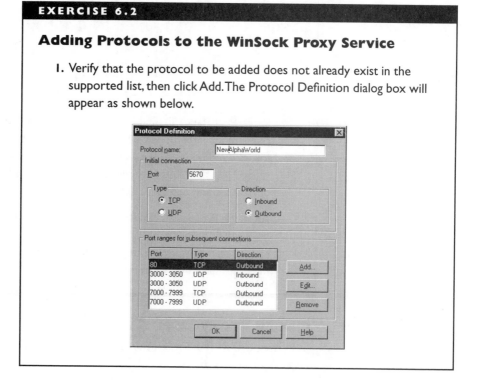

2. Type the name of the protocol in the Protocol Name box. Although the name should match the actual protocol, you may use variations as required.

3. In the Initial Connection section, select the type of communication that this protocol will use. Again, use UDP for connectionless and TCP for connection-based configurations. Remember that outbound TCP will actually enable a client to make a connection, but outbound UDP will simply pass or relay data to a destination. Next, choose the direction that the initial connection will use, either inbound or outbound.

4. In the Port Ranges for Subsequent Connections section, you may select Add, Edit, or Remove. In this case, since we are adding a new protocol, the list should be empty. In the case of our graphic above, we included some settings to illustrate example settings. At this point, we should select Add. The Port Range Definition dialog box will appear.

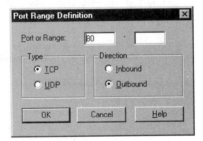

5. In the Port Range Definition window, select the port or range of ports that can be used with the newly defined protocol. Selecting 0 for inbound connections will allow the server to use any port in the range 1024 to 5000. The valid port range on the Proxy Server is between 0 and 65535. Select OK when completed.

6. After the Protocol Definition screen reappears, select OK, and the new definition will be created. Note that before this new protocol can be used, permissions must be granted to users. Refer to the Permissions tab for further details.

Defining WinSock Proxy User Access

The WinSock Proxy Permissions tab enables an administrator to define access according to users and protocol. To enable permissions, simply click the Enable Access Control box as shown in Figure 6.20.

FIGURE 6.20

Use the Permissions tab
to enable and define
WinSock access control.

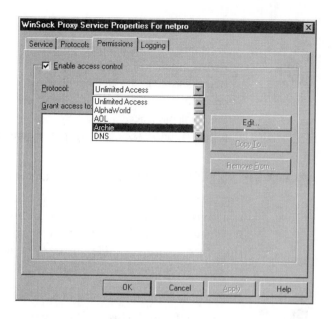

Once access control has been enabled, use the Protocol drop-down box to select the protocol for which you will define access rights. For example, you might select Archie, as in Figure 6.20. Notice that the protocols listed in the drop-down box are the same ones found in the Protocols tab. Once you've specified a protocol, you can edit, remove, or copy user assignments. Since there aren't any default rights, select Edit to assign access to a user or group of users. You'll see the window shown in Figure 6.21. Here you may add users as you would with any other security object.

FIGURE 6.21

Setting WinSock Proxy
permissions

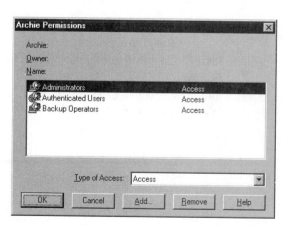

To grant access to all protocols and ports on a server, select Unlimited Access in the Protocol drop-down box on the Permissions tab. This allows all users listed in the Unlimited Access section rights to all WinSock protocols. Note that if you deny a user access to the Web Proxy Server, but grant them unlimited access to the WinSocks Server, they can still access Web pages via the WinSock Proxy, provided they have the WSP client installed.

Logging WinSock Proxy Server Activities

The event logging functions of the WinSock Proxy service are practically identical to those of the Web Proxy service, as are the steps for configuring them. As it is with the Web Proxy service, logging is an important part of securing the server. It allows an administrator to view how the Proxy Server has been used. In short, the logging options enable you to audit Internet access.

Please refer to the *Logging Web Proxy Activities* section for exact details about configuring the logging functions.

As with the Web (and Socks) logging functions, logs may be stored in text files or in an SQL database. The only major difference is that the automatically-generated log file names are as follows:

- Daily: WS*yymmdd*.log
- Weekly: WSW*yymmw*.log
- Monthly: WSM*yymm*.log.

A sample screen is shown in Figure 6.22.

Note that although the configuration of the WinSock Proxy and Web Proxy logs are identical, they each store information relative to their design. For example, the WinSock Proxy will store information regarding access to it and the respective protocol, such as Telnet. You will not find this item in a Web Proxy log.

FIGURE 6.22

Logging WinSock Proxy
activities

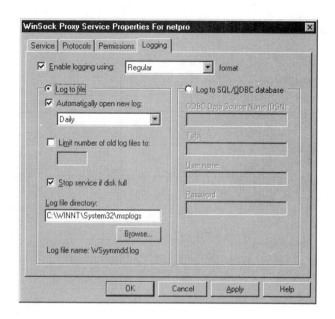

Setting Up the Socks Proxy Service

Like the other two Microsoft Proxy Server services, the Socks Proxy is configured from the Internet Service Manager. From the main management screen, select the Socks Proxy service icon. From here, you have the option of selecting which aspect of the service to control. The control parameters are broken down into three sections: Service, Permissions, and Logging. A number of the controls affect the other proxy services. The controls that span multiple services are in the Shared Services and Configuration areas of the Service tab. To avoid repeating information, these configuration items are discussed later in this chapter. The hierarchy of the Socks Proxy service controls is shown in Figure 6.23.

Viewing and Configuring Socks Proxy Service Information

The Service tab is used to view and configure general Socks Proxy service information. From this tab, an administrator can perform the same basic functions as with the Web and WinSock Proxy services. Figure 6.24 shows this tab.

FIGURE 6.23

Options configured
through the Socks Proxy
service window

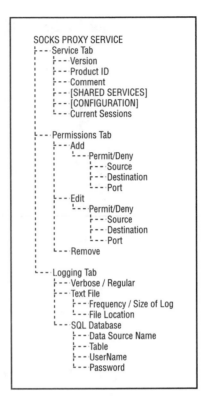

FIGURE 6.24

The Socks Proxy
service tab

From this tab, an administrator can perform the following tasks:

Review the product version Near the top of this window you'll see the version of Microsoft Proxy Server that you have installed. This information is more important for troubleshooting than anything else. As service packs and updates occur, you can use the version number to track the revision and the build.

View the product ID You can also view the product that was installed to a particular system. This is useful for keeping legitimate licensing and for support when determining which media were used during installation.

Define the server's functionality by placing a comment The comment you enter here will appear in the Internet Services Management tool's list of proxy servers, so you will typically use it to identify each server uniquely by name. However, any text typed in the Comment box will appear in the manager.

Display the current sessions This option allows an administrator to determine which users are connected to the Socks Proxy Server. The displayed information includes the connected user's name, the time connected to the server, and the duration of the connection. At times, it is useful to review what connections are in use. For example, it is useful to determine whether a system can be taken off-line, and also to see which users are being selfish with connections, possibly by leaving their system on the Internet even when they're not using the connection. The connection screen, shown in Figure 6.25, simply allows you to view this information; you cannot control the connections.

FIGURE 6.25

Displaying current sessions

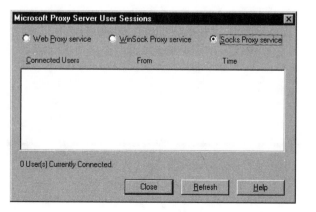

Access the shared services   This is a group of services that are shared among all three proxy services. These services include security, array controls, auto-dialing, and Web page plug-ins. Note that the Web page plug-ins do not apply to this service. These shared services are discussed in a separate section later in this chapter.

Common configuration access   Similar to the shared services, the common configuration controls are used among all three proxy services. These configuration items include client configuration, local address table settings, and server backup and restoration. Note that the Socks service does not use client configuration settings. These shared services are discussed in a separate section later in this chapter.

Defining Socks Proxy User Access

The Socks Proxy Permissions tab enables an administrator to define access according to action, such as to permit or deny access to a system. Requests to the Socks Proxy Server are supported for version 4.3a of the Socks protocol. Each entry in the permissions list contains a source, destination, and whether the request should be allowed or not. Figure 6.26 shows the Socks Permission tab.

FIGURE 6.26

The Socks Proxy Service Permissions tab

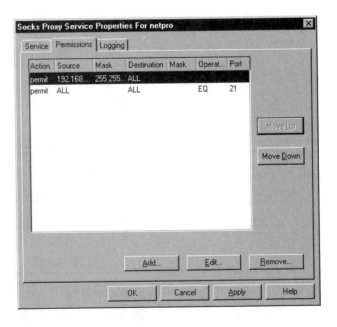

From this screen, an administrator can add, edit, or remove listed items. When adding items, an administrator must define whether the action will be allowed or denied, in addition to the request's source and destination. For both of these the options are All, a domain/zone you specify, or an IP address and mask. Additionally, you may set the port (number) interface as Equal To (EQ), Not Equal To (NEQ), Greater Than (GT), Less Than (LT), Greater Than or Equal To (GE), or Less Than or Equal To (LE) (see Figure 6.27).

F I G U R E   6.27

Setting Socks Proxy permissions

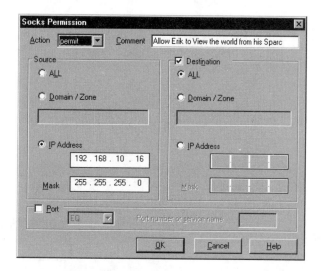

To apply this function to users, let's suppose that you wanted to block all UNIX users from using a service such as IRC. To do this, open the Socks Proxy service, select Add, and choose Deny in the Action box. To help us remember what we are doing, we should type **IRC** in the Comment box. You can be descriptive; however, short and to the point is usually preferred. Since IRC operates on port 6667, we should select the Port checkbox, select EQ in the Options box, and type **6667** in the Port box. Finally, since we want to add all users, we should select All in the Source box, and then, optionally, select Destination and choose All. The reason that the destination is optional is that we have all sources blocked that would otherwise attempt to contact any given destination.

Now, suppose that your policy on IRC changed and you wanted to allow all users to use this service. This process can be completely reversed by changing the Deny option in the Action box to Permit.

Logging Socks Proxy Server Activities

The event-logging functions of the Socks Proxy service, and the procedures for configuring those functions, are practically identical to those of the Web and WinSock Proxy services. As in the Web and WinSock Proxy services, logging is an important part of securing the server. It allows an administrator to view how the Proxy Server has been used. In short, the logging options enable you to audit Internet access.

Please refer to the *Logging Web Proxy Activities* section for exact details about configuring the logging functions. As with the Web and WinSock logging functions, logs may be stored in text files or in an SQL database. The only major difference is that the automatically generated log file names are as follows:

- Daily: SP*yymmdd*.log

- Weekly: SPW*yymmw*.log

- Monthly: WSM*yymm*.log.

A sample screen is shown in Figure 6.28.

FIGURE 6.28

Logging Socks Proxy
activities

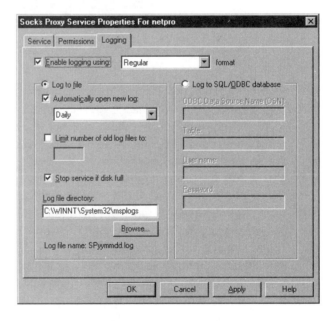

Configuring the Shared Proxy Services

You can configure the shared proxy services from the Service tab of any of the three proxy services. Typically, you should perform configurations from the WinSock or Web Proxy services tabs, as the Web plug-ins are disabled on the Socks service tab. The control parameters are grouped into four sections:

- Security: This is used to secure a network from external (Internet-based) attacks. In this section, a firewall can be configured such that static and/ or dynamic packet filters can be applied. The firewall function under Proxy Server is known as *packet filtering*. By allowing only specified packets into the network, your server can be secured from attack. However, note that security works in two ways and can limit users to use only those ports and services that the firewall is configured to allow. Also, a domain filter can be configured to allow or disallow users access to certain sites. This keeps people from spending their day on the stock market watch or at some other site. However, if access is completely restricted to just a few sites, it can be a nightmare to keep up with when users request additional sites. Exceptions must be configured for each site. This tab is discussed in detail in Chapter 7, *Controlling Access*.

- Web Plug-Ins: Add-on products that may be purchased from third-party vendors, such as on-the-fly virus scanning. Further details are provided in Chapter 8, *Internet and Intranet Access*.

- Array: This tab is used to configure and control multiple proxy servers for fault tolerance, joint caching, and so forth. The use of this tab is reviewed in Chapter 9, *Multiple Proxy Servers and Internet Access*.

- Auto Dialer: This tab is used to configure an on-demand link to the Internet. This tab is used as an extension of the RAS service, defining user account, protocol, and schedule information. This tab is discussed in Chapter 10, *RAS and Microsoft Proxy Server*.

The hierarchy of the shared services is shown in Figure 6.29.

FIGURE 6.29

Shared proxy services
you can configure from
either the Web or
WinSock Services tab

```
[SHARED SERVICES]
 --- Security Tab
     --- Packet Filters
         --- Enable Dynamic Packet Filtering
         --- Enable Filtering of IP Fragments
         --- Exceptions
             --- Add
                 --- Predefined Filter
                 --- Custom Filter
                     --- ID
                     --- Direction
                     --- Local Host
                     --- Remote Host
             --- Edit
                 --- Predefined Filter
                 --- Custom Filter
                     --- ID
                     --- Direction
                     --- Local Host
                     --- Remote Host
             --- Remove
             --- Reset Defaults
     --- Domain Filters
         --- Enable
             --- Exceptions
     --- Altering
         --- Event
         --- Conditions
         --- Email
         --- Reset
     --- Logging Tab
         --- Verbose / Regular
         --- Text File
             --- Frequency / Size of Log
             --- File Location
         --- SQL Database
             --- Data Source Name
             --- Table
             --- UserName
             --- Password

 --- Array Tab
     --- Join Array
     --- Synchronize
     --- Remove From Array

 --- Auto Dialer Tab
     --- Configuration SubTab
         --- Enable for Socks / WinSocks
         --- Enable For Web Proxy Primary
         --- Enable for Web Proxy Backup
         --- Dialing Hours
     --- Credentials SubTab
         --- Entry Name
         --- User Name
         --- Password
         --- Password Confirmed
         --- Domain

 --- Web Plug Ins -> Internet Delivered Proxy Additions
```

The Shared Configuration Controls

The Configuration proxy controls are used to define basic information that is common among all proxy services. There are four basic controls—Client Configuration, Local Address Table, Server Backup and Server Restore.

Typically, you will not perform a lot of changes in this section except when changing the network configuration. For example, if the network changed such that additional IP ranges were added, you would use this section to update the LAT. The majority of the controls, however, are less likely to be used often. Most changes are to adjust user rights, Web pages, and so forth. Shared configuration controls is intended to be more of an after-the-fact setup utility. The hierarchy of the shared configuration controls is reflected in Figure 6.30.

FIGURE 6.30

Shared configuration controls you can configure from any Service tab

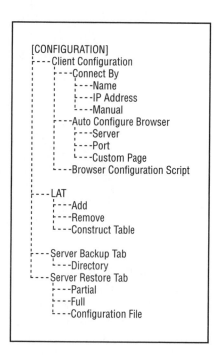

Configuring Clients from IIS

The Client Installation/Configuration tab is used to configure Web and WinSock Proxy clients automatically. From this tab, an administrator can control the values assigned to proxy clients from the MSPCLNT share on the proxy server.

The WinSock client can be defined to connect to a proxy server by name, IP address, or manually. Simply select one of these and provide the information required to define the connection.

The Web Proxy client has a more advanced configuration than its WinSock counterpart. A Web Proxy client can be configured to connect to any proxy server you define in this dialog box. From here you can use either an automatic or custom script to customize the proxy server, as shown in Figure 6.31. Note that the URL is the location where a client will download an automatic configuration script.

FIGURE 6.31

Configuring Proxy clients

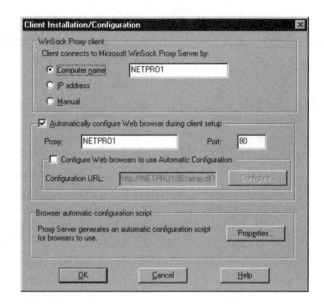

When using the automatic configuration option, the Properties button enables an administrator to fine-tune the Web Proxy service. In the Advanced Client Configuration window you define whether a client should use a proxy server for local systems, whether to skip the proxy server on given IP addresses or domains ending in a specific suffix (subnet mask), and how backup connections should be established. These options are shown in Figure 6.32.

Configuring the Local Address Table

The Local Address Table (LAT) is used to determine which systems are on the private network instead of the Internet. To view the LAT, open any Proxy service and click Local Address Table in the Configuration group of the Services tab. The Local Address Table Configuration screen is identical to the one you used during Proxy Server setup and is shown in Figure 6.33.

FIGURE 6.32

Advanced Web Proxy
client options

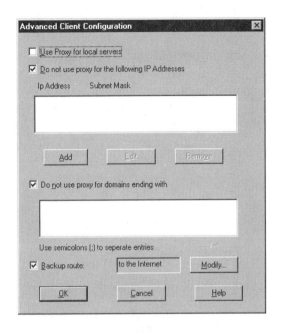

FIGURE 6.33

Editing the Local
Address Table

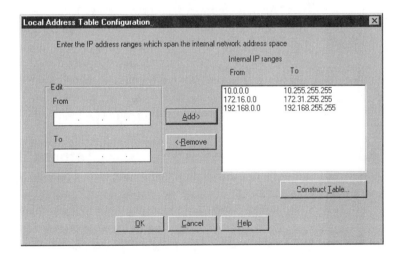

Microsoft
✓ Exam
Objective

Create a LAT.

The LAT is used to define which IP addresses are used on your private network, as well as to reserve those ranges that should not be used on the Internet. From the installation, in which you clicked the Construct Table button to create the LAT, you should have the private IP address ranges 10.x.x.x, 172.16-31.x.x and 192.168.10.x already excluded. You can click the Construct Table button again to refresh these settings, including those found in the local system's routing table. To manually add or remove ranges, click the appropriate button after selecting the range.

When creating a LAT, you should never include any addresses other than those on the private network. This means that you do not add the external interface of the Proxy Server, any Internet sites, any addresses including the DNS at your ISP, and so forth. Only add an address to the LAT when it is on the local network. If creating the LAT accidentally adds a wrong address, you should remove it.

The LAT range of the private network should include all those ranges designated by the subnet mask of the system on the network. Do not just add the IP addresses of each client, but rather the entire network range. For example, if your Proxy Server had an IP address of 192.168.10.5 and a subnet mask of 255.255.255.0, you should include the range 192.168.10.0 to 192.168.10.255. Also, if your external interface was 134.57.8.2 with a mask of 255.255.255.0, you should not include any numbers from here. Adding even a range such as 134.57.8.3 to 134.57.8.255 could allow Internet users to access the intranet through the proxy server since, locally, users could connect to the external interface, but they have a number which is included in the LAT. In other words, the external interface with its subnet mask defines a range of 134.57.8.0 to 134.57.8.255, which should not be included in the LAT.

Backing Up and Restoring Proxy Information

The server backup function is used to store information about the server's installation, client configuration, and so forth. The Backup option located in the Shared Configuration section allows an administrator to make a complete backup of all server options to C:\MSP\CONFIG or another specified directory. The backup file will be called MSP*yyyymmdd*.MPC, where *yyyy* is the year, *mm* is the month, and *dd* is the day. Note that for security reasons, the backup data should be stored on an NTFS volume. An example of the administrative backup interface is shown in Figure 6.34.

Microsoft
✓ *Exam*
Objective

Back up and restore Proxy Server configurations.

FIGURE 6.34

Backing up Proxy Server
information

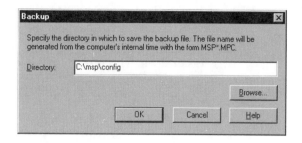

Restoring server information is just as simple as creating the backup. Simply choose the file that you would like to restore from by typing its path in the text box or select the file using the Browse function. You may restore either partial or full material. When restoring partial information, only data that's not system specific, such as information about user permissions and arrays, will be recalled. Partial restorations are sometimes used between proxy servers to ensure that both have identical permissions. Full restores tend to be used when replacing a server or when rolling back to a previous configuration. Figure 6.35 shows the administrative restore options.

FIGURE 6.35

Restoring Proxy Server
information

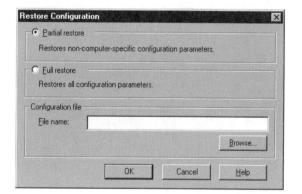

Summary

This chapter presented a general overview of the functions available in the IIS Internet Service Manager. Because most of the features of the three services that you configure with IIS Manager are covered in greater depth in other chapters, this chapter's purpose was simply to provide a basic understanding of where the various controls are located.

In the Service tab of each proxy, we essentially found miscellaneous information that could be used to describe a specific system. Information in this tab is especially useful in multi-server environments, where identification of each server is difficult. This tab is also the key point to access the shared configuration and security settings.

The user Permissions tab in all services allows an administrator to designate which users have permission to access specified protocols on a given proxy server. User rights may be granted on an individual user or group basis. Clearing the Enable Permissions box allows users to use the proxy server anonymously. In the case of Socks, authorization is more an option to perform an action on the server rather than define who has the ability to determine where users are defined according to their IP addresses. With Socks, user definition is by source IP address.

All services also provide a Logging tab, which offers full-featured information tracking capabilities. The log files may be generated based on size or frequency, such as monthly, weekly, or daily. Proxy Server maintains management capacity by allowing its log files to be stored either as plain text or in an SQL database. Reported data may be verbose, including all available data, or in a reduced (regular) format that reports only the more commonly monitored information.

The Web Proxy Server maintains only a handful of protocols (FTP Read, HTTP, Secure, and Gopher), and there is no provision for adding other protocols. However, the WinSock Proxy contains an additional tab for specifically configuring additional protocols not in the default list. The additional protocols may be either TCP- or UDP-based, and you specify an outbound or inbound port accordingly. This tab allows the WinSock Proxy to support virtually all WinSock applications. Note that of all three proxy services, WinSock is the only one that supports UDP-based connections.

Since the Web Proxy Server contains predictable data and a limited number of protocols, which tend to be used frequently, this service maintains a cache. The caching system allows data to be accessed more quickly, giving the appearance of more bandwidth. The Cache tab allows you to balance caching types and to manipulate the cache size and location.

Finally, since all of the IIS servers (WWW, FTP, Gopher) are related in that they share a browser-compatible interface, the Web Proxy service also includes a Web Publishing tab, for publishing to the Internet.

The Security subsection is used to filter traffic for all services. Security is used to either grant or restrict access to Internet resources and to block certain types of packet traffic. Likewise, the shared configuration options control common resources, such as the LAT, across all services. These options are also used to set client settings for WinSocks and Web clients as well as backup and restore server configuration settings.

Review Questions

1. Explain how logs work. What is regular logging? Verbose? When should they be used?

2. Explain how filtering helps in securing a site. How can it be limiting?

3. Will Microsoft Proxy Server 1.0 integrate with IIS 4.0? Explain.

4. How do you instruct Proxy Server not to cache certain sites?

5. Explain how to change the cache after an installation. How does the cache size differ from caching (passive and active)?

6. Where are the log files stored?

   A. \WINNT\SYSTEM32\PROXYLOGS

   B. \INETPUB\PROXYLOGS

   C. \WINNT\LOGS

   D. In an SQL database file designated during or after installation

   E. Anywhere the administrator designates

7. Without customization, how can Proxy Server be managed through HTML?

    A. By downloading PXYHTMG.EXE from www.Microsoft.com

    B. By clicking Enable Web Publishing

    C. It is already installed; no changes are required.

    D. By connecting your Web site to /PROXYMGR

    E. It is not supported at this time.

8. What operations can be performed from the Service tab of the WinSock Proxy Properties page?

    A. None

    B. Change the number of licensed connections.

    C. Enter a Comment for the server.

    D. Check existing user sessions.

9. What types of log files are supported?

    A. Text

    B. Proprietary encoded

    C. Bitmap graphical log

    D. SQL database

    E. Microsoft Word .DOC format

10. Of the following, which are the default log name formats?

    A. W3*yymmdd*.LOG

    B. WS*yymmdd*.LOG

    C. WWW.LOG

    D. WINSOCK.LOG

    E. None of the above

11. What should you do on the Logging tab in the WinSock Proxy Service Properties dialog box when trying to compile a weekly report containing the Internet IP addresses accessed by applications that use the WinSock service?

   A. Select the Stop Service if Disk Is Full checkbox.

   B. Select the Automatically Open New Log checkbox and specify Weekly.

   C. Select the Verbose checkbox.

   D. Select the Limit Number Of Old Logs To checkbox and set the value to 7.

12. You need to support Microsoft SQL Server with your Proxy Server. The initial inbound port uses port 1433 and then generates an outbound port somewhere between 5000 and 32767. How should you configure the ports on your Proxy Server?

   A. In the WinSock Proxy Server service, specify port 0 in the Protocol definitions.

   B. In the WinSock Proxy Server service, specify a port range of 5000 to 32767 in the Protocol definitions.

   C. In the WinSock Proxy Server service, specify a port range of "any" in the Protocol definitions.

   D. Create a protocol entry for the SQL Server and specify a port range of 5000 to 32767.

13. Your users are using the Internet to get weather and sports and using all the bandwidth so that your Internet connections are starting to get slow. What should you do to stop users from getting sports and weather information?

   A. Enable anonymous authentication.

   B. Add outbound filters for the sports and weather Web sites.

   C. Remove any protocol definitions for the sport and weather Web sites from the WinSock Proxy service.

   D. Enable Microsoft Windows NT Challenge/Response authentication.

14. What must you do on the Publishing tab of the Web Proxy Service Properties dialog box if you want to forward all requests from the Internet to your Web service installed on the local server network?

A. Enable Web publishing and select the Discard button.

B. Enable Web publishing and select the Sent To the Local Web Server button.

C. Enable Web publishing and select the Sent to the Local Web Server button and specify the name of the Web server.

D. Enable Web publishing and select the Sent to the Local Web Server button and specify the name of the proxy server.

15. What should you do to the Advanced Cache Policy dialog box to prevent large files from being stored in the cache?

A. Nothing

B. Set a size limit on cached objects.

C. Set a maximum TTL of 512.

D. Set the TTL to 0.

16. Your clients run only TCP/IP and connect to the Internet by way of the Web Proxy service. How do you find out what sites the users are visiting?

A. Enable Web Proxy logging.

B. Enable auditing for file and object access.

C. Nothing

D. Look in the cache.

CHAPTER

7

Controlling Access

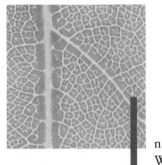

n Chapter 6 we provided an overview of the Socks, WinSock, and Web proxy service controls. In that chapter, you were shown each component of each service and how they integrate into the IIS Manager. In this section, we will build on those concepts by explaining, step by step, how you implement those functions.

Access control is designed with two goals in mind: controlling users on your network who wish to access outside information and controlling users outside your network who which to access information on your network. You will find that Proxy Server is primarily designed as an outbound service.

By the end of the chapter you should understand the following:

- IP routing

Exam objectives are subject to change at any time without prior notice and at Microsoft's sole discretion. Please visit Microsoft's Training & Certification website (www.microsoft.com/Train_Cert) for the most current exam objectives listing.

- Securing your network

- Encrypting

- Publishing Internet pages

- Enabling TCP and UDP access ports

- Setting access and protocol permissions

Creating a Secure Environment for Proxy Server

Before we progress into all the restrictions that Proxy Server can maintain, we should first consider the prerequisites of a secure environment.

Windows NT, when provided with multiple network adapters, has the ability to route IP protocols throughout your network. For example, if a network contains a live Internet address, such as on a class C network, you could use the dialup networking functions on your server to connect to the Internet without using a proxy server. I think I just heard the question, "How?" There is nothing special or different about the IP traffic on the Internet except that it is professionally structured and very large. In other words, it is like many smaller networks configured into one larger network. Simply connecting to the Internet via dialup networking using an ISDN network adapter can provide complete IP routing. In order to do so, your network must either use RIP (Router Information Protocol) or static mappings. Once the connection has been made and a route established, TCP/IP traffic can flow from your network to the Internet. However, this creates quite a large problem because anyone can send traffic to your network on any port, as well as access your network, which could be a security problem.

A Hacker Favorite

Without a strong security mechanism such as a firewall in place, simply password-protecting a network is not enough. A particular favorite of hackers and malcontents is to find an employee's name, call them on the phone, and ask them for their login ID and password. (I always ask myself what type of employee would fall for this.) Check this out:

Hacker: Hello. I'm looking for John Doe in Sales.

Employee: Yes.

Hacker: Oh, hello John. This is George in the Information Services Department. It appears that your login is…well, we think it is your login, causing problems on the network.

Employee: Really?

Hacker: Sure. I just need to verify that this is you so we can correct the problem.

Employee: OK!

Hacker: What is your login ID?

Employee: JSMITH.

Hacker: OK, John. It is you. Umm, can I get you to log out for a moment?

Employee: Yes.

Hacker: OK, now type in your login ID if it does not already appear in the dialog box.

Employee: OK.

Hacker: Now, type in your password and I will monitor your login.

Employee: OK.

Hacker: Hmm...I can't seem to see you. What network are you logging into?

Employee: Corporate-1.

Hacker: Really? I did not see you. What password did you use?

Employee: Oh, I used my wife's maiden name, doe.

Hacker: In all lowercase?

Employee: Yes…

Hacker: (making some typing noise) OK, this has to be a duplicate ID. We'll straighten this out. Thanks for your assistance John.

Employee: No problem! Bye.

From this point forward, the hacker will have a valid user ID and password to access your network. It actually has little to do with a hacker's skill or their ability to monotonously type every employee's login name and use it again, or even their willingness to try "password" for the password. Because hackers often steal passwords or try common passwords, you must secure the network so no one can access it from outside the company. You would be positively amazed at the number of organizations that are still unsecured.

The best way to keep your network secure is to have no direct links to the Internet. This means you should disable IP routing if it's enabled. This can be done by selecting Network from the Control Panel. Then go to the Protocols tab and select TCP/IP. Once the TCP/IP dialog box is open, select the Routing tab. You will find only one option, Enable IP Forwarding (see Figure 7.1). Clear the check from that box.

FIGURE 7.1

Disabling IP Forwarding allows you to eliminate direct links to the Internet.

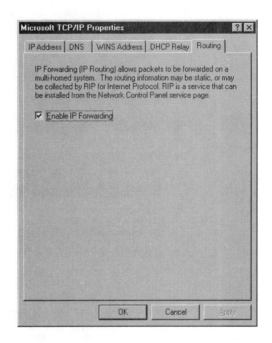

Now that the checkbox is cleared, the direct link to the Internet is severed and all communications must be established through the proxy server. However, this is not always the most desirable solution. Consider the case where hackers are not trying to get into your network, but simply trying to break your proxy server. In that case, disabling IP forwarding would not work. The best solution in this situation would be to click the Advanced button on the IP Address tab in the Microsoft TCP/IP Properties box. Then select Enable Security, and be selective about the ports that your proxy server listens to (see Figure 7.2).

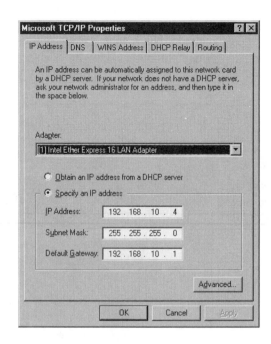

Click the Advanced button at the bottom of the screen and the Advanced IP Addressing dialog box shown in Figure 7.3 will appear. Click the Enable Security checkbox, then click Configure.

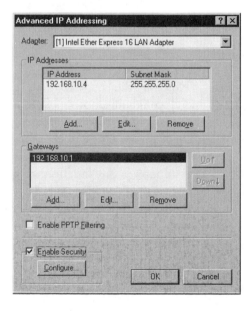

Once the TCP/IP Security screen appears, you may limit TCP/IP information accordingly. Typically, you do not have to worry about your internal users attacking your server. So for now, simply select the network adapter that is connected to the Internet. You may configure to permit or deny any TCP, UDP, or IP port or component, as shown in Figure 7.4.

FIGURE 7.4

TCP/IP Security for ports and protocols

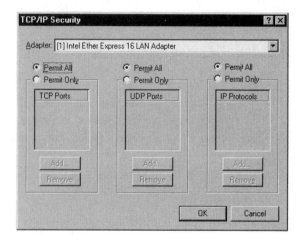

To minimize the resources drain on the server, any routing-related services such as RIP for IP should be removed.

On the surface, it might appear that management of inbound connections is not directly managed through Microsoft Proxy Server. That would be a false impression, as we will see in the next sections on Microsoft Proxy Server security and firewall implementation. Remember that regardless of all other mechanisms in place, it is very important that you configure security on inbound connections to protect your network from outside access.

Microsoft ✓ *Exam Objective*   **Given a scenario, decide which user interface to use to perform administrative tasks.**

In general, Proxy Server will pass configuration items to the Network Configuration (TCP/IP Configuration) tab, which defines which ports to accept or decline. When using packet filters or defining custom protocols for WinSock, your best bet is to use the IIS Manager to control port designations.

Although you may use IP routing on the Internet, it is important to either specify TCP/IP access restrictions on the NT Server or configure an access list (restrict functions) on the router. The most secure method is to not maintain a direct connection.

Adding unnecessary components to the proxy server may also cause security issues. For instance, you would not want to run all your major applications on this server, as there is the possibility of the added components expanding the server's functionality beyond your expectations. For example, when SQL is added, an IP interface is created that allows direct access to the server without the required use of a Microsoft Requester. Adding other products such as Steal Head or Microsoft Exchange may create additional unwanted risks. For this reason, you should always run the proxy server as lean as possible. When determining if an application can be placed on this system, always ask yourself if it creates a security hazard and if the application is mission-critical if the server goes down.

If you install RAS after Microsoft Proxy Server, IP routing will be enabled. You must disable IP routing even if you have done so before.

Windows NT Security and the Internet

If you have elected to maintain accessibility to the Internet by any mechanisms, including enabling routing, it is best to limit access by creating a new domain that is used specifically with Internet-accessed information. In this configuration, the domain would be known as a resource domain.

There are several advantages to creating this type of domain. Because Windows NT allows trusts among domains, the domain containing the proxy server can be configured so that it trusts the primary corporate master domain. This means that users' accounts can be assigned from the main domain and configured to access the proxy server's domain. Those trying to access your domain will be limited by a single-direction trust, which stops access prior to communication with the main domain. Assuming that the proxy server was configured as a PDC, additional servers can be added for e-mail, Web, FTP, and other services and managed from the main domain. In this way, Windows NT security aids Microsoft Proxy Server in creating a secure environment.

Tips for Security

Windows NT provides a fantastic security system. However, if neglected or misconfigured, even the best security system will break down. Throughout this chapter, we will explore many security topics in depth. The following material should be used as general guidelines when connecting your proxy server to the Internet:

- Enable access controls. When running the Web Proxy or WinSock Proxy services with access control enabled, the server is considered to be running in a secured configuration. This setting must be enabled to use password authentication.

- Reserve access to that which is required. Do not add users unnecessarily. Remember that all it takes is one user to compromise security.

- Limit inbound ports to those that are required. Do not allow all ports to be open. Refer to the SERVICES file for a complete list.

- Mandate such password requirements as minimum length, frequency of change, and use of numbers and letters. It is rare that a company, regardless of size, does not have at least one user who, given the opportunity, will use his or her name, login ID, or the word "password" for their password. These requirements can be set through the User Manager for the Domain utility.

- Define as few users as possible with administrator-level security. This will reduce the chance of a user with administrator clearance assigning rights with too little discretion or selecting a bad password.

- Use built-in accounts when feasible. Keep in mind that the default accounts are those used by the system for anonymous logons and are configured usually as IUSR_*systemname*. These names should be changed to unique names that are unlikely to be guessed. Also, the built-in accounts such as Administrator should be renamed so the login ID is not predictable.

- Use a browser that supports the maximum security abilities of Windows NT Challenge/Response. Internet Explorer has this support, while Netscape Navigator currently does not.

- Restrict user permissions by proxy service, then by share, and finally, by file level.

- Do not use Unlimited for Internet access. Most users only require HTTP or HTTP-secured access. Only when other applications have a requirement should security be authorized. Some applications such as Point-Cast, RealAudio, and VDO Live generate lots of traffic. It may be in your best interest not to clutter up corporate bandwidth with non–business-related applications.

- Refrain from allowing users to set DNS and gateway configurations at their workstations. This will prevent users from attempting to bypass the proxy server. The proxy server will perform all DNS lookups on the Internet for the client as well as deliver information to the correct gateway. If DHCP is in use, these settings should be removed from the server. The only time these setting should be used is if they are required on the internal network.

When using Proxy Server in its own domain, never use the same user name and password as specified in other domains.

Now that you are familiar with some of the more common security precautions, we recommend that you complete Exercise 7.1 to test your hands-on abilities.

EXERCISE 7.1

Using Web Proxy Security with Inbound Access

This exercise will take you through the process of securing a Web site by disabling anonymous user access. When a Web site is private, but is used through the Internet, disabling anonymous access will cause the user to be prompted for credentials. Note that, for security, the Web Proxy service is linked to the setting of the WWW service.

 1. From the Internet Services Manager, double-click the WWW service.

2. On the Service tab, clear the Allow Anonymous checkbox (in the Password Authentication section) and click OK.

3. Double-click the FTP service.

4. On the Services tab, clear the Allow Only Anonymous Connections checkbox.

5. Click OK and close the WWW Service Configuration window.

Securing Internet Services

Unlike inbound connections, outbound connections are configured almost exclusively through the IIS Manager. Inbound connections are slightly more complex because their abilities may span past the level of client configurations on (outbound) proxy services.

As you assign permissions to proxy clients, remember that you should only assign rights to clients that use services that they require. For example, if a client only needs WWW and FTP services, only provide permission to those protocols. It would be flawed thinking to add a service such as Gopher when it would never be used.

Filtering IP Packets

Perhaps the most powerful function for securing Proxy Server is the packet filter. Performing the actions of a firewall, the packet filter has the ability to statically or dynamically control data on the external interface. This means that the proxy server will evaluate inbound traffic before it has the chance to reach any resource. Dynamically filtering packets allows the proxy server to open and close ports on the fly while the filter adjusts for Proxy Server's needs. An administrator can disable this function and specify the valid ports. However, this tends to create configuration problems with applications. Unless you know the ports that all TCP/IP programs will use, you should enable dynamic packet filtering.

Microsoft ✓ *Exam* *Objective*

Use packet filtering to prevent unauthorized access. Tasks include:

- Using packet filtering to enable a specific protocol.
- Configuring packet filter alerting and logging.

Remember that because port controls are in place, you can disallow packets destine for a service such as SMTP, WWW servers, Web Proxy, Win-Sock Proxy, or Socks Proxy. For example, SMTP usually is linked to port 25. If port 25 is blocked, you cannot access SMTP information. When working with a dynamic filter, it is not necessary to unbind specific services from an external network adapter.

Dynamic filtering, in the context of a firewall, is sometimes referred to as *stateful* filtering.

In addition to dynamically filtering Proxy Server packets, this service can also filter IP fragments. To do this, click the Enable Filtering of IP Fragments box located on the Packet Filtering tab, which can be found by clicking the Security button on any of the proxy services. Filtering fragments is useful when filtering of packet or Datagram fragments is required. Combined, the packet filters prevent attacks from address spoofing, SYNs (synchronized aggression), and FRAGs (fragment or runt assaults).

To enable packet filtering, click any of the proxy services and then click the Security button. By default, you will be presented with the Packet Filters tab. Packet filtering can be enabled for inbound traffic, outbound traffic, or both (see Figure 7.5).

Packet filtering can define the direction of traffic, protocols, local ports, remote ports, and addresses. Because of this, certain types of traffic that are determined to be harmless are allowed to pass. For example, a Ping operates as ICMP traffic, not as TCP or UDP traffic. In a typical situation, the proxy server would not allow this type of traffic through. However, the packet filter allows for this type of exception and allows the administrator to determine if the information can pass. By default, all traffic is blocked except for those types of traffic listed in the exceptions list. If an exception to the filter does not appear in the list, as shown in Figure 7.5, it may be added by clicking the Add button. The screen shown in Figure 7.6 will appear.

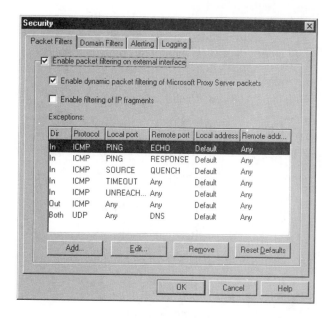

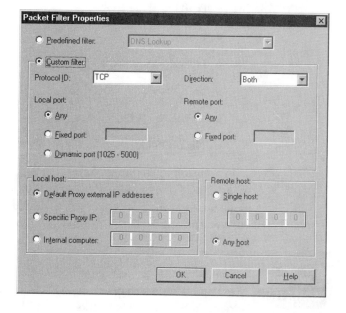

A number of predefined filters are provided within the service. To select a predefined service, simply click the radio button next to Predefined Filter, and then click the down arrow next to the drop-down box. The predefine list includes:

- DNS Lookup
- ICMP All Outbound
- ICMP Ping Response
- ICMP Ping Query
- ICMP SRC Quench
- ICMP Timeout
- ICMP Unreachable
- PPTP Call
- PPTP Receive
- SMTP
- POP3
- Identd
- HTTP Server (Port 80)
- HTTPS Server (Port 443)
- NetBIOS (WINS Client Only)
- NetBIOS (All)

In addition to enabling packet filtering, you may also be required to take other steps. For example, if we wanted to keep users from accessing NetBIOS name tables at the proxy server, we should disable NetBIOS to the external adapter and any links to a WINS server.

WARNING Some traffic types require multiple entries before they can operate. For example, Ping, which operates on ICMP, requires the controls listed above to respond to all conditions. Likewise, PPTP requires multiple filters.

When the predefined filter does not contain a function that you require, you may build your own custom filter. To do this, select Custom Filter and provide the protocol type, the direction of the communication, and the local and remote ports. Packet filters require that you define a local host computer on the internal network and the remote host system that you will be exchanging data with. The proxy server may be configured to use multiple external interfaces, each with multiple IP addresses. Note that there is a single default IP address assigned for each external interface.

If your filter does not appear in the predefined list, use the instructions in Exercise 7.2 to configure a custom filter. Remember that if the server becomes incorrectly configured by setting filters, you may always revert back to the old settings by clicking the Reset Defaults button on the Packet Filters tab.

EXERCISE 7.2

Building a Customized Packet Filter Exception

1. Open any of the proxy services (Web, WinSock, or Socks) and click Security on the Service tab.

2. Click the Custom Filter radio button.

3. The first item to configure is the Protocol ID. The protocol must be TCP, UDP, or ICMP.

4. Once the protocol has been selected, you must choose the direction in which communications will occur: In, Out, or Both.

5. Next, assign both local and remote port requirements. Local port requirements can be Any, Fixed, or Dynamic. Remote ports must be Any or Fixed. Fixed requires the port to be specified in the corresponding dialog box. Dynamic port control is used in conjunction with filtering and is automatically assigned a value between 1024 and 5000.

6. Once the basic filtering information has been established, both a local and a remote host must be specified. By default, the local host is set to the proxy external IP address. However, a specific address on the internal or external network can be defined by clicking the corresponding radio button and supplying an IP address.

7. The remote host can be defined as a single host by IP address or as Any. This completes the full definition of a packet filter exception. Click OK and you're done.

When setting packet filters, always consider that assignments are made to the server, not to users. Although you can have different proxy servers allowing different ports, you cannot make any assignments by user in this particular area. For this type of control, you must make changes to the permissions of the proxy service itself. Exercises 7.3 and 7.4 give you more experience working with packet filters.

EXERCISE 7.3

Enabling Packet Filters

As you have learned, packet filters are perhaps the most important element for securing a network. At this time, we will enable packet filters to control permitted traffic.

1. From the Internet Services Manager, double-click the Web Proxy service and click Security.

2. The Packet Filter tab should appear by default. If it doesn't, select it.

3. Next, click the checkbox to Enable Packet Filtering on External Interface.

4. Verify that the Enable Dynamic Packet Filtering option is also enabled. Then click OK.

5. You should be returned to the Web Proxy Service tab. Click OK to apply the changes and you're done.

EXERCISE 7.4

Changing the Packet Filters

Building on the previous exercise, we will make changes to the packet filters list.

1. From the Internet Services Manager, double-click the Web Proxy service and click Security.

2. The Packet Filter tab should appear by default. If it doesn't, select it.

3. Click the Add button to place an additional exception in the list.

4. Select Predefine Protocol and click the down arrow.

5. Select the entry called DNS Lookup, then select the local host computer that will exchange packets with a remote host computer. Under Local Host, do one of the following:

   ■ To allow the default IP address for each external interface of the Proxy Server computer to exchange packets, click Default Proxy External IP Addresses.

   ■ To allow a specific IP address for an external interface of the Proxy Server computer to exchange packets, click Specific Proxy IP and type a valid IP address.

   ■ To allow a specific internal computer behind Proxy Server to exchange packets, click Internal Computer and type a valid IP address. In this case, select Allow the Default IP Address for each external interface.

6. Click OK.

7. You should be returned to the Web Proxy Service tab. Click OK again to apply the changes.

8. Repeat the above steps, but this time enable SMTP by selecting the appropriate entry in step 5. You should enter either a valid server's IP address or 192.168.254.254, an address from the private class C range.

9. When completed, click Reset Defaults on the Security tab to restore the original filters.

Setting Packet Filter Alerts

When the packet filter is enabled, alerts may be set to notify an administrator of a possible security breach, an attempted security breach, dropped packets, and suspicious network events. For example, if someone is attempting to infiltrate the system and gain access to an unserviced port, an alert can be created that will warn the administrator of this. To enable alerts, first verify that packet filtering has been enabled. To do this, click the Security button on the Service tab of any proxy service. Once you have verified that packet filtering is enabled, click the Alerting tab.

The Altering tab shown in Figure 7.7 can only be accessed if packet filtering is enabled. Based on the event of Rejected Packets (packets dropped and frame anomalies), Protocol Violations (suspicious activities of packets that do not follow the accepted protocol format), or Disk Full occurrences, an administrative notice will be generated.

FIGURE 7.7

Configuring security alerts

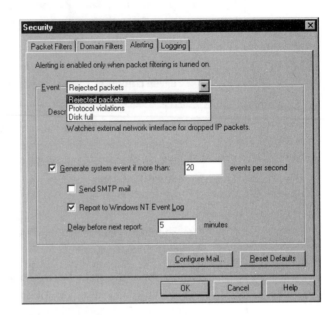

The alert specified by a given event will be reported if more than a designated number of occurrences happen within one second. The alert will be reported through e-mail and/or the system event log, depending on the options checked. To keep alert floods from occurring, alerts are delayed by a given period of time according to the value specified in the Delay Before Next Report dialog box. This box is accessed on the Alerting tab of the Security section, which can, in turn, be accessed on the Service tab of any of the proxy services.

E-Mail and Filter Alerts

When sending alerts via e-mail, user and server information must be supplied. It is recommended that you use an internal e-mail server, so if the external port is under attack, sending e-mail will not be a problem. By clicking the Configure Mail button, the administrator can set e-mail information. The Configure Mail Alerting dialog box shown in Figure 7.8 will appear.

FIGURE 7.8

Configure e-mail for
packet filter alerts in the
Configure Mail Alerting
dialog box.

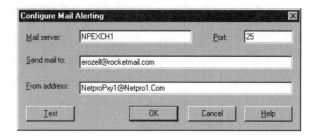

Complete the dialog box by filling in the Mail Server, Port, Send Mail To, and From Address boxes. Since some mail systems disable SMTP relay services (typically on port 25), click the Test button to verify functionality. Note that no special functionality or rights are required when sending alerts via e-mail. Use the instructions in Exercise 7.5 to set up an alert.

Remember that you will need a valid e-mail account, a MAPI profile, client software, and accessibility for the e-mail alerts to function. Simply typing information in the e-mail screen will not create an account or configure a client to read it.

EXERCISE 7.5

Setting an Alert

After completing all earlier exercises, use this exercise to extend current services.

1. In the Internet Services Manager, double-click the Web Proxy service and click Security.

2. Select the Alerting tab, and in the Event drop-down box select Protocol Violations.

3. Select to send an alert if more than one event per second occurs, as shown on the Alerting tab in the Figure 7.7.

4. By default, Send SMTP Mail should not be selected and Report to Windows NT should be checked. Click Send SMTP Mail, then select the Configure Mail button. Assuming that you have this service (SMTP mail), type in the name of your mail server, the port on which SMTP is accessed (usually 25), the name of the account that you are sending mail to, and the name of the account the mail is from.

EXERCISE 7.5 (CONTINUED FROM PREVIOUS PAGE)

5. When you're done, click OK to close the Mail Configuration screen. Then Click OK once to return to the Web Proxy screen and once more to return to the IIS Manager screen.

6. Stop the Web Proxy service and then restart it for the changes to take effect.

Logging Packet Filter Events

Aside from the alerts that can be used to inform an administrator of potential security problems, a log can be kept that keeps track of packet filter events. As with other services, logging is an important part of securing the server. In short, the logging options provide audit abilities to Internet access.

To enable the packet filter logs, click any of the proxy services and select the Security button. The event logging functions of the packet filter service can be configured almost identically to the way the Web, WinSock, and Socks Proxy services are configured.

The packet filter logs will record service, remote, local, filter, and packet information. Each entry in the log will include connection information for each end of a connection. Remember that a source will usually indicate where the network resource data is taken from, while destination tends to refer to the proxy client where data is being sent. The following entries are stored in all logs:

- Date: The day the packet was received (service info fields)

- Time: The time the packet was received (service info fields)

- SRC IP: The IP address of the originating remote system (remote info fields)

- SRC Port: The remote service port being used to open the TCP, UDP, or ICMP connection (remote info fields)

- Protocol: An entry listing that used TCP, UDP, or ICMP to create a connection (remote info fields)

- Dest IP: The IP address of the internal local system (local info fields)

- Dest Port: The port number that the destination (local) computer uses when servicing a TCP, UDP, or ICMP connection (local info fields)

- Action: A description that informs you that the packet was either accepted or dropped. By default, only dropped packets are logged (filter info fields).

- Interface: The interface on which the packet was received (filter info fields)

If verbose logging has been selected, the following two entries are also stored. Note that only a portion of the Raw IP packet is stored. A registry entry defines the number of bytes to keep in the log. An administrator should exercise caution when using verbose mode because logs can become very large.

- Raw IP Header (Hex): The complete header of the packet generating the alert (packet info fields)

- Raw IP Packet (Hex): A listing of the number of bytes in the packet generating the alert (packet info fields)

Microsoft ✔ Exam Objective   Configure auditing.

Please refer to the *Logging Web Proxy Activities* section in Chapter 6 for exact details on the logging functions.

Like the Web and WinSock logging functions, data may be stored in text files or in an SQL database. The only major difference that you should notice is that the log file names for packet filtering are as follows:

- Daily   PF*yymmdd*.log

- Weekly   PFW*yymmw*.log

- Monthly   PFM*yymm*.log

A sample screen is shown in Figure 7.9. You should again note that the Logging tab for packet filtering is virtually identical to the Logging screen that you configured for the other proxy services. Aside from the names of the files, you should also note that if the Stop All Services If Disk Full option is selected, all proxy services will be stopped in the event of a full disk. With regard to the other proxy services, this option will only stop itself. Practice working with logs by running through Exercise 7.6.

FIGURE 7.9

Packet Filtering logs

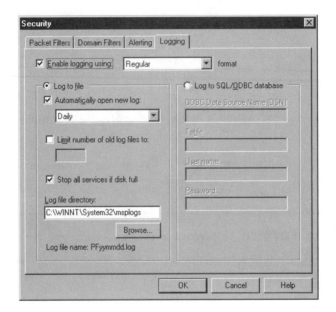

EXERCISE 7.6

Enabling Logging

This exercise demonstrates how log files are generated. If you are already familiar with log files and controls, you can skip this exercise.

1. From the Internet Services Manager, double-click the Web Proxy service and click Security.

2. Select the Logging tab, and in the Format drop-down box, select Verbose.

> **EXERCISE 7.6 (CONTINUED FROM PREVIOUS PAGE)**
>
> **3.** In the Automatically Open New Log drop-down box, select Daily.
>
> **4.** Click OK to return to the Web Proxy screen, and then click OK again.
>
> When you have a chance, review the log files. Remember that they are called PFYYMMDD.LOG and are stored in C:\WINNT\SYSTEM32\MSPLOGS. Once you have checked the logs, you should consider disabling them to preserve storage space.

Granting and Denying Access to Sites

When planning a site, it is useful to determine the way in which you will use the Internet in advance. Unlike permissions, which apply to users or groups, access to Web sites is determined using a filter to grant or deny access to a specific Internet resource.

Microsoft ✓ ***Exam Objective***   **Grant or restrict access to specific Internet sites for outbound users.**

The Domain Filters tab of the Security dialog box (see Figure 7.10) is used to block Internet access for all users to or from specific sites. There are only two modes of filtering: granting or denying access for all. The sites, group of computers, and domains that appear in the excepted list allow exceptions to the rule of "all or nothing" access. This tab can be used to keep users from accessing sites containing pornography, stock market information, or other information that a company may not want its employees to view. For example, if a company has a problem with employees who would rather read the online edition of the *Wall Street Journal* than do their jobs, they can restrict users' access to this site. If a company does not want employees to have access to stock market pages, they can censor sites by IP address or URL. Some companies are very conservative in the amount of Web access they want their employees to have and only allow access to an approved list of sites. You may also select to deny all sites, then create a set of filters that allows selected sites to be accessed.

FIGURE 7.10

Management of site filters

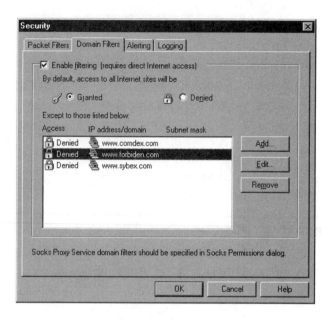

Microsoft's Domain Filter dialog box offers the following options:

Enable Filtering (Requires Direct Internet Access)   Selecting this checkbox will determine whether or not this function is enabled. Enabling the filtering will require all requests listed to be processed to meet the criteria in the order in which they are listed.

Granted   This grants access to all Internet sites.

Denied   This denies access to all Internet sites.

Exception to Those Listed Below   The systems listed here are noted as exceptions to the Granted and Denied functions. This is the allowed or disallowed filter that lists the sites clients may or may not access.

Microsoft Proxy Server's default allows all users full access to any site. To enable filtering, simply click Enable Filtering (Requires Direct Internet Access).

There are three options when specifying access to Internet resources that are shown in the Deny Access To dialog box. First, you may specify a single computer according to its IP address. Unless you see a site that is being abused, you should try not to use this option because it's like trying to cut the outfield grass at Dodgers Staduim with a pair of scissors. Next, you may choose to specify a group of computers. This can be accomplished by selecting an IP address and a subnet mask. The node portion, as designated by the subnet mask, is ignored. For more information on subnet masks and the networks they define, refer back to Chapter 2.

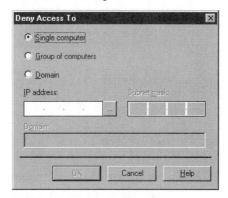

Finally, and most useful, you may choose restrictions by domain. The domain function is good in that many companies have their Internet resources spread over many different networks. However, the original flaw with domains was that they were easily bypassed by using an IP address and assigning an alias, such as what can be done with a host file. However, with Microsoft Proxy Server 2.0, you only need to specify the domain, not the domain and IP address. When a request specifies a DNS, the system name is resolved to an IP address, and both the DNS name and IP address are searched for in the Domain Filtering site list. If the client generates a request with an IP address rather than a DNS name, the IP address is searched for in the Domain Filtering site list. If at least one entry in the site list contains a domain name, the request's IP address is converted to a DNS name by doing a DNS reverse resolution, and the domain name is searched for in the site list.

If you look in Microsoft's online documentation, you will note that is says both the Domain and IP address are required to completely filter a domain. However, Microsoft has noted this as an error in their technical database. To control WinSock Proxy access to Internet sites, you only are required to create a filter for the domain name. It is unnecessary to create an additional domain filter for the IP address of an Internet site.

The exceptions list is not perfect, although it has gotten better with Proxy Server 2.0, since you no longer are required to list the IP address in addition to the domain name extension. There are many back door routes that can be used to bypass this list. For example, there are other proxy servers on the Internet that you could connect to that would be allowed by your proxy server and which could be used to access the excluded systems. For this reason, as well as companies having multiple IP address ranges, you are often best to exclude access using double entries that name both the domain name and the IP address, even though the proxy server should technically handle this internally.

Generally, filtering sites to control user access is like brushing your teeth while eating cookies. It is very difficult to keep up. While this function is generally good for blocking sites, it is typically a self-defeating task in implementation. Exercise 7.7 will take you through the steps of enabling Internet site access filters.

A wildcard may be used in the Domain Name box to exclude or include all objects. To use the wildcard, simply place an asterisk (*) in the Domain Path line.

EXERCISE 7.7

Enabling Internet Access Filtering

To enable filtering for Internet resources use the following steps:

1. From the Start menu, select Programs ➤ Microsoft Internet Server ➤ Internet Server Manager.

2. Click the Web Proxy service in the listing for the server that you want to administer.

3. In the Properties pull-down menu select Service Properties.

4. When the Web Proxy Properties screen appears, click the Security button and select the Domain Filters tab.

5. Verify that the Enable Filtering checkbox has been checked and select either Grant or Deny as the default for all Internet access.

6. Click the Add button to place sites or specific resources in the Except to Those Listed Below list.

EXERCISE 7.7 (CONTINUED FROM PREVIOUS PAGE)

7. When either the Grant Access To or the Deny Access To dialog box appears, select one of the following:

Single Computer Add either the IP address or DNS names. Click the button with the ellipses to enter the IP address or the DNS name. You will need either the computer's fully-qualified domain name or its IP address.

Group of Computers Enter a network IP address and subnet mask. You will need the group's IP address and subnet mask.

Domain Type the domain as applicable to the Internet site. (for example, **www. sybex.com**). You will need the domain name and the path.

8. Click OK to close the dialog box. Then click OK or Apply to set the changes in motion.

As you may have concluded, using the domain name and path can also be used to exclude a single computer, multiple computers, or the entire domain.

Exercise 7.8 takes you through the steps of using Web Proxy security to filter sites, while Exercise 7.9 explains how to verify security.

EXERCISE 7.8

Using Web Proxy Security to Filter Sites

1. From the Internet Services Manager, double-click the Web Proxy service and click the Security button.

2. On the Domain Filters tab, check the Enable Filtering box, choose the Granted option, and then click Add.

3. Select to deny access to a domain, type **acme.com** in the Domain box, and click OK.

4. Restart either the server or all Internet services to invoke the changes.

EXERCISE 7.9

Verifying Web Proxy Security

1. From a client system, log in as **Guest** and configure your Web browser to use your proxy server on port 80 for all protocols.

2. From the Web browser, enter **http://servername**. You should receive a forbidden access message.

3. Repeat step 2 with the FTP service (**ftp://servername**). You should receive the same forbidden access message.

4. Repeat steps 1 through 3 logging in as **Administrator**. You should have normal access.

Port Security and WinSock

Up until this point, security has been focused around applications that apply to both WinSock Proxy Server and Web Proxy Server. WinSock Proxy Server also has an additional indirect security function that allows an administrator to limit the functions of a Windows Socket application by designating valid ports. While working with ports, it is important to understand that the valid range for Microsoft Proxy Server includes all positive numbers up to 65,535 (2^{16}). The original port specification only allowed eight bits, which produced a range of 0 to 255.

Recall that in Chapter 6 we discussed that as a standard, most systems follow the port specification as outlined in the SERVICES file. Changing ports can take this ability further for services and can limit the port ranges. To limit the range, follow the steps in Exercise 7.10. Practice working with port security by following the directions in Exercise 7.11.

EXERCISE 7.10

Limiting Ranges

1. From the Start menu, select Programs, then the Microsoft Internet Server folder, and open Internet Server Manager.

2. Click the WinSock Proxy service in the listing for the server that you want to administer.

3. On the Properties pull-down menu, select Service Properties.

EXERCISE 7.10 (CONTINUED FROM PREVIOUS PAGE)

4. When the Winsock Proxy Properties screen appears, select the Protocols tab.

5. Click the Add button and the Protocol Definition screen will appear.

6. In the Port Ranges for Subsequent Connections dialog box, click Add.

7. Input the port (single) or range of ports to use.

8. In the Type section, select TCP.

9. Click OK to close the Port Range Definition dialog box.

10. Click OK to close the Protocol Definition dialog box.

11. Click either OK or Apply to set the changes in motion.

When creating WinSock protocol definitions, you may create any service you want, provided that the program you are using supports the functions that you define.

Microsoft ✓ *Exam* *Objective*

Choose a secure access strategy for various situations. Access includes outbound access by users to the Internet and inbound access to your Web site. Considerations include:

- Translating addresses from the internal network to the Local Address Table (LAT)
- Controlling anonymous access
- Controlling access by known users and groups
- Setting protocol permissions
- Auditing protocol access
- Setting Microsoft Windows NT® security parameters

Microsoft ✓ ***Exam Objective***

Grant or restrict access to the Internet for selected outbound users and groups who use the various Proxy Server services to access the Internet.

EXERCISE 7.11

Using WinSock Proxy Security with Outbound User Access

1. From the Internet Services Manager, double-click the WinSock Proxy Service.

2. On the Protocols tab, click Add and type **FTP Out** in the Protocol Name box and **20** in the Port field in the Initial Connection area.

3. Add port ranges for TCP/IP. To select the defaults, click OK twice.

4. On the Permissions tab, click Enable Permissions, then click Add and select Administrators for FTP.

5. With a live Internet account for the proxy server, attempt to open an FTP session (from a Windows DOS prompt command line) to www.microsoft.com. Type either **FTP www.microsoft.com** or **FTP**, then type **Open www.microsoft.com**. Be sure that you are at a client configured to use WinSock Proxy and are logged in as the Administrator. You should gain access.

6. Log in again as **Guest** and repeat Step 3. Access should be denied.

Port Security and the Web Proxy Service

There is not much that an administrator can do in terms of securing a proxy server for Web Proxy service port usage. In basic usage, the service only operates over port 80. While working in its normal capacity and using packet filters as required, the service is secure. However, in some cases, administrators feel the need to change the Web Proxy service port.

The Web Proxy service uses the same port as the WWW service (port 80) as its listen-on port. This value is stored in the Registry and can be manipulated through the IIS Manager by using the following instructions:

1. Start the Internet Service Manager and select the WWW service on the server with the Web Proxy service installed.

2. The Service tab should appear. Locate the TCP Port box and type in a new port number that is not in use by other applications in your environment.

3. Click OK to accept the changes. Then stop and restart the WWW service that you just changed.

If you have already installed Microsoft Proxy Server, you will need to make additional changes before your users can access the server. Each client must be updated to use the new port that you specified for Web Proxy services. Perhaps the easiest way to do this if you are using the entire proxy client suite is to edit the WebProxyPort value in the MSPCLNT.INI client configuration file. Otherwise, this port value may be specified during installation for clients using automatic configuration.

User Validation and Authentication

User validation is a process by which users are either granted or denied access to a requested resource. This process can be as simple as allowing anyone access anonymously, or as complex as using a name and password that are encoded and checked against a database for access rights.

Password authentication on the proxy server varies by service. Each type of proxy service allows certain features, which may affect security. For example, the Web Proxy service uses the same password authentication methods for client requests as those used in configuring the WWW service. These authentication methods include anonymous logon, basic authentication, and Windows NT Challenge/Response authentication, and are used to communicate between the client and the proxy server. Enabling and disabling these controls will affect the type of browser that can be used, if access control can be enabled, and so forth. Note that basic authentication is only available on the Web Proxy service, while the WinSock Proxy service uses Windows NT Challenge/Response authentication exclusively. However, when access control is disabled, it is considered anonymous. The Socks Proxy does not use any authentication and relies on a client's IP address for defining rights.

When working in a secure environment or converting to one, generally you will find that the following actions will take place:

- Anonymous authentication will be disabled.

- Accounts will be created for each user if they don't exist in the domain.

- Access control will be enabled.

- Explicit rights and permissions will be granted to each user or group.

As you add permissions, assignments should be done by group rather than by individual user. For example, create a group called "Web users" and assign them the appropriate access. This will allow an administrator to quickly create a user account without having to access multiple servers and utilities to assign various access rights.

The HTTP protocol allows password authentication only on a client-to-server basis through a single Proxy Server computer. Proxy Server-to-Proxy Server authentication should be set up when supporting proxy servers in a chained configuration.

Microsoft Windows NT Challenge/Response Authentication

Microsoft Windows NT provides an excellent set of controls for validating users and helping to create a secure environment. As such, Microsoft Proxy Server can utilize NT security to validate users to use services. This is done by forcing Microsoft Windows NT Challenge/Response authentication.

Challenge/Response authentication is an elaborate system in which a user name and password are sent in an encrypted format. This extra degree of security allows Microsoft to bypass the problem of sending passwords through the network as required with clear-text authentication. Challenge/Response authentication is supported by Microsoft Internet Explorer 3.0 and later versions. However, it is recommended that if you plan to use this type of authentication, you use Microsoft Internet Explorer 4.0. Otherwise it is possible that you may observe rejected client configuration scripts or incorrect HTTPS pages that use SLL. If a browser does not support Challenge/Response authentication and no other authentication is enabled, the user will be denied access to the proxy service. For this reason, it is suggested that if you are not using Internet Explorer 4.0, you enable basic authentication as well.

Challenge/Response authentication operates as a transparent logon procedure. In a challenge-and-response scenario, the client system uses its established user logon information to identify itself to the server. The user is not prompted to enter these user credentials. Instead, the information is presented after the user first logs on to a Windows NT–based server. The credentials are held at the client and sent to a resource as required. A client logon request is generated when a client request is sent to a server by using IIS or Microsoft Proxy Server. The logon authentication process is used to determine if a client is allowed to use a requested server resource.

Challenge/Response authentication works only where the client and server computers are located in the same or trusted domains. There are two ways to enable Challenge/Response authentication. Use the following "easy way" to configure Challenge/Response authentication for all users. You can also use the "hard way" to allow anonymous logon for specific users and require Challenge/Response authentication for all other users. Exercises 7.12 and 7.13 will guide you through the steps of configuring users to operate with Challenge/Response authentication.

EXERCISE 7.12

Configuring Challenge/Response Authentication the Easy Way (For All Users)

1. Start the Internet Service Manager, and then double-click the computer name for your WWW service.

2. In the Password Authentication section, select the Windows NT Challenge/Response checkbox and clear the Allow Anonymous checkbox.

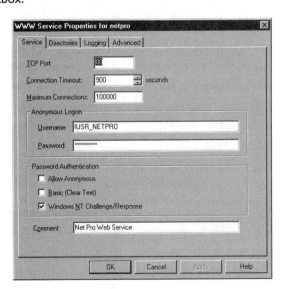

EXERCISE 7.12 (CONTINUED FROM PREVIOUS PAGE)

3. Click Apply and then OK.

4. Double-click the computer name for your Web Proxy service.

5. Click the Permissions tab and set access control for users as follows:

   ■ Clear the Enable Access Control checkbox to allow all users access to all Web Proxy services.

   ■ Select the Enable Access Control checkbox to set limited user access to Web Proxy services. You need to assign user permissions for access rights to each service (FTP, Gopher, WWW, and Secure).

6. Click Apply and then OK.

EXERCISE 7.13

Configuring Challenge/Response Authentication the Hard Way (Per Users Access)

1. Start the Internet Service Manager and then double-click the computer name for your WWW service.

2. In the Password Authentication section select the Windows NT Challenge/Response checkbox, mark the Allow Anonymous checkbox, and clear the Basic (Clear Text) checkbox.

3. Click Apply and then OK.

4. Double-click the computer name next to the Web Proxy service.

5. Click the Permissions tab and select the Enable Access Control checkbox.

6. Add users to the permissions list for Web Proxy services.

7. To allow anonymous user access, add the IUSR_*systemname* user name to the permissions list for Web Proxy services.

8. Click Apply and then OK

As you have seen, Windows NT maintains a tight integration with Microsoft Proxy Server. With the power to authenticate items that were previously unsecured, you now have the ability to take on items such as using Challenge/Response authentication for UNIX access (proxy server-to-proxy server) or to reach other segments of your internal network.

Basic Authentication

The most common type of resource security, basic authentication is supported by all Web browsers and is the easiest security mechanism to implement. However, despite easy implementation and wide support, basic authentication comes with a few problems that can make it somewhat unappealing. As a standard HTTP mechanism, basic authentication transmits secure data as non-encrypted (but encoded) or clear-text data. Under most circumstances this is not a problem. However, if a network link is being monitored with a network sniffer or another packet filtering mechanism, it is possible that others may read your password. Unfortunately, platforms other than Windows only support this authentication.

WARNING   Basic authentication uses a weak encoding scheme that can be read using a variety of utilities, such as UUdecode. Unlike a strong encryption technology that can't be decoded, basic authentication can be decoded.

The standard for basic authentication requires that the client be responsible for prompting the user for user name and password credentials. Once credentials are supplied, they are encoded and forwarded to the server. Regardless of the platform that generates the encoded information, the user name must exist as an account on the system running IIS or in a trusted domain of that system. Accounts that are accessing the server from a trusted domain must use username=domain\account as the format for supplying their credentials.

When accessing a remote server, basic authentication will be forwarded through a standard HTTP protocol in clear-text format. While the proxy server may not use this authentication for itself, the authentication can be sent remotely. The users will simply see a prompt for a name when the request is returned for authentication.

Anonymous Authentication

Anonymous authentication is not actually an authentication type, but rather a way in which a guest user can log on and access a system. The most common place that we see this type of access is with the Web and with FTP sites (as with Microsoft's IIS FTP and WWW services). Anonymous logons occur when a user accesses a system and supplies the user name **Anonymous** and their e-mail address as the password. Most Web browsers will perform this function automatically.

> To allow anonymous only access to the proxy server, disable access control and select Allow Anonymous Authentication for the IIS WWW service.

The anonymous account is created during the installation of IIS and has limited privileges on the system. Internally, the account is called IUSR_*systemname* where *systemname* is the name of the system. By default, this account is granted permission to the Web Proxy service. The user does not need to be assigned further user permissions in the Web Proxy service. The anonymous user account can be changed to a different name. However, to keep full compatibility, the replacement account should be able to log on locally to perform all IIS functions.

> When using an array of proxy servers, anonymous user rights will not replicate correctly because the user account will vary from system to system in the SAM database. Instead, use the Everyone account in its place when you want anonymous access to a local IIS server or desire to authenticate users as they access the proxy server. Verify user rights individually after you change anonymous user rights.

Microsoft Proxy Server extends the use of the anonymous account and uses it for guest access. Anonymous access can be granted to both the WinSock and Web proxy services by disabling Access Control. The Socks Proxy never logs users in or authenticates users by password. Rather, it functions by allowing or disallowing systems according to their IP address.

> When Allow Anonymous is the only checkbox enabled in the WWW service, Access Control will automatically be disabled for the Web Proxy service.

When the Allow Anonymous checkbox is cleared and basic authentication is enabled, you must grant user permission before users can access the Internet by using the Web Proxy service. If you use both anonymous and another authentication when access control is enabled, you must assign rights to the IUSR_*systemname* account. If no rights are assigned to the IUSR_*systemname* account, anonymous rights will not exist. Note that if the anonymous account is enabled, users will automatically access the system without being prompted for a password. However, at that stage of control, it would be just as simple to disable access control, unless you were restricting the use of services to everyone.

If Allow Anonymous is disabled, either Basic or Challenge Response is enabled and Access Control is disabled. Only members of the Windows NT Administrators group will have access to the Web Proxy Server.

When working with the WinSock Proxy, enabling Access Control will disable anonymous usage.

If a user is going to use Internet Explorer to go through Proxy Server, he or she receives an "Access denied" message. On other Web browsers, the user is prompted to log on but the logon process eventually fails. The user does not have Execute permission to the SCRIPTS directory at the Windows NT file system (NTFS) level or on the SCRIPTS directory. The SCRIPTS directory contains a filter .DLL that you need to execute.

Data Encryption

While we are on the topic of access control and securing an environment with Microsoft Proxy Server, we would not be thorough if we didn't bring up the topic of data encryption. Microsoft Proxy Server utilizes security that is identical to what IIS uses. As such, user login information when used with a supporting client application such as Internet Explorer will fully protect authentication. Remember that the Web Proxy establishes a tunnel by which controlled data is sent.

Microsoft Proxy Server also supports secure connections via HTTPS and HTTP with SSL. Using this protocol, all communication with a client is encrypted prior to being sent. With basic HTTP authentication and SSL, both the user name and the password are encrypted prior to transmission. For further request authentication, the ISAPI extensions can be applied to a system.

Granting and Revoking Permissions to Clients

Perhaps the most practical method for controlling users is assigning them rights to use the various proxy services. For example, if all members of the accounting team should not be using the Web for any reason, they will have no rights to any services. On the other hand, if the executive staff requires access to everything, rights should be applied accordingly. The process to add or remove client permissions is fairly straightforward. Set user security as follows:

1. From the Start Menu, select Internet Service Manager from under either the Information Server or the Proxy Server Program group.

2. Select the Web Proxy Server for the server that you wish to administer, and select Service Properties from the Properties menu.

3. After the Web Proxy Service screen appears, click the Permissions tab. Permission assignments will not work if the Enable Access Control box is not checked.

4. Add or remove users as required.

5. In the Protocol drop-down list select the service that you would like to grant access to.

6. Click the Edit button and then the Add button. Then select the group or user you would like to add rights for.

7. When you're done, click OK. The users or groups will appear in the Grant Access To dialog box. After user rights have been added, the Add Users and Groups dialog box will appear.

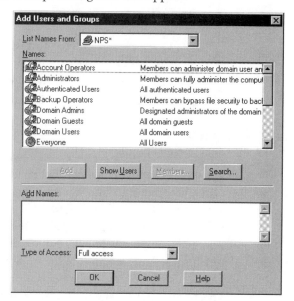

To remove granted access rights, simply click the group or user that you would like to drop and click the Remove button. You will not be prompted to verify your actions, so be sure to watch what you are doing. Follow the instructions in Exercise 7.14 to practice using Web Proxy security with outbound user access.

EXERCISE 7.14

Using Web Proxy Security with Outbound User Access

   1. From the Internet Services Manager, double-click the Web Proxy service.

   2. On the Permissions tab, click Enable Permissions, then click Add and select Administrators. (This will allow only administrators to use the service.) If your Internet browser does not support proxy authentication, you will also have to add IUSR_*systemname* to the permissions list. Note that when adding IUSR_*systemname*, permissions will be ignored.

EXERCISE 7.14 (CONTINUED FROM PREVIOUS PAGE)

3. Repeat step 2 with the FTP service.

4. Double-click the FTP service.

5. Complete this exercise by testing an account that is a member of the Administrator's group and one account that is not. You should note a difference, as stated in step 2, when IUSR_*systemname* is used.

Socks Security

While the Socks Proxy seems somewhat archaic when compared to WinSock Proxy, you must remember that this is the standard on which improvements have been built. Unlike WinSock, Socks supports virtually all client platforms including DOS (with required add-on software), Windows, Macintosh, and UNIX. WinSock merely supports the Windows platform. Also, while Socks does not support Windows NT Challenge/Response authentication, it uses Identification Protocol (the Identd Simulation service) authentication to maintain communication with clients. For example, suppose that a client was connecting to an FTP site or IRC session and the Internet server required the client to have a unique name for tracking purposes. The Identd Simulation service would provide this. The service is contained in IDENTD.EXE, found on the Proxy Server distribution media. This service generates a random, false user name to those Internet services that would normally block the connection if the identification could not be established.

The Identd Simulation service must be installed manually. Once installed, the service will start automatically when the server is restarted. You can view its boot options in the Control Panel under Services. Installing the Identd service is simple and straightforward:

1. From the proxy server, double-click My Computer, and then select a drive to which you would like to install the service.

2. Click the right mouse button and select New Folder. The folder (or directory, for you "old school" people) should be called IDENTD.

3. Double-click your CD-ROM drive in the My Computer window.

4. Open the IDENTD directory and select the subdirectory relating to your version of Windows.

5. Copy IDENTD.EXE to the IDENTD directory on the server.

6. Open a DOS box, then change to the IDENTD directory on the server.

7. Type **identd –install**.

8. After the command completes, type **net start identd**.

As a security precaution, you may want to create a packet filter for the Identd services. The packet filter should use TCP and port 113 in a bi-directional format. We will discuss how to configure packet filters later on.

Publishing to the Internet

When installed, Microsoft Proxy Server changes the configuration of the IIS installation such that requests from the Internet are ignored based on the adapter installed on the Internet. However, requests that are sent from intranet clients (sent to the LAN adapter on the private side) are still serviced.

Although secure, Microsoft Proxy Server was not originally designed or intended for Internet publishing. However, as the product has evolved, additional safeguards have been added to allow relatively safe Internet publishing. When working with Internet publishing, your best bet for security is to assume that there are no safeguards in place. In this way, maximum security is most likely to be maintained.

The main purpose of Microsoft Proxy Server is to manage connections to Internet resources from clients. In its secondary capacity, Microsoft Proxy Server has the ability to impersonate a Web server by reversing the proxy functions so Internet users become clients. Information can then safely be relayed to a system in the private network. However, the safety of the system is relative to the Web server's content. If active pages, CGI scripts, or other materials that can dynamically change a Web page are present, there is always the possibility that the page may be exploited in some way that was not tested. For this reason, it is suggested that you do not use mission-critical systems as Web servers. A preferred solution is simply for Internet Publishing to establish a small network that contains any resources that will be published on the Internet. Refer to the Figure 7.11 for a visual interpretation.

If your company does not have the resources to establish a separate network, it is recommended that you consider the use of a separate proxy server for inbound requests. The theory is that separating components as much as possible creates a situation that is more secure. Ideally, bouncing Internet requests between proxy servers and eventually to a Web server makes it harder to determine a network's structure. However, this still can introduce

FIGURE 7.11

A network between
networks

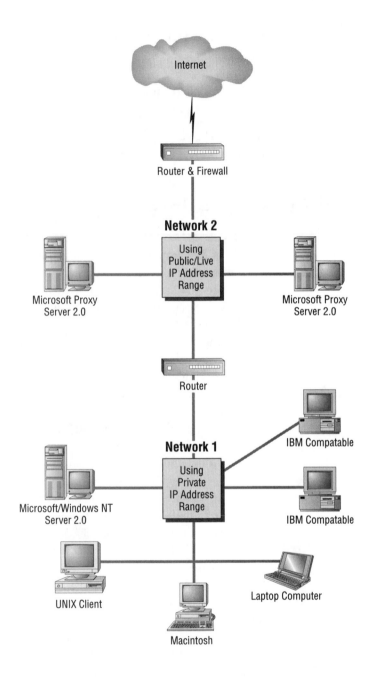

security issues. For this reason, when Proxy Server is installed to a system with IIS, the external port is disabled for listening to inbound traffic.

Another thought for publishing a Web page is to have your ISP provide the Web server. This is usually included in the price of their normal service. Typically, they start with five megabytes of storage and move up from there. Your Web page is published as an HTML file on the ISP's server. The DNS then points to the directory just as if it were the server at your site. In many cases, it is actually cheaper to buy this service from an ISP because bandwidth costs and other associated expenses are not your responsibility.

Enabling Internet Publishing

There are two methods for publishing to the Internet: reverse proxying and reverse hosting. Reverse proxying listens to requests from the Internet, then forwards them accordingly to a publishing server. Reverse hosting performs the same function as reverse proxying except that data is sent via an alternate route according to its destination path. In either case, as far as the remote client can tell, no proxy server is in place or is talking directly to the Web server. Figure 7.12 highlights the options that are available to control inbound requests to the Web server. The fact that the client is not talking directly to the server will be virtually indistinguishable.

FIGURE 7.12

The Web Proxy Publishing tab

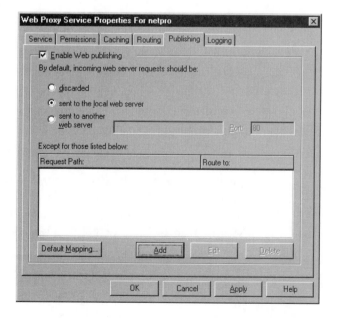

Implement Web publishing to enable reverse proxying.

Implement reverse hosting.

Before determining how to route Web requests, first consider the overall policy of the server. You should decide that all incoming Web requests either be discarded, sent to the local server, or sent to another Web server. After this determination has been made, you should then set the exceptions mappings as shown in Figure 7.13.

FIGURE 7.13

Configuring the proxy server to publish Web pages

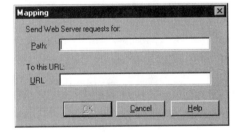

When an exception is encountered, the mapping of the request to an alternate route will allow some safeguarding of semi-sensitive material. For example, if a request is made for a certain URL such as http://www.sybex.com/ secrets, it could be redirected to a Web page that provides the author's home phone number. Since the /secrets area is not listed on any public page, it could be used to access semi-sensitive information that is not fit for public consumption, but probably would not matter if someone found it. By adding additional security such as Windows NT Challenge/Response, the /secrets area could be considered secure and a less than likely target for hackers. (They will hopefully not even know it is there.) Exercise 7.15 will take you through the steps for enabling Internet publishing.

EXERCISE 7.15

Enabling Internet Publishing

1. From the Start menu, select Programs ➤ Microsoft Internet Server ➤ Internet Server Manager.

2. Click the Web Proxy Service in the listing for the server that you want to administer.

3. In the Properties pull-down menu, select Service Properties.

4. When the Web Proxy Properties screen appears, select the Publishing tab.

5. Click the Enable Internet Publishing checkbox. At this point you can ignore all inbound requests, redirect requests to the local Web server, or specify an alternate Web system. Choose to send requests to the local Web server.

6. Define the default mapping for all inbound requests. If this information is not already set, choose your own server. (Do this just for this exercise. This is not really recommended in practice.) This step defines a reverse proxy.

7. If you have a connection to the Internet, click the Add button and type **http://www.yourserver.com/secret** for the requested path and **http://www.sybex.com** as the path to route to. If you do not have a connection to the Internet, use a second system and redirect publishing there, or use a virtual directory from your Web server. This step defines reverse hosting.

8. Click OK to close the Web Proxy Protocol screen.

Since Web publishing opens your network up to inbound traffic, you want to be certain that you apply all access controls that you can to safeguard your network. Although you are only enabling certain functions to work from the external network, there always remains the danger that security may be exploited in one way or another. For example, enabling Web publishing allows a proxy server to listen to requests from the Internet on port 80. Clearing the checkbox disables listening for port 80 requests from the Internet. As you can see, this does not open all functions. However, the data is considered unsecured and should be monitored as closely as possible.

When packet filtering is enabled, you must use the predefined packet filter for the HTTP server (port 80) to allow Internet users to access your Web server. If you are using a port other than 80, you must create a custom packet filter.

The Web Proxy publishing service has no effect on FTP (port 21) or Gopher (port 70) sites. These services do make a distinction between internal and external networks. For this reason, use ACLs (assign-limited user and share permissions) for security. If these services are not used, they should be disabled and stopped.

Tips for Publishing to the Internet

As you have learned, Internet publishing can easily be added to Microsoft Proxy Server. However, with the dangers considered, it is recommended that you use the following guidelines:

Do not add external IP addresses to the LAT   When an Internet range of IP addresses is added to the proxy server's LAT, it is believed that those addresses are local as well. As such, it is possible that the proxy server will act as a relay and connect external users to the resource that you really did not want them to see. Also, it is possible (although not probable) that an Internet user could also exploit this function even further and access other resources. Remember that both the WinSock Proxy and Web Proxy services are available.

Use separate domains for proxy servers publishing Web pages   As mentioned earlier, you should divide your master domain from the proxy server(s) that provides external services. Recall that a one-way trust will allow users on the master domain to access the resources on the other domain, but not the other way around. In the event a hacker gets into your network, chances are that the impact would be limited to the proxy server's domain.

Apply maximum security restrictions   Windows NT employs a number of security options that allow a system to be completely secured. For instance, you should set the ACL for a share to No Access for the Internet services anonymous user account. By setting security here to this level, you are assured that the account cannot write destructively or in any other way to your server. In general, the anonymous user account is called IUSR_*systemname*.

Avoid using network-mapped drives While it is considered extremely hard, if not impossible, for a connection to another system to have its credential forged and introduce the ability to form other unwanted connections. This problem is a common issue because quite often Web pages are divided to different servers based on function in order to reduce load. However, if your company is big enough that you must divide your Internet data, then you really should consider some of your other options.

Configure auditing to record events In order to monitor what activities are transpiring on your server, it is imperative to know that someone is, or has been, trying to actively break into your system. When this occurs, you should note the time that they connect, the resources that they are trying to access, and any other relevant information. If possible, perform a trace route (tracert) back to their system, attempting to resolve where they gained access. Notify the IS department of the company that allowed the hacker to use their machines. If the actions persist, consider contacting the FBI or imposing stronger security, such as a firewall. It is illegal to hack into a system. And remember, never place a welcome message to secured data!

Minimize the use of active scripts and input forms There are two major flaws with implementing these functions on a Web page. First, you have accepted data from an external resource. And second, the scripts may have hidden access to other points on your server. Active scripts perform activities other than merely providing the download of data. The other activities include, but are not limited to, CGI, Microsoft Visual Basic, implementations of ActiveX, and Java. If you need to use server scripts, be sure to limit user access down to the file level. This will, of course, require NTFS as the implemented file system.

Disable IP forwarding This will keep unauthorized packets from being routed into your network uncontrolled.

Run only applications which are required This will reduce the chance that a security hole will be left open. For example, if you are not using the Gopher service, do not enable it. If you do not require an application such as Exchange on that server, do not install it.

Disable the server service on the Internet adapter This will deny access to the share set on the service regardless of whether the user is accessing it from the Internet side. If you decide to leave the service enabled, always verify settings on shares that exist on the server. Any default access should be set to read-only or None. Also, if any services are unnecessarily bound to the Internet adapter, they should be removed. For example, there is no reason to have the WINS client bound to the Internet adapter. Allowing WINS on the external interface could potentially allow client computer names to be visible from the Internet.

All drives on the proxy server should be configured as NTFS volumes NTFS contains many features and improvements over FAT that makes it more secure. You may use the Convert utility to change a FAT volume to NTFS. Refer to the Windows NT Online help for further information.

Disable ports 1024 through 1029 These ports are used for RPC listening on the Internet interface. Once disabled, RPC listening will only be available on the internal network. Alternatively, you may also use packet filtering to request that these ports be ignored. Nonetheless, you should disable at both points in the event packet filters.

Summary

This chapter addressed the configuration and safeguarding of Microsoft Proxy Server. It covered the security interface, which is accessed through the Security button on any of the services. The security service provides packet filtering, site blocking, altering, and logging. At this point, you should be fairly comfortable with the basics of securing your network.

In providing a secure network, we discussed the idea that a network is only as safe as the administrators who configured it and the users who assist in keeping the environment safe. Direct connections to the Internet are not advisable, and as such, no IP routing should be implemented. In situations where routing in unavoidable, administrators should consider alternatives, such as maintaining a separate network. Microsoft Proxy Server disables access to the internal LAN by not listening to requests received from the Internet. This means that when allowing inbound access, an administrator should limit the TCP and UDP ports in the Advanced section of the TCP/IP Configuration tab.

The packet filtering aspect of the security service can be configured as either static or dynamic. When operating as static, an administrator can finely tune the server such that only certain ports are open at any given time. When configured as dynamic (recommended), ports that are opened can be closed as required by IIS. All traffic must match an IIS request or be included in the exceptions list. The exceptions list provides a mechanism by which traffic may be allowed to pass to a configured IP address. Through the exceptions list, ICMP traffic is allowed and the Ping program is functional to test connectivity.

The site filters also allow an administrator to define if a site should be accessible or not. When planning a site, it is useful information to predetermine its function on the Internet. In determining user access, first all sites must be defined as either blocked or accessible, then exceptions can be created.

Altering and logs are used as written notification to allow an administrator to monitor potential system hazards. Alerts may be sent to the Event Viewer log or via e-mail to an account. This allows an administrator to track problems. The log file support provides a holistic view as to what the security involvement with the proxy service has been.

Review Questions

1. Explain how IP routing could effect and compromise security on your network.

2. Describe how implementing a separate domain for your proxy server aids in protecting your network from unauthorized Internet access.

3. How are inbound connections managed from the Internet at the proxy server?

4. How are outbound connections managed from clients at the proxy server?

5. Is activating Internet Web publishing on a proxy server considered a good practice? Explain.

6. Where do you set protocol permissions?

    A. Web Proxy Service Permissions tab

    B. WinSock Proxy Service tab

    C. Web Service Permissions tab

    D. FTP Service Permissions tab

    E. Gopher Service Permissions tab

7. Where is IP forwarding enabled or disabled?

    A. Web Proxy Service Permissions tab

    B. WWW Service tab

    C. At the client

    D. TCP/IP configuration

    E. At the router

8. What are the two ways Microsoft Proxy Server secures a network from external users?

    A. Disabling IP forwarding

    B. Assigning a filter

    C. Disabling listening on inbound service ports

    D. Setting user permissions

    E. Rejecting user requests listed in the LAT

9. When filtering a single computer into the exclude list on the Domain Filters tab, how can you use the DNS name rather than IP address?

    A. Type the name in the Domain box.

    B. Browse the computer list and double-click the computer.

    C. Select Learn by Example, type the URL, and click Accept.

    D. Click the ellipses button next to the IP address and type the name.

    E. Click the Construct LAT button.

10. What type of trust relationship should be set up between a Proxy Server domain and a main company domain?

  A. One-way trust

  B. No trust

  C. Two-way trust

  D. Meshed trust with SSL links

  E. None of the above

11. You want to be alerted when your proxy server running packet filtering is dropping packets. What should you do?

  A. Using the Alerting tab of the Proxy Server Security dialog box, create an alert for Rejected Packets.

  B. Using the Alerting tab of the Proxy Server Security dialog box, create an alert for Protocol Violations.

  C. Using Microsoft Windows NT Performance Monitor, create an alert on the Packets Received Discarded counter.

  D. Using Microsoft Windows NT Performance Monitor, create an alert on the Packets Received Unknown counter.

12. You enable filtering on your Windows NT Proxy Server and deny access to www.newstoday.com. However, you have one client that needs to get to this site for business purposes. The client is configured for the Win-Sock Proxy and Web Proxy services. How can the client access this site?

  A. The client can't.

  B. Use the WinSock Proxy Server, then enter the host name.

  C. Use the Web Proxy Server, then enter the host name.

  D. Use the Web Proxy Server, then enter the IP address.

13. Your Proxy Server is configured to allow Anonymous Authentication and Challenge/Response authentication. The Sales department and the Shipping department are both granted access to the WWW protocol in the Permissions tab of the Web Proxy Service Properties dialog box. Which Windows NT groups can access the Internet by using HTTP in the Web Proxy service?

    A. None

    B. All group in the domain

    C. Only the Sales and Shipping departments

    D. Any groups with local logon rights to the domain

14. NBTSTAT displays the NetBIOS name cache. How can you keep someone from running this command on your Proxy Server? (Choose two answers.)

    A. Enable packet filtering.

    B. Disable RAS on the external adapter.

    C. Enable access control on the WinSock Proxy service.

    D. Disable the NetBIOS interface.

    E. Remove the workstation service from the external adapter.

15. Which three of the following events can your Proxy Server alert or notify you of that might affect performance on the local network?

    A. When the hard disks are full

    B. When packets are rejected by the Proxy Server

    C. When the internal network is down

    D. When users access restricted Web sites

    E. When proxy services are stopped

    F. When protocol violations occur

CHAPTER

8

Internet and Intranet Access

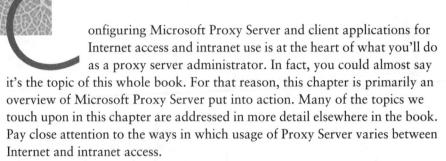

onfiguring Microsoft Proxy Server and client applications for Internet access and intranet use is at the heart of what you'll do as a proxy server administrator. In fact, you could almost say it's the topic of this whole book. For that reason, this chapter is primarily an overview of Microsoft Proxy Server put into action. Many of the topics we touch upon in this chapter are addressed in more detail elsewhere in the book. Pay close attention to the ways in which usage of Proxy Server varies between Internet and intranet access.

In this chapter, we are focusing on the short-term configuration of Microsoft Proxy Server and client software for Internet and intranet access. By the end of this chapter, you will be able to do the following:

- Configure Microsoft Proxy Server and clients for Internet access

Exam objectives are subject to change at any time without prior notice and at Microsoft's sole discretion. Please visit Microsoft's Training & Certification website (www.microsoft.com/Train_Cert) for the most current exam objectives listing.

- Identify a client application and the appropriate proxy component to service it

- Determine security requirements

- Maximize Proxy Server performance

- Configure Microsoft Proxy Server for an intranet

- Set up Microsoft Proxy Server as an IPX-to-IP gateway

- Troubleshoot Internet access problems

Internet Proxy Server Configuration

Configuring Microsoft Proxy Server for use as an Internet proxy server is pretty straightforward; it makes little difference which Internet services your users will work with or where the end resource is located. There are few special considerations that need to be examined. This section is a quick-start guide to Microsoft Proxy Server. It will also provide a preview of the more complex intranet configurations discussed later on.

Client Setup

Microsoft Proxy Server supports most TCP/IP-based applications. However, proxy support for each type of application varies according to its compatibility with supported services. Generally, compatibility is broken into two types: CERN-compatible and non-CERN–compatible (all others).

Microsoft
✓ *Exam*
Objective

Configure Proxy Server and Proxy Server client computers to use the Proxy Server services. Configurations include:

- Microsoft Internet Explorer client computers
- Netscape Navigator client computers
- Macintosh® client computers
- UNIX client computers
- Client computers on an IPX-only network

Configuring CERN-Compatible Applications

As discussed in Chapter 3, CERN-compatible Internet client applications are those that conform to the proxy protocol developed at CERN as part of its definition of the original HTTP standard. Most of the widely used clients, such as Internet Explorer and Netscape Navigator, are CERN-compatible. Microsoft Proxy Server directly supports CERN-compatible applications, which means that users can directly configure such programs to communicate with Proxy Server. No other configuration is necessary. Of course, each program's configuration is unique. However, the basic configuration is to specify the server and the port. Figure 8.1 shows Internet Explorer 4.0 being configured to work with a Proxy Server.

FIGURE 8.1

Configuring a CERN-compatible application to use a Proxy Server for Internet access

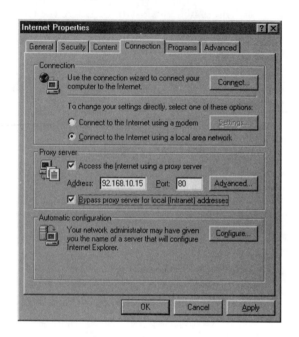

Configuring Non-CERN–Compatible Applications

Many smaller applications are not CERN proxy-compatible. Some of these may require no configuration. For example, the FTP utility in Windows NT and 95 simply loads and runs on top of a given IP stack. On the other hand, non-compatible applications also include those for which IPX was implemented as the transport. For example, running Netscape Navigator with the WinSock Proxy client uses a non-CERN–compatible configuration. In either case, these applications are known as non-CERN, WinSock-based Internet applications.

As you are working with non-CERN proxy-compatible applications or IPX-based clients, verify that you have installed WinSock.DLL for 16-bit Windows applications and WSOCK32.DLL for 32-bit Windows applications. Note that Windows 95 installations require both files.

When installing the WinSock Proxy client, you should verify the settings to ensure that you have a working and secure installation. Begin by checking that the correct Proxy Server appears in the WinSock Proxy client configuration icon in the Control Panel. If your system is running IPX, the client should be enabled and the Force IPX box should be checked. Finally, make sure the MSPLAT.TXT file contains all the correct local entries for the private network.

A client can quickly and easily be installed by running the Setup program located on the MSPCLNT share in Microsoft Proxy Server. This program is the Microsoft Proxy client support program. All proxy server client components will be installed and configured based on the MSPCLNT.INI file. You should recall that either Netscape Navigator or Internet Explorer will auto-configure to use the proxy server; however, others may require manual intervention. The configuration setting for each client varies slightly. Typically, these services only require a server name and an IP address; if they are using WinSock, they may even run as-is.

A client may also be set up by following the instructions in HTTP://*systemname*/ MSPROXY in any browser.

Mixing and Matching Proxy Compatibility

For security reasons as well as to reduce system overhead, you should only install and enable the proxy components that are required by your users. If, for example, you have no UNIX or Macintosh clients, you should not enable the Socks Proxy service. There are no problems having all the proxy services as well as all IIS services installed and enabled; you should just install only what is necessary. Overall, you should find that most clients only require the Web Proxy service.

The Web Proxy can be used by all clients including Microsoft Windows 3.*x*, Windows 95, Windows NT, UNIX, and Macintosh. Likewise, the Socks Proxy supports all system platforms but is limited to TCP connections only. WinSock is compatible with Windows-based systems only.

Have you ever made breakfast and not cleaned up your mess? Well, the setup program has been known to do the same thing. For some unknown reason, the setup program may leave a directory called ~MSSETUP.T on a client's hard drive. There are absolutely no valuable files in this directory. Feel free to delete it.

Server Setup

In configuring Proxy Server for Internet access your main concern is to deliver the services required safely, without compromising your network security. We have reviewed these topics in great detail in chapters 4 and 7; however, here is a quick overview of the setup procedure.

First, determine the necessary services required by users. For example, you have installed IIS and performed all the upgrades. Will your users require WinSock Proxy? Will they need the Web Proxy as well? The best solution is to limit the services by blocking those components that you truly do not need. This will spare a great deal of overhead on the system and will help to secure the server. For example, very few organizations use the Gopher services that ship with IIS. What do you think should be done? Our suggestion would be to disable the service. Remember that the positioning of the server in a domain environment as either a member server or not will in part determine local performance.

Second, determine which users require access and limit the available services and protocols strictly to those users. Remember that as you add permissions, assignments should be done by group rather than by individual user. For example, create a group called "Web users" and assign them the appropriate access. This will allow an administrator to quickly create a user account without having to access multiple servers and utilities to assign various access rights.

Finally, determine whether Internet publishing is going to be active. When Internet publishing is enabled, some Internet traffic is allowed into the private network. To decrease the possibility of a hacker exploiting security gaps, it is best for an administrator to configure the proxy server on its own network and domain. In this configuration, it will not be possible for the proxy server domain to access the main domain. A one-way trust should be established such that users from the main domain can access the one containing the proxy server. At this stage, you will want to limit those accounts that have the ability to publish pages. This will protect the network from those who are unfamiliar with security procedures, and it will also ensure that items published to the corporate Web page meet the company's standards and integrity levels.

When allowing Internet traffic into your network, you should always use packet filtering. In the case of Web publishing, you must use the predefined packet filter HTTP server (port 80) to allow users on the Internet to see your Web page.

Use the instructions in Exercise 8.1 to set up and configure Microsoft Proxy Server for Internet access. When completed, test your implementation with the steps in Exercise 8.2.

EXERCISE 8.1

Setting Up and Configuring Microsoft Proxy Server to Work with the Internet

Before beginning this exercise, you must have installed Windows NT 4.0 with two network adapters, IIS 3.0 or greater, service pack 3 or greater and hot fixes, as well as Microsoft Proxy Server 2.0.

This exercise was designed to give you the foresight required to implement Microsoft Proxy Server. By the time you have completed this exercise, you will have verified your abilities to troubleshoot problems, secure the network environment, and ensure performance.

In this exercise, you will want to either team up with a friend or have two systems configured as described above and one system to act as the Internet service, if you are not connected to the Internet. Ultimately, you will have a network that consists of one client and the proxy server. You should probably use a private IP address, such as 192.168.x.x, followed by a second network or link to the Internet.

This exercise requires you to disable a client from using an actual IP address, and then configure it to use the one on the proxy server.

On your first system, stop and disable the Web Proxy and WinSock Proxy services:

1. Click the Uninstall icon located in the Microsoft Proxy Server folder in the Programs group on the Start menu.

2. Click the Control Panel and select Add/Remove Programs.

3. Select IIS to be removed and click OK to accept.

EXERCISE 8.1 (CONTINUED FROM PREVIOUS PAGE)

Note that depending on the version of IIS, you may also be able to perform the uninstall by clicking Control Panel ≻ Network Services and selecting to remove the service from there.

4. Next, disable the network adapter on the network with the Internet Service.

5. Either right-mouse click the Network Neighborhood icon, or click Network in the Control Panel.

6. Click the Bindings tab; then select All Adapters in the Show Bindings For dialog box.

7. Select the network adapter that is connected to the system with the Internet Services and click Disable.

8. Click Close and allow the system to reboot.

The system where you disabled and removed both Proxy Server and IIS above should now be configured as a proxy client.

9. Browse the network and locate the second system that is still configured as a proxy server. Double-click the MSCLNT share and run Setup.

10. Click OK on any defaults to complete the installation.

11. Reboot.

EXERCISE 8.2

Accessing the Internet

Before beginning this exercise, ensure that you have completed Exercise 8.1. You should have one system configured as a proxy server and another as a client. If the proxy server is not connected to the Internet, you must have an additional system on the network (Internet side) that has TCP/IP services such as FTP, WWW, etc.

Begin by using the Ping utility on the proxy server to verify a connection to the Internet or system configured to simulate the Internet.

1. Ping 127.0.0.1 (TCP/IP loopback). If the system replies, TCP/IP is configured correctly. If an error occurs, verify your setting in the Network control panel. This could possibly indicate a hardware problem, such as the network card not responding as configured.

2. Ping the IP address of the system that is configured to simulate the Internet or an actual Internet system, if connected. Continue by pinging the same system by its host name. You should get a reply and a time. If not, try another system. Repeat the same steps from the client. You should get a message indicating that the destination is unavailable or that the request timed out. The error will depend on your configuration. For example, if you are pinging without a gateway, you will get the first message. Otherwise, it is possible that a route was configured but not available, and so the Ping timed out. If it's available, you may also use the Ping command from the Internet simulation system to see a similar message when attempting to ping the client system.

3. Verify that you can access the Internet with either Internet Explorer or Netscape Navigator. Begin by clicking the Program icon. On the URL line, type the name of the proxy server. You should most likely get a screen with the Default IIS Web page. Assuming you're successful, test your Internet access by typing the following IP address on the URL line **http://206.100.29.83**. You should see Sybex's home page. Note that this is a URL that does not require DNS resolution.

Plug-Ins

In addition to the basic Proxy Server product, add-on services are available from third-party manufacturers to extend the usability of Microsoft Proxy Server. An example of these services is a monitoring utility to scan data on-the-fly for viral infections. Microsoft posts vendor product information at:

```
http://www.microsoft.com/proxy/plugins/vendors2
```

To obtain plug-in modules, simply open any of the proxy services and click the Plug-Ins (Web Page) button located on the Service tab. This will spawn a session of Internet Explorer open to the location designated above, as shown in Figure 8.2. Currently, plug-in products are available for Anti-Virus, Content Filtering, Analysis, and Reporting. Each product has its own installation procedure. Please connect to the Web site for further product details.

FIGURE 8.2

Plug-Ins Web page

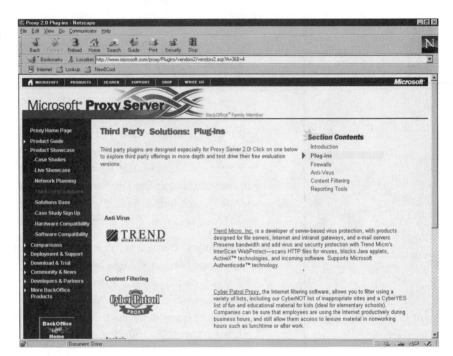

WINS, DNS, DHCP, and SNMP

The Windows NT Server services include some components that are not part of the core technology of the server. The four main server services that we need to be concerned with while configuring Proxy Server for the Internet are WINS, DHCP, DNS, and SNMP. Access from the Internet to any of these services on your network should be restricted or denied completely.

WINS

The WINS service is Microsoft's solution to NetBIOS name resolution in the enterprise environment. Typically, WINS is combined with other services and operates on a central server. Because WINS maintains a database of all systems on the network, it is absolutely necessary to deny all external access to WINS or the WINS database from external resources. However, it is perfectly acceptable for the proxy server to be a WINS client. To block this type of access, disable the WINS client on the external port by clearing its bindings in the TCP/IP configuration section of Windows NT, as shown in the graphic below. (Note that the 3Com Etherlink III adapter is external in this configuration.) If packet filters are used or a third-party firewall is in place, port 139 for NetBIOS name traffic should be blocked. In the event that no WINS servers are used on the network, an LMHOSTS file may be used in its place. However, the same rule applies to the LMHOSTS file as to the WINS database—there must be no external access.

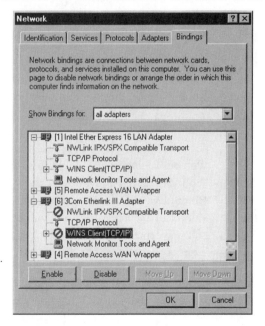

Since we don't care about registering the external adapter with the WINS database, you may leave this WINS entry blank, as shown below.

DNS

Like the WINS service, DNS should also be restricted. However, you cannot deny access completely, because some information may have to be available if Web publishing is enabled. In this case, you may want to have only these services defined in the DNS, while all others use WINS. If you are using an Internet DNS server or your DNS is configured as a secondary DNS to an Internet DNS, blocking DNS access will not matter. Typically, a primary DNS is configured that is independent of the Internet's, which is used for clients. However, since all Internet requests sent to the proxy server are resolved by the proxy server itself, there is usually little concern for DNS security. Configuring clients to use an Internet DNS may allow them to bypass the proxy server when accessing the Internet. You should probably avoid this configuration. Again, safeguard the DNS database as you would WINS or the LMHOSTS file.

DHCP

When addresses are dynamically assigned via DHCP, you need to exercise caution primarily in protecting the database and by not assigning an address to the external interface. Typically, an ISP will assign a static address to the server regardless. It is not recommended that the Proxy Server use DHCP as a client since addresses can change. Assign the information as static. This is done on the TCP/IP Configuration screen located in the Network Setup area on the Protocol tab. With the external interface not reading DHCP requests, the server may be used as a DHCP relay; however, it is not a good idea to tie this type of traffic to the proxy server. DHCP is useful in configuring clients to work with the proxy server. If you are adding a proxy server to a network and are using a DNS strictly for Internet resources, you should remove the DNS entries from the DHCP server and place the assignment on the proxy server only. DHCP changes should be made with the DHCP Manager. Remember that when using a proxy server, the client is not resolving names to IP addresses—the proxy server is.

SMTP

Finally, some companies like to perform remote site administration via RMON and SMTP. Overall, this is not a problem; however, data is not encrypted and it is possible for security to be breached. Secure the proxy community, the trap address, and so forth before implementing SMTP. In no event should you allow this traffic to the Internet. These restrictions can be applied directly in the SMTP Configuration screen in TCP/IP under Networking on Windows NT. Working with SMTP is discussed in Chapter 11.

Performance Considerations

Whether it's used for Internet access or within an intranet, the speed and responsiveness of Microsoft Proxy Server will vary directly with the number of users, the bandwidth, and the cache size. When allocating cache, you should always add more than is necessary. This will constantly increase throughput and help maximize bandwidth. When the available bandwidth is completely used, you should consider upgrading the connection to the Internet.

Microsoft ✓ *Exam* *Objective* | **Choose the location, size, and type of caching for the Web Proxy service.**

Once bandwidth has been maximized, additional cache will no longer make a significant difference. For example, if 100% of the available bandwidth is in use, adding additional cache will not allow you to facilitate more users. By increasing the cache, your goal is to redirect users from the Internet to a local resource. However, when at a constant full utilization, the bottleneck is the available bandwidth, and increasing the cache will provide more space. However, users will still see slow performance of non-cached items. At this stage, an administrator should definitely consider increasing bandwidth or adding additional servers, as required.

Microsoft ✔ ***Exam*** ***Objective***

Optimize performance for various purposes. Purposes include:

- Increasing throughput
- Optimizing routing

Remember that performance is partly based on perception. Caching assists in providing the perception that more bandwidth is available than really is. However, caching does not necessarily enhance a system's performance. To put this in perspective, imagine that instead of using a 56k data line to the Internet, you are using a 2400-baud connection. Guess what? No matter what level of cache you use, the connection is bound to reach maximum usage almost immediately.

You can use Performance Monitor to see how efficiently the system is performing at any time. You can check data from over a period of time by configuring a chart with a duration scale. Information in the Performance Monitor is useful for maximizing the speed of the proxy server.

Sometimes it's not enough to monitor the proxy service; other events on the server can lead to decreases in performance that require you to review the entire system. The Event Viewer records system messages as they occur. As such, any problems initializing Proxy Server, IIS, TCP/IP, dial-up networking, and so on will be listed here. Both the Event Viewer and the Performance Monitor are discussed in Chapter 11, *Monitoring and Tuning*.

System Analysis

Now that we have reviewed some of the basic configuration items, we can take a quick look at system analysis—how to be attentive to your system's needs and when to recognize that action must be taken.

While the majority of this information is presented elsewhere in the book, we highlight a few points here as a matter of discussion for working specifically with the Internet.

Performance Monitoring

The performance of a proxy server is mainly concerned with cache and throughput. As you attempt to tune the server, you will need to review what the utilization is over a given period of time. You can then use this information to note busy periods of a day or week. There are again only two questions to be answered: Is the cache size high, low, or just right? What materials are being requested that are cached or not cached?

When determining cache size, we are only interested in maximizing bandwidth. We can only do this by knowing peak hours of use and where data is coming from. Think of it this way, would it be completely effective to have a T1 link to the Internet that was maximized for only five minutes a day and then used at only 15% thereafter?

Since caching aids in throughput, the obvious question that you must ascertain is whether data is being retrieved from the Internet or from cache. Clearly, if data is constantly being retrieved from the Internet, and the cache is hardly being utilized, then increasing it will not do a lot for performance. For this reason, requests with ?**Keyword** in the URL are not cached. It is unlikely other users would make the same types of queries.

The hard part of gauging performance is determining if speed issues are related to your connection, the site that you are connecting to, or caching. Internet performance is not always within your control since your best speed is equal to the slowest link along a route to a site. Tips on streamlining Internet configurations will be presented in Chapter 11, *Monitoring and Tuning*.

Reviewing Logs

Let's assume that your organization has invested in equipment that will provide adequate bandwidth, and you have turned on system logging. You are reviewing the logs to determine three pieces of information:

1. Are there any security problems?

2. Is performance adequately covered by the system in place?

3. Which sites are being accessed, and are they found in the cache?

Finding the answer to these questions will usually determine the type of logging you implement: Verbose or Regular. Microsoft has anticipated that these are the most common questions and attempts to answer them with a minimal amount of data; so you can usually choose Regular logging. For statistical purposes or other reasons, perhaps defined by your management, you may determine that logs of site access by users must be kept verbosely. That is to say, all possible information about proxy access is recorded in verbose mode, while regular mode contains more limited information. Verbose information will include items such as the amount of data transferred, which proxy server was used, the client agent, the client platform, processing time, transport, referring server name, destination address, operation name, and authentication status. The level of paranoia that each company expresses varies as much as the smog level in Los Angeles from day to day.

Troubleshooting Internet Access Problems

There are no NRA membership requirements to find trouble and shoot it; however, you should select your weapon wisely. While Chapter 12 provides a complete guide to Proxy Server troubleshooting, this section will give you a quick start with Internet access problems.

As you sift through user complaints, you will find that issues usually can be narrowed down to the following four topics:

Application does not work   Usually a user will report this situation when there are incorrect port assignments to a given protocol or an error in one of the LATs. In either case, to the user it will appear that their application is not working correctly with the proxy server. Remember that in order for a WinSock application to operate, you must have installed the Microsoft Proxy client program. Otherwise, these applications will be limited to operations on the local network using TCP/IP.

Access is denied   This message appears when a user attempts to access a resource for which they have not been granted permissions. These situations will arise as users are directly or indirectly removed from the authorized user list. When a user is indirectly removed, it's generally because a group has been deleted from a list. A user is directly removed when their rights have been specifically disabled. In any event, the user will not be able to access a given resource. Verify the user's access rights and verify that the account is for the correct domain and so forth. Keep in mind that Internet access to HTTP (Web) resources may be accessed through the Web Proxy or the Win-Sock Proxy. Access errors can be caused by a configuration at the local workstation as well as the security assignments at the server. In this instance, Internet access may work for HTTP, but not for other Web browser services.

Complete failure (of all Internet applications)   This error tends to occur after a new application is installed. Typically, what will happen is that the Microsoft Proxy WinSock.DLL will be replaced by one from the application being installed. Then, when other applications are called, it appears that the system is in complete failure. Also, if you attempt to use the wrong CERN name and port, you will see the same situation, since there will be no end-to-end communication. That is to say, no connection is established from the proxy client to the Internet site via the proxy server. Finally, if the LAT is incorrect, your system may not be able to distinguish what network the destination system is on; and it may fail for this reason as well.

The network seems broken!   There really is no starting or ending point for this issue. Often users will say that the proxy server is slow when in fact it is the entire network. Be that as it may, assume that a user cannot communicate with anything on the network. Verify that the network electronics are functioning, that there are no duplicate names on the network, and that the DNS (at the proxy server) is in order. Resolving a name to an incorrect IP address, or to no IP address, will create the appearance that no services are working.

As you can see, while there are only a limited number of basic things that can go wrong, the possible variations in the ways users may describe them seem endless. Again, Chapter 12 discusses these and other user-related problems in more detail. For the time being, review your current problem-solving skills by trying out Exercise 8.3.

EXERCISE 8.3

Problem-Solving Client Issues

You have gotten a complaint that the Accounting department in your company cannot access the Internet. However, further research reveals that Accounting is the only department with this problem and that all others are fine. You check with the network and telecom group and find that the department is on its own subnet. What is the problem? Use the following steps to locate the difficulty:

1. Check that the address range of the Accounting department is listed in the LAT.

2. Verify that the proxy server they are using can communicate with the Internet. To do this, log in as Administrator, try to Ping an Internet server, and use a Web browser to view its Web page.

3. While still logged in as Administrator, open Event Viewer and look for system events or security-related issues.

4. Log out of the Proxy Server (as Administrator). Log in again as one of the accounting users and try to connect. Determine if the problem is related to the user or the network configuration. For example, if any user in Accounting can connect, then the problem is with the other users, not the network.

5. Verify that the proxy client is installed and enabled at the client. If not, you may want to try reinstalling the client.

6. Check communications to the proxy server with the Ping command from the DOS prompt. Note that since Ping uses ICMP and not TCP or UDP, it cannot be used to verify Internet access from a client.

7. Attempt to access the same Internet resource as you had from the proxy server. Having checked all the key components related to the proxy server, we will assume that at this point you have access and the problem is solved.

Configuring Proxy Server for Intranet Access

Yet another fifty-cent buzz word to add to your collection...An intranet is a scaled-down version of the Internet that usually plays host to a private secured network only. An intranet can contain anything that is found on the Internet—Web pages, FTP sites, and so forth. No one particular element is required to define a network as an intranet, however, they commonly include a Web site.

Microsoft ✓ *Exam* *Objective*

Plan an Internet site or an Intranet site for stand-alone servers, single-domain environments, and multiple-domain environments. Tasks include:

- Choosing appropriate connectivity methods
- Choosing services
- Using Microsoft Proxy Server in an intranet that has no access to the Internet
- Choosing hardware

Intranets are generally used only in medium-size to larger firms. Unless a smaller company is developing applications or has a very specific need, such as heterogeneous operating systems, intranets are typically too costly to build and maintain. However, a large organization can utilize intranet Web pages effectively for everything from e-mail to updating systems. In an intranet, a proxy server is excellent for caching across slow links, protecting certain parts of the network from unauthorized users, and so forth. Remember that when you design caching, this function only works with the Web Proxy Server. In other words, IPX-only clients will not benefit from caching because their Web browser will operate via the WinSock Proxy Server.

Sample Uses of the Intranet

There are a number of resources that a company may want to place on their intranet. These are generally informational, however, they may also allow for input.

HR listings   Quite often, a human resource department at a given company will want to place job listings where employees can easily access them. Usually, they are hoping to find a good referral and are not necessarily looking to have these positions open to the public.

Company information and reports   Internal information such as the company's plans, current values, future products and so forth tend to be listed in this type of area. For obvious reasons, this is usually kept under wraps.

Telephone information   Larger firms sometimes keep an online telephone directory of employees. For instance, to contact a person in Development, you may be able to search for people by department.

Policies and procedures   Companies often publish this information so that users can have an understanding of how to navigate through the organizational red tape. Commonly these listings include travel information, instructions for purchasing work-related materials, and other rules and guidelines.

Technical support   Depending on the type of company, a knowledge base is sometimes integrated into an intranet. This allows a company to maintain a single, up-to-date listing of bugs, changes, etc.

File updates   We tend to see this type of service in organizations with MIS departments where updates to programs and system files are made available for employee download. Remember that it is no longer practical for all users in an organization to download the same updates and fixes from a given site.

Reducing e-mail   Company-wide postings are typically placed on a corporate Web server. This mechanism allows employees to see current information regarding a company's actions. This is far easier than sending e-mail to all employees. Consider that most users will simply ignore the message anyway. Then, they will not delete it and it will consume your e-mail storage capacity.

Unification of heterogeneous networks   Organizations that support multiple desktops consisting of Macintosh, PCs, UNIX, and so forth may have a central common information/application source.

Selective news feeds   Information from Internet newsgroups is often too risky to allow users unlimited access. As a substitute to this situation, some businesses will configure a "news feed" over the NNTP protocol, specifying which newsgroups to receive. Received information can then be viewed by any and all clients at full network speed.

Sales reports   As an up-to-date listing, accounting departments will often show employees how they are performing compared to expected sales performance. This type of information is hardly ever shown to the public as it reveals too much.

A proxy server in the intranet clearly has its place. Between its caching abilities, support for heterogeneous networks, and security, Microsoft Proxy Server is much more than an Internet gateway. The sample items listed above are just a few of many uses for an intranet. As stated earlier, there is no need to have any one component in order to have an intranet. As far as new technology is concerned, it is expected that an intranet's functionality will increase over the next several years.

Configuring Proxy Server to Act as an IPX Gateway

Microsoft Proxy Server is automatically configured to support IPX clients. However, the server on which Microsoft Proxy Server is installed must include the protocol with the correct frame type. This will allow the server to read packet information. Typically, companies will implement Microsoft Proxy Server to support existing NetWare installations. This is usually cheaper than defining an IP structure, configuring clients, assigning addresses, and maintaining the design. The major downfall to this configuration is that clients will operate on the WinSock Proxy and not take advantage of the Web Proxy service's caching capabilities. The configuration of Proxy Server with IPX is highlighted in Figure 8.3 and in Exercise 8.4.

If the internal network does not run TCP/IP, Proxy Server assumes that all attempts by Windows Sockets applications to communicate over TCP/IP are to be redirected to the Internet. Obviously, if TCP/IP is not present on the local network, no TCP/IP request should be sent there.

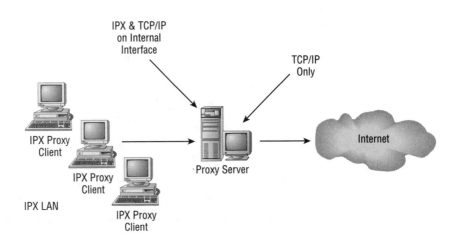

FIGURE 8.3

Proxy Server configured with IPX

 IPX is connectionless-based, as is UDP.

IPX/SPX communications operate identically to TCP/IP, except that the control channel is established over IPX. As applications attempt to establish communications via TCP/IP, the proxy version of WinSock DLL converts the Windows Sockets API input to the equivalent for IPX/SPX. At this time the addresses are converted, and communications between the client and the WinSock Proxy Server are handled over IPX/SPX. Since IPX-to-IP is not a perfect translation, the following additional tasks are handled by the Proxy version of the WinSock DLL:

socket() API   When an application attempts communications via TCP or UDP in a socket API call, the proxy version of the WinSock DLL changes the request to the corresponding IPX/SPX protocol.

bind() API   As an application attempts to link to a specified socket on the local IP network, the proxy version of the WinSock DLL changes the designation to a local IPX/SPX address. This function is compatible with the Bind to IP_ANY request as well.

connect() API   In order to connect to an Internet IP-based service, the proxy version of the WinSock DLL must first use the IPX address of the Proxy Server's internal interface to have the Proxy Server establish communications.

sendto() API   When an application makes this API call, the destination IP address needs to be converted to the IPX address of the Microsoft Proxy Server.

recvfrom() API   As applications attempt to respond to a request, the source IP address returned needs to be converted from the IPX address of the Proxy Server to the IP address of the Internet application.

Now that you better understand the WinSock Proxy portion of the IPX gateway we must also explain the IP gateway. Typically, under IP, connecting to the IP gateway is plug-and-play. However, since the proxy service does not resolve domain names until communications with the server are established, a Web browser will not find the proxy server by its host or DNS name. To work around this problem, an administrator should designate the proxy server by its IP address. The WinSock DLL will be able to convert the request. Recall that you set the IP address in the Configuration screen from Internet Explorer or Netscape Navigator. You may specify the port address.

Remember that this process can be automated by using an IP address rather than a host name during the setup of Proxy Server. This will automatically configure Netscape Navigator and/or Internet Explorer.

Also, because of the higher overhead involved in converting IPX to IP, administrators should attempt to balance the server load between servers when multiple proxy servers are in use. Chapter 9 discusses multiple proxy servers.

Using an IPX-only configuration has some potential side effects other than just high overhead. These potential problems include configuration refreshing or redirection by certain Windows NT services running on WinSock Proxy IPX clients. To prevent this from happening, you need to verify that the following information appears in the MSPCLNT.INI file to disable the WinSock Proxy client for those services:

```
[Services]
Disable=1
[Spoolss]
Disable=1
[Rpcss]
Disable=1
```

One of the major shortcomings of Microsoft Proxy Server is that IPX clients must run either in Windows 95 or in NT. Windows 3.*x*, Windows for Workgroups, and Novell 16-bit IPX clients are not supported.

When configuring IPX clients, you should set the frame and network number according to your environment, as shown in Figure 8.4. If you are running a NetWare server or router that forwards IPX information, IPX will automatically configure itself with the correct frame type. This will automatically create a section called Servers IPX Addresses in the WSPCLNT.INI file, which contains a network string in the format of Addr1=(Internal Network Number)-(MAC Address).

FIGURE 8.4

The Advanced tab of the IPX/SPX-compatible Protocol Properties screen

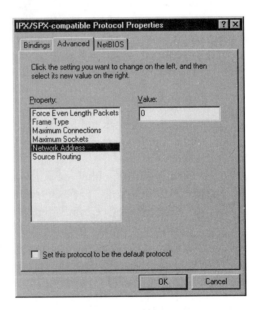

However, if your network contains neither a router that forwards IPX information nor a NetWare server, you must manually select the network number to be identical to all others on your network. The frame type must match that used at the server. Ethernet will use Ethernet 802.2 or Ethernet 802.3. Token Ring networks will use either Token Ring or Token Ring Snap.

Also, you must configure the MSPCLNT.INI file to reflect the following information:

```
[Servers Ipx Addresses]
Addr1=55555555-000000000001
```

Note that regardless of what the internal network adapter's MAC address is, you should use 000000000001 as the MAC address in the MSP-CLNT.INI file.

When working with Novell's 32-bit client, IPX information must also be set to match the proper frame type, as shown in Figure 8.5. Under normal circumstances, if you have a client that is communicating to a NetWare server, no additional configuration is necessary. The frame type will obviously match the NetWare server. However, you should verify that it also matches with the proxy server. If you are working with a Windows 95 system that is still using the DOS-based ODI or VLM drivers (16-bit), you will need to update to the 32-bit NetWare Client driver before operations with the proxy server can take place.

FIGURE 8.5

Novell's 32-bit IPX Client Setting screen

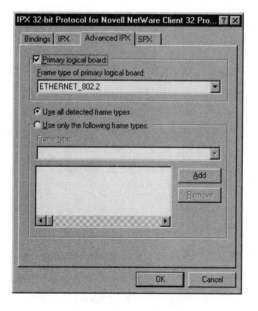

Microsoft ✓ **Exam Objective**

Configure Microsoft Proxy Server for Internet access. Situations include:

- Configuring Proxy Server to provide Internet access through a dial-up connection to an ISP.
- Configuring Proxy Server to act as an IPX gateway.
- Configuring multiple Microsoft Proxy Servers for Internet access.
- Configuring multiple Proxy Servers spread across several different geographic locations.

TIP

To allow IPX name resolution when using CHKWSP32 /F, install the SAP Agent Service on the Windows NT Server. Be aware that you will generate SAP (service advertisement protocol) traffic.

On the server side, the configuration of IPX will, of course, depend on whether you have to define the IPX configuration. For instance, if you have a NetWare server, you will set the frame type and network number to be configured automatically. Otherwise, as with clients, it will be necessary for you to set it. The procedure in Exercise 8.4 can be applied to configuring the Proxy Server.

EXERCISE 8.4

Adding IPX Support

As you have seen, Microsoft Proxy Server can perform the functions of an IPX gateway. To do so, the server must be configured with IPX. Use the following steps to enable your server to function in an IPX environment.

1. Open the Network icon from the Control Panel and select the Protocols tab.

2. Click Add; then select IPX/SPX Compatible Transport from the list of available protocols.

3. When prompted, provide the CD-ROM or the location of the i386 directory from the Windows NT CD-ROM. You may use the defaults and auto-detect frame time for IPX.

4. Locate the external network adapter. Click Disable, then click Move Up until the selected external network adapter is at the top of the list. Although this is counter-intuitive since the protocol is disabled, this is a requirement.

5. Select the Protocols tab and open NWLink IPX/SPX Compatible Transport.

6. Type the 8-digit address in Internal Network Number on the General tab. This is a unique number to identify the server on an IPX network.

7. If your network has a NetWare server or router that provides IPX information, click Auto Frame Type Detection, as shown in the graphic below and go to step 8. Otherwise, click Manual Frame Type Detection, and in the Manual Frame Detection dialog box click Add. Select the frame type (for example, Ethernet 802.3) that is used on your network. Type the 8-digit network number, and click Add to close the Manual Frame screen. Repeat this step for each manual protocol that must be added.

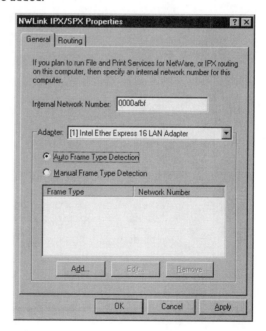

8. When finished, click the OK button, then click Close. When prompted, reboot the server.

Now, to enable the IPX gateway, you must reinstall Microsoft Proxy Server:

1. Run the Setup program from the root of the Proxy Server CD-ROM.

2. A menu will appear. Select Reinstall.

With the IPX gateway functioning, enable user access to the WinSock Proxy service:

3. While in the IIS Manager, click the WinSock Proxy system name.

4. Click the Permissions tab. In the Protocol box, select Unlimited Access.

5. If no users or groups are listed, click Add and then select the Everyone group.

6. Click OK to apply the changes.

To configure the client, use the system from which you removed the Proxy Server in Exercise 8.1.

1. Click the Network icon in the Control Panel.

2. Click the Service tab and remove any TCP/IP-related services such as WINS, DNS, IIS, Simple TCP/IP, TCP/IP printing, and so forth.

3. Click the Protocol tab and remove TCP/IP.

4. Click Add, and then select IPX/SPX Compatible Transport from the list of available protocols.

5. When prompted, provide the CD-ROM or location of the i386 directory from the Windows NT CD-ROM. You may use the defaults and auto-detect frame time for IPX.

6. Click the Bindings tab and disable IPX from the second (Internet) network adapter, as shown here.

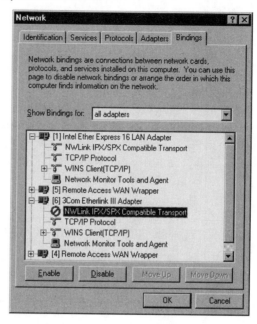

7. Click OK to accept the changes, and reboot when complete.

Reinstall the Proxy client. Since this system was previously configured with IP and the proxy client, you may either remove all components and reinstall, or just reinstall:

1. Browse the network and locate the second system that is still configured as a proxy server. Double-click the MSCLNT share and run Setup.

2. Click OK for any defaults and to complete the installation.

3. Reboot.

EXERCISE 8.4 (CONTINUED FROM PREVIOUS PAGE)

Start monitoring the performance of the Proxy Server. Verify that IPX traffic is being sent to a remote server.

1. From the Proxy Server group on the Start menu, select Performance Monitor.

2. Using the File pull-down menu, select Open and choose the cache workspace.

3. From a proxy client, open either Netscape Navigator or Internet Explorer and browse the proxy server. Note that you most likely need to use the IP address since name resolution is performed from the server itself (**HTTP://ipaddress**). Repeat the same test with FTP and Gopher.

Finally, review the Performance Monitor results:

1. On the Proxy Server, switch to the Performance Monitor screen.

2. Examine the Winsock Proxy Server object. Note that the results show that all traffic is sent to a remote server, whether local or not.

One final tip for working with IPX: Secure the network by forcing this protocol. If there is no need for clients to use TCP/IP directly, you may limit access by forcing IPX access through the WinSock Proxy client. At the server, you should only bind IPX to the internal network adapter. Obviously there is no reason to bind IPX to the external interface since the Internet operates over TCP/IP only. Leaving this protocol bound could potentially cause a security breach because there would be a common protocol by which you could access the internal network. Also, since the IPX protocol will be your primary means of communicating with the internal network, you should consider moving the protocol binding to the top of the list in the service settings, as shown in the graphic on the next page.

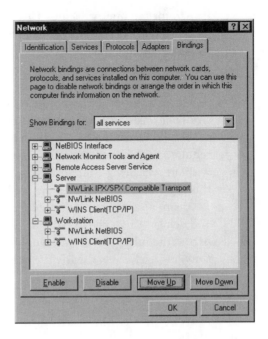

 Protocols other than TCP/IP and IPX/SPX, such as DLC, LAT, and NetBEUI, will not communicate with the proxy server. Do not bother to add these protocols to the proxy server unless clients will be using file, print, or other service that are installed on the proxy server. NetBEUI-only clients must add IPX or TCP to use the proxy server. In general, the external interface should only have TCP/IP bound to it.

Caching Intranet Resources

Caching of intranet resources is identical to caching those on the Internet, with a few exceptions. First, an application must communicate with a service via the proxy server. If the proxy server is bypassed, there will be no way for it to maintain a copy of the data. For this reason, you may want to use a proxy server on the local intranet. There are some very good application reasons to do this.

Suppose a company has a number of its clients based on NetWare, who also need to connect to UNIX resources. No problem; the communications can be established via Proxy Server using the same basic configuration as what is used for the Internet setup. This was discussed earlier in this chapter in the section *Configuring Proxy Server to Act As an IPX Gateway*.

Next, suppose that the same company is diverse and spread across multiple countries with several slow links and many users who need to retrieve various corporate memos and notes. Proxy servers can be chained such that they are downstream from the corporate office. Each link via the Web Proxy is cached from one location to the next. In this way, if the same Web page or FTP site is accessed through the WAN, the data only needs to be downloaded once, or as required by TTL timeouts. In this configuration, the proxy servers may act without ever being configured to access the Internet. A functional example of this is given in Chapter 9 in the section *Arrays and Chains of Proxy Servers*.

Again, after the site is cached, Proxy Server can retrieve the information and deliver it to a client. Now if a client is configured for IP only, they could bypass the proxy server, but would have to get their data directly across the slow link each time. Clearly the proxy server would be much faster for each additional time data is requested.

Summary

This chapter was primarily concerned with the configuration and setup of Microsoft Proxy Server on the Internet as well as its placement in the intranet. The focus of this chapter was to provide a quick reference to implementing Microsoft Proxy Server so that the big picture of how the service works could be seen. In many of our examples, we focused on the topic of integrating with IPX networks so we could demonstrate real-world applications of the proxy technology.

The first half of the chapter looked at configuring client applications, and Proxy Server itself, for Internet access. We reviewed the types of proxy compatibility—CERN or WinSock and the appropriate proxy component to service each type of application. We also generally described the troubleshooting procedures for problems that users of the proxy server may experience.

This chapter also looked briefly at determining security requirements. As discussed in Chapter 7, a proxy server is only as secure as your configuration of it. In other words, if configured incorrectly, it is a possible hazard to network security.

We also provided an overview of maximizing Internet proxy performance. A general rule is that you can add cache to increase performance until your bandwidth capacity is reached. We will discuss this is greater detail in Chapter 12, *Monitoring and Tuning*.

In the second half of this chapter, we focused on Microsoft Proxy Server in the intranet. The same caching technology that enhances Internet performance extends the ability of an intranet by providing the same speed enhancements. As an intranet device, Proxy Server also provides security enhancements by helping to segment a network and using Windows NT Challenge/Response authentication for user validation. This improved security allows a UNIX system to be configured so that its accessibility is virtually integrated with Windows NT.

And finally, we discussed how Microsoft Proxy Server acts as an IPX-to-IP gateway. In this mode, all WinSock requests are treated as being sent to a remote system. As such, the entire protocol stack is converted from IPX to IP and back again.

Review Questions

1. Explain how the Event Viewer should be used in system monitoring to identify problems with the proxy server.

2. What is the key factor in determining the type of support that an application requires? Is there any mixing of proxy services within a supported application?

3. Why would a large company want to maintain an intranet?

4. Explain how Microsoft Proxy Server's user validation for all users differs from validation of specific users.

5. Why is caching limited by bandwidth?

6. As a gateway, which parts of an IPX message does Microsoft Proxy Server not convert?

   A. Data in the message

   B. All addressing

   C. The Request command

   D. The protocol

7. Which of the following customer complaints should you analyze using the proxy server or related components?

   A. Duplicate IP address error

   B. Proxy Server timeout in the Web browser

   C. Cannot see other systems on the network

   D. Access denied to any FTP site

8. The caching mechanism of Microsoft Proxy Server benefits an intranet. True or False? Why?

9. The IPX gateway on Microsoft Proxy Server is enabled by default. True or False? Why?

10. When configured correctly, Windows NT security can be applied to a UNIX system through a proxy server. True or False. Why?

11. You want all your Web Proxy client computers to have access to the sales.com domain, but do not want them to access any other Internet domain. You deny access to all Internet sites through domain filtering, but you need to do one more thing. What is it?

   A. Create a domain filter to grant access to the sales.com domain.

   B. Add sales.com to the list of actively cached sites.

   C. In the Web Proxy service, enable access control.

   D. In the WinSock Proxy service, enable access control.

12. Your clients run IPX and the proxy server runs both IPX and TCP/IP. You want to use the caching features of the Web Proxy service. What must you do on each client computer?

A. Clients cannot use the caching feature when they are only running IPX.

B. Install the Proxy Server client, and configure the Web browser so that it does not use the Web Proxy service.

C. Install the Proxy Server client, and configure the Web browser so that it uses the Web Proxy service.

D. Install nothing on the clients, but enable the Web browser to use the Web Proxy service.

13. On your network you have Windows for Workgroups, Windows 95, and Windows 3.1 clients. They run IPX to connect to your Netware server. You install a proxy server running IPX, but the Windows for Workgroups and Windows 3.1 users cannot access the proxy server services. What is most likely the problem?

A. You must install TCP/IP on the proxy server so it can communicate with the Windows for Workgroup and Windows 3.1 clients.

B. Microsoft Proxy Server only supports the Microsoft IPX/SPX protocol.

C. Microsoft Proxy Server only supports older Novell VLM clients.

D. Microsoft Proxy Server does not support IPX client software on Windows 3.1 and Windows for Workgroups.

14. You want your IPX clients to access the Internet by using the WinSock Proxy service. During the setup of Microsoft Proxy Server, you want to specify the Proxy Server computer name in the Client Installation/Configuration dialog box. What must you specify?

A. The computer name of the Proxy Server computer

B. The DNS name of the Proxy Server computer

C. The hardware address of the Proxy Server's internal adapter

D. The IPX internal network number of the Proxy Server computer's internal adapter

15. You want all your IPX clients to use the WinSock Proxy service to access the Internet. What should you do in the Client Installation/Configuration dialog box?

A. Select the IP Address option button and type the IP address of the internal adapter.

B. Select the IP Address option button and type the IP address of the default gateway.

C. Select the IP Address option button and type the IP address of the external adapter.

D. Select the Computer Name option button and type the NetBIOS name of the Proxy Server.

E. Select the Manual option button and edit the WSPCFG.INI file on every client computer.

CHAPTER

9

Multiple Proxy Servers
and Internet Access

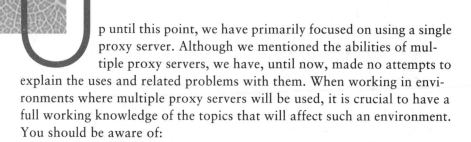

p until this point, we have primarily focused on using a single proxy server. Although we mentioned the abilities of multiple proxy servers, we have, until now, made no attempts to explain the uses and related problems with them. When working in environments where multiple proxy servers will be used, it is crucial to have a full working knowledge of the topics that will affect such an environment. You should be aware of:

- Load balancing

Exam objectives are subject to change at any time without prior notice and at Microsoft's sole discretion. Please visit Microsoft's Training & Certification website (www.microsoft.com/Train_Cert) for the most current exam objectives listing.

- Determining a deployment site

- Geographical issues

- Security problems

- Interactions of DNS and WINS

- Logging proxy events

Load Balancing

As your proxy server begins to reach its capacity and expansion is required, you are faced with several options. First, you can locate the bottleneck that causes the proxy server to be at capacity, or you can add an additional proxy server. For example, your organization may have a server that has a 128k ISDN link to the Internet that is maximized. After performing a study, you may decide that you need to add another ISDN adapter and line to the server. However, if further research shows that the system itself is at capacity and also suffers from somewhat unreliable hardware, you may want to consider upgrading the machine. Or, your decision may be that you would rather implement a second proxy server for redundancy and divide your users.

Depending on the services that you are using, you may be able to implement the use of multiple servers per service. The Web Proxy Server, for instance, can contain separate entries for different services such as FTP, WWW (HTTP), and Gopher, as depicted in Figure 9.1. On the other hand, the WinSock service relies on a single server to provide the service, as it only contains one proxy server entry for all protocols, as shown in Figure 9.2.

FIGURE 9.1

In the Manual Proxy Configuration screen (inside a browser), you can configure multiple proxy servers.

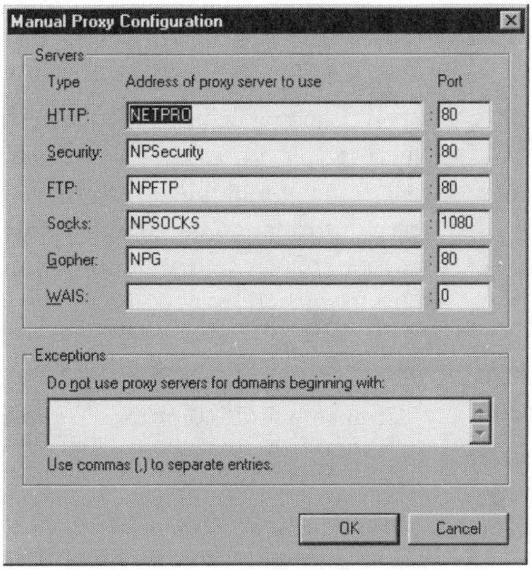

FIGURE 9.2

In the Microsoft WinSock Proxy Client screen, you can see that there is only one proxy server entry for all protocols.

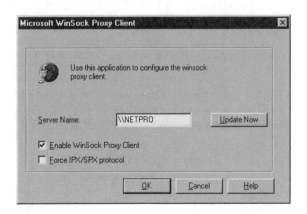

When configuring load balancing, there are many ways to perform the operation. For example, you may load balance simply by assigning some users to one server and the rest to another. Alternatively, you may have Proxy Server's array and chaining abilities perform this action for you. Some administrators prefer another approach, such as having a proxy server for WinSock applications, one for HTTP requests, another for Web and FTP requests, and so on. Additional methods for load balancing, such as with the DNS, will be presented later in this chapter.

The WinSock Proxy Server is configured automatically during setup and is defined in the MSPCLNT.INI located on the Setup share, MSPCLNT, of the proxy server.

Arrays and Chains of Proxy Servers

As you should recall, caching is one of the primary functions of a proxy server. Caching helps define the performance level at which users receive data. Microsoft Proxy Server 2.0 includes the ability to share and distribute its cache among multiple installations. With this capacity, the receipt of local server information maximizes bandwidth, while fault tolerance and shared security are achieved. Microsoft accomplishes these features in two configurations: *chains* and *arrays*.

Microsoft Exam Objective

Choose a fault tolerance strategy. Strategies include:

- Using arrays
- Using routing

Chaining is designed to work in a WAN configuration where an "upstream" server delivers data across the network. In an upstream system, you create a route or data path which is used to resolve client requests. The proxy servers and proxy arrays that comprise that part of the chain are then in a hierarchical configuration. We will discuss this topic in more depth when we review routing requests among multiple servers later on in this chapter. When data is not located on the first proxy server checked, the next in the chain is used until the request is resolved by the cache or the actual resource. In a chained configuration, systems can be linked in arrays or individually, as shown in Figure 9.3.

FIGURE 9.3

Proxy servers in a chain configuration

<table>
<tr><td>Proxy Client</td><td>Proxy Server</td><td>Proxy Server 2</td><td>Internet</td></tr>
</table>

Microsoft ✓ Exam Objective

Configure hierarchical caching.

Arrays allow multiple computers to act as if they are all the same system. In this configuration, the systems are automatically load balanced, security is shared, fault tolerance is active, and scalability is enhanced. By using a distributed cache, downstream servers may unload some of their caching burden on other systems. Furthermore, with multiple computers acting as one larger computer, more hits occur on the cache and clients experience faster access.

Arrays are typically found in companies with large numbers of users concentrated in a single location. When multiple locations are present with large numbers of users, arrays can be chained to each other. This is especially common where proxy servers are placed behind some type of firewall. Also, array configurations are used to consolidate multiple Internet/ISP connections. For example, when a company is spread out geographically, proxy servers may be configured to route traffic through a single connection at a home office. However, sometimes two (or more) Internet connections are used and one is designated as a backup to the primary ISP link. A basic array configuration is shown in Figure 9.4.

FIGURE 9.4

An array of proxy servers

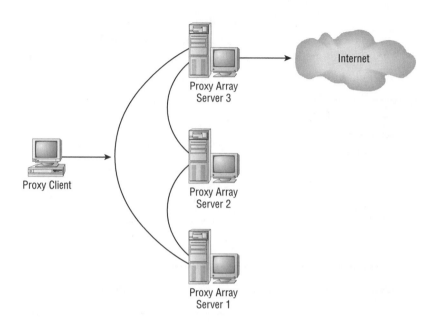

Array Operations

An array can easily be established among two or more installations of Microsoft Proxy Server 2.0. The array can be configured by clicking the Arrays button on the Service tab of any of the proxy services running on a particular server. On an established array, only one system should be administered at any given time. If configuration changes are made at the same time, an Array Update Errors screen will appear denoting a configuration change, as shown in Figure 9.5. After clicking OK, your options are to overwrite changes, refresh changes, or to cancel. Typically, an administrator should cancel to avoid problems. Refreshing will allow in-place changes to occur while adding additional changes from the current session. If overwriting is applied, the results may be undesirable because you will have no way of knowing what it is you are overwriting or whose work you may be affecting.

While working in an array, load balancing is achieved through an algorithm known as the *hash procedure*. In this array configuration, each server maintains a list of all other servers in the array and their operating status. When a system is down, it is placed on hold while other systems take on their responsibilities. The hash procedure formulates its operation based on the number of servers the URL requested, and the load on each system. Using this information, user requests are assigned within the array. Given the identical operating conditions, the algorithm will always assign the same server.

FIGURE 9.5

The Array Update Errors
dialog box

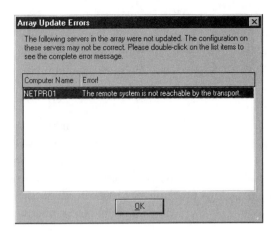

Each array is independent of all other arrays. Configuring one array will have no effect on other arrays.

When the status of an array is verified, only a single member system of the array needs configuration changes applied. For instance, once changes are made to a member of the array, those changes will be applied to all other members without additional steps. Each member contains the same information regarding other systems within the array. Although any system can request to verify the status, only the system administrator (or a member of the Administrators group) can change array membership. In this configuration, the system is fault tolerant against any member system being off-line. Also, because all array member systems keep information on each other, they can also be synchronized to the configuration of a particular member. Synchronized information includes:

- Client configuration file

- Domain filters (security)

- LAT (Local Address Table)

- Logging information for each service (not the directory storing the logs)

- Web Proxy advanced caching options with cache filters

- Web Proxy publishing information

- Web Proxy upstream routing options

- Web Proxy user permissions

- WinSock Proxy protocol definitions

- WinSock Proxy user permissions

The information maintained by the array members is constantly updated so the system's status (up or down) is current in an array table. This table is managed independent of the other systems. As a result, each system is constantly queried regarding its status. To ensure that information is current and accurate, a TTL (Time to Live) period is assigned to the table. When the TTL period has concluded, the system begins querying other array member systems again.

To improve routing performance, client browsers may download an auto-configuration file (JavaScript) from an array member.

Controlling Array Membership

As you have read, proxy servers may operate in a stand-alone configuration or in groups of systems known as arrays. When working in an array, there are three ways in which membership can be controlled: Join/Create, Remove, and Leave. These options appear under the Array Controls. If no array is established, the button will be displayed as Join; otherwise it will be displayed as Leave. The Remove button appears on the Array List screen and is discussed later in this chapter. Depending on the type of operation you are attempting to perform, each control option can be of use to you. The controls of the array are simple, straightforward, and fairly fool proof. However, for security reasons, you should enable Windows NT Challenge/Response authentication for all interactions involved with array membership, since any member can control the entire array.

Microsoft ✓ *Exam* *Objective*   **Configure Proxy Server arrays.**

Joining or creating an array translates into either forming a new array between two or more stand-alone systems, or becoming a part of a currently established array. When joining an array, an administrator may simply type the name of any system in an array to become a member. Use the steps in Exercise 9.1 to join an array.

EXERCISE 9.1

Joining an Array

1. From the IIS Manager, double-click a proxy service for the system you want to administer.

2. On the Service tab, click the Arrays button.

3. An Array screen will appear. Make note of whether or not the check-box for Synchronize Configuration of Array Members (currently grayed out) is checked. Then click the Join Array button.

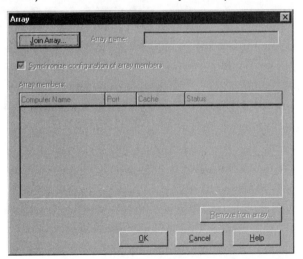

4. Type the name of the system that you would like to join with an Array. That system may be a stand-alone machine or part of an existing array.

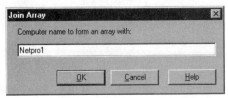

EXERCISE 9.1 (CONTINUED FROM PREVIOUS PAGE)

5. If no array currently exists, you will be prompted to enter an array name in the New Array dialog box. Once you have entered a name, click OK.

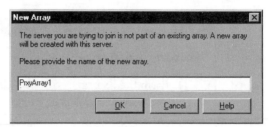

6. Verify that the system now appears in the Array Members list in the Array dialog box. Note that the Join Array button is now called Leave Array. Click Apply and then OK to complete the array settings.

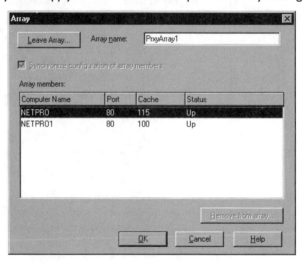

7. If the Synchronize Configuration of Array Members checkbox in step 3 was not checked, repeat steps 1 and 2. When reviewing the Array Members list, click the Synchronize Array Members checkbox. Click Apply, then OK.

Leaving and removing an array both accomplish the same function, but the premise behind each operation is different. Leaving an array is accomplished from the system that is being administered, while removing from an array is done remotely. Remember that only the administrator can make changes directly to a system. Removing a system from the table is not an action that is performed directly on the system you are deleting. Exercise 9.2 will walk you through the necessary motions required to remove a system from an array.

EXERCISE 9.2

Removing Systems from an Array

1. From the IIS Manager, double-click a proxy service for the system that you want to administer.

2. On the Service tab, click the Arrays button.

3. An Array screen will appear. Check the box for Synchronize Configuration for Array Members.

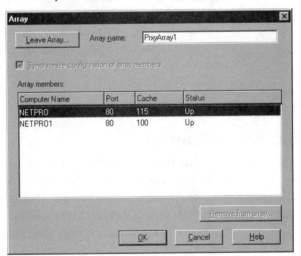

4. To remove the local machine, click Leave Array on the Array screen, then click Yes to exit the Leave Array dialog box. You must click Apply and/or OK for Leave Changes to be applied once on the Service tab.

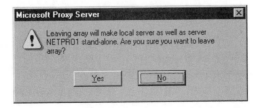

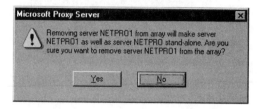

> **EXERCISE 9.2 (CONTINUED FROM PREVIOUS PAGE)**
>
> **5.** To remove a system from the Array list, select the server from the list you would like to remove it from, then click the Remove from Array button on the Array dialog screen. A dialog box will appear. Once you click Yes, changes will take place immediately. Click OK or Apply on the Service tab to make the changes permanent.

After changing array membership, you should stop and restart the service. This will ensure that all functions that were involved previously are updated. Since each system maintains data on the others, the load will be redistributed evenly. When a system is off-line, no request will be sent to that system until it is back online.

Other Array Controls

There are two other methods through the IIS Manager by which arrays may be controlled. The first method is via a command line using a utility called RemotMSP. The command offers multiple options. To view command options, execute RemotMSP –H from the C:\MSP directory. Because commands are chained, you must type the command plus the modifier with a –H switch to view Help for any subject. For example, to view help on array status, you would type **RemotMSP STATUS –H**. Or you may just want to review the status by typing **RemotMSP status –member:*proxyservername* –V**. This will yield the following output for a stand-alone machine:

    C:\msp>remotmsp status -member:netpro -v

    Array configuration information from proxy NETPRO1
    Version 02.00.0372
    Stand alone Proxy Server

Stamp 345e0f90 345e0f90 21924f
Operation completed successfully

And the following output for an array:

C:\msp>remotmsp status -member:netpro -v

Array configuration information from proxy NETPRO1
Version 02.00.0372
Proxy Array
Array Name: ProxyArray
Synchronize Array Configuration: Enabled
Distributed Cache: Enabled

Machine Cache Load Time
Name Status Size Factor Version Stamp
NETPRO OK 115 100 (%50) 02.00.0372 345e1617 345e1617 3
b13bd
NETPRO1 OK 100 100 (%50) 02.00.0372 345e1617 345e1617 3
b13bd
0 machines are down.
The array is synchronized
Operation completed successfully

Another useful URL for finding arrays is `http://proxyservername/`
`ARRAY.DLL?Get.Info.v1`. This site lists the array information version, if the
array is enabled, the configuration ID, the array name, and the array list TTL,
in addition to information about each member server (as in the example
above). Do not confuse the `GET.INFO.V1` URL with the automatic client configuration `GET.Routing.SCRIPT` discussed in Chapter 3.

The RemotMSP command can be used to administrate the starting, stopping, status, load factor, synchronization, membership, and configuration
backup/restore for an array. This command line utility is useful in managing
remote proxy servers for which using IIS Manager is too difficult due to bandwidth restrictions and geographic problems, and when configuring multiple
servers via a script. The utility is commonly used with WSPProto.EXE, which
is used to define WinSock Proxy protocols via the command line. Both utilities
are excellent for remote management.

Configure Microsoft Proxy Server for Internet access. Situations include:

- Configuring Proxy Server to provide Internet access through a dial-up connection to an ISP.
- Configuring Proxy Server to act as an IPX gateway.
- Configuring multiple Microsoft Proxy Servers for Internet access.
- Configuring multiple Proxy Servers spread across several different geographic locations.

Another method for viewing array information is with a Web browser. To view Web information, you must have Execute access to the Web page that you are connecting to. In the URL line, you should type **HTTP://proxyservername/ ARRAY.DLL?Get.Array.List**. This URL will list some basic array configuration information. Note that the proxy is enabled. Call out a configuration ID, an array list, and the list's TTL. Following this synopsis of the array, members will be listed as follows:

- Proxy Server name or IP address
- Port number
- URL for ARRAY.DLL
- Version of Proxy Server
- Time in seconds Proxy Server has been in its current state
- Current status of the server (up or down)
- Load factor
- Cache size

Array.DLL is only delivered with the purchased release product.

Routing Requests among Multiple Servers

When multiple proxy servers are joined together, many benefits are available. In a wide area configuration, perhaps the most value benefit is the ability to route Internet traffic. Microsoft Proxy Server 2.0 allows requests to be forwarded between proxy servers. Requests that are forwarded may be sent between individual machines, arrays, or directly to the Internet. Optionally, clients may be configured such that they attempt to resolve their requests from an array prior to forwarding the request upstream.

Changes in the routing configuration will be detected and dealt with automatically. For instance, if the operating status of a proxy server shows a fault, the configured backup path will automatically be used. Also, if an array member is faulted (has an error), the other participants in the array will not forward requests to it.

Upstream Routing

Web Proxy client requests may be routed among individually chained proxy servers and arrays, or directly to the Internet. Since security among servers may become questionable, such as when certain departments add unauthorized proxy servers, password authentication can be enabled. By enabling this level of authentication, downstream systems can be identified more easily.

Microsoft ✓ *Exam* *Objective*	**Configure arrays to provide fault-tolerance for Web Proxy client requests.**

As a factor of configuring fault tolerance, multiple upstream paths may be defined. The primary path will be used under normal conditions. In the event of a failure, however, a backup path may be used. The fault tolerance switchover to a backup path is automatic. The backup path typically is completely functional and has all the capabilities the primary path has. In this configuration, no single point of failure is present. The failed server will continuously be checked for availability. Once online, the primary path will be restored without intervention.

Since Microsoft Proxy Server cannot automatically determine which proxy servers and arrays are downstream, routes must be configured statically by an administrator. To configure a static route, follow the steps in Exercise 9.3.

EXERCISE 9.3

Configuring a Static Route

1. Open the IIS Manager and select the Web Proxy service.

2. Click the Routing tab. The Web Proxy Service Properties screen will appear.

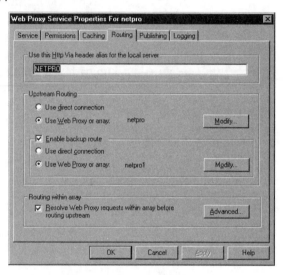

3. In the Upstream Routing section, select either Use Direct Connection or Use Web Proxy or Array. When forwarding data to another Web proxy or array, you must supply a valid server or array name plus a port. To do this, click the Modify button and the Advanced Routing Options screen will appear.

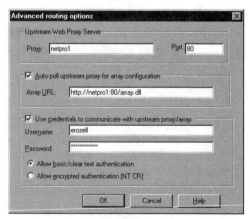

EXERCISE 9.3 (CONTINUED FROM PREVIOUS PAGE)

4. At this point, you also have the opportunity to configure upstream polling and credentials. Generally, you should not change polling of upstream servers, since this mechanism is used to detect faults. However, if you have a reason to do this, you may disable it or change the URL array DLL. This most likely would not change unless you were either attempting to connect to a third-party proxy server or troubleshooting a fault. To set credentials, supply a user name and password, and select either Allow Basic/Clear Text Authentication or Allow Encrypted Authentication (NT CR).

5. A backup route can also be defined by selecting the Enable Backup Route checkbox in the Web Proxy Service Properties dialog box. The backup route can either use a direct connection or a Web proxy or an array. Once the checkbox for the backup routing is selected, you have the same options available as with the primary route. Commonly, backup routes do not use credentials as the primary route does.

Resolving Web Requests within an Array

An administrator may want to attempt to resolve Web proxy requests within an array before routing upstream. Since clients may be connecting to an array, this can be performed from the same Routing tab on the Web Proxy Service dialog box. To enable this function, simply click the checkbox in the Routing within Array section at the bottom of the Routing tab. For advanced configuration of this function, click the Advanced button in the Web Proxy Service Properties screen. The Advanced Array Options screen shown in Figure 9.6 will appear.

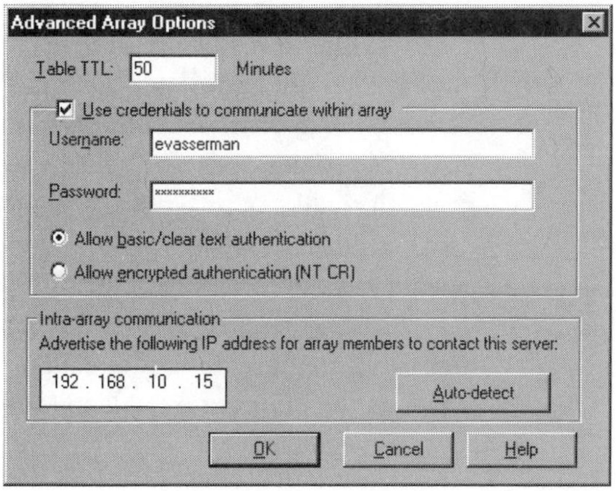

FIGURE 9.6 The Advanced Array Options dialog box

In this screen, you can set the Time to Live (TTL) duration of the array table, set credentials to communicate within the array, and include intra-array communications information. The TTL duration is the period of time that the array table will be considered current. By default, the TTL is set to 50 minutes. The credentials in the array are used in the same context as upstream routing, with the exception that credential information is used between routes in the array rather than between chains. Finally, intra-array communication is advertised by announcing its IP address to other systems. To automatically set this value, click the Auto-Detect button. Only when a server is using multiple IP addresses or when you are manually trying to redirect requests from other proxy servers within the array should you change this value.

Routing should not be used in an upstream configuration with a system or array that is not based on Microsoft Proxy 2.0. Results may be unpredictable.

To the user, the array structure is invisible. Web Proxy client requests are sent to a single member of the proxy server array. Assuming that the member does not contain the requested information, the request is forwarded either to another array member of the array that may have the item cached or to an upstream proxy server computer or proxy server array. Finally, if the request cannot be filled from an upstream proxy server, the request is forwarded directly to the Internet. Only one hop is performed within an array before the request is sent upstream. When working with a client that auto-configures and supports CARP, only one hop is required to access the cache, regardless of where data is in an array. Client requests are routed within an array using the Cache Array Routing Protocol (CARP).

An array may be addressed as a logical structure, and a client may communicate to it either directly or through a DNS *round robin* configuration (The round robin configuration is discussed later in this chapter in the section *Load Balancing DNS Networks with Proxy Servers Other than Microsoft Proxy Server 2.0*). When addressing the array as a logical structure, an array-aware client can route to a proxy array based on the CARP algorithm. Because CARP is a deterministic algorithm, the client can determine where an item should be cached (if in the cache). If a client does not support CARP, they will need to access an array member that will then route the request for them, if, in a round robin DNS configuration, the request will be resolved in a load-balanced way. However, the information will still require redirection by an array member.

WinSock and Socks clients do not support arrays or chained configurations. Remember that an array's primary concern is load balancing and sharing cached information. This means that alternative methods for load balancing must be used. Other load balancing methods are discussed later in this chapter.

Cache Array Routing Protocol

The primary technology behind Microsoft Proxy Server 2.0's array caching system is known as Cache Array Routing Protocol (CARP). CARP was inspired by and designed to replace the Internet Cache Protocol (ICP). ICP's main flaw was that it had to be manually configured to query neighboring proxy servers. The problem, of course, was that in checking with the neighboring systems, there was no deterministic pattern for where data could be found. As arrays with the ICP technology grew, they become self-limiting due to internal requests (negative scalability). This flaw meant that proxy servers in an array were unaware of what their neighbors had in their caches, effectively creating a highly redundant cache. CARP does not have this drawback.

The CARP technology makes efficient use of resources by providing the following features:

- Compatibility with today's technology: Regardless of the client browser, CARP can be applied to provide efficiency in a request. A CARP-aware client will use a Proxy AutoConfig file (PAC). Clients with this feature can anticipate where cached data is stored and retrieve data directly from the server in the array with only one hop. If a client does not have this compatibility, the server can perform the redirecting operation at the cost of an extra hop. Essentially, this means that a Web browser that is not capable of configuring itself will retrieve an object from the cache with a maximum of two hops. Because CARP operates over the HTTP, no new protocols are introduced, thus maintaining compatibility with firewalls and other devices. The original ICP technology only existed on proxy servers, but CARP exists at both the client and server levels.

- Imaging an array so the server can behave as a single cache: As an advanced caching system, CARP has the advantage of not replicating data between proxy servers. For example, if data were requested from a specific site, the same server in an array will always be queried for that data. In this way, there is no overlapping of cached data. This helps in producing an efficient use of cache disk space.

- Distributed caching without queries: The deterministic nature of CARP means that a system seeking information will know exactly where the requested data is stored. CARP is a hash-based algorithm that resolves requests for the same information to the same data path every time. A client such as Internet Explorer or a downstream server will be aware of the cached data's location without a query and can access this data in a single hop.

- Dynamic array adaptations: A key feature of the CARP technology is its ability to remain dynamic (ICP was manual). When a server fails or is taken off-line, no changes are required to reconfigure a Microsoft Proxy Sever array cache. The only change that occurs is the redirection of requests from that server to its peers.

- Scalability: Since the algorithm for caching is hash-based, adding additional servers does not require inner-array searching to find data. This feature means that the proxy array actually will become faster rather than slower with more servers. (The ICP, as you've likely guessed, got slower with more servers.)

When put into action, all CARP clients and servers follow a set of rules that assist in yielding the efficiencies discussed above. First, all proxy servers are noted in an array membership list that maintains a TTL listing as to the last time an array member's status was checked. Next, a hashing function is applied to compute a scoring value based on the name of the proxy server. This same function is later used for URL requests when determining the location of cached data. Effectively, adding the hash scores of the URL and the proxy server determines which server owns the cache. Finally, each request for the same data will automatically be directed to the same owner for the cached data. The function for determining a cache owner is so involved that data becomes distributed by statistical values (scores) $- 2 \wedge 32$ or 4,294,967,296. With this algorithm, no large caching table is required. The hashing formula simply produces the same outcome without the table.

Issues with an Array Configuration

Since Proxy Server 2.0 is relatively new, very few known problems exist with its arrays. However, there are problems that occur that are not due to error. Here are some problems you may encounter:

- Array members may have difficulty communicating with each other during times of extreme traffic. Systems may assume that other systems are down and that they will remain down for long periods of time. This assumption may be due to the available bandwidth between servers.

- An array configuration is only effective if it has no more than 20 members.

- Multiple changes made to the Proxy Server at the same time can create conflicts. This is especially true when changing permissions on servers that are part of the array.

- The routing configuration is such that downstream proxies and clients are too few. The result is a poor distribution in the array that does not enhance performance. More lateral requests are made, resulting in an overload within the array.

DNS-Based Networks and Proxy Gateways

A DNS-based network is one where a primary DNS server performs name resolution. These names hold a hierarchical design that distinguishes each device with a host name from all other devices with the same name. For example, you may have two systems that are known as WWW at two different companies. The domain name followed by the organization type distinguishes the two. For instance, www.microsoft.com and www.sybex.com share the same name, but are identified according to their domain and suffix.

Microsoft
✓ ***Exam***
Objective

Choose a strategy to balance Internet access across multiple Proxy Server computers. Strategies include:

- Using DNS
- Using arrays
- Using Cache Array Routing Protocol (CARP)

Microsoft
✓ ***Exam***
Objective

Choose a rollout plan for integrating a Proxy Server with an existing corporate environment.

DNS networks are common to environments where TCP/IP-based applications handle the majority of network utilization, such as with UNIX-based systems. In a DNS network, host names are used to assign each device a user-friendly name rather than an IP address. For example, it is much easier to think of the Web server at Sybex as www.sybex.com rather than 206.100.29.83. When requesting to resolve the name, the system checks the name against a list provided through the DNS. If that DNS does not have an entry, it makes a referral request to another server that also checks for the requested IP address until it is resolved.

Each DNS-based network that is integrated with the Internet is required to maintain two DNS servers. This requirement is set forth by InterNIC (Internet Network Information Center). This allows a redundancy, which ensures that the network name can always be resolved. In many cases, two companies will team up and share DNS services such that each provides the secondary server for the other. Also, it is not uncommon for DNS services to be provided by the ISP. In either case, the DNS provides resolution to host names as requests are received from users on the private network as well as on the Internet. Since the DNS is linked as a secondary server to a primary DNS on the Internet, name resolution takes place in a hierarchy.

For more information on the operations of a DNS, refer to Chapter 2.

Load Balancing DNS Networks with Proxy Servers Other than Microsoft Proxy Server 2.0   A key method of load balancing is a DNS procedure known as round robin. This procedure earned its name from the DNS request procedure, which revolves in a circle. In this procedure, a DNS is configured with all proxy servers compiled into a list. This list is defined by a generic alias such as "proxy" or "WWW." When a user attempts to resolve the proxy server's name, a list of servers is delivered. The client will use the first name that appears in the list. Then, on subsequent requests, the second server will be used, then the third, and so on. When the list is exhausted, the process repeats from the first system down (with the round robin approach). Proxy servers in the list are defined by a CNAME or an alias. If a server's actual host name is used, the server will be accessed directly, rather than in a way that promotes load balancing.

Clients must be configured to use the generic alias assigned to the proxy array in order to work. For instance, suppose that you have a set of three servers called NPXY1, NPXY2, and NPXY3. All three systems are configured at the DNS to resolve to the name PROXY.NETPRO.COM. Your clients should address the proxy servers as PROXY.NETPRO.COM rather than by their host name or IP address. Performing load balancing via a DNS is very important, but there's a little conflicting advice about it. Use the DNS for load balancing (explained in Chapter 9), but remove DNS entries from the client (explained in Chapter 7). There is a trade off of security for functionality. Make a call as to what works best for you. Typically, using the DNS is the better choice.

Another approach to this situation would be to load balance through the login script or according to an assigned IP address. For example, if you have multiple DNS servers, you may configure all clients to use the proxy servers by alias and use different IP addresses between DNS servers. Suppose that DHCP was used to assign IP addressing information. Two pools could be used to assign half the users to one DNS and half to another. When the alias is resolved, load balancing will be achieved because the DNS servers point to different resources when using the same name. Those that are assigned addresses from one range can resolve the address to the first proxy server, and those from the next range to another. However, this scenario has limitations, since you may have difficulties with a third (or fourth, or fifth, etc.) proxy server. Since the search order for resolving names uses the host file before it uses DNS or another method, you may also define in the user login script to copy a host file from the validating domain controller. The result will be that load balancing is determined according to which server you log on to. Of course, this has the limitation of erasing any HOST file that users may have in place for other uses.

Yet another method is to define a different server according to an alias stored in the HOST file. Depending on which HOST file was delivered, each client will be assigned to a proxy server via the HOST file. The HOST file is located in the Windows directory for Windows 3.11 and Windows 95 clients, and in SYSTEMROOT\SYSTEM32\DRIVERS\PATH for Windows NT.

The bottom line is that every gateway requires a DNS entry. Depending on what the administrator wants, load balancing can be achieved in many different ways; it all depends on how creative you want to be. There are no direct mechanisms for performing load balancing since we are no longer exclusively working with just Microsoft Proxy Server 2.0 in this section. Implementation is purely methodical. Exercise 9.4 demonstrates the use and configuration of multiple proxy servers in a DNS-based network.

EXERCISE 9.4

Configuring Multiple Proxy Servers in a DNS-Based Network

In this exercise, your goal is to configure the DNS service on the Proxy Server so the client will use both DNS systems. This means that you will be required to configure the client to use the DNS.

To configure the DNS service:

1. If the DNS service is already installed, skip to the section of this exercise that discusses controlling your server from the DNS Manager. If the DNS service is not installed, double-click the Network icon in the Control Panel.

2. Click Services. Then click the Add button and select Microsoft DNS Server.

3. When prompted, enter the location of the i386 directory or insert the Windows NT Server CD.

4. After the files have completed copying, click the Close button and restart the system.

To control your server from the DNS Manager:

1. Select Start ➢ Programs ➢ Administrative Tools, and click the DNS Manager icon.

2. From the DNS pull-down menu, click New Server.

3. Enter the IP address of the DNS server. Assuming that you have installed this on the same server as the proxy service, the IP address should be the same.

To Create the primary zone for your DNS:

1. Select Start ➢ Programs ➢ Administrative Tools, and click the DNS Manager icon.

2. From the DNS pull-down menu, click New Zone and select Primary Zone.

3. On the next screen (DNS Wizard), type the domain name. In this exercise, use **MCSETEST.COM**. Push the Tab key. The rest of the boxes in the dialog box should be filled in automatically. Assuming the Zone File information is acceptable, click Finished.

EXERCISE 9.4 (CONTINUED FROM PREVIOUS PAGE)

To define the Proxy Server to the DNS:

1. Select Start ➤ Programs ➤ Administrative Tools, and click the DNS Manager icon.

2. From the DNS pull-down menu, select New Host.

3. Type **MSPROXY** in the Name dialog box followed by the IP address of the proxy server. When finished, click Add Host.

4. Configure the second system as a proxy server, if it isn't already configured as such.

5. Add a record for the second proxy server using the same name, MSPROXY, and the IP address of the second server. When finished, click Add Host, and then click Done.

To configure the client to use the DNS server:

1. Double-click the Network icon in the Control Panel, select the Protocols tab, and click TCP/IP.

2. Click the DNS tab and type **MCSETEST.COM** in the Domain box.

3. Clear any entries in the DNS Services Search order.

4. Add the IP address for the server that contains the (Primary) DNS service.

5. Add the secondary proxy server in the DNS listing (assuming it contains the DNS service).

6. Click OK, then select the WINS tab and click Enable DNS for Windows Resolutions.

7. When complete, click OK and reboot.

Load Balancing without a DNS or with IPX Clients   The obvious question that is probably on your mind is, "What do I do if I have no DNS server in my network?" As far as functionality of the proxy server is concerned, it will not matter as long it has access after it attaches to the Internet. However, for load balancing, the process is a little more complex. To communicate with the array, you must either use the IP or IPX address of the server or member server in an array. This information (the IP or IPX address) can be found in the LOCAL-ADDR.DUMP file located in the C:\MSP\CLIENTS directory on your Proxy Server. Copy this information from each array member's LOCAL-ADDR.DUMP file and merge the data from the files into the [Servers IP Addresses] and [Servers IPX Addresses] sections of the client MSPCLNT.INI file. Note that the LOCAL-ADDR.DUMP file will be different from server to server, and that is why you must compile them. After the merge is complete, manually copy this information to the other members of the array so load balancing can take place.

Microsoft ✓ ***Exam*** ***Objective***

Configure Proxy Server and Proxy Server client computers to use the Proxy Server services. Configurations include:

- Microsoft Internet Explorer client computers
- Netscape Navigator client computers
- Macintosh® client computers
- UNIX client computers
- Client computers on an IPX-only network

Remember that when working with IPX clients, the clients will always use the WinSock client software. The *WINS-Based Networks and Proxy Gateways* section provides an alternative method for addressing this problem.

WINS-Based Networks and Proxy Gateways

WINS is DNS's name resolving counterpart for NetBIOS names. WINS servers are commonly implemented with DNS servers within Windows NT–based networks. Because the majority of clients in these networks rely on the WINS server, there are special considerations when configuring multi-homed servers such as Microsoft Proxy Server. WINS operates with the following parameters, which help to automatically load balance. There are three stages to name resolution. The first involves the WINS server, which pairs up a client's request to the client's IP address. The WINS server attempts to locate a proxy server with the

Implementing and Supporting Microsoft® Proxy Server 2.0

Exam 70-088: Objectives

OBJECTIVE	PAGE
Planning	
Choose a secure access strategy for various situations. Access includes outbound access by users to the Internet and inbound access to your Web site. Considerations include translating addresses from the internal network to the Local Address Table (LAT), controlling anonymous access, controlling access by known users and groups, setting protocol permissions, auditing protocol access, and setting Microsoft Windows NT® security parameters.	139, 233, 311
Plan an Internet site or an intranet site for stand-alone servers, single-domain environments, and multiple-domain environments. Tasks include choosing appropriate connectivity methods, choosing services, using Microsoft Proxy Server in an intranet that has no access to the Internet, and choosing hardware.	133, 345, 520
Choose a strategy to balance Internet access across multiple Proxy Server computers. Strategies include, using DNS, using arrays, and using Cache Array Routing Protocol (CARP).	239, 383, 531
Choose a rollout plan for integrating a Proxy Server with an existing corporate environment.	383, 531
Choose a fault tolerance strategy. Strategies include using arrays and using routing.	366
Installation and Configuration	
Create a LAT.	143, 160, 267
Configure server authentication. Authentication options include anonymous logon, basic authentication and Microsoft Windows NT Challenge/Response authentication.	205, 233
Configure Windows NT to support Microsoft Proxy Server.	134
Configure the various Proxy Server services.	227
Configure Microsoft Proxy Server for Internet access. Situations include configuring Proxy Server to provide Internet access through a dial-up connection to an ISP, configuring Proxy Server to act as an IPX gateway, configuring multiple Microsoft Proxy Servers for Internet access, and configuring multiple Proxy Servers spread across several different geographic locations.	352, 376, 404
Select and use software configuration management tools (for example, Control Panel, Windows NT Setup, Regedt32).	420, 478
Configure auditing.	243, 295
Given a scenario, decide which user interface to use to perform administrative tasks.	226, 281, 421
Identify the licensing requirements for a given Proxy Server site.	135
Configure Proxy Server arrays.	370
Configure arrays to provide fault-tolerance for Web Proxy client requests.	377
Use packet filtering to prevent unauthorized access. Tasks include using packet filtering to enable a specific protocol and configuring packet filter alerting and logging.	286
Configure hierarchical caching.	367
Setting Up and Managing Resource Access	
Grant or restrict access to the Internet for selected outbound users and groups who use the various Proxy Server services to access the Internet.	232, 304

 NOTE Exam objectives are subject to change at any time without prior notice and at Microsoft's sole discretion. Please visit Microsoft's Training & Certification Web site (www.microsoft.com/Train_Cert) for the most current listing of exam objectives.

OBJECTIVE	PAGE
Setting Up and Managing Resource Access	
Grant or restrict access to specific Internet sites for outbound users.	297
Choose the location, size, and type of caching for the Web Proxy service.	134, 236, 339
Configure active caching and passive caching.	234
Implement Web publishing to enable reverse proxying.	318
Back up and restore Proxy Server configurations.	268
Implement reverse hosting.	318
Integration and Interoperablility	
Use the Proxy Server client Setup program to configure client computers.	150
Configure Proxy Server and Proxy Server client computers to use the Proxy Server services. Configurations include Microsoft Internet Explorer client computers, Netscape Navigator client computers, Macintosh® client computers, UNIX client computers, and client computers on an IPX-only network.	165, 329, 388
Configure a RAS server to route Internet requests.	415
Write JavaScript to configure a Web browser.	146
Change settings in Mspclnt.ini.	155
Monitoring and Optimization	
Configure Proxy Server to log errors when they occur.	244, 462
Monitor performance of various functions by using Microsoft Windows NT Performance Monitor. Functions include HTTP and FTP sessions.	440
Analyze performance issues. Performance issues include identifying bottlenecks, network-related performance issues, disk-related performance issues, CPU-related performance issues, and memory-related performance issues.	429, 475
Optimize performance for various purposes, including increasing throughput and optimizing routing.	340, 440
Use Performance Monitor logs to identify the appropriate configuration.	440
Perform Internet traffic analysis by using Windows NT Server tools.	451
Monitor current sessions.	229
Troubleshooting	
Resolve Proxy Server and Proxy Server client installation problems.	486
Resolve Proxy Server and Proxy Server client access problems.	486
Resolve Proxy Server client computer problems.	486
Resolve security problems.	506
Resolve caching problems.	488
Troubleshoot a WINS server to provide client access to Proxy Servers.	489
Troubleshoot hardware-related problems such as network interfaces and disk drives.	482
Troubleshoot Internet/intranet routing hardware and software. Software includes Microsoft Routing and Remote Access Service (RRAS).	415

same subnet as the client. Next, WINS tries to find a proxy server on the same network as the client. When all else fails and none of the methods have worked, the WINS server will simply pick the gateway at random from an internal list. This scenario, of course, assumes an automatic configuration rather than one where a proxy server is specifically designated.

Now that you have configured a network environment that supports multiple proxy servers (refer back to Exercise 9.1), you must verify that you can connect automatically to a second server in the event that the primary server is unavailable. To learn how to do this, complete Exercise 9.5.

EXERCISE 9.5

Verifying Connectivity with Multiple Proxy Servers

To verify your DNS client settings:

1. At the workstation that is configured as a proxy client, type **IPCON-FIG ALL** (or **WINIPCFG** for Windows 95).

2. Inspect the DNS entries. You should see both proxy servers listed in the DNS section.

To configure the client to use the proxy server:

1. Run the client setup utility from the primary proxy server. To call the setup utility, select Run from the Start menu and type *servername*\ **MSCLNT\SETUP**.

2. After setup has completed, verify that the system is not set to use the proxy server for local systems.

3. Shut down the computer and restart.

To verify that the implemented configuration works:

1. On the client system, open a DOS prompt and type **PING WS PROXY**.

2. Repeat the Ping command three to four times more. Note the IP address of the system that is responding.

3. Disable one of the proxy servers by shutting it off or unplugging the network cable.

EXERCISE 9.5 (CONTINUED FROM PREVIOUS PAGE)

4. Repeat step 1. Note the IP address of the system that is responding.

5. Run Internet Explorer or Netscape Navigator and connect to a system that is on the Internet or a separate network that simulates the Internet. Click the Refresh button to ensure that you are not looking at the proxy server's cache.

6. Re-enable the server that was disabled in step 2 and restart you Web browser. Connect to the same Internet Web site and click Refresh.

7. Repeat steps 2 to 5 with the other proxy server disabled. Note how the DNS load balances your system on the proxy servers.

Issues with Multiple Proxy Servers

There are a number of issues that arise when using multiple proxy servers. Unlike other servers, such as WINS, where information is shared between systems, proxy servers other than Microsoft Proxy Server 2.0 do not exchange data with each other. In other words, Netscape Proxy will not communicate its cache with any other proxy server; Microsoft Proxy Server 1.0 will not talk to Microsoft Proxy Server 2.0, and so on.

Because there is no communication between all servers (other than Microsoft Proxy 2.0), the cache will be unique to each installation. This means that systems that are configured to use different proxy servers may experience different access times when requesting data. Typically, this situation is not noticed because caching occurs on the first request, and then as needed. Nonetheless, users may complain about a performance problem when they switch between workstation systems that utilize different proxy servers.

Also, as an effect of no communication between servers, security is explicitly set to only the server that the user was configured to. For this reason, we recommend creating groups such as "Web Proxy Users" and defining security equally between servers. This is a manual process. However, when using groups, security can be defined at the User Manager for Domains level without having to change each proxy server for each user. Note that this is less of a problem with arrays since they share security information. However, you would still have to use the IIS Manager to assign user rights rather than just working within User Manager for Domains.

When working in an environment that consists only of Microsoft Proxy Server 2.0, caches can be shared among all systems; and in an array configuration, they can be administered as a single system. However, if a proxy server is not listed in the DNS CNAME list or alias list, it will not be accessed via the round robin approach. The server will only be accessed directly and by load balancing from redirected requests from other array members.

Finally, because there is no communication between servers (unless in an array), LAT changes, filter updates, permission modifications, and so forth must be repeated for all proxy servers in the network.

Geographical Considerations

One of the major concerns about using multiple proxy servers is the geographical configuration of the servers. Typically, this problem occurs in a campus environment or in wide area networks. In either situation, the server should be placed where it will be used the most. For example, a company with an office in Los Angeles with 50 users and an office in New York with 300 users should not run proxy services across their 56k frame relay link. Instead, they should consider using two separate servers so the rest of the network does not become congested.

In this example, the geographic configuration may define the proxy configuration depending on the network's configuration and abilities. An administrator may want to consider dividing users according to their region. Administrators should avoid placing proxy servers across slow links. In situations where a proxy server must operate across a slow link, proxy server chaining should be implemented.

Suppose, for example, that you were in an environment where your company had a main office and 10 departments spread across a campus, all linked together with a common network line (back bone). The proxy server currently resides on the back bone itself. If you noticed high volumes of HTTP traffic, the application of the proxy server would be to place one in each department so caching would decrease the load on the back bone. Each of the 10 departments could then be chained to an array on the back bone such that caching could help off-load the number of requests on the back bone. If one of the departments had an additional link to the Internet, that department could be used as a backup route in the event the proxy array on the back bone failed.

Additionally, each department could be configured with a dial-up backup. Note that this scenario will also apply to a wide area network.

If load balancing is the largest consideration, consider defining each proxy server according to the protocol it serves. For example, if only a few users in Los Angeles use Web services, but many of them use FTP, and the opposite was true for users in New York, you may want to define each proxy server by function. Of course, this would require you to know what portion of the 56k bandwidth was free. For a management-free environment with a large concentration of users, an array configuration of servers generally works best.

Remember that your network IP address ranges are likely to vary, and will cause the LAT on each proxy server to appear different. If you want to use the proxy server between locations on the WAN for caching, you may not want to make the LAT the same.

Server Placement Considerations

The other considerations that come into play when using multiple proxy servers are minor in comparison to the geographic issues. Nonetheless, they may be concerns that are just as valid depending on the environment. For example, you could encounter problems with server placement. To prevent this, you should place your servers according to the largest number of users. This will allow your users to have proxy representation where they most need it. On the other hand, suppose that the mass of users did not actually utilize the proxy server and that a group of developers within your organization did. In this case, you should consider placing your proxy servers according to their utilization.

Recommendations

We have presented a number of ideas about how to load balance and what other factors to take into consideration in setting up your servers, but since there is no way to know the specific considerations that apply to your network, you should determine your own solution to the load balancing issue.

Typically, in larger environments where applications are placed on servers, an administrator will configure directory replication so there is a redundancy between systems. The administrator will then use a net use command followed by a resource to link users to a common path. For example, if all users in a company require common information, one BDC (Backup Domain Controller) on the network may have the command net use s: \\server1\commonapps while another has `net use s: \\server2\commonapps` placed in the login script. However, when the servers are placed in a farm (a grouping of systems) configuration rather than distributed, the first server in the network chain usually responds to the validation request. In this case, you may have to write your own custom utility to determine which resource to use.

The recommended method is still to configure the available proxy servers in a location in an array.

A load balance utility may take an IP address or use a random algorithm to link users to resources. For example, a theoretical utility may appears as follows:

```
RANLINK resources1 resource2 resourceN
```

In the case of this utility, a link may be defined at random according to the resources listed on a given line. The results can then be passed to a common line or another utility to issue the actual command. Even if the utility does not exist, that is no reason not to write your own or locate a third-party utility to perform the changes you desire. Be creative: This type of load balancing does not have to apply strictly to proxy servers.

Logging Multiple Servers

Most organizations tend to want their network to act as a single entity rather than as a bunch of smaller networks or resources strung together as a single network. When configuring multiple proxy servers, an administrator should consider using a single location for proxy logs.

When using a single location, an administrator can easily get a holistic view of Internet utilization. Furthermore, with logs in a central location, an administrator can review and manage resources more easily than if those reports were spread across multiple locations.

Separate your log files from the proxy server. Since you are working with multiple servers and placing logs from at least one server in another location, what is the difference if all servers are configured to place logs in other locations? None. Your system's management should be separated from the proxy server, and log files should be stored together.

When working in multi-server environments, Microsoft SQL tends to be the best choice for database management due to its multi-user capabilities. While you may use text files or a product such as Microsoft Access, you will not observe the flexibility that you would with SQL.

Summary

The primary reason for adding an additional proxy server is to expand on resources that have reached their limits or to provide a better class of services. In this chapter, we focused on load balancing a given network so the load will be evenly distributed among servers.

The use of multiple proxy servers within an environment introduces a number of additional steps and concerns. The inevitable problems that arise as a function of having multiple proxy servers include security-related problems, issues with logging, different LATs, and a lack of communication between servers.

In determining the potential problems and requirement of load distribution, we examined geographic, demographic, and other information to ensure that we met the requirements of the end users. Together, these factors help an administrator determine deployment sites and configurations for the proxy servers.

When multiple proxy servers are used, redundancy can be created through a variety of mechanisms. The bottom line in implementing load distribution is to analyze the problem carefully and to use creativity in developing a solution.

Review Questions

1. Explain how load balancing can be difficult to implement without arrays.

2. Explain how an array can be an effective solution to load balancing and fault tolerance.

3. Provide some examples of load balancing for a two-location wide area network, a system where users tend to use one protocol, and a system that is completely mixed.

4. The type of Name Resolution (WINS versus DNS) used by clients makes no difference when configuring multiple proxy servers. True or false?

5. Which of the following are not issues when implementing multiple proxy servers?

A. Servers do not communicate.

B. Cache is different between servers.

C. Security is different.

D. Clients are Windows 95–based.

E. The Proxy Server also contains the DNS service.

6. How do proxy servers communicate with each other?

A. PSIP (Proxy Server Information Protocol)

B. RIP (Router Information Protocol)

C. TCP (Transmission Control Protocol)

D. UDP (User Datagram Protocol)

E. CARP (Cache Array Routing Protocol)

7. Which of the following are problems when working with an array?

   A. Multiple administrators making changes

   B. Number of array members

   C. Array members not communicating with each other

   D. Proxy server's video can't display all requests

   E. None of the above

8. What options are available when working with arrays?

   A. Leave array

   B. Join array

   C. Synchronize configuration of array members

   D. Remove from array

   E. None of the above

9. Resolving requests within an array is slower than attempting an upstream Internet connection. True or false? Explain.

10. Chaining Microsoft Proxy Server with other proxy servers such as on a UNIX system optimizes the network. True or False? Explain.

11. If you are running three proxy servers in an array, how must you configure the DNS entry for the proxy server array?

   A. An MX record must be created for each proxy server.

   B. Each computer must have a separate DNS record created.

   C. A DNS record that points only to one of the proxy servers must be created.

   D. Nothing should be done.

12. Your network has grown to 10 departmental LANs. On your main back bone connecting all the departmental LANs together, you have a proxy server that provides Internet access. However, as your LANs have grown, you have noticed a degradation in service to the Internet. What should you do to decrease the amount of network traffic on the back bone LAN?

A. Disable caching on the proxy server.

B. Install a proxy server on each departmental LAN.

C. Install 10 proxy servers on the back bone LAN.

D. Use on-demand dialing on the proxy server computer.

13. Your network has grown to 10 departmental LANs. The network uses an array of three proxy server computers located on the back bone LAN to provide Internet access to all the users. How should you configure caching to reduce the network traffic generated between a departmental LAN and the back bone LAN?

A. Configure the array to use hierarchical caching rather than distributed caching.

B. Configure the array to use distributed caching instead of hierarchical caching.

C. Install a second array of three proxy servers.

D. Install a proxy server on each departmental LAN, and configure them to use the proxy server array on the back bone.

E. Increase the size of the Web Proxy cache on each proxy server in the array.

14. When using the Microsoft Windows NT remote console to remotely administer your proxy server, how do you back up the configuration on your proxy server?

A. Use the Internet Service Manager.

B. Use the HTML-based administration tool.

C. Use the WspProto command-line utility.

D. Use the RemotMsp command-line utility.

15. You have an array of six proxy servers to handle 4,000 clients on your network. However, the Web browsers used on the client computers are incapable of automatically configuring themselves. What is the maximum number of hops that a Web browser will make to retrieve an object from the cache?

A. 2

B. 3

C. 4

D. 5

CHAPTER

10

RAS and Microsoft Proxy Server

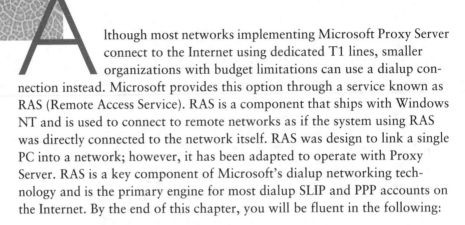

Although most networks implementing Microsoft Proxy Server connect to the Internet using dedicated T1 lines, smaller organizations with budget limitations can use a dialup connection instead. Microsoft provides this option through a service known as RAS (Remote Access Service). RAS is a component that ships with Windows NT and is used to connect to remote networks as if the system using RAS was directly connected to the network itself. RAS was design to link a single PC into a network; however, it has been adapted to operate with Proxy Server. RAS is a key component of Microsoft's dialup networking technology and is the primary engine for most dialup SLIP and PPP accounts on the Internet. By the end of this chapter, you will be fluent in the following:

- Setup and configuration of RAS

Exam objectives are subject to change at any time without prior notice and at Microsoft's sole discretion. Please visit Microsoft's Training & Certification website (www.microsoft.com/Train_Cert) for the most current exam objectives listing.

- RAS requirements
- RAS options
- Using PPTP and RAS
- Automatic dialup networking with RAS and Proxy Server
- Limiting dialup hours
- Troubleshooting RAS problems

Remote Access Services

RAS allows remote client computers (RAS clients) to access a network as if they were connected directly to it. Unlike PC Anywhere, Timbuktu, Reach Out, and other dialup software, RAS is designed to have clients act as part of the network rather than to remotely control another machine. For this reason, most Internet client systems use RAS in a SLIP (Serial Line Interface Protocol) or PPP (Point to Point Protocol) configuration. RAS supports clients running MS-DOS, Microsoft Windows 3.1, Windows 95, or Windows NT.

As an RAS server, Windows NT Server supports up to 255 connections. Of course, this number is limited by the number of physical connections (modems or ISDN adapters) that can be added to the server. The RAS service can be configured to have each independent device configured either as dial-in, dial-out, or both.

Windows NT Workstation also supports RAS service as a server with a limit of one concurrent inbound connection.

RAS requires that a system contain one of the following communication devices:

Modem   Any modem that is supported by Windows NT may be used with the RAS service. Although slower modems are supported, at least a 28.8k modem is recommended.

ISDN adapter   An ISDN adapter is a digital type of modem that supports speeds of 56k and more. Typically, ISPs (Internet service providers) offer the option (for a service charge) of ISDN connections with the ability to use more than one dialup channel to support additional bandwidth.

To maximize bandwidth, you can combine multiple connections—modem, ISDN, or both—using the multi-link option (discussed later on).

To avoid problems, always use a modem that is certified to work with Windows NT. These modems can be found on Microsoft's hardware compatibility listing. The most current version of Microsoft's hardware compatibility listing can be obtained from Microsoft's Web site at www.microsoft.com. Typically, any modem will work; however, it's always better to use a modem that has a specific listing than to use one that operates in compatibility mode such as "Hayes Compatible." Often, you will have problems with disconnecting, hand shaking, and performance with these unsupported modems. Items on the hardware compatibility list have been tested under Windows NT and approved to help ensure installation ease.

We recommend using a name-brand modem such as Hayes, US Robotics, Motorola, etc. These modems tend to have better support and updates than lesser known brands. Also, it is often beneficial to use the same modem that your ISP is using. However, many ISPs have switched from using conventional modems to using access server devices such as Cisco's AS5200. With these devices, a single T1 line is connected to the access server and the connection is multiplexed to support multiple lines. To take advantage of this, 2X and K56 Flex analog modems are available that support up to a 56k connection if available from the ISP. Note that tests of 2X and K56 Flex modems have not found them to be as quick or as reliable as their ISDN counterparts; however, they can be cheaper. Check with your ISP, the NT documentation, and magazines that review current products when making this decision.

WARNING   Installing RAS will enable IP forwarding and the WINS client on the dialup adapter. These functions should be disabled.

Installing a Modem

Before RAS can be configured on a Windows NT Server, a modem must be set up and configured in the system. To set up a modem on the server, take the following general steps:

1. Shut down the server and physically install the modem as outlined in the manufacturer's directions.

2. Power on the NT Server.

3. Double-click the Modems icon in the Control Panel.

4. Use the on-screen instructions for the modem as shown in Figure 10.1.

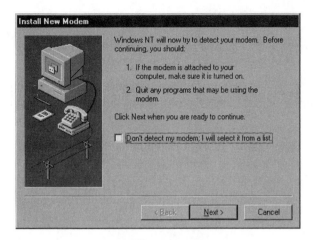

FIGURE 10.1

Installing a modem

Note that some modems require special installation steps. Refer to the manufacturer's documentation for these instructions. In addition, Windows NT does not support some name-brand modems, such as US Robotics' Win-Modem. Be sure that you match the model and manufacturer name on the compatibility list for certified support.

Installing an ISDN Adapter

For a time, ISDN stood for "I Still Don't kNow" or "It Still Does Nothing." While the original specification was first proposed in 1984, only in the last year or two have price reductions by the phone companies made ISDN the Integrated Services Digital Network that users have been promised. ISDN is a digital communications mechanism that generally provides much faster connection speeds than POTS (plain ordinary telephone system) analog lines. ISDN can operate at speeds of 64k or 128k per second, with a portion of the bandwidth set aside to facilitate data flow control. Also, since the ISDN lines are conditioned better, they will have a clearer signal with less reduction of connection speed.

While most modems use the same signaling technology, particularly within a given area such as the United States, ISDN uses many different types. As such, the ISDN adapter must support the same signaling technology as the local phone company or ISDN provider. In rare cases, some adapters are incompatible and an alternative must be selected. Before purchasing an ISDN modem, check with your ISDN provider for the types of signaling they are using or support and ask for their recommendation on a modem. When you have found an

ISDN product, you should cross-check it with the Windows NT hardware compatibility listing to ensure support. Often it is tempting to purchase a cheap device. Unfortunately, these products sometimes do not work as well as advertised and degrade performance or require additional setup time, to the point where they are not worth using. As with conventional modems, you should check the usual publications for product reviews.

Take the following steps to install an ISDN adapter:

1. Shut down the server and physically install the adapter as outlined in the manufacturer's directions.

2. Power on the NT Server.

3. Double-click the Network icon in the Control Panel.

4. Use the on-screen instructions to select or install a device driver for the ISDN adapter.

5. When you're finished, reboot the system. If you don't reboot, some drivers may not load or some ports may not be available.

Installing and Configuring RAS

The Remote Access Service (RAS) operates as an add-on service to the Network component of Windows NT and can be installed during initial Windows NT Server setup or added later on. Assuming that you did not install RAS during server setup, you will want to use the instructions outlined in Exercise 10.1 to add the service. Note that you will need to be an administrator (or equivalent) and should already have the TCP/IP protocol installed and configured.

Microsoft ✓ *Exam Objective*

Official Microsoft Exam Objective: Configure Microsoft Proxy Server for Internet access. Situations include:

- Configuring Proxy Server to provide Internet access through a dial-up connection to an ISP.
- Configuring Proxy Server to act as an IPX gateway.
- Configuring multiple Microsoft Proxy Servers for Internet access.
- Configuring multiple Proxy Servers spread across several different geographic locations.

EXERCISE 10.1

Installing and Configuring RAS

1. From the Start Menu, click Settings and open the Control Panel. Click the Network icon in the Control Panel and select the Services tab.

2. Click Add, select Remote Access Service from the Options dialog, and then click OK.

3. Use the on-screen instructions to install Remote Access Service. When completed, a screen similar to the one shown below will appear for system configuration.

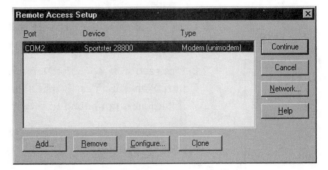

4. Select a modem from the dialog's listing and click the Configure button. In the next dialog (shown below), select Dial Out Only for the port that will be used to connect to the ISP. Note that if you want to allow remote users to dial into your server, you should use this same procedure, but configure a separate adapter to dial in with. (If you use the same adapter for both purposes, your network may be without Internet access longer than your users find acceptable.)

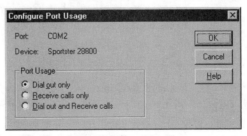

EXERCISE 10.1 (CONTINUED FROM PREVIOUS PAGE)

5. Click the Network button to display the next dialog box. When configuring the Dial Out Protocols, be certain to use only TCP/IP. The checkboxes for IPX/SPX and NetBEUI should be blank.

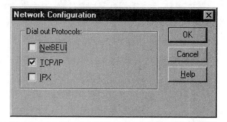

6. Click OK to close the Network dialog box; then click Continue on the Remote Access Setup dialog box.

7. Before rebooting, open the Network Configuration screen from the Control Panel again. Verify that IP forwarding is disabled and the WINS client is not bound to the dialup network adapter.

8. When prompted after closing the Network Configuration screen, reboot the system.

For further information about configuring RAS, you should consult the Windows NT Server instructions.

Note that a number of fixes and updates are available for the Remote Access Service. As with Microsoft Proxy Server, always verify that you are using the latest service pack and hot fixes. If you have applied the service pack and hot fixes to your server prior to installing RAS, you must reinstall them.

Installing RAS in server mode with Microsoft Proxy Server is not recommended. If you are considering using RAS for dial-in, or if you configured an RAS server during installation, you may want to disable it. Later in the chapter, we'll look at the dangers of combining these services.

Auto Dial, Dial-Up Networking, and Proxy Server

Microsoft Proxy Server supports dial-up networking into your Internet service provider through the use of an Auto Dial utility; the filename is ADIALCFG.EXE. Auto Dial maintains a "phonebook" of URLs, IP addresses, and related information. Once an RAS client is installed and configured on the proxy server, you can create a phonebook entry for dialing into your ISP. This entry can then be set as the default during the Auto Dial installation.

Auto Dial will then be called automatically for Web, WinSock and Socks Proxy services whenever a request is issued that cannot be filled from cache. As discussed later in this chapter, you can limit this access by defining hours of operation for Auto Dial.

Verifying RAS Options

Before attempting to configure dialup support for Microsoft Proxy Server, verify that the Remote Access Service has been installed and set accordingly. Use the following directions to verify or reconfigure an RAS client:

1. Double-click the Network icon in the Control Panel.

2. Select the Services tab; then click Remote Access Service in the list of installed items. Click Properties.

3. From the list of available ports, select one to be configured. If only one port is available, it will be selected by default. Click Configure Port.

4. Check that Dial Out Only is selected and click OK.

5. You will be returned to the original screen. Click the Network button. In the list of dial-out protocols, verify that only TCP/IP is selected and clear any others. Click OK to continue.

6. When returned to the main screen, click Continue, then click Close. At this time, if you have made changes, you will have to restart the system.

If RAS was previously installed with any ports configured as dial-in, you must reconfigure them as dial-out.

After making any changes requiring files, you should reinstall the current service pack and add any hot fixes.

The Auto Dial Manager

After RAS services are set up and configured for dial-out support, you must reconfigure the Auto Dial Manager to utilize the correct resource. Use the following instructions to reconfigure Remote Access Service for dialup support:

1. Double-click the Services icon in the Control Panel.

2. Locate Remote Access Auto Dial Manager in the list of services.

3. Click Startup; then select Disabled from the list of startup types. Click OK.

4. Locate Remote Access Connection Manager in the list of services.

5. Click Startup; then select Automatic from the list of startup types. Click OK and then Close.

Creating RAS Phone Book Entries

Before adding a new entry to the phonebook, make note of the name of your ISP, their dialup phone number, and any specific required settings to log in to the server, scripts, domain information, and so on. This information is required to create the first phonebook entry. If you start the Dial-Up Networking service, you should enter any information such as the office's main line. You will have the option to change this information later. The RAS phonebook may be maintained either as a personal book for the user logged in or as a system phonebook to be shared among all users.

There are five tabs available in the new book entry: Basic, Server, Script, Security, and X.25. The Basic tab is used to configure information such as entry name, phone number, and the device to dial with. When configuring devices from the Basic tab, you can also enable multi-link (using multiple phone lines as one). Multi-link works by having each line attached to an RAS client dial a target service, such as the ISP, then combine the two lines for greater bandwidth. An example of a hardware product that performs this action is Diamond MultiMedia's ShotGun Product. The Script tab is used to automate ISP services that require manual intervention upon dial-in. The Security tab is used in conjunction with all other services to determine the type of authentication/encryption to use while establishing communications. The X.25 tab is used to select an X.25 carrier and to configure the connection as required. Most Proxy Server networks will not use the X.25 tab. The Server tab is used to set the dialup server type. Commonly, the server should be set as PPP and TCP/IP only. When configuring TCP/IP on the Server tab, you will need to provide an IP address (or specify DHCP) and the IP address(es) of the names servers. You'll also need to choose IP header compression and use a default gateway on the remote network. Using the default gateway on the remote system allows packets that are bound for the external network to be routed as such when deemed unroutable on the local network.

WARNING

It is crucial that you complete the first RAS entry in order to create a phonebook. Often, users will begin Dial-Up Networking and click Cancel while creating the first entry, thinking they can return to it later. Occasionally, however, a bug in the program will prevent the phonebook from opening later on. This problem appears to be intermittent and affects only some systems; others re-create the partial phonebook entry as expected.

To create the RAS phonebook for dialup support, use the procedure shown in Exercise 10.2.

EXERCISE 10.2

Creating a Phonebook Entry

Take the following steps to create a phonebook entry for dialing out from the Proxy Server to your ISP:

   1. Log onto the service using an Administrator account or equivalent.

EXERCISE 10.2 (CONTINUED FROM PREVIOUS PAGE)

2. Click Start ➢ Programs ➢ Accessories ➢ Dial-Up Networking as shown below.

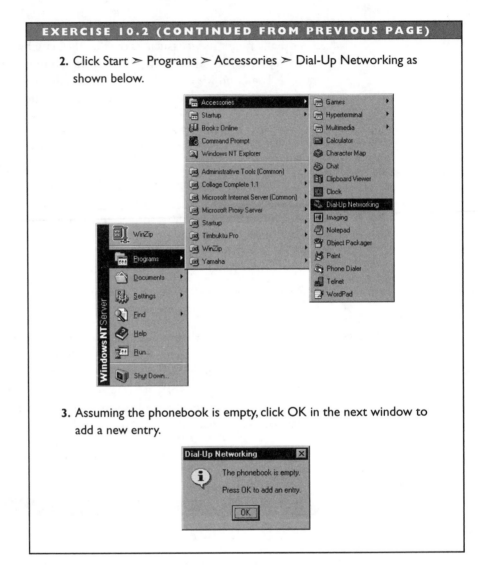

3. Assuming the phonebook is empty, click OK in the next window to add a new entry.

4. This launches the New Phonebook Entry Wizard, shown here:

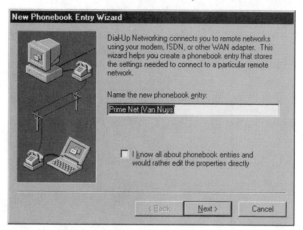

5. On the input line, type the name of the new phonebook entry. Usually this entry will be the name of the dialup service plus the name of the city that you are calling; for example, "Prime Net (Van Nuys)." Click Next to continue.

6. At this point, you can either edit the phonebook directly by clicking the "I know all about..." checkbox or continue using the wizard to guide you through setting your ISP account information. When you're finished entering the basic information (name and password), NT returns you to the Dial-Up Networking window, where you can do further configuration.

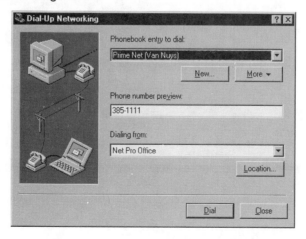

7. Click the drop-down list, select the entry you created in step 4, and click More to fine-tune your settings.

8. In this case, we want to configure Logon Preferences. Notice that the More button offers additional abilities:

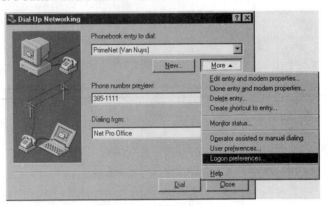

9. To ensure that RAS will always disconnect after each dialing attempt, change the Idle Seconds Before Hanging Up value from 0 to 1 as shown here. Click OK, then click Close.

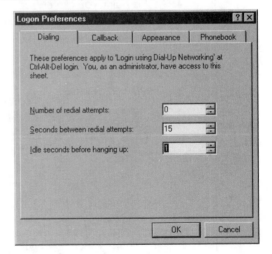

10. Back in the Dial-Up Networking window, clicking More ➤ Edit Entry and Modem Properties.

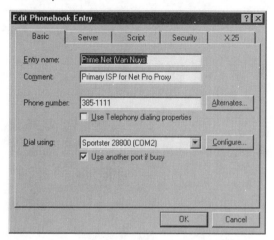

11. At this stage, you may edit the entry for multiple numbers according to your ISP's abilities, and you can set scripts, IP options, and so forth. One useful option is to define additional COM ports in the event that one is in use while trying to connect to the ISP. This can be found while editing the phonebook on the Basic tab. Use the checkbox and Alternates button to adjust settings.

Logon Scripting

Note that some ISPs require certain login procedures to connect to their service. Microsoft Proxy's Auto Dialer does include an option for automated dialup connections and requires the use of RAS dial-out scripting options. These options can be set in an RAS script file as designated in SWITCH.INF.

ISP Dialup Credentials

Before Microsoft Proxy Server can connect to an ISP, it must be configured with the dialup information and valid credentials. As stated earlier, these credentials include user login name (for the ISP account), password, and domain login for a given phonebook entry. Here are the steps for configuring credentials:

1. From the IIS Manager, double-click a proxy service for the system that you want to administer.

2. On the Service tab, click the Auto Dial button.

3. Click the Credentials tab, then display the drop-down list to select a phonebook entry as shown in Figure 10.2.

FIGURE 10.2

Setting dialup credentials

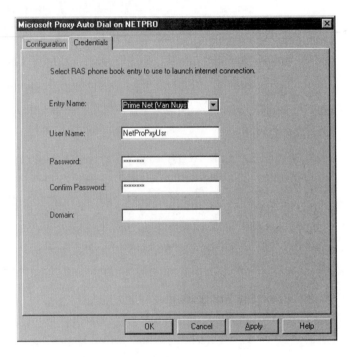

4. In the spaces provided, enter the user name for logging in to the ISP, the required password, and the domain if required. Typically, domains are used in linking to a wide area NT network. The Domain field is not used by most ISPs and is usually left blank.

5. Click Apply, and then OK. The information that you entered will be used each time Microsoft Proxy Server makes a dialup connection to the ISP, regardless of the user who made the request (as long as that user has rights to use the services).

Routing and Remote Access Service (RRAS)

Routing and Remote Access Service (RRAS) is an add-on product that provides dialup routing between two networks. Typically, RRAS is used to create virtual private networks (VPNs) across the Internet. When creating VPNs, you must use the PPTP protocol. This will provide secure encrypted communication across the Internet. The RRAS PPTP Server service can co-exist with Proxy Server 2.0, provided that the following conditions have been met:

- The predefined filter PPTP Receive must be enabled when using packet filtering.

- The predefined filter PPTP Call must be enabled when using packet filtering.

- The RRAS hot fix must be applied.

Microsoft ✓ *Exam* *Objective*   **Configure a RAS server to route Internet requests.**

The PPTP filters are used to allow traffic in inbound and outbound directions between your network and the Internet. The PPTP filters allow data to flow via port 1723. Fortunately, Proxy Server 2.0 comes with these filters, so the port number is not as important as it would have been otherwise.

As discussed in earlier chapters, hot fixes may be obtained from Microsoft's Web page. You should always check for hot fix updates before installing any applications. For instance, if you were to attempt to add RRAS to Proxy Server 2.0, you would have a number of errors in the operation, and you would encounter interference with each other's services.

Microsoft ✓ *Exam* *Objective*   **Troubleshoot Internet/intranet routing hardware and software. Software includes Microsoft Routing and Remote Access Service (RRAS).**

In some scenarios where RRAS is used with Proxy Server, some changes must be made. These changes help promote product functionality as well as security. Some examples of these changes are listed below:

- When operating RRAS with Microsoft Proxy Server 2.0 as a department server, packet filtering should be disabled. Typically, there is only one network adapter used.

- Configuring a connection to the Internet with RRAS and Microsoft Proxy 2.0 on an Edge server typically requires that you enable packet filtering and the PPTP packet filter. No other filters should be required. In this configuration, two network adapters are used. The external network adapter may be a modem.

- In the same configuration as above, and having an Extranet or a barrier-LAN segment in addition to the Edge server, three network adapters are used. Note that an Extranet is a network between networks or a live network that does not require the proxy server to access the Internet. Live IP addresses are used on the Extranet LAN. The LAT must not include the IP address of the adapter connected to the Extranet. This network (with the Extranet) is often referred to as a *DMZ network*. In most configurations, routing is enabled such that communication can occur with the clients on the Extranet LAN and between its own network and the external network. RRAS, in this case, is used to configure routing for each interface. All communication to the Extranet LAN with the internal private network should be done via Proxy Server 2.0.

You may access the Extranet LAN through RRAS rather than through Proxy Server by enabling IP forwarding to that segment. This configuration, however, has greater security risks and is not recommended.

Other RAS-Related Issues

Using RAS in dial-in (server) mode on the same machine as Microsoft Proxy Server is not recommended. Although this configuration is allowed, it creates a number of problems. For instance, if you connect clients using the same lines for both the proxy server and RAS server, there may be times when the client has no Internet access. This is very undesirable. You can create a time schedule to work around this problem, but you would then be unable to access the Internet from the dial-in client. In addition, when the dial-in (server) mode RAS features are in place, additional overhead is placed on the server regardless of which line is used for dialing in.

If you need to allow clients to dial into the server, use a separate dial-in line than the one used to connect to the Internet. The dialup adapter may be configured as either Dial Out and Receive Calls or Receive Calls Only. For RAS clients, IP information can be assigned either by a reserved pool of addresses stored with the RAS server or by the DHCP service. Although RAS clients will appear as if they are directly connected to the network, these systems may be configured to use the Proxy Server with all other clients on the network.

WARNING The main problem with this configuration is that the dial-in clients should be limited by selecting This Computer Only and clearing the Entire Network Access checkbox in the Remote Access Service setup procedure. If access to the entire network is enabled, however, IP forwarding will be enabled; this will create a severe security hole.

After performing any changes to the RAS server, always verify that your changes did not enable routing. As you may recall from earlier chapters, RAS will automatically enable routing when installed or when certain options are changed. When routing is enabled, you run the risk of external users bypassing the proxy server services to access your network. You may check this by looking at the TCP/IP protocol in Network. Check that the Routing tab has not had any options (there is only one) enabled.

PPTP and Microsoft Proxy Server

Windows NT 4.0 introduced a new networking protocol known as PPTP (Point-to-Point Tunneling Protocol). This protocol offers the ability to create a virtual network with multi-protocol support, known as a Virtual Private Network (VPN). When used correctly, PPTP provides a secure end-to-end link through the Internet.

Since PPTP is a two-way communications mechanism, Microsoft does not recommend installing it with Microsoft Proxy Server. If PPTP is installed on the same system as Proxy Server, modify the PPTP-configured port usage settings in Remote Access Service setup from Receive Calls Only to Dial Out Only. This change effectively converts the RAS system from server to client mode. The concerns about enabling PPTP are based on the default installation, where IP forwarding is enabled and RAS is configured as a dial-in server. Whenever IP forwarding is enabled, there is always the concern that you are opening security holes that may be attacked through the Internet.

In short, PPTP usage should be avoided whenever possible in a proxy server environment. This protocol works very well for what it was designed to do; however, it may cause countless headaches as a network grows and is reconfigured. Depending on your security requirements, you may find the protocol acceptable; however, use extreme caution when implementing it, and monitor system activity closely.

Scheduling Auto Dial

Earlier in the chapter, we looked at Microsoft Proxy Server Auto Dial's convenient phonebook feature. Equally important are its money-saving capabilities. Typically, business phone lines and ISDN calls have per-minute charges. Depending on the distance to the ISP, there may also be a long distance charge with each call. To reduce these costs, the Auto Dial will link to the Internet as requested and disconnect after a given period of no activity.

Since there are some hours that a company may desire for a workstation not to use the Internet, dialing hours may be set in the Auto Dial utility such that the proxy server will not place a call even if requested during restricted hours.

Dialing Hours

To save on dialup costs and add security to the network, an administrator can restrict AutoDial's operation to a given set of hours. A number of organizations place this limit not to block users from the Internet, but to keep costs down. Some programs, such as Point Cast Network, may create situations where the level of activity never drops and the line remains on constantly. When users leave their systems on, these programs may auto-load themselves (like screen savers) and start the proxy server link to the Internet. Once set for a given RAS phonebook entry, the dialing hours will be stored with that entry. Exercise 10.3 shows how to configure dialing hours.

EXERCISE 10.3

Setting Dialup Hours

To configure dialing hours, use the following list of instructions:

1. From the IIS Manager, double-click a proxy service for the system that you want to administer. This step will be required for each Proxy Server that uses dialup connectivity. However, you only need to check the Enable box on the Configuration screen of the Auto Dialer tab to enable dialing for other services on the same server.

2. On the Service tab, click the Auto Dial button.

3. Select the Credentials tab, and then select a phonebook entry.

4. Once you have picked a connection to define call hours, click the Configuration tab.

5. In the Dialing Hours grid, you can disable the Auto Dial service during specified hours of the day or for days of the week by clearing cells. The default configuration allows the proxy server to dial at any time on any day. As shown below, proxy server has a customized schedule of M-F 6am-10pm, and Sat 6am-4pm. To dial as requests are received, the Enable Dial checkboxes must be selected. This allows dialing for WinSock Proxy, Socks Proxy, Web Proxy Primary, and Web Proxy Secondary routes.

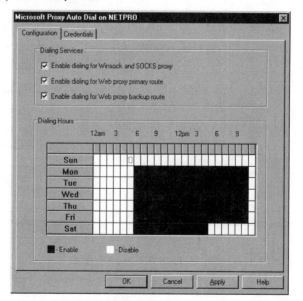

EXERCISE 10.3 (CONTINUED FROM PREVIOUS PAGE)

6. To accept the changed hours, simply click Apply and then OK. The set hours will be stored permanently and will not change unless reconfigured by the administrator.

If you specify hours when Auto Dial is disabled, Proxy Server will do active caching only at those times.

Updating Services After a Dialup Service Change

In some cases, when a dialup connection is used in conjunction with the Auto Dial utility, NT's WWW, Web Proxy, Socks Proxy, and WinSock Proxy services must all be restarted. This restarting is used to register the service request and link it to the dialer. It's necessary in two situations:

- Auto Dial is being used for the first time. When the auto dialer is first added, the services listed above must be notified to use the dialer. Think of this as enabling Auto Dial with respect to related services.

- The Auto Dial configuration is cleared. Once a change such as disabling the dialer is implemented, the associated services that use the dialer must be reloaded so that they are no longer linking to Auto Dial. Think of this as disabling the auto dialer with respect to the other services.

Note that the above changes really only reflect enabling and disabling the dialer. Unless you are commonly performing this function, subsequent use of the auto dialer in the same configuration will not require restarting the WWW, Web Proxy, Socks Proxy, and WinSock Proxy services. If you implement the auto dialer and it appears that the service is initially broken, try rebooting before you call Microsoft's technical support.

Microsoft ✓ ***Exam Objective***　**Select and use software configuration management tools (for example, Control Panel, Windows NT Setup, Regedt32).**

The WWW, Web Proxy, Socks Proxy, and WinSock Proxy services can be stopped with the Internet Service Manager, through the Control Panel, or from the command line. To stop the service from the Internet Service Manager, simply click the service and then the Stop toolbar button, or right-click and choose Stop from the context menu. When the services have all been halted, you may restart them by clicking the Start button as shown here:

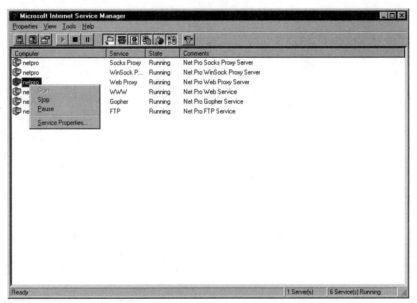

If you prefer, you may use the command line as follows to stop and start the related services. Notice that there is no need to stop the Web Proxy service separately as this is performed automatically at the same time as the WWW service:

```
Net STOP w3svc
Net STOP wspsrv
Net STOP spsrv
Net START w3svc
Net START wspsrv
Net START spsrv
```

Microsoft ✓ Exam Objective

Given a scenario, decide which user interface to use to perform administrative tasks.

Using the Service icon in the Control Panel to stop or start these services is error-prone and not recommended. The only time you may want to do this is when remote-controlling a system through the System Manager tool. However, you can perform the same functions through the Internet Service Manager for any server in the organization, so there is no point in performing management tasks through the Control Panel.

RAS Troubleshooting

There are a number of problems that can occur with RAS. Here we will focus on those that are most commonly related to the Proxy Auto Dial service:

- Connections are not disconnected, or hangup fails. This situation generally occurs when either a modem initialization string is set incorrectly, or there is no timeout on the connection. Either obtain an updated modem driver/firmware change or set a value in seconds for Idle Seconds Before Hanging Up in Logon in the RAS phonebook.

- The dialing properties for the RAS phonebook entry that is used by Microsoft Proxy Server for dial-out are not displayed. When a non-user service (one that is run by the system, such as the auto dialer) accesses the phonebook, user preferences are not used. The logon preferences must be set by selecting More from the Dial Up Networking dialog box.

- No connections can be established. This problem usually occurs on the ISP side where your system has connected to a modem; however, the host system has not had enough time to reset its login program. Retry the connection. If the problem persists, contact your ISP. If they do not have a reasonable solution, either try a different dial-in line or try another provider. ISPs that are servicing too many accounts often have this problem. Also, verify that your modem settings are correct and that your modem has the latest firmware. Discuss this with the ISP.

- No common protocol could be negotiated. This error typically occurs as a matter of a bad hand shake or dirty phone lines. Verify that IP is enabled, and that the IP information is as stated from your ISP, such as using DHCP or a static address.

For additional information about troubleshooting RAS connections that don't involve Proxy Server, see the Windows NT documentation, the RAS documentation, Microsoft's online knowledge base, or Microsoft TechNet.

Summary

Again showing its integration with Windows NT, Microsoft Proxy Server utilizes the Remote Access Service (RAS) for dialup networking into the Internet. RAS is a key component of Microsoft's Dial-Up Networking technology and the primary engine to most dialup SLIP and PPP accounts on the Internet.

In this chapter, we demonstrated how to set up and configure RAS for use with Microsoft Proxy Server. We showed how to use some capabilities or configurations that, while possible, are not recommended because they either lead to complex problems that are difficult to solve or create security-related issues. For example, we showed how to use PPTP because a number of users now implement this protocol to expand their networks cheaply. As we saw, however, it's not a good idea to use PPTP with Microsoft Proxy Server if you can avoid it.

The Auto Dial feature provides a mechanism for reducing the cost of connecting to an ISP. With this service, Proxy Server can connect to the Internet as required using logon information supplied through the auto dialer by an administrator. As a further cost-saving measure, Proxy Server also implements the ability to limit dialup hours in Auto Dial. This both helps to secure the network and saves additional expenses that could be incurred if systems are left running unattended and make automated requests.

Finally, we also included a brief listing of problems that an administrator may encounter while working in a dialup configuration, and their solutions.

Review Questions

1. What are the two types of adapters that can be used with RAS and how are they configured?

2. Discuss how connecting with RAS differs from using a connection established with PC Anywhere, Timbuktu, Reach Out, and similar software.

3. Why is RAS dial-in (server) mode not recommended for use with Proxy Server? What problems might you have when configuring RAS to allow access to the entire network?

4. Why is PPTP filtering typically not used with Microsoft Proxy Server?

5. When Proxy Server is configured in a dialup network, in what ways are users limited in access?

6. What is the filename of the Auto Dial utility?

   A. AUTOCFG.EXE

   B. DIALER.EXE

   C. WINDIAL.EXE

   D. PRXDIAL.EXE

   E. ADIALCFG.EXE

7. After installing Auto Dial, what servers need to be restarted?

   A. WWW service

   B. Browser service

   C. WinSock Proxy service

   D. Web Proxy service

   E. Domain Name service

8. What utility is used to schedule dialing hours of operation?

   A. ADIALCFG.EXE

   B. IISMGR.EXE

   C. PRXYTIME.EXE

   D. W3DLTM.EXE

   E. WINSOCK.DLL

9. The system containing Microsoft Proxy Server cannot service RAS dial-in users. True or False?

10. PPTP should be installed on the Proxy Server to secure Internet access. True or False?

11. You want to set up your proxy server by using a dial-up connection to your already existing ISP. You create a Dial-Up Networking phonebook entry for the dial-up account. What else must you do?

   A. Configure the Auto Dial utility and enable dialing for the Web Proxy backup route.

   B. Include the assigned IP address in the LOCALLAT.TXT file on the client computers.

   C. Include the entire dial-up IP address pool from the ISP in the LAT.

   D. Configure Auto Dial and specify which phonebook entry and credentials to use to connect to the ISP.

12. You want to set up your proxy server by using a dialup connection to your already existing ISP. You need to provide a valid user name and password for the ISP account. What should you do?

   A. Configure the Auto Dial in the Proxy Server services by specifying the phonebook entry and the corresponding ISP account credentials.

   B. Manually dial in to the ISP by using Dial-Up Networking, and provide a valid user name and password for the ISP account.

   C. Configure the Auto Dial in the Proxy Server services by specifying the phonebook entry and the Proxy Server Administrator account and password.

   D. No action is necessary, the proxy server will log in to the ISP by using a built-in account.

13. You have a proxy server with one NIC card and a modem with RAS installed. What should you do to minimize the risk of unauthorized access to your Intranet? Choose all that apply.

A. Disable IP forwarding.

B. Disable the WINS client on the dialup adapter.

C. Add the dialup network adapter's IP address to the LAT.

D. Install PPTP.

E. Add a packet filter for DNS lookup.

14. You want your proxy server to use on-demand dialing to access the Internet whenever a client request is received. What should you do?

A. Dial in to your ISP by using Dial-Up Networking and maintain the connection for as long as necessary.

B. Add the dynamically-assigned IP address to the LOCALLAT.TXT file on each workstation.

C. Add the dynamically-assigned IP address to the MSPLAT.TXT file on the Proxy Server.

D. Configure Auto Dial on the Proxy Server services by specifying the phonebook entry and the corresponding ISP account credentials.

15. Which Proxy Server service(s) can use on-demand dialing to access the Internet?

A. Web Proxy

B. WinSock Proxy

C. Both Web Proxy and WinSock Proxy, but not Socks Proxy

D. Web Proxy, WinSock Proxy, and Socks Proxy

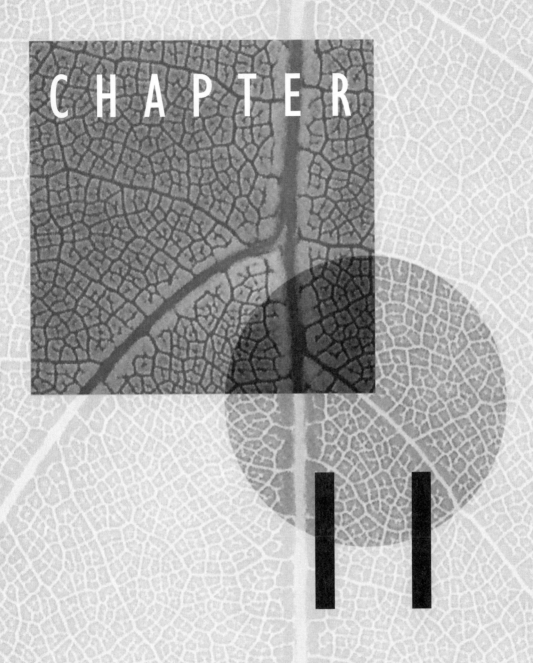

CHAPTER

11

Monitoring and Tuning

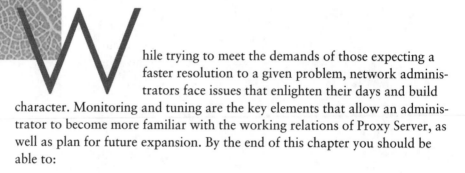

hile trying to meet the demands of those expecting a faster resolution to a given problem, network administrators face issues that enlighten their days and build character. Monitoring and tuning are the key elements that allow an administrator to become more familiar with the working relations of Proxy Server, as well as plan for future expansion. By the end of this chapter you should be able to:

- Distinguish between various Performance Monitor indicators

Exam objectives are subject to change at any time without prior notice and at Microsoft's sole discretion. Please visit Microsoft's Training & Certification website (www.microsoft.com/Train_Cert) for the most current exam objectives listing.

- Recognize items that degrade Proxy Server performance

- Identify caching efficiency

- Note memory-related issues

- Sense CPU bottlenecking

- Reveal disk deficiencies

- Configure logs to report on system status

Performance

All too often, administrators are informed that the network is too slow or seems sluggish in some area. Internet performance is one area where performance problems can be introduced. There are a number of factors that can contribute to this problem that are beyond the administrator's control. So ideally, for any given network, an administrator should configure those items for which they have authority, to give them as much control as possible.

Microsoft ✓ Exam Objective

Official Microsoft Exam Objective: Analyze performance issues. Performance issues include:

- Identifying bottlenecks
- Identifying network-related performance issues
- Identifying disk-related performance issues
- Identifying CPU-related performance issues
- Identifying memory-related performance issues

Before we get too deep into performance issues, there are a few terms you should be familiar with:

- Bottleneck: Used to describe the most constrained part of a system or communications path. A bottleneck can be thought of in terms of an actual bottle. If you pour water out of a bottle, where is the slowdown for emptying the container?

- Load: The amount of work that a specific device has to do. For example, if your PC was used as a file server, an Exchange e-mail system, a DNS server, a print server, and an intranet Web server, you could say that your system has a heavy load.

- Optimization: The act of reducing as much overhead as possible and maximizing device output abilities.

- Processes: A software-utilizing resource that generates throughput. Any program or device driver is considered a process.

- Resources: The physical hardware devices that are used by software to generate throughput. Resources include items such as memory, disk space, disk I/Os, network bandwidth, and so on.

- Threads: The unit of measure used to describe a process that runs concurrently with other processes. A process can utilize one or many threads. The number of threads used, combined with CPU time, determines the overhead of a process on the entire system. When Microsoft states that Windows NT is a preemptive multitasking system, they are referring to its ability to run multiple programs as if there were multiple CPUs.

- Throughput: The measure of data output by any given device. For instance, a hard drive output is measured by its ability to transfer data between its medium and the controller. Remember that the throughput always is totaled with the overhead removed.

The Internet is a compilation of networks and devices that communicate, so the connection to any one site is only as fast as its slowest link. For this reason, if a company's Web page was connected to an ISP at 56k and you had a 1.544MB link to your service provider, the maximum speed that you could hope to achieve is 56k. And bandwidth is also shared with other users on that company's Web page as well as those who have outbound connections at the company. So even though your system has the ability to connect much faster than its current rate, it is too hopeful to expect to achieve maximum speed. Even 56k lines are not very likely to get 56k as a connection speed.

If you are asking yourself why 56k is not achievable, consider that the link from the ISP to the site contains approximately 20% overhead. That translates to approximately an 80% throughput of data, less your protocol overhead, which is about another 15%. This overhead is used to manage the flow of data, and monitor and correct errors. In cases of frame relay connections, the phone company assigns a value known as the CIR (Committed Information Rate), which typically tops out at 38.4k. As a factor of overhead, bandwidth shared between multiple users, numerous pathways to connect to a destination (hops), and other traffic on the Internet, it is not reasonable to assume that all or even most problems with the Internet are related to your network. The best test is always to benchmark a site that is fairly unpopular, and draw your conclusions from there. Time how long it takes to bring up the site. Then calculate the bytes per minute on file transfers. However, this method is not even guaranteed as the best way to calculate speed. If performance is dropping while under the same configuration, time of day, day of week, and so forth, you may need to fine-tune your system.

The data that is used in comparing the problemed system to the original data is known as *baseline* or *control data*.

Resources

Microsoft Proxy Server is fine-tuned based on five areas of your system. These five areas include the Network, Disk, Memory, CPU, and Cache. Each item is responsible for providing smooth operations and has the potential to be a bottleneck to all the other areas.

Cache

The cache memory, as it applies to the proxy server, is the amount of space that is reserved to hold commonly-requested pieces of data from the Internet. Adding cache to a system will continue to increase its overall speed until another bottleneck is reached. Ideally, the cache will balance with utilization and with other resources to ensure quality performance. Too little of a cache will mean that some items will have to be downloaded from the Internet more often, thus reducing the speed of the system. We will talk in more detail about this subject later on in this chapter.

CPU

The CPU is the heart of the Windows NT system. While Microsoft Proxy Server is not very CPU intensive, this may still have an impact on performance because other aspects of the server may be slowed. These other degradations may eventually lead to a loss of performance. However, this tends to be less of an issue for dedicated proxy servers. If massive CPU processing is required, multiple CPUs may be used with Windows NT. Again, while this item is typically not a problem, it is still one to watch.

Disk

Disk drives have long been a problem for many systems when dealing with a large amount of data. Developments to address this problem have included RAID (Redundant Array of Inexpensive Disks) systems and caching controllers.

RAID, as opposed to SLED (Single Large Expensive Disk), boasts the collective throughput of all drives as limited to the controller and an average seek-time share by all devices. Caching controllers also aid the ability of disk performance by buffering data. Microsoft is aware of this obvious bottleneck and includes its own caching routine with Windows NT. While Microsoft Proxy Server is usually not a disk-intensive application, if your service is caching large amounts of data, a bigger, faster drive may be an option. If your service is caching a few sites, this type of upgrade is not likely to have a large impact unless the system is used for another purpose as well.

Memory

Microsoft certainly raised the stock values of a number of integrated circuit and RAM manufacturers when they developed Windows for public and commercial markets. As a general rule, the more memory, the faster the system. However, do not be fooled into believing that this rule doesn't have exceptions. When evaluating your server, determine how much RAM is necessary to satisfy all services of the server. When memory is low, *disk thrashing* generally occurs. This is where the system continuously swaps memory to disk. The actual swapping of memory to disk is known as *paging*. You could say that thrashing is the constant paging of memory to disk. In reality, disk thrashing is any occurrence where the hard drive is constantly running (usually serving the paging request). This process of paging is normal. Microsoft extends memory by writing it out to disk. The frequency with which this occurs is directly related to the amount of RAM in the system. Even after disk thrashing has been alleviated, additional RAM may be used for caching or for some other benefit. You must always evaluate if more memory will help a system when performing this type of expansion.

Network

As the transportation mechanism between clients and the proxy server, the network plays a key factor in ensuring performance. There are a number of factors that will create a bottleneck between the clients and a server. First, we must examine what the actual throughput of the topology is. For example, suppose that a given network based on a coaxial Ethernet back bone has 100 users. While the topology itself supports rates up to 10MB per second, the topology itself may be maximized by overhead. In the case of this example network, the 100 systems share the available bandwidth (10MB per second less overhead). Since Ethernet works by broadcasting all information to all systems on a segment, the network will eventually be saturated just by internal user access of resources. As utilization of the network increases, after a certain threshold, data throughput will decrease as a whole. While a network with two users may experience performance rates of 8MB per second output, one with 100 users may only see 1MB per second. You may use Network Monitor to analyze these situations. Ultimately, you need to take into account the number of users per network segment, the available bandwidth, and the type of topology, usage, and number of services offered. Let us examine them individually:

- Number of Users Per Segment: It should be fairly obvious from the example that a network usually works better with fewer users. If you were to look at the extremes, 1000 users will individually get much slower network response than a configuration with two users.

- Available Bandwidth: Various topologies offer different speeds. For instance, Ethernet is available in 2, 10, 100, and 1000MB. Clearly, the number of users placed on a given network will also vary according to the amount of bandwidth available. Imagine trying to run video conferencing on a 2MB Ethernet network compared to a 100MB network.

- Type of Topology: When determining the amount of overhead associated with a given topology, we must examine many factors. For instance, Ethernet maximizes itself at about 25% to 30%, whereas Token Ring networks tend to grow more efficiently to about 65%. Adding switches in place of concentrators so that only certain parts of a network hear a request helps ensure performance. All parts of the topology can be a factor.

- Usage: A network with users who are only printing and sharing data files will see much better throughput than the same network where users are running their applications from the server and performing all operations through the network rather than performing them locally. How a network is used is as important as the throughput that will be received.

- Number of Services: As with usage, the number of services that are available on a network can also increase traffic. For example, for every workgroup and domain in Windows NT, a system must act as a browser and must listen to broadcasts made from resources notifying them of their availability. (NetWare contains a similar form of resource advertising called a SAP, or Service Advertisement Protocol).

Performance Monitoring

Performance Monitor is a utility that ships with Windows NT that can be used to determine the optimization of a service, system, network, and so forth. When using Performance Monitor, an administrator can monitor individual components that comprise a server rather than the server as a whole. This has the benefit of allowing the fine-tuning of a single components of the server. A number of components can be monitored as standard features of the Performance Monitor. In some cases such as proxy server, additional monitor items are provided as add-on components.

Using Performance Monitor

Performance Monitor is available for any user logged in at the Windows NT Server console. No special rights or privileges are required to use Performance Monitor. However, to perform some additional resource probes such as viewing disk performance, you must be a member of the Administrator's group.

To turn on disk monitoring, an administrator must use the DiskPerf utility. After changing disk monitoring to on or off, the system must be restarted. The options for DiskPerf are noted in Figure 11.1. Before continuing with the monitoring process, it will be necessary for you to enable this feature. Remember that observing the disk, CPU, network, cache, and memory monitors the performance of the proxy server.

FIGURE 11.1

Working with the DiskPerf command

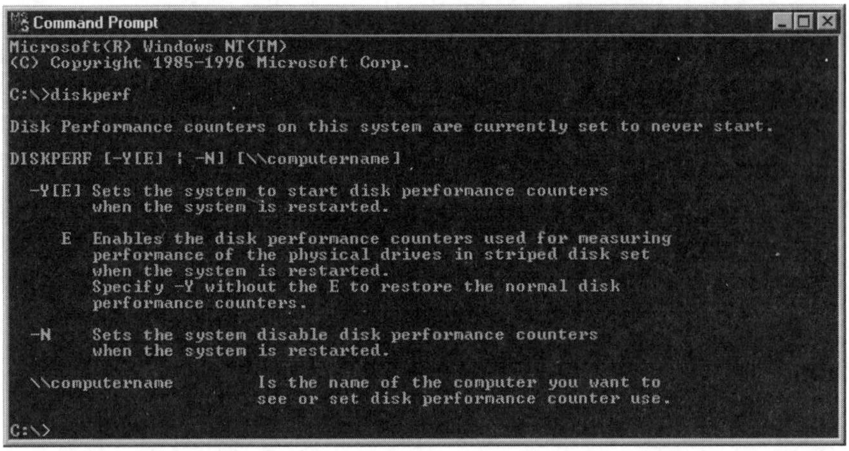

WARNING Enabling disk performance monitoring may decrease performance due to additional overhead. If your system is not using a large cache or doesn't already have a fast drive, you may consider omitting this item.

Performance Monitor can be started by clicking the Performance Monitor icon located in the Administrator's Tools folder under Programs on the Start Menu. However, as far as Proxy Server is concerned, Performance Monitor can be started with a pre-configured template. To start Performance Monitor using this approach, simply click the Microsoft Proxy Server Performance icon in the Microsoft Proxy Server folder under Programs on the Start Menu. The screen shown in Figure 11.2 will appear.

FIGURE 11.2

Performance Monitor in action

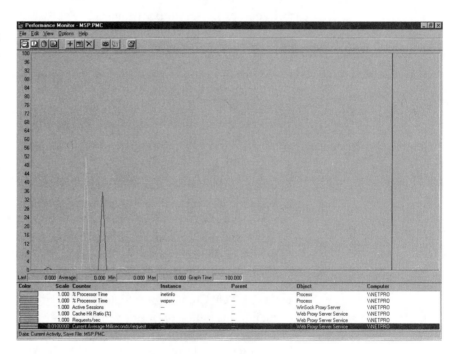

A little criticism of the template is that Performance Monitor does not automatically provide suggestions based on standard diagnostics. This means that some items that could be determined for an administrator, are not. The administrator must make the changes manually, and therefore must recognize when this needs to be done. Since Microsoft has the ability to determine changes, they should also include an option to change those settings automatically. NetWare, for example, is self-tuning and gains efficiency over a period of time.

Performance Counters to Watch

A number of performance meters are included with the default installation of Windows NT. These meters can be used by an administrator to actively tune the server for better performance and determine what upgrade is required to eliminate bottlenecks. The default counters that are included with Windows NT provide the ability to evaluate the drive system, network (and related protocols), CPU, memory, and so forth. When you work with the meters, you will observe a number of counter items that directly relate to the five items that ensure good proxy server performance.

Network

The network can greatly affect the speed of the proxy server. When monitoring this category of equipment, unless you know a specific problem that you are trying to find, you should primarily watch these counters. They will allow you to determine when it is time to add another proxy server, segment a network, and so forth:

- Active Sessions: This indicator notifies an administrator as to the total usage of the WinSock server at any given time. Since there is no rating scale for use, the number of users per server will vary with the identical equipment. A high number of users could indicate that it's necessary to add a second proxy server. Note that the active session counter in Performance Monitor will show the same information as in the Microsoft Proxy Server Current Sessions dialog box.

- Active TCP Connections: Similar in function to the NETSTAT command, this indicator notifies an administrator as to the number of connection-based sessions that the server is performing. This indicator should be used in conjunction with Active UDP Connection and is a subset of the Active Sessions Counter.

- Active UDP Connections: Complementing the Active TCP Connection Monitor, this indicator reflects connectionless-based requests from clients. This monitor is a subset of the Active Sessions Counter and can be used to gauge the load on a proxy server.

- Bytes Read/Sec: Perhaps the most descriptive of the default indicators, this monitored item can be used to determine the location of a problem. When followed over a reasonably long period of time, an administrator may see a decrease in this value, thereby suggesting a problem with the efficiency of data going though the system. On the other hand, if this count remains high and performance decreases, the monitored item indicates a problem with the system. Note that this item is configured to operate on a scale of 0.001 to 1.

- Network Interface Output Queue Length: The length of the output packet queue waiting for transmission. This length is measured in number of packets. If this number is greater than two, this usually indicates that the network is congested. This could be caused by too little available bandwidth, a slow processing network adapter, too many systems on a segment, and so forth. You must examine other properties of the network structure to determine what is causing the problem.

- Network Interface Bytes Total/Sec: The total number of bytes sent and received per second on a network interface. If this number is near the maximum capacity of your network line, you may have a bandwidth bottleneck and need to segment the network. Check the Network Interface Output Queue Length for output congestion to determine if this is a bandwidth issue.

- Network Interface Packets Outbound Discarded: The number of outbound packets that were discarded. The packets may be removed even though no errors have been detected to prevent their being transmitted. This commonly occurs to free up buffer space.

CPU

The key component of the Proxy Server is its CPU. When too many requests are received, the proxy server may begin buffering requests that may appear to be other problems. Before checking other services, you should always verify that the CPU is not the root cause.

- % Processor Time: Monitors the instance of the WSPSVR. Higher values may indicate that a faster CPU is required or that the proxy services need to be divided. If the counter ever goes over 80%, according to Microsoft, the server has a bottleneck and must be upgraded to improve performance.

Memory

The main reason to watch the memory component is the effect that it can have on serving all other requests. Although you may have a fast CPU, the system itself may bottleneck if there is just not enough memory in the system to have all processes active at once. This counter will indicate when it is necessary to add additional RAM to the file server.

- Page Fault/Sec: Adding memory almost always increases performance. However, once a system is optimized, the benefit of more memory is outweighed by the cost versus return argument. As this value increases, it means that the file server has to swap its memory to the disk system and that the server most likely requires more RAM.

Cache

The only cache counter of serious importance is the hit ratio. Essentially, you are trying to create a balance where this value is as high as possible for the amount of disk space it has to work with. While the minimum recommendation is 100MB plus 0.5MB per user, the actual optimum number will vary with proxy server use.

- Cache Hit Ratio %: A high value for this counter indicates that your caching is on target. An administrator should use this indicator to determine when changes are required. After changes are made, always observe if this number has gone up. The cache should be monitored over a given period of time to determine the efficiency of the cache. If, for example, you were adding users and wanted to know if the current cache was adequate, you would look at this counter.

Disk

The disk is an integral part of delivering requests to clients from the cache more quickly. By default, no disk counters are enabled. The reason is that the disk can only be monitored when specifically enabled through the DiskPerf utility. An administrator should use the default disk counters after activating monitoring with the DiskPerf utility.

- Disk Queue Length: The length of the queue waiting for transfer to disk. If this number is greater than two, this usually indicates that there may be a problem with the system's disk I/O subsystem. Typically, an administrator will be concerned with the overall I/O. However, for filling requests, performance will be based on how fast information can be read. Too much queued data indicates that the disk is too slow.

Performance Counters Added to the Installation of Proxy Server

Since it is not possible to include all counters in the basic Windows NT product for all add-on products, Microsoft Proxy Server ships with a number of its own. The performance counters or indicators that are installed with Microsoft Proxy Server (in the MSP.PMC template) are arranged into five groups:

- Web Proxy Server cache

- Web Proxy Server service

- WinSock Proxy Server service

- Socks Proxy Server service

- Packet filter (firewall) service

When starting Performance Monitor from the MICROSOFT PROXY folder, these categories are available. As with any other counters, an administrator may use the performance meters to create charts, logs, or reports. Additionally, an administrator may set threshold limits for any monitored item. When the utilization of that item reaches its threshold, an alert may be sent. The Performance Monitor alert system relies on the Windows NT messenger server. You may view the performance counter by clicking the Add button in Performance Monitor shown in Figure 11.3.

FIGURE 11.3

Adding counters to the performance chart

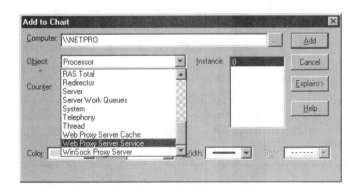

Microsoft
✓ *Exam*
Objective

Use Performance Monitor logs to identify the appropriate configuration.

When an alert is triggered, a message is sent through the network to notify a specified administrator or user. The message notes the reason for the alert, the event that caused the error, and the time and date the error occurred. If those options are selected, this information is then stored in the Applications log of the Event Viewer.

Microsoft
✓ *Exam*
Objective

Monitor performance of various functions by using Microsoft Windows NT Performance Monitor. Functions include HTTP and FTP sessions.

When restarting the Web Proxy or WSP services, the majority of counters will reset themselves. Only a few services that have information stored in cache or contain values for URLs are preserved.

Web Proxy Server Cache Counters

The Web Proxy service cache is designed specifically to help tune Proxy Server's cache. For the most part, administrators will only look at a few counters to determine if the cache system is adequate. Below is a list of cache counters. It is not important to memorize every cache counter. However, we strongly recommend that you are able to recognize those caches in bold, as they tend to be the ones that are most commonly used in the cache monitoring process.

Microsoft
✓ *Exam*
Objective

Optimize performance for various purposes. Purposes include:

- Increasing throughput
- Optimizing routing

- **Active Refresh Bytes Rate:** Represents the amount of activity in bytes per second retrieved from the Internet to update the active cache. Recall that the active cache is used to proactively refresh popular URLs in the URL cache. This indicator's main purpose is to determine if the active cache needs to be adjusted.

- Active URL Refresh Rate: This counter is similar to the Active Refresh Byte Rate, except that it functions by URL rather than by byte count. This means that it counts how many sites are accessed every second.

- Bytes Committed Rate: The speed in bytes per second sent to disk storage in the URL cache.

- Bytes in Cache: Displays the current size in bytes of the URL cache. When this counter approaches its maximum size, an administrator should consider increasing the cache size.

- Bytes Retrieved Rate: The rate at which data is recalled from the URL cache in bytes per second.

- Max Bytes Cached: Similar in function to the way we record weather temperatures, this meter identifies the maximum size the cache has reached. If this indicator is constantly at the maximum size, the cache should be increased.

- Max URLs Cached: Indicates the maximum count of URLs stored in the URL cache.

- **Total Actively Refreshed URLs:** As with the active refresh site count, this counter monitors the cumulative number of URLs in the URL cache refreshed proactively from the Internet.

- Total Bytes Actively Refreshed: As with the active refresh byte count, this counter monitors the cumulative number of URLs in the URL cache refreshed proactively from the Internet.

- Total Bytes Cached: The total cumulative bytes stored in the URL cache.

- Total Bytes Retrieved: The total cumulative bytes retrieved from the URL cache.

- Total URLs Cached: The total cumulative number of URLs stored in the URL cache.

- Total URLs Retrieved: The total cumulative number of URLs retrieved from the URL cache.

- URL Commit Rate: The speed at which URLs are committed to the URL cache in sites per second.

- URL Retrieve Rate: The speed at which URLs are retrieved from the URL cache in sites per second.

- URLs in Cache: The current number of URLs in the URL cache.

Web Proxy Server Service Counters

The Web Proxy service counters are designed to help gauge the proxy server's activities. As with the cache counters, administrators will only look at a few indicators to determine how the system is being used. Below is a list of indicators. It is not important to memorize every indicator. However, we strongly recommend that you are able to recognize those indicators in bold, as they tend to be the ones which are most commonly used in analyzing the Web Proxy service.

- Array Bytes Received/Sec: The rate at which data is received from other proxy servers to respond to a request.

- Array Bytes Sent/Sec: The rate at which data is sent to other proxy servers to respond to a request.

- Array Bytes Total/Sec: The total send and receive rate at which data is transferred between proxy servers to respond to a request.

- **Cache Hit Ratio (%):** The number of requests that were filled with cached information out of the total requests sent to the Web Proxy Server. This indicator is used in the default counters listed earlier in this chapter.

- Client Bytes Received/Sec: The speed at which a clients send data to the Web Proxy Server. This is useful when examining if the local network is creating a bottleneck.

- Client Bytes Sent/Sec: The speed at which the Web Proxy Server sends data to a client. This is useful when examining if the local network is creating a bottleneck.

- Client Bytes Total/Sec: The total combined transfer speed (bytes sent and received) between the Web Proxy Server and the Web Proxy clients. This is useful in determining if the local network is creating a bottleneck.

- **Current Average Milliseconds/Request**: The mean average, in milliseconds, that is required to service a request. If this value is high, this could indicate too high of a load on the server.

- Current Users: A current count of the number of users connected to the Web Proxy Server.

- **DNS Cache Entries**: The current count of DNS domain name entries cached by the Web Proxy Server. If you change IP addresses on systems and users either get no answer or access the wrong server, this is most because the proxy server will cache DNS entries.

- DNS Cache Flushes: The number of times that the DNS domain name cache has been "flushed" (cleared) by the Web Proxy Server.

- DNS Cache Hits: The number of times a DNS domain name was used from the DNS cache.

- DNS Cache Hits (%): The percentage of DNS domain names retrieved from cache out of the total DNS entries that were retrieved by the Web Proxy Server.

- DNS Cache Retrievals: The cumulative number of DNS domain names that have been retrieved by the Web Proxy Server.

- FTP Requests: The number of FTP requests that have been received by the Web Proxy Server.

- Gopher Requests: The number of Gopher requests that have been received by the Web Proxy Server.

- HTTP Requests: The number of HTTP requests that have been received by the Web Proxy Server.

- HTTPS Sessions: The total number of secure HTTP sessions serviced by the Secure Sockets Layer (SSL) tunnel.

- **Maximum Users**: The highest number of users that have connected to the Web Proxy Server at any one given time. This counter is useful in determining server usage and expansion.

- Requests/Sec: The number of requests the Web Proxy Server is receiving per second.

- Reverse Bytes Received/Sec: The rate at which inbound requests for published material are received by the Web Proxy service.

- Reverse Bytes Send/Sec: The rate at which inbound requests for published material are replied to by the Web Proxy service.

- Reverse Bytes Total/Sec: The rate at which inbound requests for published material are received and replied to by the Web Proxy service.

- Sites Denied: The total number of Internet sites to which the Web Proxy Server has denied access. If this count is too high, it is likely that you have restricted access to sites that may be required in normal activities.

- Sites Granted: The total number of Internet sites to which the Web Proxy Server has granted access. Combined with Sites Denied, an administrator can gauge the number or requests made for different sites.

- SNEWS Sessions: The total number of SNEWS sessions serviced by the Secure Sockets Layer (SSL) tunnel.

- SSL Client Bytes Received/Sec: The speed at which Secure Sockets Layer (SSL) data is received by the Web Proxy Server from secured Web Proxy clients.

- SSL Client Bytes Sent/Sec: The speed at which Secure Sockets Layer (SSL) data is sent by Proxy Server to secured Web Proxy clients.

- SSL Client Bytes Total/Sec: The total combined transfer speed (bytes sent and received) between Web Proxy Server and secured Web Proxy clients. This is useful in examining if the local network is creating a bottleneck.

- SSL Sessions Scavenged: The number of Secure Sockets Layer (SSL) sessions closed because of the idle timeout and excessive SSL demand.

- Thread Pool Active Sessions: The number of sessions being actively serviced by thread pool threads.

- Thread Pool Failures: The number of requests that could not be serviced due to the thread pool being over committed. A high count could indicate that the server (usually the CPU) is inadequate.

- Thread Pool Size: The total number of threads in the thread pool.

- Total Array Fetches: The total number of requests that have been serviced by other proxy servers in an array.

- Total Cache Fetches: The total number of requests serviced by using cached data from the Web Proxy Server cache.

- Total Failing Requests: The total number of Internet service requests rejected due to errors by the Web Proxy Server. Errors can be caused by the Web Proxy Server failing to locate a requested server URL on the Internet or by a client being denied access to the requested URL.

- Total Requests: The total number of Internet requests that have been sent to the Web Proxy Server.

- Total Reverse Fetches: The number of inbound requests that have been serviced by servers that publish Web pages.

- Total SSL Sessions: The total number of Secure Sockets Layer (SSL) sessions serviced by the SSL tunnel.

- Total Successful Requests: The total number of Internet requests successfully processed by the Web Proxy Server.

- Total Upstream Fetches: The total number of requests retrieved from Internet servers or from proxy servers up the chain.

- Total Users: The total number of users that have connected to the Web Proxy Server.

- Unknown SSL Sessions: The total number of unknown Secure Sockets Layer (SSL) sessions serviced by the SSL tunnel.

- Upstream Bytes Exchanged: The total rate at which data is exchanged with the Internet or an upstream proxy server in response to a request for this proxy server.

- Upstream Bytes Received: The rate at which data is received from the Internet or from an upstream proxy server in response to a request for this proxy server.

- Upstream Bytes Sent: The rate at which data is sent to the Internet or to an upstream proxy server in response to a request for this proxy server.

WinSock Proxy Server Counters

The WinSock Proxy Server (WSP) counters are designed to help gauge WinSock activities. As with the Web Proxy counters, administrators will only look at a few indicators to determine how the system is being used. Below is a list of counters. It is not important to memorize every counter. However, we strongly recommend that you are able to recognize those counters in bold, as they tend to be the ones which are most commonly used in analyzing the WinSock Proxy service.

- Accepting TCP Connections: The number of connection objects waiting for TCP connections from the client after a successful remote connection.

- **Active Sessions**: The number of active WinSock sessions including TCP and UDP connections. This same information can be found on the Service tab in IIS by clicking Current Sessions.

- Active TCP Connections: The number of active TCP connections.

- Active UDP Connections: The number of active UDP connections.

- Available Worker Threads: The number of worker threads available and waiting in the completion port queue.

- Back-Connecting TCP Connections: Total number of connections waiting for an inbound connect ( ) call to be completed. These are connections from the WSP service to a client after the Proxy Server accepted a connection from the Internet on a listening socket.

- Bytes Read/Sec: The rate at which bytes are read by the data-pump (the program or activator that pulls data).

- Bytes Written/Sec: The rate at which bytes are written by the data-pump.

- Connecting TCP Connections: The total number of connections waiting for a remote connect ( ) call to be completed.

- DNS Cache Entries: The current number of DNS entries cached due to WinSock Proxy service activity.

- DNS Cache Flushes: The total number of times that the DNS cache has been cleared.

- DNS Cache Hits: The total number of times a DNS request was found in the DNS cache.

- DNS Cache Hits (%): The percentage of DNS names serviced by the DNS cache out of the total number of all DNS entries that have been retrieved.

- DNS Retrievals: The total number of DNS domain names that have been retrieved.

- Failed DNS Resolutions: The number of API calls to `gethostname`/`gethostbyaddr` that have failed.

- Listening TCP Connections: The number of connection objects that wait for TCP connections from the Internet (after a successful listen).

- Non-connected UDP mappings: The number of mappings for UDP connections.

- Pending DNS Resolutions: The number of API calls to `gethostname`/`gethostbyaddr` that have not yet been returned.

- Successful DNS Resolutions: The number of API calls to `gethostname`/`gethostbyaddr` that have been returned successfully.

- Worker Threads: The number of control channel worker threads and data-pump worker threads that are active.

Socks Proxy Service Counters

The Socks counters are arranged such that they are integrated with the Web Proxy service counters. While logically these items should be considered separate, they are not. The Socks counters are used to determine what sort of performance levels clients using Socks 4.3a–compatible stacks and applications are experiencing. Below is a list of counters for this service, the most important of which are presented in bold. You will probably note that there are very few of them. Aside from core Socks counters listed below, additional items can be visible through other counter listings, such as the Web Proxy counters and those delivered with Windows NT.

- Socks Client Bytes Received/Sec: The rate at which data is received from Socks Proxy clients.

- Socks Client Bytes Sent/Sec: The rate at which data is sent to Socks Proxy clients.

- Socks Clients Bytes Total/Sec: The total bytes sent and received per second for Socks Proxy clients. This value reflects the total communications in bytes transferred between Proxy Server and Socks Proxy clients.

- Socks Sessions: The total number of Socks Proxy client sessions serviced by the Socks Proxy service.

- **Total Failed Socks Sessions**: The total number of Socks Proxy client requests that were not serviced by the Socks Proxy service either because the client did not have access rights to satisfy the request or because of an initial protocol error.

- **Total Socks Sessions**: The total number of Socks Proxy client sessions.

- Total Successful Socks Sessions: The total number of Socks Proxy client requests that were successfully serviced by the Socks Proxy service.

Packet Filter Counters

The Packet Filter counters measure the performance of Microsoft Proxy Server 2.0 as a firewall. You should note that the counters are only effective when packet filtering has been enabled in the Security section of any proxy service. The items listed below define different types of failures from a total number of connections, and the most important items are listed in bold.

- **Frames Dropped Due to Filter Denial**: The total number of frames dropped because of data rejection by the dynamic packet filter.

- **Frames Dropped Due to Protocol Violations**: The total number of frames dropped as a result of a protocol irregularity.

- Total Dropped Frames: The total number of dropped or filtered frames.

- Total Incoming Connections: The total number of incoming connections established through filtered interfaces.

- Total Lost Logging Frames: The total number of dropped frames that cannot be logged.

Network Monitor

In addition to Performance Monitor, Windows NT includes a product called Network Monitor (see Figure 11.4). Network Monitor acts as a network sniffer. In typical usage, it is used to analyze network traffic as it occurs instantaneously.

FIGURE 11.4

Network Monitor

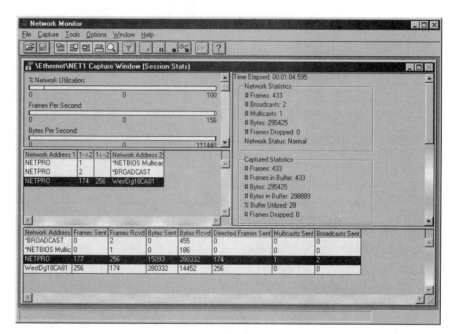

Network Monitor is advantageous for monitoring traffic to verify that a certain type of traffic is present. In most implementations, Network Monitor can be used to examine the traffic of any network interface. That is to say, all traffic that is sent past the wire in which the proxy server is attached may be read. This is perhaps one of the more commonly known ways in which non-encrypted passwords are stolen.

To view statistical information, however, you must use Performance Meter. Performance Meter is typically used to monitor traffic over a period of time, while Network Monitor is used to view the actual information in a packet as it is sent. Figure 11.5 demonstrates what an administrator may observe while reviewing data captured through Network Monitor.

FIGURE 11.5

Data captured using
Network Monitor

FIGURE 11.5

Data captured using
Network Monitor

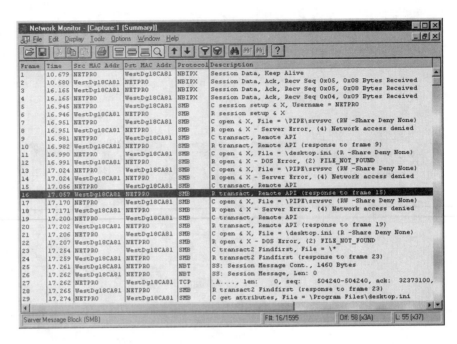

If you plan on using a server other than Proxy Server with Network Monitor, you are required to run a Network Monitor agent. To install Network Monitor, follow the steps in Exercise 11.1.

EXERCISE 11.1

Installing Network Monitor

1. Open the Network icon from the Control Panel, and select the Services tab.

2. Click Add, then select Network Monitor Tools and Agent from the list of services.

3. When prompted, provide the CD-ROM or the location of the i386 directory from the Windows NT CD-ROM.

4. When complete, click the Close button.

5. When prompted, reboot.

Perform Internet traffic analysis by using Windows NT Server tools.

Network Monitor requires that your network adapter support promiscuous mode. This is a special mode that allows an adapter to read all network information, regardless of whether it is destine for it or not.

Cache Monitoring and Tuning

As you may recall, caching is perhaps the single most important component of Proxy Server for increasing speed. However, before assuming that a system's caching mechanisms are set and continuing onward, it is 100% necessary to review your configuration because a misconfigured cache can lead to failure as easily as one configured correctly can lead to success.

Presumably, an administrator could simply increase the cache, then gauge the changes as they occur over the next week. However, this type of approach is hardly scientific. When working with the cache, an administrator should examine if the hit rate is low as compared to the basic configuration of expected cache hits, and then tune the server accordingly. You may use the Performance Monitor to acquire this information. Once you have acquired it, you should consider the size of the objects being cached, the size of the cache itself, and the attributes of the object being cached, such as the expiration period.

The active cache is perhaps the most influential mechanism for delivering an optimized system, since it continues to adapt once the server is placed into production. An administrator should also consider the prospect of pre-loading the cache or using third-party tools. Pre-loading the cache can be performed in such a way that the object being retrieved need not be downloaded before it's cached. This helps create the illusion that the server was working at its optimum capacity when it was implemented. Typically, this effect is achieved automatically when chaining systems or resolving requests within an array.

Cache Settings

The cache may never be fully optimized to function effectively in all situations, especially if the environment and system requirements are constantly changing. For this reason, the cache configuration may consistently change as well. Always look into your crystal ball and ensure that the equipment you are using will meet your needs. My *Ouiji* board and *séance* procedures (better known as consulting) usually includes the following:

- Note that your hard drive can facilitate growth.

- Verify that the cache is being used correctly and the TTL settings for HTTP and FTP items are correct for your environment.

- Review the maximum size and number of objects cached. Distribute the cache among multiple servers.

When making changes to the cache settings, note that the cache expiration policy will determine the frequency at which updates are required and if more cache hits should take place by extending the TTL life. Also, the active cache can be configured for faster responses with more pre-fetching, or for fewer requests to the Internet with less pre-fetching. For example, if the cache was configured for few network accesses (more cache hits) on the expiration policy, and faster user response is more important (more pre-fetching) on the active caching, the result would be that the pages in the cache have the maximum TTL and the largest percentage of popular cached objects are updated. Remember that when you deal with problems such as users retrieving old information, this problem is related to having fewer network accesses (more cache hits).

When downsizing a cache, you may not observe changes until the Web Proxy Server is restarted and the cache is validated. Older objects in the cache will be the first to be removed.

Once an administrator has decided to change the cache, they may do so through the IIS Manager, as reflected in Figure 11.6. To configure the cache, refer to Exercise 11.2.

FIGURE 11.6

Configuring cache settings

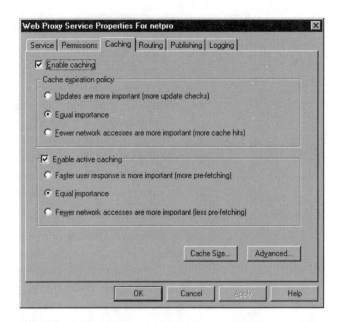

EXERCISE 11.2

Configuring the Cache

1. Open the IIS Manager and double-click the Web Proxy service to be modified.

2. Click the Caching tab and verify that the Enable Caching checkbox is selected. This will enable Proxy Server to store information requested by a client and later respond to an identical request to the same resource.

3. Set the freshness level of cached items by selecting from among the Cache Update options. The duration set by the expiration policy is determined by your selection: Updates Are More Important, Fewer Network Accesses Are More Important, or Both Are Equal. Selecting fewer Internet requests reduces traffic significantly and sets the cached object's TTL period to the maximum duration, as defined in the Advanced section.

The cache expiration policy can mean greater efficiency to the system. Be aware, however, that it may also respond to clients with older data. Typically, Web sites do not change that often relative to the length of their longest TTL, but this can be an issue.

4. Enabling the active cache by clicking the corresponding checkbox is a time- and traffic-saving measure. Typically, this option is used such that the updates are made while system utilization is low. When users request updates, little, if any, information is actually sent at that time to the requested area. Items are actively cached according to their popularity. The active caching mechanism can be adjusted for fewer, more, or equal pre-fetching. Selecting more pre-fetching will provide the most updates. Note that if a dialup connection is used, active caching will not operate during those hours when the dialup service is disabled.

5. Adjust the cache according to your network configuration. Begin by noting the total cache size on the screen. To modify this value, select Change Cache Size. It is a bad idea to allocate a small cache size, since objects are dropped from the cache based on their popularity as it reaches its capacity. While changing the cache size, you also have the ability to define the drive location. Note that although it is possible to use setup to change the cache size and location, it is not recommended. You should always use the IIS Manager instead. Remember that reducing the cache may delete items, and setting the cache to 0 will disable caching.

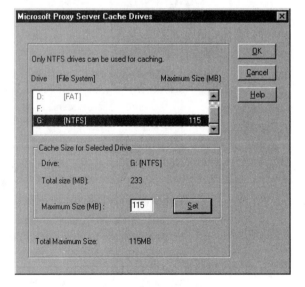

EXERCISE 11.2 (CONTINUED FROM PREVIOUS PAGE)

Typically, the best performance is obtained by selecting an NTFS-formatted drive that neither the Microsoft Proxy Server nor the Windows NT operating system is installed on. That is not to say that you should select a different partition, but rather a physical drive. Note that caching on non-local drives is usually ineffective, and defining alternate drives on RAID-striped systems is only advantageous to set the cache on partitions with more free space. When multiple drives are available, using multiple caches often adds speed. When using a RAID-striped storage system, the cache is automatically spread across multiple physical drives.

To ensure that your drive does not reach capacity unexpectedly, place the cache and log files into separate drives.

6. To customize cache settings, click the Advanced button. The material covered in the Advanced section is discussed in the next section, *Customizing the Cache*. You may either review the section on cache customization or click OK to continue.

When configuring the cache after booting up, you must wait for the system to complete its initialization. While you are able to access the associated page and read information, you will get an error if any changes are made. If you are in a Web Proxy service tab while initialization completes, you will need to close and reopen the tab before changes will take effect.

Customizing the Cache

The cache can be further fine-tuned in the Advanced Cache Policy in the Caching tab of the Web Proxy service. In the Advanced section, you may define the size of cached objects to use expired objects to fill requests when a site is unavailable, set the TTL defaults, and filter which types of resources are cached. To access the Advanced Cache Policy screen, follow the instructions in Exercise 11.3. Once you've completed Exercise 11.3, use the instructions in Exercise 11.4 to configure the cached sites filter.

EXERCISE 11.3

Accessing the Advanced Cache Policy

1. Open the IIS Manager and double-click the Web Proxy service to be modified.

2. Click the Caching tab.

3. With the Enable Caching checkbox selected, click the Advanced button located at the bottom of the tab to reveal the Advanced Cache Settings dialog box.

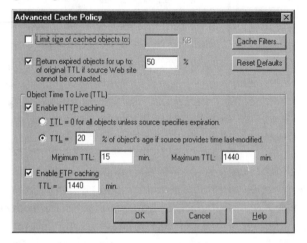

4. Five options are available on the Advanced Cache Settings screen and are discussed in full detail here:

- Limit Size of Cached Object To: Clicking this checkbox allows an administrator to define the number of megabytes to be reserved for a given object. An object that exceeds this specified size will not be cached. When this value is set to 0, the IIS Manager interprets the value as impossible and clears the checkbox, disabling the function. This option is not enabled by default.

- Returned Expired Objects for Up to X% of Original TTL If Source Web Site Cannot Be Contacted: Selecting this checkbox returns expired stored information when a site is unavailable. While this has the advantage of providing information when an object cannot be updated or reached, it can also provide a false impression if the data retrieved truly has changed. Setting the percentage of the original TTL acts as an extension so that the original expiration date can be bypassed. When this box is cleared and an Internet resource is not available, no information will be returned to the client (except perhaps an access error). This function is enabled by default.

- HTTP TTL: This item is used specifically with Web-based requests. You may select 0 to not assign a TTL period unless defined by the Web page itself. Otherwise, you may choose to define the TTL as a percentage of the time since the object was published (assuming time last modified is provided). With this percentage option, both a minimum and maximum TTL period may be established.

- FTP TTL   This is the counterpart of the HTTP TTL setting, and it defines file transfer protocol caching. Since FTP items will not define any time information, an arbitrary time is set. By default, the TTL value is 1440 minutes or one day.

- Cache Filters: Cache filters are configured by selecting the Cache Filters button. Once selected, an administrator may Add, Edit, or Remove any entry or object. This option allows you to define which objects are stored in the cache. Entries that appear may include as little as the URL, or as much as an entire URL with an object path or a wildcard (*). Note that the wild card can be set in the path or before the domain name. These objects can be set as Always Cached or Never, as shown in Figure 11.7. Generally, Proxy Server will determine and cache an object for you. Cache filters are useful when disabling caching for an entire site by filtering out data. However, a portion of a site that has its caching disabled may be re-enabled by adding an entry to always cache a subtree of that site. This function is especially useful for an administrator when they observe a highly utilized site. To help alleviate traffic, that site can be set to always be cached.

F I G U R E   11.7

Defining a cache-
filtered site

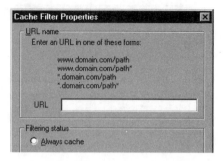

> **EXERCISE 11.4**
>
> **Configuring Cache Filters**
>
> 1. From the Internet Services Manager, double-click the Web Proxy service you want to access.
>
> 2. Click the Caching tab.
>
> 3. With the Enable Caching checkbox selected, click the Advanced button located at the bottom of the tab.
>
> 4. Click the Cache Filter button.
>
> 5. Click the Add button, type ***.sybex.com/*** on the URL line, and select Never Cache. This will prevent the caching of any servers or objects located at sybex.com. The URL must include a forward slash. The asterisks are wild cards used to denote any address information. Once complete, click OK.
>
> 6. Click the Add button once more, type **www.sybex.com/books*** on the URL line, and select Always Cache. This will enable caching specifically for all items located at or below the BOOKS directory on the WWW server at sybex.com. The URL must include a forward slash. The asterisks are wild cards used to denote any address information. Once complete, click OK.

Using Proxy Server for Caching Purposes Only

In many implementations, security is not an issue and may be handled by other devices, such as a router or a firewall. For example, an ISP is only concerned with retrieving data, not with security that is relayed to the end-user.

For this reason, Microsoft Proxy Server can be set such that caching is the only function performed. This means that the server essentially allows access and caching on all network adapters.

Avoid using WinSock Proxy and Socks Proxy applications when a Web Proxy–based substitute is available. Neither WinSock Proxy nor Socks Proxy perform caching.

When using Microsoft Proxy Server in a caching capacity only, include all networks in the Local Address Table (LAT). If public users from the Internet are going to access your network as well, add 0.0.0.0 through 255.255.255.255 to the LAT. In this way, the proxy server will process all objects and clients, regardless of location.

The inverse for proxy server also applies. Rather than have proxy server perform caching functions, it may also be used for its security features. In this scenario, caching is disabled, and security items such as packet filtering and reverse hosting are applied. Typically, this configuration is only placed where a fast Internet connection that is used by few users is in place.

Log Usage

As we have said time and time again, an administrator should maintain logs so they can determine the usage of the server, evaluate performance, follow security, and so forth. Log files may be stored in a text file or an ODBC/SQL database. Logs that are stored as text files can be viewed with any text editor. However, for longer files, you may consider using Wordpad and storing any changes in text format. Virtually any database can be used with the log files, since most database products today, such as Microsoft Access, Microsoft SQL, Sybase, and Oracle support ODBC or SQL.

Although we do not suggest running the logs over the Internet, if you access a Microsoft SQL database that is on a network protected by Microsoft Proxy Server 2.0 with packet filtering enabled, you must set up a packet filter for port 1433, which allows traffic to be passed to the IP address of the SQL server (local host).

Setting a Standard Using Logs

To ensure performance, you must observe your server's utilization over a period of time, such as a week or a month. It is recommended that you do this when the server is first brought online, then periodically thereafter. The initial reading should be kept as a standard or a control set (of data) so you can judge how the server is performing. Unless there are massive changes in the number of users or Internet IP applications, you should see similar results each time. A drastic change may indicate a problem with the disk, CPU, cache, network, or memory.

It is not a good idea to perform these tests and observations on weekends and holidays, as they usually do not reflect actual usage.

Most administrators tend to keep a standard on all servers and services. For instance, some companies monitor how often toner cartridges are changed on laser printers by reading the page count. This allows them to note and anticipate costs. If you are not doing so already, it is recommended that you keep a notebook with each server so you can keep track of changes that are made by different administrators at different times.

Log Reports

In order for logs to be useful, they must first be compiled into reports. The reports may be detailed, providing all information regarding the use of the server, or thinned down, providing as little information as just site access. In short, reports can be configured to answer any query that an administrator composes. Common tools for creating reports include batch files, Windows-based applications, and SQL table filters.

A database is also referred to as a table.

One of the more brilliant moves by Microsoft was to create automatic report generation. These automatically produce documents, known as *production reports*, are typically distributed to various managers in the MIS, telecommunications, management, and operations departments. Each group usually examines the report for different reasons. For instance, the MIS department looks at the report to determine utilization and performance, while management reviews the report to justify expenses.

Commonly, daily reports are posted so that curious users can see how Internet access is managed. It is not uncommon to find this type of document on a corporate intranet Web page. By allowing users to view the report, they are typically more conscience of their own actions. Weekly and monthly reports are also useful, particularly in understanding a big-picture view of how the Proxy Server operates over a period of time.

Text-Based Logs

The majority of the information discussed here has already been covered in Chapter 6. However, as a key component of monitoring and tuning a proxy server, we will review it again in brief here.

Logging data to a text file provides application-independent tracking of system usage and flaws. The text-based logs are enabled by clicking Enable Logging and selecting Log to a File in the Logging tab of any service. Each service maintains separate logs from the other services. You may distinguish the log files from each service according to the log file name. Typical logging options include the following:

- Automatically Open New Log: This action is performed daily, weekly, or monthly depending on administrator selection.

- Limit Number of Old Logs To: This option clears old log information from the hard disk by preserving only the most current logs up to the number specified. By default, this option is not enabled and the number of logs is limited to available hard disk space.

- Stop Service If Disk Full/Stop All Services If Disk Full: This option will halt a given service if the disk is full. If this option is enabled, all services will be stopped. Free space must be available to restart the service(s).

- Log File Directory: This is the location where your log files will be stored.

There are a number of uses for log files. Text files are easily imported to analysis tools that do not provide an SQL or ODBC connection. In many cases, log files are not used. However, we recommend keeping at least one active log to ease troubleshooting if the need ever arises.

Interfacing Logs with a Database

As you have seen, in order for a log to produce useful information or be tailored for a specific query, an ODBC- or SQL-compatible database must be used. As a general rule, any database application that supports ODBC 2.5 or SQL will operate with Microsoft Proxy Server's logs. ODBC (Open Database Connectivity) is a standard Windows API that allows database information to be configured in a common format that can be transported between Windows applications. By design, ODBC is structured to operate as a CLI (Call Level Interface) for any database system including those that are non-relational DBMSs (Database Management Systems).

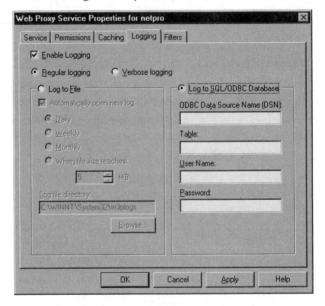

Microsoft* ✓ *Exam Objective   **Configure Proxy Server to log errors when they occur.**

When calculating the server requirements for Proxy Server, always be sure to include logging as an activity. While not an extreme abuser of system resources, logging on a heavily used system can be quite intensive. To add SQL or ODBC to a system, follow the steps in Exercise 11.5.

EXERCISE 11.5

Adding SQL or ODBC to a System

1. Verify the system requirements of your database package, and install the package accordingly. Note that if the database is to be stored with the proxy server, you must combine both system requirements accordingly.

2. Configure a table such that all related fields are added.

3. Install the ODBC driver.

4. Define a system Data Source Name (DSN) for the table.

5. Configure the Logging tab of the Web Proxy and WinSock Proxy services as required by your database.

When using Microsoft SQL Server or Microsoft Access, use the information in Tables 11.1 and 11.2 to structure your tables as guidelines for data from the Web Proxy, WinSock Proxy, or Socks Proxy services.

	Field name	SQL data type	Access data type	Length
TABLE 11.1	BytesRecvd	Int	Long Int	N/A
Proxy services database structures for Microsoft SQL and Access	BytesSent	Int	Long Int	N/A
	CacheInfo	Int	Long Int	N/A
	ClientAgent	Varchar	Text	100
	ClientAuthenticate	Char	Text	5
	ClientIP	Varchar	Text	50
	ClientUserName	Varchar	Text	50
	DestHost	Varchar	Text	255
	DestHostIP	Varchar	Text	50
	DestHostPort	Int	Long Int	N/A

TABLE 11.1 *(cont.)* Proxy services database structures for Microsoft SQL and Access	Field name	SQL data type	Access data type	Length
	LogTime	Datetime	Datetime	N/A
	MimeType	Varchar	Text	25
	ObjectSource	Varchar	Text	25
	Operation	Varchar	Text	255
	ProcessingTime	Int	Long Int	N/A
	Protocol	Varchar	Text	25
	ReferredServer	Varchar	Text	100
	ResultCode	Int	Long Int	N/A
	ServerName	Varchar	Text	50
	Service	Varchar	Text	25
	Transport	Varchar	Text	25
	Uri	Varchar	Text	255

For Packet Filters use the information in Table 11.2.

TABLE 11.2 Packet filter database structures for Microsoft SQL and Access	Field name	SQL data type	Access data type	Length
	DestinationAddress	Varchar	Text	25
	DestinationPort	Varchar	Text	8
	FilterRule	Varchar	Text	10
	Interface	Varchar	Text	25
	IPHeader	Varchar	Text	255
	Payload	Varchar	Text	255

	Field name	SQL data type	Access data type	Length
T A B L E I I.2 *(cont.)* Packet filter database structures for Microsoft SQL and Access	PflogTime	Datetime	Datetime	N/A
	Protocol	Varchar	Text	8
	SourceAddress	Varchar	Text	25
	SourcePort	Varchar	Text	8
	TcpFlags	Varchar	Text	255

For further information on database structures, refer to the online HTML documentation provided with Microsoft Proxy Server.

SNMP

The TCP/IP suite of protocols includes a built-in management channel known as SNMP (Simple Network Management Protocol). While at times this protocol is not so simple, it provides a common method of accessing various devices and reporting on their status. SNMP can commonly be found in devices such as network hubs, routers, switches, printers, uninterruptable power supplies, and a number of server products including Windows NT and Proxy Server.

Each device that operates with SNMP must use an SNMP management software package to read its information. The information is kept in a common format noted as an MIB (Management Information Base). In the case of Microsoft Proxy Server, the .MIB files are W3P.MIB (Web Proxy service) and WSP.MIB (WinSock Proxy service). The installation will not install these files by default. To use the .MIB files, an administrator must manually copy the two files from the distribution compact disc. The files are located in the PERFCTRS directory in the appropriate processor architecture directory: ALPHA\PERFCTRS (Alpha AXP) and I386\PERFCTRS (Intel). Note that the .MIB files are processor-specific and are not interchangeable.

Before any of the .MIB files can be used, you must first compile them with the compiler that is shipped with your SNMP management package. Many larger corporations have SNMP products such as HP Openview, IBM Netview, Microsoft Systems Management Server 1.2 (SMS), and so forth. Microsoft also includes one in the Microsoft Software Development Kit (SDK): MIBCC.EXE. Since each compiler varies, you should refer to your respective compilers for compilation information.

Once compiled, the SNMP service uses Object Identifiers (OIDs) for .MIB processing. The OID for the W3P.MIB is 11 and WSP.MIB is 12. Note that the .MIB files are readable through any text editor while in their uncompiled form.

To initialize SNMP's capabilities, an administrator must start the Web Proxy and WinSock Proxy services prior to configuring or starting the Windows NT SNMP services on Proxy Server. After initialization, you must start the related services before they can be monitored. For example, if the Web Proxy service has not been started, you have nothing to monitor. These servers should be started before installing or re-installing the Windows NT SNMP services. After the SNMP service has been started on Proxy Server (locally), you may use a configured system to read the management information (remotely).

To configure SNMP on the Windows NT Server, use the steps in Exercise 11.6.

WARNING

A major problem with SNMP on an insecure gateway is that routing information may be visible to unauthorized users.

EXERCISE 11.6

Configuring SNMP on the Windows NT Server

1. From the Control Panel, double-click the Network icon.

2. Click the Services tab, then click Add.

3. From the list of available services, select SNMP. Windows will prompt you for the i386 directory location.

EXERCISE 11.6 (CONTINUED FROM PREVIOUS PAGE)

4. When the SNMP Configuration screen appears, select the Agent tab. Type the related contact name and location. Also, select the appropriate services for the products you plan to monitor (Physical, Datalink, Application, End-to-End, and Internet).

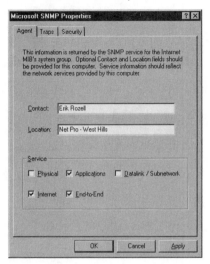

5. Click the Traps tab. Select or input the community name that your SNMP management tool will be a part of. Most implementations default to Public. However, to better secure your environment, we recommend against this. Also, provide the IP address(es) of the system(s) to receive messages from the SNMP agent.

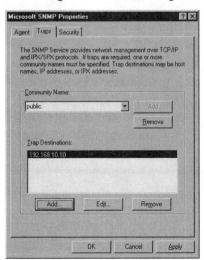

6. Select the Security tab and configure it according to your security requirements. For example, select the Send Security Trap option to verify management nodes authority. Also, define the accepted communities and whether to accept management requests from all or specific IP addresses.

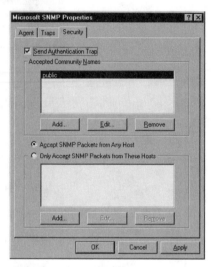

7. When completed, click OK to accept and then Close to close the dialog box. You must reboot for the changes to take effect.

Summary

Performance is an issue that has been a concern long before the introduction of the computer. In this chapter, we focused on the specific points and issues that could create bottlenecks or performance problems in a given system. Five specific items are generally reviewed as a matter of diagnosing Proxy Server's performance: the disk, CPU, memory, cache, and network. Any of these performance hot spots can create a significant reduction is server efficiency.

A number of system issues can be identified through the Performance Monitor. While a number of counters are included with the default installation of Windows NT, Microsoft Proxy Server includes five of its own: Proxy Server Cache, Web Proxy Server Service, Socks Proxy Server, Packet Filter Service, and WinSock Proxy Server. Each item contains several counters and indicators. However, an administrator will typically only review a few. Microsoft includes these counters for diagnostic as well as statistical functions.

As an administrator reviews each item, they can use the Performance Monitor data to review changes in the system's behavior. Once completed, an administrator will compare the results of the proxy server having problems to readings that were taken while the system was running optimally. Concluding from this information which component is causing the problem, the administrator can correct the problem by taking the appropriate action. The data that is used in comparing the problemed system is know as baseline or control data. This control data is taken from reports in the Event Viewer, log files, and the Performance Monitor. When trying to answer questions, the database interface is useful in extracting only relevant data to answer queries.

There are a number of items that affect the overall throughput of the proxy server. Remember that, as a rule, increasing the cache size will almost always increase the throughput. As a factor of caching, if active caching is not enabled, it should be. However, be aware that on dialup connections, active caching is subject to the hours defined by an administrator. To extend caching capabilities, you may increase an object's TTL so it is refreshed less often. Moreover, avoid using WinSock Proxy and Socks Proxy applications when a Web Proxy–based substitute is available. Neither WinSock Proxy nor Socks Proxy perform caching.

A final component in ensuring your Proxy Server's functionality is its support for SNMP. Using a third-party SNMP package such as HP's Openview or IBM's Netview, an administrator can configure a system to perform automated notification of system problems. This greatly helps decrease work hours in system support.

Review Questions

1. Discuss the five key components that can bottleneck a proxy server.

2. Explain how Performance Monitor operates as opposed to the Event Viewer.

3. What are the three counter groups that Microsoft Proxy Server provides to integrate with Performance Monitor?

4. Describe how DISKPERF operates with Performance Monitor. Does it add any overhead to the system?

5. Explain the connections between SNMP and Microsoft Proxy Server.

6. Which of the following items could create a bottleneck for the proxy server?

   A. Video monitor type

   B. Video adapter speed

   C. System power supply

   D. Hard drive transfer speed

   E. None of the above

7. While using Microsoft Proxy Server, which items can be affected by a slow network?

   A. Data transmission rates

   B. Number of users that can use the proxy server at a time

   C. Access to specific sites

   D. Hard drive transfer speed

   E. None of the above

8. What items can be affected by too small of a Web Proxy Server cache?

   A. Data transmission rates

   B. Number of users that can use the proxy server at a time

   C. Access to specific sites

D. Hard drive transfer speed

E. None of the above

9. Microsoft Proxy Server automatically adjusts itself by fine tuning its internally controlled switches. True or False? Explain.

10. Enabling SMNP on a unsecured gateway could potentially allow your network routing information to be seen from the Internet. True or False. Explain.

11. You want to build a new proxy server, but you want to keep the configuration changes you made on the old proxy server. How should you do this? Choose all that apply.

A. Copy the WSPCFG.INI file to the new computer.

B. Copy the MSPCFG.INI file to the new computer.

C. On the Service tab of the Web Proxy service Properties dialog box of the current Proxy Server, click the Server Backup command buttons.

D. On the Service tab of the Web Proxy service Properties dialog box of the new computer, click the Local Address Table command button.

E. On the Service tab of the Web Proxy service Properties dialog box of the new computer, click the Server Restore command button.

12. When looking at the proxy logs, you notice that 30% of all users are accessing www.work-related.com. You want to decrease the network traffic and ensure that Web pages from this site are still cached. What should you do?

A. Disable caching.

B. Enable active caching and then select the Fewer Network Accesses Are More Important (Less Pre-Fetching) option button.

C. Set the cache expiration policy to Updates Are More Important (More Update Checks).

D. Create a cache filter for the www.work-related.com domain and set the Filtering Status option to Always Cache.

13. You want to check performance on your IDE drive. You open Microsoft Performance Monitor and add the % Disk Time counter from the PhysicalDisk object to examine the time spent reading and writing files to disk. However, no activity is shown for the % Disk Time counter. What must you do to monitor disk activity through the Performance Monitor? Choose all that apply.

A. Run the Diskperf command.

B. Restart the Web Proxy service.

C. Restart the Proxy Server computer.

D. View the % Disk Time counter from another computer on the network.

E. Replace the IDE drive with an SCSI.

14. In the Web Proxy Service Properties dialog box you select Enable Caching and Use Fewer Network Accesses Are More Important (More Cache Hits), and you also select Enable Active Caching and Use Faster User Response Is More Important (More Pre-Fetching). How does this configuration affect the cache?

A. The pages have a maximum TTL with the largest percentage of popular cached objects updated.

B. The pages have a minimum TTL with the smallest percentage of popular cached objects updated.

C. The pages have a minimum TTL with the largest percentage of popular cached objects updated.

D. The pages have a maximum TTL with the smallest percentage of popular cached objects updated.

CHAPTER

12

Problem Solving

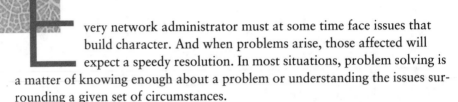

Every network administrator must at some time face issues that build character. And when problems arise, those affected will expect a speedy resolution. In most situations, problem solving is a matter of knowing enough about a problem or understanding the issues surrounding a given set of circumstances.

This chapter is not meant to give the impression that an administrator should expect frequent problems with Proxy Server. Instead, our focus is on preventing problems and on finding quick solutions to issues as they arise. Typically, these issues arise as a product of monitoring the system, a topic covered in Chapter 11. This chapter will teach you where problems arise most and how to fix them. We will look at sources of information an administrator should consult when trying to correct a problem.

By the end of this chapter you will understand the following:

- Identifying problems as they occur

Exam objectives are subject to change at any time without prior notice and at Microsoft's sole discretion. Please visit Microsoft's Training & Certification website (www.microsoft.com/Train_Cert) for the most current exam objectives listing.

- The use of tools available for troubleshooting

- The Registry and related materials

- Using the Event Viewer to diagnose problems

- Web Proxy service problems

- WinSock Proxy service problems

- Where to find information on problems

- Troubleshooting Internet access problems

Troubleshooting Resources

Windows NT and Proxy Server provide a number of tools for troubleshooting. While there are no specific tools to fix all situations, knowing the right tool to use can certainly reduce downtime. The key areas you'll need to troubleshoot are the Registry, software, hardware, and the network. You may note that these items involve performance as much as problem solving. That is because there is not always a clear distinction between improving performance and troubleshooting.

Microsoft ✓ **Exam Objective**

Analyze performance issues. Performance issues include:

- Identifying bottlenecks
- Identifying network-related performance issues
- Identifying disk-related performance issues
- Identifying CPU-related performance issues
- Identifying memory-related performance issues

For the Proxy Server administrator, the best sources of system information are the Registry Editor, the Event Viewer, the Windows system configuration applications like MSD (Microsoft Diagnostics), and Performance Monitor. Each application has its own distinct use as discussed throughout the chapter.

NOTE Some problems that you encounter may be specific to the operating system. Although we have performed our own testing with both Windows 98 and Windows NT 5.0 and found no problems, that doesn't mean you won't encounter a problem related to the operating system. You should consult Microsoft's knowledge base or TechNet prior to installation to verify that no problems with the operating system you're using are known. If there is a problem, you will be prepared to deal with it.

The Registry

Microsoft Proxy Server is installed with a number of default settings that you cannot change through the IIS Manager. These settings are stored in a database of settings known as the Registry.

The Registry was developed in Windows NT as a replacement to the .INI files that stored program settings in previous Windows versions. There were two basic problems with .INI files. First, there was no distinct format defining how vendors would write data to them and in what directory they would reside. Second, the .INI files lacked a hierarchy that would designate which user the settings were for and in what working order. For example, two users might use the same system to perform different tasks. One uses Microsoft Word as a publishing tool while the other uses it to filter data with macros. If settings are preserved in the .INI files, preferences must be reset for each user. In short, the Registry was a necessary step toward advancing the operating system.

Every time an administrator makes a change through the IIS Manager, updates are made to the Registry. For example, if an administrator changes the active cache update, the corresponding entry in the Registry will be updated. You've seen throughout this book that configuration changes to Proxy Server and other NT services typically involve restarting the affected service; restarting is necessary so that NT can go back to the Registry and use the updated information at the system level, where changes cannot be made directly once the operating system has loaded.

The Registry is structured as a tree, made up of categories called *subtrees*. Windows NT has five subtrees, each of which contains keys and possibly subkeys. Each subtree controls a broad area of system operations; for example, the HKEY_LOCAL_MACHINE subtree contains the settings for the system itself, which is stored in keys. Each key contains the settings for a specific function within a subtree area; for example, the HKEY_LOCAL_MACHINE\ SOFTWARE\MICROSOFT\WINDOWS\CURRENTVERSION\RUN key contains the settings for a list of applications that are automatically run when a Windows session is started.

The settings within a key are known as values, and these are the actual Registry entries. Each value has two parts: its name and its data. Values are of two types: binary and string.

Another buzz word used in discussing the Registry is *hive*, which refers to a group of keys.

The Registry structure is shown in Figure 12.1.

FIGURE 12.1

The Registry structure

```
TREE ROOT
├---SUBTREE
├------KEY
├-------SUBKEY
├-------SUBKEY AND VALUE
├---SUBTREE2
├---SUBTREE3
├---SUBTREE4
└---SUBTREE5
```

In some cases, after you remove a program and then reinstall it, the application may pick up some of its old settings, such as User Preferences. The manufacturer may have done this deliberately to simplify reinstallation, or they may simply have been too lazy to clean up after themselves. In cases like this, you may want to delete all occurrences of the application in the Registry by using a keyword search. For example, if a hypothetical company, Acme Software, installed an application, and then when the application was removed it left remnants in the Registry, you would most likely want to search the Registry for all entries containing the application name or references to Acme. When any are found, you would delete either the entire subkey or the line containing the search text (in this case, Acme Software).

Never guess at Registry entries. You know the consequences. Also, even though a software manufacturer has recommended a specific Registry change, there is no guarantee the change is right for your system. For this reason, never make too many changes at once.

When you need to change the Registry, do so with the absolute understanding that the changes you make can destroy the functionality of your server. That is not to say that your machine will stop working if you modify specific settings. Rather, if the wrong settings are implemented, the system may not boot thereafter. The best suggestion for dealing with this problem is to keep constant system backups. You can perform imports of the Registry so you can refer back the way things should be. However, if the system is not booting this will not be too useful for correcting the problem.

Some of the changes that are applied to the Registry may come from patches or hot fixes that are added to the service pack. These fixes can be downloaded from Microsoft's Web site.

Registry Tools

The Registry is stored among files that cannot be directly read by a text editor. Instead, certain utilities known as Registry tools must be used. By default, Microsoft ships two editor tools with Windows NT: Regedit and Regedt32. These utilities are independent and used for separate purposes.

Microsoft Exam Objective

Select and use software configuration management tools (for example, Control Panel, Windows NT Setup, Regedt32).

Although it's tempting to make routine adjustments to the system by editing the Registry directly, we don't recommend that. Whenever possible, use the correct configuration tool. In Layman's terms, "You can really mess up big!"

Regedit

There are two Registry editors included with Microsoft Windows NT. The standard editor, which is also used for Windows 95, is called Regedit. Regedit can be run from the DOS command prompt or be selecting Start ➤ Run from the Windows desktop. Once Regedit is active, an administrator can use it to import/export other Registry files, search, edit, add, delete, and so on. The two most common things that you will do with your Registry are searching and editing.

Importing the Registry can be as simple as double-clicking a .REG data file. Entries in the file are instantly merged into the current Registry database. Regedit is best suited to working with general problems that span multiple subtrees, particularly when searching keys, values, and data. For example, if you are looking for all occurrences of Microsoft Word, you should use this utility. This way you can find all occurrences regardless of their location in the Registry. Figure 12.2 shows part of the Registry, viewed in the Regedit Editor window.

FIGURE 12.2

Viewing Web Proxy parameters in the Regedit Editor

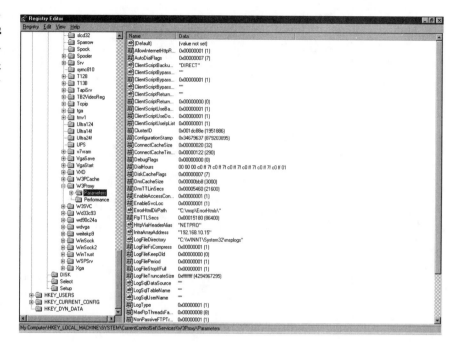

When working with Regedit, the left panel is used to migrate through the Registry tree, while the right side is used for change values. Keys can be added to either side.

Regedt32

The 32-bit editor that ships with Windows NT is named Regedt32 (see Figure 12.3), and you can run it from a DOS command prompt or by selecting Start ➤ Run. For the most part, Regedt32 has the same functionality as Regedit; however, it is designed to work with individual subtrees rather than the entire Registry. In Regedt32, you may set permissions, auditing, and ownership for specific keys. However, a major disadvantage of this editor is that its Search feature can only locate keys, not data or values.

FIGURE 12.3

Using the Regedt32 Editor

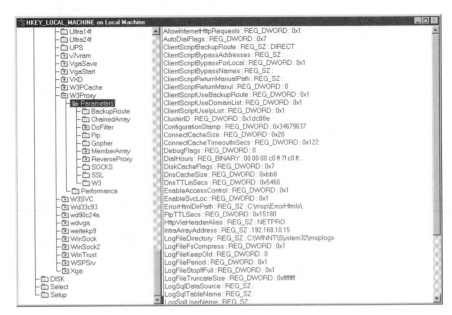

The Regedt32 view is virtually identical to that of Regedit. However, the subtrees are separated into individual windows. Operations can take place only with one window. The left side of a window is still used for navigation, while the right is for changing values.

Windows NT Resource Kit

The Windows NT Resource Kit contains a number of utilities for working with the Registry. These utilities include programs to search and replace entries, merge trees, delete keys, and so forth. Although the ability to perform all the functions of the Registry tools is available in both Regedit and Regedt32, the extra tools generally contain specific utilities for performing certain functions, such as in batch or command line.

Registry Entries

Now that you are familiar with the Registry and the tools used to manipulate it, we can examine the entries as applicable to the Microsoft Proxy Server services. Remember that when you work with the Registry, you should never make changes to items you are uncertain of. Also, when making changes, be certain to keep a log of exactly what you have changed and the reason for the action. Trying to repair a corrupted Registry can be like finding a needle in two haystacks (a little harder than one haystack!). You may consider performing a system backup before continuing.

Registry entries related to proxy services are stored in five basic key locations, all within the HKEY_LOCAL_MACHINE\SYSTEM\CURRENT-CONTROLSET\SERVICES subkey. However, third-party add-ons may use other locations. Use the following as a guideline as to where to look:

Service	Key Location
WinSock Proxy service	WSPSRV\PARAMETERS
Web Proxy cache	W3PCACHE\PARAMETERS
Web Proxy service	W3PROXY\PARAMETERS
Socks Proxy service	W3PROXY\PARAMETERS\SOCKS
Reverse Proxy service	W3PROXY\PARAMETERS\REVERSEPROXY

There are also some Registry items common to all Proxy services:

Entry	Key Location
Domain filtering keys	W3PROXY\PARAMETERS\DOFILTER
Array membership	W3PROXY\PARAMETERS\MEMBERARRAY
Chained array	W3PROXY\PARAMETERS\CHAINEDARRAY
Packet filtering	MSPADMIN\FILTERS
Logging	MSPADMIN\PARAMETERS

Tools for Verifying Communications

There are a number of commands you can use to verify communication between a client and the proxy server. In general, you should begin by checking the transport (IP or IPX) communications, then concern yourself with others. For example, if a workstation cannot see any other systems on your network, its communication with the proxy server obviously will not work either. You should begin by verifying the protocol stack by checking to see that your other networked machines are using the same settings. If that does not work, you may consider verifying the network card, then the cable, and so on.

Microsoft Exam Objective Troubleshoot hardware-related problems such as network interfaces and disk drives.

You use the following commands and utilities when debugging a system. If your system is using TCP/IP for its transport, use the TCP/IP utilities accordingly. On the other hand, if your system is running Windows NT or Windows 95 and IPX as the transport, use the IPX utilities. Remember that IPX communication is limited to these two 32-bit operating systems.

TCP/IP Utilities

A number of communication utilities are included as part of the TCP/IP suite. Microsoft further extends these utilities by adding a few of their own. While reviewing this list, remember that not all utilities (for example, hostname, ipconfig, and nslookup) are included with Windows 95. Since the majority of these utilities were covered in Chapter 2, we will not go into great detail here. For further information on most utilities, include /? on the command line for help.

- ARP   Used to view data pertaining to the resolution of IP addresses to hardware addresses (-g or –a option). ARP stands for Address Resolution Protocol.

- HostName   Used to view the current configured host name associated with the system where the command is executed.

- IpConfig   Displays the current settings for TCP/IP. Commonly used with the /ALL command to display all settings.

- NbtStat   Reveals the current status of NetBios over TCP/IP communications. This command can be used to view the NetBios name cache, reload an lmhosts-defined cache, etc. Command options are case sensitive.

- NetStat   Lists network interface statistics and status.

- NsLookup   Used to verify name information by querying domain name servers (DNS).

- Ping   Checks TCP/IP communications and establishes accessibility of a remote system. Commonly used with the -a option to perform address-to-name resolution. Also used with the -t option to extend packet life over slow links. This command is commonly used when troubleshooting communication problems where no network is seen. If, for example, a TCP/IP client could not Ping the IP address of the proxy server, you can assume that either TCP/IP is not configured correctly or there is a hardware failure.

- Route   Used to add, view, and create static routes on a Windows NT system. The route command is the interface to the Windows NT router.

- TraceRt   Verifies step-by-step (or hop-by-hop) access to a target resource.

- WinIpCfg   Windows 95 GUI version of IpConfig. This command is also included with the Windows NT Resource Kit.

IPX Utilities

The IPX protocol suite is a plug-and-play stack that delivers instant access to network resources. Unlike TCP/IP, IPX includes no support commands. Microsoft, however, extends basic troubleshooting by providing a command called IPXRoute.

Typically, IPX does not require any troubleshooting and is operational unless a fault occurs in a router, server, or a workstation's network adapter/cable. In normal conditions, workstations should be set to automatic configuration, Ethernet/Token ring type, and network detection. This means that the system will be configured as automatic frame type and network 000000. However, in some instances where no router or server can automatically configure this information, it must be set manually. Always verify that the data matches the correct network and frame type. If you know the frame type and number, do not leave it to chance—set it.

Remember that Proxy Server supports IPX only if it was installed on the physical server before Proxy Server. The protocol must be bound to the adapter on both the client and the server. To verify that IPX was installed before the Proxy Server installation, you can check the MSPCLNT.INI file. The file should include one and only one IPX address for the internal network adapter on the proxy server machine. Note that if the network card was exchanged, it is very likely that you will experience problems communicating with clients since the hardware address is directly associated with the adapter.

The IPXRoute command has a number of uses. However, it's most commonly used with the modifiers config and servers, as shown below:

IPXRoute Config: This command will display the client's network number, IPX frame type, network card hardware address, and IPX address. For communication to occur, this information must match that of the configured server.

IPXRoute Servers: The command in this context will display the IPX address, server type, and name.

Because IPXRoute verifies IPX communications, the transport must be loaded on both the client and the server. Also, since communications are propagated through the service advertisement protocol (SAP), you must have the SAP agent in the network configuration loaded as well.

Proxy Utilities

Because of the complexity of the WinSock Proxy service, Microsoft includes a diagnostic utility you can use to display the installed protocols, the WinSock files/locations/version, the name of the configured Proxy Server, and the status of the client's connection to the proxy server. The utility is installed in the MSPCLNT directory during client setup and comes in two varieties:

- CHKWSP16.EXE   Used with 16-bit operating systems

- CHKWSP32.EXE   Used with 32-bit operating systems

In the default installation, no icon is included on the Start menu for this utility. Instead, an administrator must run the utility from a DOS prompt. As with the CHKDSK (check disk) command, you can use the –f option to display full information. For example,

```
CHKWSP32.EXE -F)
```

will provide a detailed report like the following:

```
********************************************************************

**** Winsock Proxy Diagnostic Information ****

********************************************************************


WAIT...
```

```
CONFIGURATION:
Winsock Proxy Service - Configuration Location: C:\mspclnt\
Proxy Name (IP Addr):
NETPRO
IP: Installed
IPX: Installed

WAIT...

16-bit RWS CLIENT:
Winsock Name: C:\WINDOWS\winsock.dll
Version: 1.0.194.2
Description: Microsoft Remote Windows Socket 16-Bit DLL

32-bit WSP CLIENT:
Winsock Name: C:\WINDOWS\SYSTEM\wsock32.dll
Version: 1.0.194.2
Description: Microsoft Remote Windows Socket 32-Bit DLL
Version Type: FREE
Client version of control protocol: 9


--------------------------------------------

Remoting is disabled. You can enable it via WSP Client control
panel applet.
```

Specific Proxy Server Problems

From time to time, your network will experience problems that may or may not be triggered by an event or a change on the server. This section lists a number of specific errors or problems and their solutions. Although it is not necessary to memorize all the details, reviewing these errors will be extremely useful in understanding Microsoft Proxy Server. Problems specific to the Web, Socks, and WinSock Proxy services are listed in their own sections.

Microsoft ✓ ***Exam*** ***Objective*** | **Resolve Proxy Server and Proxy Server client installation problems.**

Microsoft ✓ ***Exam*** ***Objective*** | **Resolve Proxy Server and Proxy Server client access problems.**

Microsoft ✓ ***Exam*** ***Objective*** | **Resolve Proxy Server client computer problems.**

Setup could not find the IIS virtual root scripts (during proxy setup).
The error occurs when the Proxy Server installation program could not find the default SCRIPTS directory set by IIS. Typically, the directory will have been renamed or deleted. To correct the problem, re-create the directory (SCRIPTS) and set it with Execute access in the properties under the VIRTUAL directory.

You receive the message "Proxy: Error Log full." This error is slightly confusing. You will receive this message when the system event log (viewed with Event Viewer) is full, rather than when the log you've specified in the IIS Manager is full. To work around this problem, open the Event Viewer and change the log options so that the Manual option is set to Off, or increase the maximum log size, or select a lower number of days to Overwrite Events Older Than. If you have selected to stop services (from any proxy service's Logging tab), proxy services may be stopped until the problem is corrected.

Internet sites can only be accessed by IP address. This problem commonly occurs on new installations when a DNS server is not defined. Contact your ISP for a DNS IP address.

Internet sites can't be accessed via the proxy server. There are a number of items that must be available for the proxy server to access the Internet. The easiest way to verify the ISP configuration is to use a browser at the proxy server itself. Assuming that you have a failure, it is likely that you do not have a default gateway, a DNS, or some other component. Otherwise, it could be a permission problem at the client. When no default gateway is specified, clients will not be able to resolve requests. Typically, information will not be in the cache either, because this is usually only related to problems with new installations.

You receive a message stating that "A duplicate name exists on the network" even though there is no duplicate name. Windows NT requires that multiple network adapters in a given system be on different networks. These networks may be physically separate networks or different logical networks with different transport protocols. However, if you use the same protocol such as NetBEUI on both adapters and the adapters are connected to the same network, you will receive this error.

You receive a message stating that "None of the proxy server's computer's addresses are internal." This issue is related to incorrectly configuring the LAT. The internal network adapter must have its IP address in the LAT to function properly. The IP address may be specified directly or through a range of IP addresses.

Users without access can connect to Internet sites. This problem generally occurs as a factor of poor protocol security. First, check that IP forwarding is disabled. If enabled, users will have a path other than through the proxy service. Second, check if you are restricting users from the Web Proxy but not the WinSock Proxy or perhaps the other way around.

Web Proxy Service Problems

A number of problems are specific to the Web Proxy Server. Again, it is not necessary to know all the errors; however, reviewing them will improve your understanding of this service.

You receive the message "HTTP/1.0 500 server error. (An attempt has been made to operate on an impersonation token by a thread that is not currently impersonating a client.)" This message can occur when changes are made to the home directory properties for the WWW service while the Web Proxy service is being used. For example, suppose that the home directory is redirected to some given UNC path such as \\NETPRO\WWWNEW. Because the share on the remote system is not mapped to a drive letter, all requests processed via the Web Proxy service will fail.

Restarting both the WWW and Web Proxy services or rebooting the system can easily solve this problem. A better solution would be to create a virtual directory entry instead of modifying the default local drive path for the home directory when adding directory names that use UNC path names.

You receive the message "HTTP/1.0 500 server error (-*number*)."
This error appears while using Windows NT Challenge/Response authentication on the Proxy Server for proxy client validation. This is the password authentication set in the WWW service Properties screen to validate Web Proxy clients. Use the IIS Manager to verify the type of password authentication in use for WWW services. These services should match. Verify that the client is using a newer version of Internet Explorer or select Basic (Clear-Text) Authentication. Ideally, you should use Internet Explorer 4.0 or better, as problems are known regarding earlier version of Internet Explorer and secured pages. If you are unable to correct the problem, contact Microsoft's technical support.

You receive the message "HTTP/1.0 500 server error. (The specified module could not be found)."   This is a common problem that occurs when certain proxy binaries are not installed in the correct directory for proxy scripts. Review the location of the IIS SCRIPTS directory and verify that a PROXY subdirectory appears. If not, create the directory.

The cache seems to change too often.   The cache may appear to change often because of the TTL value set for an object. This is the period that the cache will hold an object in memory. The TTL value for a given cached item is determined by a number of factors. First, the Web page that is being cached may have an expiration date in its header. If so, this value is used as the TTL value. Next, if no value has been set in the page, the Proxy Server will configure itself according to an explicit caching period set in the Registry. If the explicit value has not been set, the proxy server will set the TTL to the duration defined in the Advanced section of the Web Proxy Caching tab. An example of these settings would be 20% of the period since the page was last modified with a minimum of 15 minutes and a maximum of one day.

Microsoft
✓ *Exam*
Objective

Resolve caching problems.

You receive the HTTP 500 server error "System cannot find the specified path." This error occurs when the WWW service has been configured with all home directories linked to virtual servers. To correct this problem, add a physical directory that is not linked to a virtual server, and make this your home directory. You will need to restart the WWW service.

Web Proxy Client-Specific Issues

A number of problems are specific to the Web Proxy client. It is not necessary to know all the errors; however, reviewing them will improve your ability to troubleshoot and fix problems related to the Proxy client.

A user can't browse external Web pages. Typically, a client will have no problem browsing the internal sites when this error occurs, but connectivity to the external sites fails. This is generally a problem related to either an incorrect proxy setting in the Web browser or a failure to connect externally. Verify the settings, and then Ping the Web Proxy Server to verify name resolution and connectivity. If a failure occurs at this point, you should either correct the problem at the DNS, WINS server, or workstation (possibly the error is in a host file), or use the IP address of the proxy server instead. Note that the WINS server may be operating such that it provides information to the DNS. You must remember that NetBIOS names are resolved while working within a Microsoft client's redirector (such as the Net use and Net view commands), However, all TCP/IP-based utilities, such as telnet and FTP, are based on host name resolution.

If access control is enabled, this problem could also appear due to a lack of rights. Remember that internal Web pages can be accessed without the proxy server on IP networks, but external sites require explicit rights.

Microsoft ✔ ***Exam Objective***   **Troubleshoot a WINS server to provide client access to Proxy Servers.**

A user can't browse internal Web pages. The inverse of the previous error, this typically has one of two possible causes: Either you have not included your internal servers on an exclude list, or you have failed to specify that Proxy Server should not be used for internal Web sites. Also, if you are using name resolution via WINS, you must verify that you are actually resolving the given host name of an internal system. If the host name, for example, can't use the Ping utility (i.e. PING SERVER1), you must add a static record to the WINS database, create a HOSTS file, or add the host name to the DNS.

FTP with Netscape Navigator displays received files as text rather than downloading them.   This problem is common with older versions of Netscape Navigator. The file to be downloaded is seen as an HTTP page, because Netscape does not examine its contents. Hold the Shift key when clicking a link to download a file to bypass this problem.

You receive the message "HTTP error 5 occurred."   This error occurs when a connection has been refused for a proxy client. When working in an anonymous configuration, verify that IUSR_*systemname* appears on the Web Proxy service sheet for the requested protocol (FTP, HTTP, Secure, or Gopher). The IUSR_*systemname* is used in this context to authenticate clients. If the system is not configured for anonymous access, verify that the users are authorized to have access.

You receive the message "HTTP error 12 occurred."   This problem is associated with errors in the configuration of the Local Address Table (LAT). Verify that the server's IP address for the local network is listed in the LAT.

You receive the message "HTTP error 18 occurred."   This problem occurs when a Web browser is operating with the FTP service and viewing an empty directory. This is not an issue with the WinSock Proxy service.

You receive one of these messages: "HTTP error 10060 occurred," "The Operation Timed Out," or "A connection with the server could not be established."   These errors typically indicate a timeout while attempting to connect to a URL. The timeout can occur if the foreign host is off-line, too busy to reply, or located on an unavailable network. A connection failure can be attributed to a server that is not responding or is unavailable at the time of the request.

You receive the message "The server returned an invalid or unrecognized response."   When an HTTP request is corrupted by transmission errors or is sent in an incompatible format, this error may occur. Try the operation again. It is possible that the server you are accessing may require reduced security or other adjustments. If all else fails, send e-mail to the site owner for assistance. In some rare cases, the browser may cause the problem. This occurs when a site requires Netscape Navigator, Internet Explorer, or another specific browser and does not function with any other client.

You receive one of these messages: "The service has not been started (stopping the WWW service)" or "An instance of the service is already running (starting the WWW service)." After the proxy server has been installed, the Web Proxy and WWW services are linked, so stopping or starting one service will do the same for the other service automatically. If the IIS Manager screen is slow in displaying updates, you can press F5 to show the current status of all services.

The log file for the Web Proxy Server does not list IP addresses associated with a given site. This occurs when all requested pages are being retrieved by the Proxy Server's Active Caching mechanism. Since the process makes the request, the client never actually connects to the site and an address is not logged.

A "Connection timed out" error occurs when the client is configured with multiple default gateways. This error reflects the fundamental design of TCP/IP. When a system has multiple network cards, only one gateway should be configured as the default. Since the proxy server connects the private network to the Internet, in effect it is a router that uses the default gateway as an outlet for any traffic that has no specific route assigned. The proxy server will assume that two default gateways are a redundant path, which may cause it to send traffic to the wrong network. You should disable the default gateway to the internal network (in Advanced TCP/IP Settings) and use the Route command to create static mappings. You can also use the –p command switch to create a persistent route. Also use Route /? to get help or refer to the Windows NT manual for further details on creating static routes.

A secured SSL site asks for its password three times and then replies "Access denied." This problem is inherent to Internet Explorer 2.*x* and some later versions with Windows NT Challenge/Response authentication on the Proxy Server. Depending on the level at which this error occurs, the solution will vary. Try the following:

1. Upgrade clients to Internet Explorer version 3.01 or later (preferably Internet Explorer 4.*x*); then apply the service pack on the Proxy Server to version 3 or greater along with any hot fixes. Test the configuration.

2. Install the WinSock Proxy client. Then clear the Proxy Server entry for Secure in Internet Explorer. This will cause the client to use WinSock Proxy for Windows NT Challenge/Response. Test the configuration.

3. Disable Windows NT Challenge/Response and use basic authentication through the WWW service Properties screen.

4. Disable all proxy functions in the Proxy Server and use those in the Win-Sock service only.

5. Disable the access control functions of the Web Proxy service. This will allow all users to use the server as the anonymous account, regardless of any prior security.

6. Modify the secure protocol so that the permissions include the IUSR_servername account. SSL security will be effectively disabled, and access will be configured as anonymous.

Web Proxy Cache-Specific Issues

The major concerns up until this point have been related primarily to the quirks of different products interacting with the proxy server. As you have seen, not all proxy clients are equal and the issues they face are not always intuitive. A number of problems are specific to the Web Proxy cache. It is not necessary to know all the errors; however, reviewing them will improve your ability to troubleshoot and fix problems related to the cache.

Caching fails to occur.   Verify that there is adequate drive space available for caching. Verify that caching is enabled and increase the drive if necessary.

Requests to a given site yields data retrieved from the cache that is out of date.   Some sites incorrectly set the TTL value of their site such that cached data appears current to the proxy server but is actually out of date. To correct this problem, you should create a cache filter to not cache that site. The other possibility for receiving this error is that you have set your cache expiration policy as Fewer Network Accesses Are More Important (More Cache Hits) and the TTL is being set to the maximum possible length, thus causing this problem.

When systems are moved and the DNS is updated, the proxy server still attempts to use the old IP address.   In addition to caching data, the Proxy Server will cache DNS entries. When changes in the DNS occur, it will take some time for the DNS to flush some of its older entries. You can view the DNS caching activity through Performance Monitor.

You receive one of these messages: "Web Proxy cache initialization failed due to an incorrect configuration. Please use the administration utility or manually edit the Registry to correct the error and restart the service" or "Web Proxy cache failed to initialize the URL cache on disk." Since Microsoft Proxy Server performs an automatic check on the cache file, this error rarely occurs, even when incomplete objects are stored, the server is not shut down properly, a device hangs, or the like.

Using Internet Service Manager, stop the WWW service (the Web Proxy service will automatically stop). Click the Advanced button in the Caching tab of the Web Proxy service. Locate and select the Reset Default button. Restart the WWW service. If the failure still occurs, run the setup utility that ships with Microsoft Proxy Server and select the Reinstall option. If this does not alleviate the problem, stop the WWW service, delete the cache directories manually, and then reinstall.

If the problem still occurs, it is most likely related to a problem with the hard drive. Try typing **chkdsk /r** at the command prompt to recover readable information, or delete the cache directories and move the cache to a different drive location.

You are required to stop the WWW service before you can delete Web Proxy cache directories.

You receive the message "The Web Proxy cache corrected a corrupted or old-format URL cache by removing all or part of the cache's contents." This error occurs when cached objects are deleted or removed from the cache. Typically, the error will be displayed, but no further action is necessary. If the message recurs, run chkdsk /r at the command prompt to verify that there are no disk errors and to recover readable information from the disk drive if any errors are found.

You receive the message "The hard disk used by the Web Proxy Server to cache popular URLs is full. Space needs to be freed, or the Web Proxy cache needs to be reconfigured to resume normal operation." This problem is usually attributed to a highly active proxy server. Delete cached objects from the hard disk or reconfigure with a larger cache.

Before we move on to look at problems with the WinSock Proxy service, try Exercises 12.1 and 12.2 for hands-on experience with Web Proxy troubleshooting.

EXERCISE 12.1

Fault Finding and the Web Proxy

The first part of this exercise requires that you create a fault. You will be simulating a Web page that delivers text but not graphics to a specific system. All other systems at other sites are able to get full functionality.

We recommend that you try out this exercise with a partner. One of you (Person 1) will be responsible for generating the error and the other (Person 2) for resolving it.

To set the stage for Person 1 and Person 2:

1. Open User Manager and create two accounts. The first account should be your name and the second the name of the person that you are working with. If you are working alone, simply call the account testuser.

2. Assign both accounts to the Domain Administrators group. This will ensure that both users will be able to log in, regardless of your configuration.

To create the fault (Person 1):

1. Open the C:\INETPUB\WWWROOT folder and right-click the SAMPLES folder. (If the sample folder does not appear, reinstall the IIS server and add the files.)

2. Select the Security tab and select Permissions.

3. After marking both Replace Permissions on Subdirectories and Replace Permissions on Existing Files, remove the Everyone group and add the account you've just created as a user with full control. Then click OK to close the Add box.

4. Click OK again to close the Directory Permissions box. You will be prompted to confirm that you want to update the security attributes for the files and directories. Click Yes.

5. After the update has completed, click OK to close the directory's Properties box.

6. Log out.

EXERCISE 12.1 (CONTINUED FROM PREVIOUS PAGE)

To troubleshoot the flaw (Person 2):

1. Log on as the test user or as the second account created for Person 2.

2. Start Internet Explorer or Netscape Navigator and open HTTP://
   servername.

3. Since the system may be reading the page from cache, try refreshing
   the page (use F5 in Internet Explorer).

4. Note what is displayed—not much. Notice that access is denied.
   Work through the problem and note what needs to be changed.
   Review the properties of the page that you are working on. If necessary, get Person 1 to help you correct the problem by reversing what
   they did to create the fault.

EXERCISE 12.2

Fault Finding and Web Proxy Caching

The first part of the exercise requires that you create a fault. You will be
simulating a Web page that delivers older information. Again, you may want
to work in teams of two, with Person 1 and Person 2 carrying out their
own specific instructions.

To create the flaw (Person 1):

1. Using the IIS Manager, select the Web Proxy service and select the
   Caching tab.

2. Move the slider to Fewest Internet Requests so that caching takes place.

To troubleshoot the cache (Person 2):

1. Using Internet Explorer, open a Web page on HTTP://*servername* via
   the proxy server. Your client must be configured to use the proxy
   server.

2. Modify the Web page and then reopen it. Notice that no changes are
   shown.

3. Review the caching properties to solve the problem. If necessary,
   work with Person 1 to resolve this issue by reversing the steps used
   to create the problem.

WinSock Proxy Service Problems

With the WinSock Server you may experience many problems that are similar to those experienced with the Web Proxy. Most of the WinSock issues, however, tend to appear while configuring clients to operate with the service. This is due to the diversity of applications and protocols that WinSock may encounter, whereas the Web Proxy service is typically host to only one program.

As you continue to work with the WinSock Proxy, you may note one or more of the following difficulties. Often these problems are inherent to the design of Proxy Server and are not flaws. Again, understanding the technology is your best bet for creating an effective and efficient Proxy Server.

Only the administrator can use/configure protocols for the WinSock Proxy service.   The basic installation configures the system so that only the administrator can make changes to configure protocols and ports, despite other settings shown (as available). In order to allow others to do this configuration, you need to set all the permissions correctly. Begin by verifying that the LAT correctly includes the node or network with the client PC. Next, check that the WinSock protocol they are attempting to access is included in the protocol list along with the appropriate port information. Finally, verify that the user or group has been granted permission to access the protocol. To completely bypass security, you may disable access control.

Ping does not appear to function.   The Ping utility does not use TCP or UDP protocols. Typically, Ping uses ICMP to verify connectivity. Often, only the name resolution part of Ping will appear to work. This is typically caused by using a third-party TCP/IP stack or a WinSock driver, or by a Ping utility that doesn't support the ICMP format. If the problem occurs while trying to resolve a DNS name, verify that the DNS server's IP address appears in the LAT. You may view the LAT by clicking the Local Address Table button on the Service tab of any of the proxy services. You may experience difficulties with programs that use third-party Ping utilities because of the unpredictability of the ICMP responses. If packet filtering is enabled, you should enable ICMP filters such as ICMP All Outbound, ICMP Ping Response, ICMP Ping Query, ICMP SRC Quench, ICMP Timeout, and/or ICMP Unreachable.

Local hosts are not resolved by the DNS.   The WinSock Proxy Server performs the DNS lookup functions. When working with local systems, do not use fully qualified or dotted name specifications. Also, verify that the local host names are stored on the DNS and that the DNS server's IP address is included in the LAT. If WINS is used to manage local hosts with or without the assistance of a DNS, verify that both the HOST and NETBIOS names are stored in the WINS database.

WinSock Proxy Client-Specific Issues

Since Microsoft has developed the WinSock Proxy almost exclusive from other vendors, you will not find too many additional problems arising. As you progress through the issues related to the WinSock Proxy client, you will notice that the majority of them deal with usage rather than actual bugs or problems.

RealAudio fails to operate when configured to use the Proxy Server. Microsoft's Proxy Server transparently handles all WinSock traffic. Therefore, there is no need to manually configure individual components separately. Disable the Proxy option under Preferences on RealAudio's View pull-down menu.

WinSock Proxy–aware applications fail to operate when configured to use the Proxy Server.   When the WinSock client is installed, all WinSock requests will automatically be redirected. You should not make any special settings for the application itself to use a proxy server. If you attempt this, you will have redirected requests before they ever reach the client and create a conflict. If the WinSock application you are using is 16-bit, it may be necessary to enter additional information during a client logon procedure. This is due to the fact that Windows 95's 32-bit security may not match up correctly with the application's requirements.

An IPX client with a Web browser configured to run with WinSock Proxy fails to operate.   Since protocol translation is required to determine the destination of a request, upper layer protocol commands will not work without the aid of the proxy server. In this case, clients running the IPX/SPX protocol must enter the Proxy Server computer's IP address and not the computer name. This rule applies to any WinSock application where IPX is used as the transport protocol.

Windows for Workgroups WinSock Proxy clients are required to log on when accessing the proxy server.   Windows for Workgroups clients must define a logon domain or this error will continue to occur. The logon domain can be set through the Control Panel by clicking Network. Also, in addition to this problem, users will continuously be prompted to log on each time they access the WinSock Proxy services unless a Winsock application is left open at all times.

Changes to MSPLAT.TXT file are lost.   When making changes to the LAT, you must either make changes to the MSPLAT.TXT file on the server or create one called LOCALLAT.TXT on the local PC. When changes are made to the MSPLAT.TXT file at the workstation, these changes will be lost because this file is overwritten with data from the server on a regular basis.

FTP connections via the Winsock Proxy are refused.   While operating with a stand-alone FTP application, client connections may be refused. The Microsoft WinSock Proxy implementation supports only passive FTP sessions, known as PASV. With a PASV FTP session, the FTP server is notified as to which port it must send the return data to. This is a typical implementation and does not cause problems with most FTPs configured for a Web browser. On the other hand, stand-alone FTP stacks typically contact the FTP server and then wait in a listen mode for the FTP server to assign a port for the connection. Often these stacks include an option to switch to PASV mode. Use this mode if available, or consider an alternate FTP product.

Parts of the local network are not accessible with applications via the WinSock Proxy.   This is a common issue, which is typical of expanding or changing networks. Verify that the network you are attempting to contact is included in the LAT. If the connection is still not accessible, try disabling the proxy client and verifying that you can connect in a standard configuration.

The dialup ISP services fail after installing the WinSock Proxy client. Since the WinSock Proxy client redirects WinSock traffic, the ISP will not receive your WinSock application's traffic. To correct this problem, you must disable the Winsock Proxy client in the Control Panel and reboot your system. This problem commonly occurs with home users who use RAS to dial into a corporate network and also have their own dialup ISP account.

Third-party TCP/IP stacks cause problems with the WinSock Proxy service.   Microsoft Proxy Server has only been certified to operate with the Microsoft TCP/IP stack. Microsoft does not assume responsibility for other implementations of TCP/IP. Contact the third party for support.

Windows for Workgroups IPX systems can't use the WinSock Proxy service.   This is a significant shortcoming of Microsoft Proxy Server. The typical 16-bit audience that is commonly working on the NetWare platform is not supported. WinSock Proxy supports IPX only for Windows 95 and Windows NT.

IPX/SPX clients can't communicate with the server.   Under normal conditions, this problem will occur if the server and clients are not configured the same way, or if no IPX address is set in the MSPCLNT.INI file in the [Servers Ipx Addresses] section for the server. You may manually add the address as Addr1=*xxxxxxxx*-MAC_ADDRESS where *xxxxxxxx* is the network followed by a hyphen and the NIC's MAC address. If the network does not have routers or Netware servers to define the network, you must manually set the address. The MAC address in this case should be 000000000001, regardless of the actual address.

NetBEUI protocol systems can't use the WinSock Proxy service.
Microsoft Proxy Server 2.0 only supports TCP/IP and IPX. TCP/IP is supported on all platforms. IPX is supported only on Windows 95 and NT.

Domain credentials are required each time a new WinSock application is started.   This problem is directly linked to the permissions for WinSock. When all Winsock applications are closed, the validation is lost. Reopening the application is equivalent to logging out of the server and then logging back in. If the first application is left open and minimized, the credentials will pass automatically.

Client refreshing should not be implemented on our network. How can we disable it?   For a number of security reasons, it may be desirable to disable refreshing. To do so requires that you change an entry in the MSPCLNT.INI file, located in the SYSTEM directory under CLIENTS. Locate the Common Refresh Rate Time, which should be in the [COMMON] section. Modify the number of hours from the default of 6 to 1000000000. This does not actually disable the function totally, but by the time one billion hours pass, you will have no interest in the refresh rate or much else.

WinSock applications are slow on the local network.   In some instances, the proxy server will redirect local traffic if LAT information has been supplied incorrectly. Verify that the system or network you are connecting to is listed in the LAT.

The Microsoft WinSock client fails during setup. When installing the Microsoft WinSock Proxy client, a number of possible errors may occur. To locate and resolve these errors, review the setup log file located in C:\MPCSETUP.LOG. A sample log is shown below:

```
Microsoft Proxy Server Setup Log of 11-21-1997 16:52

---------------------------------


MSP Setup: LangId=1033

MSP Setup: IsWinsockInWinDir camf=1 ois=0 or=90 DstDir=NULL

MSP Setup: winsock found in windir=1 in sysdir=0

MSP Setup: IsWinsockInWinDir returned DEFAULT!!! camf=1 ois=0
or=90 DstDir=NULL

MSP Setup: CheckFixInconsistency camf=0 ois=0 or=600 DstDir=NULL

MSP Setup: handle winsock2 = 1

MSP Setup: winsock2 exists = 0

MSP Setup: cleaning temp files

MSP Setup: IsCurrentDllRwsWin95_16 returned 1 result=0

MSP Setup: cleaning temp files

MSP Setup: wsock32.dll - InternalName: WSOCK32

MSP Setup: wsock32.dll IsCurrentDllRws = no

MSP Setup: CheckFixInconsistency returnd OK!!! camf=0 ois=0
or=600 DstDir=NULL

MSP Setup: IsWinsockInWinDir camf=13 ois=0 or=90 DstDir=NULL

MSP Setup: IsWinsockInWinDir returnd OK!!! camf=13 ois=2 or=90
DstDir=NULL

MSP Setup: IsWinsockInWinDir camf=13 ois=2 or=90 DstDir=NULL

MSP Setup: IsWinsockInWinDir returnd OK!!! camf=13 ois=2 or=90
DstDir=NULL

MSP Setup: IsWinsockInWinDir camf=13 ois=2 or=90 DstDir=NULL

MSP Setup: IsWinsockInWinDir returnd OK!!! camf=13 ois=4 or=90
DstDir=NULL

MSP Setup: IsWinsockInWinDir camf=5 ois=4 or=90 DstDir=NULL
```

MSP Setup: IsWinsockInWinDir returnd OK!!! camf=5 ois=4 or=90 DstDir=NULL

MSP Setup: CheckFixInconsistency camf=15 ois=4 or=600 DstDir=C:\mspclnt\

MSP Setup: CheckFixInconsistency returnd OK!!! camf=15 ois=4 or=600 DstDir=C:\mspclnt\

MSP Setup: CheckWinsockApps camf=15 ois=4 or=700 DstDir=C:\mspclnt\

MSP Setup: CheckWinsockApps returned DEFAULT!!! camf=15 ois=4 or=700 DstDir=C:\mspclnt\

MSP Setup: CheckFixInconsistency camf=24 ois=4 or=600 DstDir=C:\mspclnt\

MSP Setup: warning - RemoveBeta2Wsock Delete file returned 2

MSP Setup: warning - RemoveBeta2Wsock Delete file returned 2

MSP Setup: CheckFixInconsistency returned DEFAULT!!! camf=24 ois=4 or=600 DstDir=C:\mspclnt\

MSP Setup: SetReg camf=24 ois=4 or=800 DstDir=C:\mspclnt\

MSP Setup: opened find Software\Netscape\Netscape Navigator\Users

MSP Setup: opening subkey Software\Netscape\Netscape Navigator\Users\erik

MSP Setup: will put shortcuts in C:\WINDOWS\Start Menu\Programs

MSP Setup: will put shortcuts in C:\WINDOWS\Start Menu\Programs

MSP Setup: SetReg returnd OK!!! camf=24 ois=4 or=800 DstDir=C:\mspclnt\

MSP Setup: SwithWsockdll camf=24 ois=4 or=1000 DstDir=C:\mspclnt\

MSP Setup: wsock32.dll - InternalName: WSOCK32

MSP Setup: wsock32.dll IsCurrentDllRws = no

MSP Setup: succeeded - rename wsock32.dll To _msrws32.dll

MSP Setup: succeeded - rename rws32.dll To wsock32.dll

MSP Setup: IsWinsock16Loaded_w95 returned 1 result=0

MSP Setup: LazyRename=0

MSP Setup: IsCurrentDllRwsWin95_16 returned 1 result=0

MSP Setup: succeeded - rename winsock.dll To _msrws16.dll

```
MSP Setup: succeeded - rename rws.dll To winsock.dll
MSP Setup: SwitchWsockDll returnd OK!!! camf=24 ois=4 or=1000
DstDir=C:\mspclnt\
MSP Setup: InstallWinsock2Remoting camf=24 ois=4 or=1100
DstDir=C:\mspclnt\
MSP Setup: InstallWinsock2Remoting returned DEFAULT!!! camf=24
ois=4 or=1100 DstDir=C:\mspclnt\
```

While reviewing this log, you should note the events that have taken place. For example, you should note the directories that were used in installation, any failure messages, warnings, deletion notices, and so on.

Microsoft Exchange client is slow when starting on a Winsock Proxy client machine. This problem occurs on IPX networks where the proxy server uses dialup networking to connect to the Internet. The problem stems from a known issue with the Exchange client for Windows 95, where a Win-Sock DNS lookup call is made regardless of whether TCP/IP is installed on the system. The delay is the time it takes for the auto dialer to establish the connection and the DNS name to be resolved. To keep this from happening, modify the MSPCLNT.INI file entries for the installed mail client. Note that you must update the client through the Control Panel or wait six hours for the changes to make their way down to the proxy client.

Microsoft Exchange clients:

```
[exchng32]
Disable=1
```

Microsoft Outlook clients:

```
[outlook]
Disable=1
```

Clients with applications using the MAPI spooler:

```
[MAPISP32]
Disable=1
```

If you add the previous three sections, your clients will not be able to access an Exchange server via the Internet, unless that server is Web based or uses a POP3 client that does not require the MAPI spooler.

Microsoft Exchange Server and/or SMTP servers are sluggish during installation. When packet filtering is enabled, the Identification Protocol (Identd) cannot complete a request without the predefined filter (Identd). To correct this problem, open IIS and select any proxy service. Click the Security button and select Add on the Packet Filtering tab. Select the Identd filter and click the OK button until all windows are closed.

The MSPCLNT.INI configuration is creating problems. A number of problems that occur with clients are directly related to the MSPCLNT.INI file. This is the configuration file that all clients use and automatically download every time they log on or every six hours. As such, you can use this file to make broad configuration changes. Note that if the share name is to be changed, the path in the master configuration file must also be updated.

Here is a typical MSPCLNT.INI file. Notice in particular the comments in the sample file, some of which point out controls for disabling certain services:

```
[Internal]
scp=9,10
Build=2.0.372.2


[wspsrv]
Disable=1


[inetinfo]
Disable=1


[services]
Disable=1
;Disable Service controller and services


[spoolss]
Disable=1
;Disable Spooling subsystem for printing support


[rpcss]
Disable=1
;Disable Remote Procedure Call Subsystem
```

```
[kernel32]
Disable=1

[mapisp32]
Disable=0

[exchng32]
Disable=0

[outlook]
Disable=0

[raplayer]
RemoteBindUdpPorts=6970-7170
LocalBindTcpPorts=7070

[rvplayer]
RemoteBindUdpPorts=6970-7170
LocalBindTcpPorts=7070

[net2fone]
ServerBindTcpPorts=0

[icq]
RemoteBindUdpPorts=0
ServerBindTcpPorts=0,1025-5000
NameResolutionForLocalHost=P

[Common]
WWW-Proxy=NETPRO
Set Browsers to use Proxy=1
```

```
Set Browsers to use Auto Config=0
WebProxyPort=80
Configuration Url=http://NETPRO:80/array.dll?Get.Routing.Script
Port=1745
Configuration Refresh Time (Hours)=6
Re-check Inaccessible Server Time (Minutes)=10
Refresh Give Up Time (Minutes)=15
Inaccessible Servers Give Up Time (Minutes)=2
Setup=Setup.exe


[Servers Ip Addresses]
Name=NETPRO


[Servers Ipx Addresses]


[Master Config]
Path1=\\NETPRO\mspclnt\


[Inaccessible Servers]
NETPRO=106
```

ChkWSP16 or ChkWSP32 reports a client configuration error.   When running either check utility with the /F switch, you are informed that the client is not installed correctly. Check that the SYSTEM.INI includes a section called Microsoft Proxy Server with a configuration location key.

This error will also appear if the proxy-delivered WINSOCK.DLL file is missing, the original WINSOCK.DLL that shipped with your operating system is missing, or if the WinSock Proxy client has been disabled in the Control Panel.

Configuration files do not refresh or can't communicate with the server.   This problem occurs infrequently. When a client is configured with both TCP/IP and IPX/SPX, it may experience difficulties linking to the Proxy Server. Effectively, you must either disable TCP/IP or select Force IPX in the

WinSock Proxy Client configuration of the Control Panel. Disabling TCP/IP simply means removing the server's IP address from the MSPCLNT.INI file. You may also experience this problem if the MSPCLNT share does not exist on the proxy server, if rights have not been granted to clients, or if your PC is either not a member of the domain or is not logged into it.

Microsoft
✓ Exam
Objective

Resolve security problems.

Now that you've seen some of the problems most commonly encountered with the WinSock Proxy service, try Exercise 12.3 for hands-on experience.

EXERCISE 12.3

Working with WinSock Permissions

The first part of the exercise requires that you create a fault. To best experience this exercise, we again recommend that you work with a partner. If you are working with the same partner as in Exercise 12.1 and 12.2, you should reverse roles. Person 1 should become Person 2 and Person 2 should be Person 1. (Again, each partner should follow only their own instructions.) In this exercise, you will be simulating an FTP site that rejects users.

To create the flaw (Person 1):

1. Using the IIS Manager, select the WinSock Proxy service and select the Permissions tab.

2. Verify that access control is enabled and that the Unlimited access group listing is empty.

3. Select the FTP Permissions listing and add your account. No other accounts should be listed.

4. Remove the second user from the Domain Administrator's group.

To troubleshoot the FTP (Person 2):

1. Log in to your account, if you haven't already done so.

2. If your client system is not already configured as a WinSock Proxy client, do so at this time. Using the Windows NT/Windows 95 command line–based FTP, open the server running the FTP service.

3. After the failure is reviewed, check the Event Viewer. Note any changes.

4. Use CHKWSP16 or CHKWSP32 to verify your WinSock Proxy client configuration.

5. Verify that FTP is working by logging in with the Administrator account.

6. Take the appropriate steps to correct your access based on what you have learned in this chapter. If you have difficulty, work with Person 1 and reverse the steps taken to create the problem.

Socks Proxy Service Problems

There are very few issues with the Socks Proxy service. Typically, the problems are related to usage more than anything else. Most client software uses either the Web Proxy or the WinSock Proxy. As such, the Socks server tends to have less utilization. Once it is working, it is very likely that you may never encounter a problem.

Socks Proxy fails to operate without the Web Proxy running. As you saw while setting up Performance Monitor in Chapter 11, the Socks Proxy is integrated into the Web Proxy service. If the Web Proxy service is stopped, the Socks Proxy will also be stopped. If the WWW service is stopped, both the Web Proxy and Socks Proxy services will also stop.

Socks applications fail at random or connections are never established. This problem typically occurs when dynamic filtering is disabled. In a manual configuration, all used ports must be defined. If you don't know which port to use or are experiencing problems with a port you believe to be correct, enable dynamic filtering. Also, if a version of Socks other than the standard 4.3a version is used, results may be unpredictable.

The Socks Proxy service is not available.   The only time this problem occurs is when the service has been disabled in the Registry by an administrator. To re-enable the service, modify its Registry entry to read:

```
HKEY_LOCAL_MACHINE
\System\CurrentControlSet\Services\W3Proxy\Parameters\Socks=1
```

Socks Proxy allows all users full access.   Security on the Socks Proxy service is not handled in the same manner as it is for other services. If authentication is disabled, everyone has access to everything. This situation may occur if there is an incompatibility between authentication and your application. In that case, the administrator must disable the security functions.

UDP applications such as RealAudio fail to operate.   Microsoft's Socks Proxy does not support UDP applications. Only the WinSock Proxy Server supports this functionality. UNIX clients, for example, will be unable to use such an application unless they can convert the protocol to TCP.

Other Proxy Service Problems

In some instances, you may find that certain components of the proxy server interfere with other installed applications. For example, in a dialup configuration, Microsoft Proxy Server would have difficulty working with Lotus Notes, which may also use a dialup adapter. Obviously, you should try to avoid these situations ahead of time. Do not assume that resources can be shared. In the case of Lotus Notes, you will need two modems and two phone lines. If you then decide to add a product such as Symantec's WinFax, you will need yet another line and modem.

Packet Filtering

Often, administrators are tempted to add all the components of a product and enable all of its features. In the case of Proxy Server, that might cause problems. Proxy Server's options are designed to tailor the program to its environment. Not all options are applicable to every system. For example, an administrator may attempt to install packet filtering without an external network interface. In some configurations, there may be a reason to do so; such as if the server is in an upstream routing orientation. However, two interfaces are required. Packet filtering may prove to be more of a problem than it's worth on the internal network. Also, if packet filtering is enabled, sometimes the external network interface is placed in the LAT. This may cause all sorts of connectivity problems when put in production. Furthermore, when using packet filtering with a DHCP or dynamic address that is assigned to the external interface, you may have difficulties when that address changes. Plan ahead for these situations and you will not be surprised with intermittent outages.

Array Problems

Chapter 9 described the problems sometimes encountered with proxy server arrays. Typically, these problems are caused by placing too large of an array in an environment that does not require it. For example, an array may have too many lateral resolutions, which produces poor performance. At most, you should have no more than 20 members in an array. For most implementations, that number is much too high. If there are too many members, or if members are overutilized, it is possible for array members to lose contact with other members briefly. Resolving data within an array is not a bad thing; however, it can potentially make an array with a small back bone perform as if only one system was functioning.

Finally, if multiple administrators configure the array at the same time, you may see synchronization errors or problems. Typically, this type of problem only occurs in larger array environments. It is possible to have problems even in a two-system array. Plan ahead: one administrator per array at a time.

Step-by-Step Problem Resolution

We've just looked at quite a few of the problems that can occur in Proxy Server networks. It's important to understand what causes specific errors, but you also need a general method for troubleshooting. Here is our step-by-step problem resolution plan for Proxy Server:

1. Verify that the connection to the ISP is active.

2. Check the IIS Manager to determine if any services have been stopped or paused.

3. Examine the LAT. It should contain only local addresses.

4. From the Proxy Server itself, log in as an administrator and connect to the Internet.

5. Assuming that auditing is enabled, review the event logs in the Event Viewer.

6. Log on as a client that should have Internet access and attempt a connection. If successful, repeat the test at a client workstation.

7. Verify that the client and server are using the same protocol and configuration. Remember that only TCP/IP is supported for all clients and IPX support is limited to Windows 95 and Windows NT.

8. On the client, check the MSPCLNT.INI and MSPLAT.TXT files for proper content.

9. If the client is using TCP/IP, use the Ping command to verify the connection to the server. If using IPX, verify the necessary requirements and use IPXROUTE to verify connectivity.

10. Repeat step 6 from the workstation only.

11. Use CHKWSP16 or CHKWSP32 as applicable to verify the WinSock Proxy client's operation.

Sources of Information

One of the biggest problems facing an administrator is a lack of information. Problem solving means implementing a solution, not just identifying a problem. When a given problem has more than one potential solution, you need as much information as possible to determine which solution is best for your network.

The following are the best and most valuable locations to find information about Microsoft Proxy Server and related products. Note that some items have fees associated with them while others are free.

- **TechNet** A subscription-based service that costs approximately $300 annually, TechNet is perhaps the most valuable of all information tools for Microsoft products. TechNet ships monthly on CD-ROM and includes service packs, patches, updates, Microsoft's knowledge base, utilities, and a number of online books. When it comes to a one-stop solution, TechNet is the best bet for the price. TechNet may be purchased directly from Microsoft at 800-344-2121. Online information can be obtained at www.microsoft.com/technet. The following keywords may be used on a

TechNet search line to find information about specific parts of Proxy Server:

- **Pxsclient**   Clients (Internet Explorer, Netscape, etc.)

- **pxsconfig**   Configuration and Tuning

- **pxsdocerr**   Errors in Help and Documentation

- **pxsgeneral**   General, Other

- **pxshowto**   How To

- **pxsinterop**   Interoperability (Windows for Workgroups, Windows 95, Netscape, etc.)

- **pxsmsn**   MSN access component

- **pxsodbc**   Access, SQL, ODBC logging/connectivity

- **pxsperm**   FTP, Gopher, WWW proxy permissions and issues

- **pxssetup**   Setup

- **pxsui**   User Interface

- **pxsRegistry**   Registry

- **pxsrpc**   RPC issues

- **Internet**   Microsoft's knowledge base and many downloadable files are available online. You can access the knowledge base by connecting to www.microsoft.com/kb. The downloadable files can also be accessed online by connecting to ftp.microsoft.com or by using the links associated with each product page. Usually the online knowledge base is useful when TechNet is not handy or when you need very current information. No costs are associated with the Internet service.

- **Technical Support**   Microsoft's telephone technical support operates on a per-incident fee that varies according to product. Customized support is provided by connecting an administrator to a qualified Microsoft engineer. If this engineer cannot solve the problem, they will refer it to someone with more specialized training. Microsoft technical support uses an internal online version of the knowledge base, containing information that is either in the process of being published or is not fit for public consumption.

- **MSN**   The Microsoft Network is generally only useful when dealing with support forums. This has never been a first choice for solving problems.

- **MSDL**   The Microsoft Download is useful for those administrators who do not have access to the Internet. This is a BBS (bulletin board service) that users can connect to directly. The service is free; however, the user assumes the responsibility for paying any tolls associated with the modem phone call.

- **Online Services**   A number of online services provide third-party support for Microsoft products. Typically, a fee is associated with this kind of service. For example, CompuServe and AOL both have monthly access fees for services that include their forums. Other services, such as Web sites, have free postings of tricks and tips as reported by users. One of my particular favorites is www.windows95.com. These are typically useful, undocumented features, but finding one that is relevant to your needs can be difficult.

- **User Groups**   As an administrator, it is a good idea to join a local user group. User groups tend to get free support and share knowledge between members who may have had similar problems or issues.

- **The Manuals**   Believe it or not, the first place that you probably should look for solving a problem is the manual. The manual for Proxy Server is accessed online by installing the documentation to a Web server. While you may also view the documentation without publishing it, most will experiment with the related directories on the CD, as opposed to those installed on the Web server.

Summary

This chapter covered the basic problems that an administrator may encounter in working with the Microsoft Proxy Server product. Although many of these problems actually reflect the way the product is designed to work and interact with other software, others are symptomatic of changes in the network or an incorrect configuration.

A key component of keeping the proxy server running efficiently and effectively is to monitor the server so that you can identify problems as they occur. The Event Viewer is a fundamental part of locating and identifying problems. Through the Event Viewer, an administrator has the ability to track occurrences that can lead to various failures but may not be identifiable through the error that they produce.

Microsoft recommends that all management should be done through the IIS Manager. However, some items can only be customized through the Registry. An administrator should only make changes here if they are thoroughly familiar with the item they are modifying. Setting the Registry incorrectly could lead to server failure.

The Registry can be modified with any number of tools. Regedit and Regedt32 both ship with Windows NT. The primary difference between the two is that Regedit is designed to work with the entire Registry and search all items, whereas Regedt32 is used usually with specific keys and only to search for a key, not for data values. Unlike Regedit, Regedt32 has the ability to assign permissions.

Additional problems may appear that are specific to particular services. Both the Web and WinSock Proxy Server share a number of common elements that typically have similar solutions. Most of these include configuring the LAT correctly and verifying a client's configuration.

Finally, we briefly reviewed some sources of information that can help with troubleshooting.

Review Questions

1. When researching a client problem, where should you begin? What are the most likely problems the client experiences?

2. What are some of the sources for information when researching a problem?

3. Some settings cannot be configured through the IIS Manager. Where can these items be set? How do you set them?

4. What are the differences between Regedit and Regedt32?

5. Suppose that you recently modified your network, changing the location of the Proxy Server and adding subnetworks. What should you do to the Proxy Server? What about the clients?

6. Which of the following utilities should be used to check a WinSock client's configuration?

   A. CHKWSP16.EXE

   B. CHKDSK16.EXE

   C. CHKWSP32.EXE

   D. CHKPROXY.EXE

   E. None of the above

7. On which platforms does Microsoft Proxy Server support IPX?

   A. Windows NT

   B. Windows 3.11

   C. UNIX

   D. DOS

   E. Windows 95

8. It is important to memorize all problems and issues on Microsoft Proxy Server so that you may find problems quickly. True or False?

9. Regardless of the LAT configuration, a client should be able to operate with any local WinSock application. True or False?

10. You need name resolution on your local network, so you install a DNS server. You already have a proxy server that uses a DNS server on the Internet. When trying to resolve a WinSock name on the local network, you receive the error "Host Not Found." The IP address of the destination computer you are trying to resolve is on the LAT. What should you do?

   A. Add the host name to the LACLLAT.TXT file on the client computer.

   B. Add the host name to the MSPLAT.TXT file on the Proxy Server.

   C. Point all clients to the new DNS server.

   D. Add the address of the new DNS server to the Proxy Server.

11. You have installed a proxy server on your network with one NIC card going to your local network and one NIC card going to the Internet. However, you have received an error stating that the user name of your proxy server is already in use. You check all the computers and don't find a duplicate name. What is most likely the problem?

   A. The same IP address is assigned to both network adapters.

   B. NetBEUI is bound to both network adapters.

   C. Each network adapter has a different host name.

   D. Both adapters have the same hardware address.

12. You have installed a proxy server, but you did not provide a default gateway address on your external NIC card. What happens when a user tries to request an object from the Internet?

   A. It retrieves it from the Web Proxy cache.

   B. The object is retrieved from the Internet site.

   C. The requested object is retrieved from a host computer on the intranet, regardless of whether the object is in the Web Proxy cache.

   D. The request fails, regardless of whether the object is in the Web Proxy cache.

13. Your clients are configured with the WinSock Proxy service, and the Web browsers are configured to use the Web Proxy service. You configure the LOCALLAT.TXT file to contain the IP address 192.168.10.6, which is the IP address of a Web server on the intranet and is not configured in your LAT. When you try to access a site, what happens?

A. The Web browser uses the Web Proxy service to access the Internet.

B. The Web browser uses the Web Proxy service to access the intranet.

C. The Web Browser uses the WinSock Proxy service to access the Internet.

D. The Web Browser uses the WinSock Proxy service to access the intranet.

14. You have two internal Web servers, one for Marketing and one for Shipping. All clients use these two Web servers by using the Web Proxy service. DNS is used for name resolution. You switch the IP addresses of the Web servers and now both departments report that the Shipping department is displaying the pages from the Marketing department. What is most likely the problem?

A. The Web Proxy service is caching Web pages from both Web servers.

B. The Web Proxy service is caching DNS entries.

C. The client computers are caching Web pages from both Web servers.

D. No domain filters are configured.

15. Your UNIX computer works fine when using the Web Proxy service, but RealAudio does not work. What is most likely the problem?

A. The Web Proxy service does not support the RealAudio protocol.

B. The SERVICES file on the UNIX computer is not configured to use RealAudio.

C. The Web browser is not configured to use the Proxy Server services for RealAudio.

D. The client computer has been denied access to the RealAudio protocol in the WinSock Proxy service.

CHAPTER

13

Planning and Deployment

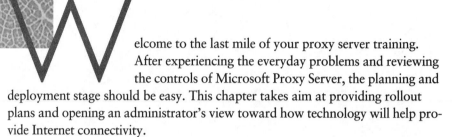

elcome to the last mile of your proxy server training. After experiencing the everyday problems and reviewing the controls of Microsoft Proxy Server, the planning and deployment stage should be easy. This chapter takes aim at providing rollout plans and opening an administrator's view toward how technology will help provide Internet connectivity.

In smaller organizations, product implementation tends to be somewhat haphazard since standards are usually not in place. On the other hand, intermediate and larger firms tend to configure these systems with a predetermined plan. Regardless of the size of your organization, there are important steps to take and facts to consider for any product rollout. With this in mind, we set your expectations for this chapter's discussion of implementing Microsoft Proxy Server 2.0.

After completing this chapter, you will have the knowledge necessary to implement Proxy Server in virtually any organization. This chapter will provide thorough coverage of the following materials:

- Determining Proxy Server hardware requirements

Exam objectives are subject to change at any time without prior notice and at Microsoft's sole discretion. Please visit Microsoft's Training & Certification website (www.microsoft.com/Train_Cert) for the most current exam objectives listing.

- Selecting an ISP

- Gauging user volume

- Setting project goals

- Identifying problems as they occur

- Addressing rollout concerns

- Recognizing organizational needs

Selecting Hardware

Before you can determine what equipment you will need to get Proxy Server up and running, you must first determine what services (HTTP, FTP, IRC, e-mail, etc.) and what usage level for each service users will need. In order to determine this information, you must query your users about the types of applications they are currently using and which applications they may need in the future. Once you know which applications will be used and how much room you need to allow for growth, you will have to determine the level of traffic, and the load that level will place on the proxy system. To do this, you should assume that each user will create a certain amount of traffic. Depending on each user's job description, the company's policy about access to the Internet, and other similar considerations, your determination about traffic and the resources you'll need may need to be adjusted. It will also be necessary for you to make certain assumptions regarding the proxy server's architecture. This will be determined according to the number of people at a site along with their physical distribution. For example, many users in one area may merit the implementation of an array, while users in different areas may require a chaining structure. And many users in multiple areas may require multiple arrays chained together. After determining which applications will be in use and the potential sharing of equipment among users, you need to ascertain which users will require access and relate that to the plans according to their location.

Once a list of applications has been compiled and the level of user use has been determined, this data can be further refined and categorized for use among the Web, WinSock, and Socks proxy services. While the Web proxy tends to be platform independent, the WinSock and Socks proxies are based on each application's compatibility to WinSock. From this information, you can then assume an estimated load that will be placed on the server hardware. It will be your goal to obtain the necessary hardware and configure it to meet your estimated required needs.

<table>
<tr><td>**Microsoft** ✓ **Exam** **Objective**</td><td>**Plan an Internet site or an Intranet site for stand-alone servers, single-domain environments, and multiple-domain environments. Tasks include:**

• Choosing appropriate connectivity methods

• Choosing services

• Using Microsoft Proxy Server in an intranet that has no access to the Internet

• Choosing hardware</td></tr>
</table>

Designating a System to Meet Requirements

It is almost impossible to gauge the right equipment for a company if you are not a part of that organization because every company has different needs. However, we can give you some basic guidelines to follow. Your proxy implementation should probably include (at a minimum) those items listed in Table 13.1. In the table, we assume that the proxy service is the only component installed. Other services can and will increase the system requirements. If your company is arranged in a geographical condition that suits chaining or a proxy array, requirements can be set according to group. However, remember that an upstream server will still have to carry a full load and meet the general requirements. Considering the price of systems these days, the requirements are reasonable for a company of any given size to afford.

T A B L E   13.1:   System Selection Guidelines

Company Size and Use	Processor	Storage	RAM
Training, basic setup, and evaluation	Intel 486 or better, or any supported RISC processor	Excluding Windows NT Server and service pack 3, 10MB are needed. To enable caching, at least 5MB on an NTFS volume with a recommended configuration of 100MB and 0.5MB per user for testing	A minimum of 24MB, 32MB for RISC-based systems

TABLE 13.1: System Selection Guidelines *(continued)*

Company Size and Use	Processor	Storage	RAM
Small LAN (2 to 300 workstations)	Intel Pentium 133 MHz or better, or any supported RISC processor	2GB, but this could vary depending on Web and FTP usage	32MB or more
Intermediate LAN (200 to 2,000 workstations)	Intel Pentium 166 MHz or better, or any supported RISC processor	Approximately 2 to 4GB, depending on Web and FTP usage	64MB or more
Large LAN (2,000 to 3,500 workstations)	Intel Pentium 200 MHz Pro with 166 MHz or better, or any supported RISC processor	Approximately 8 to 16GB, depending on Web and FTP usage	128 to 512MB, or more (depending on what other services you run)
Very Large LAN (3,500 or more workstations)	Multi-processor Pentium Pro 200 MHz, Alpha 300 MHz or better. Number of CPUs should be adjusted according to monitoring of services.	At least 16GB in a RAID striped configuration	128 to 512MB, or more (depending on what other services you run)
Internet service provider with 1000 concurrent users	Alpha 300 MHz or better, Intel Pentium Pro 200, and perhaps multiple processors.	At least 16GB	128 to 512MB, or more (depending on what other services you run)

The server hardware recommendations in Table 13.1 may seem like general knowledge, but keep in mind that Microsoft uses this listing in determining a starting point for purchasing hardware. For example, without this chart, what would you answer for a starting hardware solution for a network with 1800 users? The chart makes these calculations simple. Array requirements can be calculated based on load. For instance, if you want to know how many proxy servers with Pentium 166 MHz CPUs in an array are required to service 4500 users, you could estimate that if one system can support up to 2000 users, two could support 4000, and three could support 6000. In this case, you would require three proxy servers with 166 MHz CPUs to service 4500 users. (Always round up for more equipment.)

By looking at Table 13.1, many people will assume they only need a single server. However, in most conditions it is better to use an array because it will tend to provide equal performance, but with fault tolerance. This configuration is also applicable when purchasing storage. Use smaller disk drives as in RAID, or a larger drive as in SLED.

When determining equipment to purchase for a group, do not allow the price of the server to obstruct your judgment. Spending good money on an inadequate system is a waste. Users will not be happy and you will eventually have to replace the system with the correct hardware and spend more money and time than if you had just done it correctly in the first place.

Arranging Connections with an ISP

There are a number of factors that will influence the type of connection that you will establish between your company and an Internet Service Provider (ISP). While these factors are cost driven, you shouldn't lose sight of your user's requirements. Match user needs to the final connectivity solution.

Your Internet domain name can be obtained either through your ISP as a service or directly through the InterNIC. The URL for registration services at the InterNIC is RS.INTERNIC.NET. You are typically better off to go directly to InterNIC so you can control the ownership of your domain name.

Determining a Connection Technology

Your speed requirements will most likely be decided by the cost of implementation, the reliability, and other similar considerations. More than anything else, your speed requirements will determine the necessary hardware for implementing the connection technology.

Connectivity solutions are abundant. There are so many ways in which you can connect to an ISP, we would hate to limit you to just our suggestions. However, for explanatory purposes, here's a list of ways you could connect to an ISP:

- Analog Lines: Generally implemented due to affordability, analog or dialup lines can, in actuality, be the most expensive connectivity product to select. Since these connections are limited to speed ranging from 28.8k to 56k (when you have a clean link and a bit of luck), the user's time is wasted on slow transfers. This idle time is a loss of productivity. Further, in some companies, dialup connections are arranged one per user. This means that no one user can use all lines, so the company pays for unutilized bandwidth. A dialup connection of this sort will use either Serial Line Interface Protocol (SLIP) or Point-to-Point Protocol (PPP). This connection is only recommended for one to five users, depending on usage. Although multiple lines may be linked, an ISDN line is probably a better solution.

- ISDN Connections: This type of solution is ideal for small to medium companies that are spread across wide areas. On the low end of this type of connection, a user may purchase an ISDN BRI (Integrated Services Digital Network Basic Rate Interface) which supports either 64k or 128k connections. On the other end of the ISDN options spectrum is PRI (Primary Rate Interface), which boasts speeds up to 1.544MB. A standard ISDN line includes two channels, which can be linked to double-bandwidth (multi-link); or a company can configure the ISDN send channel as a backup connection. An ISDN connection is commonly used with both voice and data, unlike what is done with a regular phone line. And with ISDN, you are not committed to connecting to any one ISP. Like a modem, you may dial any ISP that you subscribe to that supports an ISDN connection. However, be aware that charges accumulate by the minute, plus toll charges. For typical usage on a network with five to 500 users, this solution is ideal. After 500 users, you need to re-evaluate what it is that your users will be doing with the Internet. A connection device for ISDN may be either an ISDN modem in a Windows NT Server or a router with an integrated ISDN interface.

- Frame Relay Links: This is a reliable and solid connection technology that is made of virtual connections, similar to a leased line. Unlike a leased line where the same path is always used to establish a connection, frame relay utilizes a network, which directs data between points. Unlike dialup connections, a frame relay link is always active. Frame relay operates based on fixed connections. However, multiple connections can be assigned to any point. Points are easily switched when existing services are in place. Frame relay lines require a router and a CSU/DSU (Channel Service Unit/Data Service Unit). Frame relay costs are easy to assess because you are charged a flat rate regardless of distance or time used. Also, when using capacities greater than 56k, bursting allows more data to be sent than the link was actually assigned (assuming the frame network has available bandwidth). This connection technology is generally ideal for 10 to 750 users. After 750 users, you must evaluate usage. In cases where many users are actively accessing the Internet, 50 users could saturate a line. When assessing your needs, consider, for example, how often your network would have 50 users simultaneously downloading material from the Internet.

- Leased Lines (T-1, T-3, etc.): Leased lines are the lead competitor of frame relay for reliability. Since frame relay has multiple paths available, there is less concern of a line being severed within the phone companies network. On the other hand, with the leased line a line is delivered directly to your network and is uninterrupted by anything else. This technology starts at fractions of a T-1 line and goes up from there. A T-1 line is 1.544MB, T-1C is 3.152MB, T-2 is 6.312MB, T-3 is 44.736MB, T-4 is 274.176MB, and so forth. These lines can be incredibly expensive, but most phone companies are reasonable about providing a line that meets your needs. Remember that since this is a leased line, it is connected from end to end, so changing ISPs can be an expensive task. Depending on the line you select, hardware may vary. Leased line connections are typically good for 100 or more users.

You should always try to maximize your network to perform as well as possible. Naturally, you would not implement a dedicated Alpha 500 MHz system with 32GB of storage and 1024MB of RAM to work from a single dialup line. You would also not purchase a T-3 connection for five users with a 486 processor–based proxy server. Be certain to match your hardware and user requirements to the bandwidth selected. And remember that on the other end of the spectrum, a bottleneck at any point in your system can ruin the entire implementation.

A connection to any Internet resource is only as fast as the slowest connection to the site. If you company has a T-1 line and the Internet resource is connected via a 56k line, your best speed will be 56k.

Selecting an ISP

Before you begin your selection of an ISP, you should first understand what one does for you. The Internet is a compilation of multiple networks all linked together by large telecommunications companies. These large companies provide a high-speed, large-capacity conduit, which they sell in pieces to smaller companies. These smaller companies are typically local telephone companies and national ISPs. In turn, these companies resell their time and bandwidth to larger companies and smaller ISPs. Finally, the ISPs sells their time to you. In short, an ISP is a broker that sells an Internet connection and connection time.

Both national and smaller ISPs sell time to end-users. Depending on your requirements, you will rule out different vendors. For example, let us assume that we have a 5,000 node network that we would like to establish an Internet connection for. The Internet connection is specified to only be used for e-mail and Web traffic. At the current stage, the company believes it needs a T-1 connection, but may expand later to a T-3. The company administrator will have to take this into consideration in deciding on an ISP.

We don't presume that everyone who calls an ISP will be a connectivity expert. However, if you are not sure what to ask, try this question, "Why should I use your ISP service as opposed to someone else's?" Then let them do the talking. Or, use some of these questions:

- Can you facilitate a T-1 connection?

- What price is the T-1 connection? (You also need to check with the phone company about establishing the link.)

- Currently, what kind of link do you offer to the Internet?

- What type of router equipment is in place, and what type of capacity does it have?

- How much of the link to the Internet is in use?

- Assuming that we are seeing poor performance, will you assist in correcting the problem? And if you would help, what sort of assistance would you provide?

- If you experience growth, will you increase your link's bandwidth to the Internet? (Remember that it's not your link to the ISP, but the ISP's link to the Internet that your information must travel on.)

- Do you provide Web publishing services?

- Do you have a DNS service?

- Can you assist in providing IP addresses for a group of computers?

- If we need to expand to a T-3 connection, can you support us?

- What price is the T-3 connection? (You also need to check with the phone company about establishing the link.)

- What is the expected down time of your network for maintenance?

- Does your connection to the Internet have redundant backup paths?

- What other large companys do you currently service?

- What is the hold time for technical support?

The ISP should have no problem answering these questions. Obviously, an ISP with a T-3 connection to the Internet who provides home services and has multiple customers with T-1 links would be a bad selection. Clearly, they are overselling their network. Also, if you call their technical support and they are slow to answer the above questions or you are stuck on hold too long, either the company is too popular for their own good or they have too few people at the help desk. Their ability to provide quick and knowledgeable information will greatly influence your implementation time and overall optimization of the ISP connection.

If, on the other hand, you were looking only to make a small dialup connection, you should concern yourself less with their capacity and more with their price. Just make sure that you can get quick technical support and that you are not receiving busy signals while dialing. Also, since toll calls cost money, first verify that they have a local number to connect.

In the end, you should note that ISP selections usually comes down to bandwidth and the costs related to the connection. Remember that not all companies will use the Internet 24 hours a day. In such cases, purchasing nine hours of connection time per day with reduced traffic for the other 15 hours may affect your price greatly.

Cost Reality Check

Before continuing any further, you should consider if your organization has the budget to perform the Internet connection. For example, it would be entirely unreasonable to assume a flower shop would use a T-1 link. If your bottom-line number reveals that you can not afford the connection you want, consider determining the type of services that you need and either limit your access to Internet browsing and e-mail, or note that the system will only support a given number of users.

We hate to sound like we're mocking Scott Adams (the creator of *Dilbert*), but the manager who gets ahead is not always the one who performs the job correctly. It's sometimes the one who stays within the budget. It is an ever-changing world, and you should probably discuss Internet connectivity up the chain before making any assumptions that may cost you your job. Be sure to rationalize your choice and show how the benefits will increase profitability and/or productivity. Businesses are in business to make money. Never try to promote a project because it is cool. Instead, always use the approach that it is a cost-saving measure. The value of data is something most companies understand. We recommend explaining the Internet as a cheap resource.

Site Analysis

With all our ducks now in a row, we are ready to analyze the site. Typically, we try to group companies into one of four sizes: small, intermediate, large, and very large. You will probably not see many very large companies that are not already on the Internet. However, you are likely to find one that requires maintenance or remodeling. Ask yourself how often companies rotate PCs. If you're not sure, think back to the XT, then the AT, then the 386, and so on, and you'll get the idea.

Companies are almost always in need of new technology implementations. Surprisingly, smaller companies tend to be more cutting edge and faster to adapt to change. Large and very large firms simply can not afford the massive changes and usually are slower to respond to technological changes. This goes to show that you should make no assumptions regarding a company, regardless of who they are.

Calculating the Number of Users

Most integrators will tell you that the best rule to follow for calculating the number of Internet users is to estimate according to the number of employees at a firm. We think this is bad advice. Suppose that you worked for the post office. There are far many more employees than system users.

To calculate the number of users on a network, generally, the best solution is to use a hybrid calculation of the number of users listed in a network directory service, bindery, and so on, and compare that with the number of systems on the network. Each system is a potential user of the Internet, regardless of the employee's current function. While administratively user rights may be limited, it is also likely that expansion will demand some level of service for all users. E-mail is a prime example of this.

You must be careful when analyzing users. For instance, suppose that you have a 5,000 person organization, and your organization needs Internet access. If only 50 of those 5,000 people use an Internet application, what would you recommend? Imagine now that those 50 people transfer 100MB of data or more per day to other organizations. Now what?

Suppose that you ran User Manager for domains and found 1,500 users listed with 1,000 systems in the organization. At best guess (for this organization or any other), you will have no more that 1/3 of your systems connecting to the Internet (or other Internet-related services such as e-mail or FTP) at any one given time. This means that with 1,500 users, you should only concern yourself with a peak of 333 users. The assumption that 1/3 of a company is currently on the Internet is probably too generous. However, there are always going to be some Internet application developers in the startup phase that prove otherwise by accessing Internet-related applications more than their share of the time. Remember that these figures are guesstimates (slightly less reliable than estimates). No one can tell you if they are accurate for sure. Managers and executive-level personnel are usually great resources for estimating their user involvement. Always guess high, never low. Internet bandwidth has a tendency to consume itself (at least until users get bored or get back to work!).

Determining Usage

Usage is more that merely counting the number of users; it is also gauging the applications that are on your network and the amount of data your users will transfer. To determine usage, first ask your users what applications they use. These applications should then be narrowed down to include only those requiring the Internet. From here, you need to make a call as to the frequency in which the programs are used and the amount of bandwidth they will require.

In determining usage, you must make some assumptions. For example, let us assume that your company does not use RealAudio, Telnet, FTP, Web browsers, e-mail, or video conferencing. All Internet traffic is intended to support only a custom application that performs sales and inventory analysis. You first must know if the application is run locally or remotely. If it's run locally, does the application reside at the remote site or on the local PC? For this stage, we can note the size of data files, and, if necessary, the application execution and overhead.

Now that we have formulated that this organization only has a single application that requires the Internet, we must now turn our focus to which applications will be added. Naturally, you should consider e-mail, Web browsing, and FTP. Query your users to make an actual determination. Be certain to ask what information they will be looking for on the Internet and what kind of files they will be transferring using e-mail and FTP.

Rollout Concerns

With all the preliminary field work accomplished, we need to now turn to our internal information services group to determine the following:

- Which workstations will require which clients

- What type of training will be required for users, the help desk, and administrators

- What kind of impact the addition of an Internet application will have on the existing network

- What types of security holes are open

- How to provide maximum fault tolerance

The first question is easily answered with the types of systems and applications that your users have voiced as requirements. However, training may become an issue. For the same reasons that many companies have hesitated to update their clients to Windows 95, they are also hesitant about adding Internet access and training employees. In general, we would recommend not worrying too much about this; just be cautious.

Setting Standards

Set a standard for e-mail, file transfers, and Web browsing. All other applications that are not in the standard list are unsupported. Provide training to administrators and help desk personnel. Those who will be supporting the application should have access to the resource, documentation, and service well in advance of the end-users. This will help to iron out problems before they are reported by users and to educate the support staff.

Now, begin the project by evaluating user input to determine the equipment and the connection bandwidth required. Review the positioning of internal users and their relative usage of the Internet service. At this time, you should note what other changes may be required for the existing network to support added applications and Internet load. Next, purchase or locate proper server equipment and order a connection from the phone company and ISP. Note that the phone company may take two months to install the lines you need depending on what you order. Internally, you may test the initial implementation with a dialup connection until your service is installed.

Internet Security

The Internet is notorious for being a security hole. Before enabling Internet access, review the impact it could have with the administrator responsible for security. Typically, that person will be concerned about people breaking in or viruses entering the network. Accordingly tune your security. If viruses are a concern, consider purchasing an add-on product for Microsoft Proxy Server that monitors for this type of activity. You should recall that add-ons can be accessed by clicking the Web Plug-Ins button located on the Service tab of any proxy service.

Regardless of the scenario, you may want to convert a domain to act as a master domain to a resource domain where your proxy server is kept. In this configuration, a one-way trust should be placed such that the master domain can access any servers and services in the resource domain.

Fault Tolerance

In many situations, fault tolerance and performance are issues. Recall that configuring an array satisfies both of these concerns. An array can automatically load balance requests between member servers using CARP and cover the duties of a server in the event that one goes down. Load balancing can be achieved through a DNS (see Chapter 9). However, this has the disadvantage of not providing fault tolerance when a system goes down. Each time the server that is down is called, there will be a failure. For this reason, an array is a must.

A backup route can also be maintained at the server level of each proxy, such that if the next server or Internet resource is not available in the upstream, an alternate path can be used. When multiple direct links are used, they should not be placed on the same system. For example, two T-1 lines that are installed in one company should be arranged such that they connect to two different systems in an array. Remember that chaining will not support load balancing and would most likely not support a good fault tolerance system since it is, by design, used to channel data.

Microsoft ✓ **Exam** **Objective**

Choose a strategy to balance Internet access across multiple Proxy Server computers. Strategies include:

- Using DNS
- Using arrays
- Using Cache Array Routing Protocol (CARP)

Microsoft ✓ **Exam** **Objective**

Choose a fault tolerance strategy. Strategies include:

- Using arrays
- Using routing

Putting It All Together

There is no way for us to simply pour practical experience into your head. So instead, we will present some basic scenarios that are common to many companies, which should assist you in your implementation. Perhaps no model will fit your particular organization, but perhaps a hybrid of a presented solution will fill the bill. We will present scenarios for small, intermediate, large and very large LANs.

Microsoft ✓ **Exam** **Objective**

Choose a rollout plan for integrating a Proxy Server with an existing corporate environment.

Let's begin by doing some simple math. If we want every user to constantly have at least 28.8k of bandwidth available, we could assume that a T-1 line could support approximately 54 users. This requires a connection of 1.552 MB (54 x 28.8). A T-1 is 1.544 MB; this should be close enough. But, we should also consider that these users are going to be reading cached information at times (assuming a 5% cache hit rate, which is low) and that while reading Internet information, only 10% of users will actually be transferring data beyond the proxy server (at any single instance). To maximize the usage of the T-1, we could assume that 540 (54/10%) users could then use the Internet at a given time. Assuming that 1/3 of a company was on the Internet, that T-1 line would be effective for up to 1620 (3x540) users. (In this example, we dropped the 5% from our estimations so that we could compensate for peak usage.)

Each environment is unique. However, this is the basic formula you should use for most calculations.

Small LANs

A small LAN (see Figure 13.1) typically contains anywhere from two to 300 users. In such a configuration, only one or two network protocols should be defined. If this is a Novell network, your two protocols should be IPX and TCP/IP. In any other configuration, only TCP/IP should be used. If you are using OS/2 file servers, which require NetBEUI, you should probably upgrade them to Windows NT or a newer version of LAN Server. This will help streamline network operations. Although NetBEUI is an option, it should not be used for any network with over 50 systems, as it is not routable.

FIGURE 13.1

A small LAN network only requires one or two network protocols.

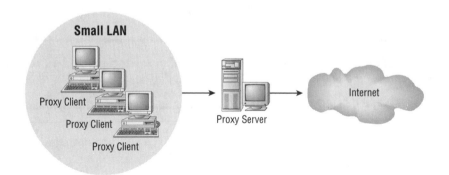

Depending on your security requirements, you may structure your network to either operate as IPX, TCP/IP, or both. With IPX as the only protocol, it will protect your network from IP-based attacks. Considering the size of this network, you may want to either request a block of active IP addresses from your ISP or use a private Class C range. Considering that all traffic will be directed through the proxy server, you are probably best off using a private range. The Class C private address range is 192.168.x.x. If your network has more that 256 devices, you may either use multiple Class C address ranges super-netted together or a private Class B range.

Your connection to the Internet will most likely be best suited to an ISDN option. In this configuration, you will normally have one of each of the following systems located in the internal LAN: e-mail, Web, and FTP. If you used a private IP address, the LAT will automatically configure itself with no side effects when you click Construct Table. Remember that if you add external addresses to the LAT, you create security holes. Since the private IP address range will not route across the Internet, this is not a problem.

A small LAN is determined to be one that has up to 200 workstations. This figure is based on NetBEUI's designed operations capacity.

Intermediate LANs

A medium-sized LAN (see Figure 13.2) is usually arranged in a campus or multiple-site environment. This type of network should consist of multiple segments in the main location, with the potential for several smaller sites to connect to it. In this configuration, the network should have a user count between 200 and 2000 nodes (or users). As in the small LAN configuration, only one or two network protocols should be defined. If this is a Novell network, your two protocols should be IPX and TCP/IP. In any other configuration, only TCP/IP should be used. If you are using OS/2 file servers, which require NetBEUI, you should probably upgrade them to Windows NT or a newer version of LAN Server. This will help streamline network operations. NetBEUI in this configuration is not an option, as it is not routable.

Branch offices may be configured with dial-on-demand connectivity to the central site, or they may be connected by other means such as frame relay. In either case, a proxy server should be configured at each branch that is forwarded (in a chain of upstream and downstream proxy servers) to the central office. This will help consolidate traffic and streamline network usage. Placing proxy servers in this configuration will benefit from caching only when the Web Proxy service is used. While WinSock Proxy and Socks Proxy will operate, they will not perform any caching.

FIGURE 13.2

A medium-sized LAN should consist of multiple segments in the main location.

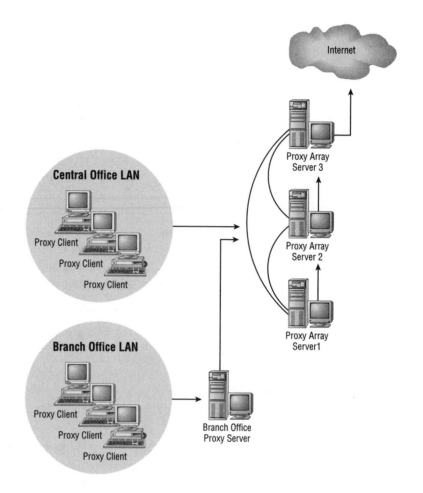

Assuming that the branch office performs most of its own operations internally, the dialup connection would most likely only be used for e-mail, file transfer, and Web browsing. It is very unlikely that a branch would run applications through the proxy server if it required them to be downloaded for local execution. Terminal-based applications are more than feasible at this level.

A private class B address should be used in this type of configuration. To avoid confusion, each site may be granted its own range. The private Class B address range is 172.16.x.x to 172.31.x.x. Depending on the number of users, sites, and so forth, your site is perhaps best suited to a frame relay link or fractional T-1 line. Remember that if you plan to exceed 1.544MB in speed, you will most likely want to use a leased line.

The LAT at all locations should include all networks in your company. The proxy server that you dial into should be set such that it includes two network adapters (one for the local network and another for the router) with as many dialup connections as there are sites that need to dial in. Dial-in connections are established via RAS and subject to all dialing conditions of the service.

A LAN with multiple connections within a campus or city is sometimes referred to as a MAN (Metropolitan Area Network).

Large LANs and WANs

Large networks typically follow no pattern and are usually compiled of several smaller networks (see Figure 13.3). These networks normally begin with 2,000 users and include up to 10,000 users. Remote sites are usually connected through a frame relay or leased line system with dialup connectivity at smaller locations. It is not unusual to find every network protocol ever created being used in some arrangement or another. Typically, this type of environment standardizes communications based on TCP/IP, but may use IPX. TCP/IP is usually the more common of the two due to VAX, UNIX, and mainframe connectivity. No matter what, NetBEUI traffic should not be bridged throughout the system because it creates lots of overhead without generating the throughput.

Branch offices may be configured with dial-on-demand connectivity to the central site, or connected by other means such as frame relay. Naturally, the drawback to using a dialup configuration is toll charges, lack of speed, and perhaps questionable reliability. In either case, a proxy server should be configured at each branch that is chained to the central office. The object here is a to maximize the available bandwidth.

In some instances, you may want to limit the hours that a dial-up branch office can contact the central office. You may do this to prevent users from unintentionally interrupting maintenance processes such as backups. This can be done through the Auto Dial Manager. The restriction must be placed on the server that is performing the dial-up action. Additional restrictions can be applied to the RAS account at the dial in server.

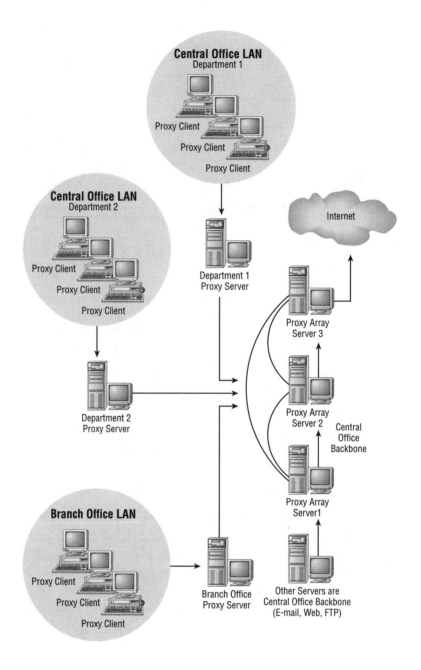

Assuming that the branch office performs most of its own operations internally, the dialup connection would most likely only be used for e-mail, file transfer, and Web browsing. It is very unlikely that a branch would run applications through the proxy server if it required them to be downloaded for local execution. For example, no one should be using a slow link to execute a program that resides at the corporate LAN where processing is distributed to the branch office. All applications that are used should be terminal-based (UNIX, As400, Mainframe, centralized SQL systems, etc.) such that the processing is performed by the host where the application resides. Branches that are linked with higher speed communications, such as T-1 lines, can be treated more like a LAN. This is, of course, subject to the number of users and applications used.

The proxy server at the central site should most likely be one or two arrays configured with the other as a backup. In addition to those proxy servers configured at the branch offices, you should also have proxy servers as required at the departmental level. Not only does this raise Microsoft's stock, it ensures higher speed security access to Internet resources while keeping MIS personnel employed.

Commonly, larger organizations are linked to suppliers and other companies in an arrangement known as an extranet. An extranet usually involves two private networks that are separate from each other, and are treated as private. The use of a proxy server on each end will limit the types of traffic that are routed through this type of link and provide an auditable path (a path that maintains logs) to usage.

A private Class B or Class C address should be used in this type of configuration. To avoid confusion, each site may be granted its own range. The private Class B address range is 172.16.x.x to 172.31.x.x. If more sites and systems are required that are allowed through a Class B configuration, the Class C range should be used. The Class C range is 10.x.x.x. This site should have at least one T-1 line, but perhaps two or three. Routers linking the network to the Internet should be able to support high volumes of traffic. Array groups should be configured at least one per T-1 line using the alternate arrays on other T-1s or better links as backups.

Very Large LANs and WANs

Very large networks (see Figure 13.4) are usually multiple large networks that have been merged together. Boeing is a good example of a very large network. In recent years, they have acquired a number of companies, including Rockwell International's Aerospace divisions and McDonnell Douglas. Each of these networks already were considered large. Combined, these networks are very large. A very large network commonly has multiple connections to the Internet, each isolated to the larger portion of the network rather than to a central facility. It is not uncommon for these networks to combine multiple class networks together.

FIGURE 13.4

A very large LAN usually
results from smaller LANs
being merged.

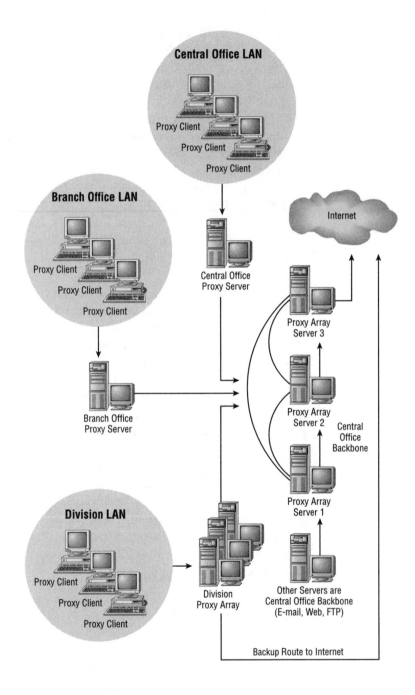

Because these networks are true compilations of different technologies, topologies, and heterogeneous systems, all protocols may be found within them. All the rules that apply to a large network are also applicable here. Multiple arrays should be used in these configurations with redundant paths configured within each area of data concentration.

Each array should be configured on a high-speed back bone with the equipment described at the beginning of this chapter. At this level, all networks may be migrated to a private Class A address based on 10.x.x.x. Other addresses may eventually be sold to other corporations or an ISP that requires live Internet addresses.

Summary

This last mile chapter is what most of us consider to be the most exciting part. It's when we get to see all that we have studied and learned come together. Planning and deployment are designed to demonstrate the stages needed to implement a proxy server. Technically speaking, most administrators are able to establish a proxy service with the knowledge gained before this chapter. However, the goal of this section is to help you achieve better results in a shorter period of time. Also, in examining the industry usage for Proxy Server, this chapter informs you about the capabilities of the product at all levels.

In planning, Proxy Server is fit to run on any number of systems. The number of users, types of applications being used, and configuration of Proxy Server will determine the necessary hardware for implementing this product as a useful tool. The push from the user community for resources to use more applications and data usually help define hardware requirements, although each company can differ drastically in its use.

Once hardware has been chosen, an adequate pipeline or link to the Internet can be established. There are several options for connecting to the Internet, and the option that is best for your organization depends on what sort of services your users need and how many users will be using those services. Dialup modems are typically only sufficient for one to five users. Technologies such as ISDN (PRI) can provide support for 10 to 500 users. Although ISDN in its maximize configuration can provide up to T-1 speeds, its dialup requirements can make it less desirable than ISDN due to the costs associated with per minute usage and faults from dropped lines. Frame relay tends to be the best choice in connecting to an ISP where no more than 750 users are connecting. Multiple frame relay connections may be established for larger organizations, and leased lines are recommended for medium-sized companies.

When selecting an ISP, your ultimate goal is to verify that they can serve your needs, and do so in a timely manner. You should make your decision based on cost and their ability to meet your current needs as well as the needs you anticipate having in the future. Think about this decision carefully because once a network is established, switching ISPs can be a chore.

The key to setting up a proxy server is planning. First, you must gauge your users, then their applications, and then future requirements. Once you determine all of this, you'll need to consider acquiring the necessary hardware, telecommunications equipment, and connections. You'll also need to think about training staff to use the equipment and services you decide to use. And always remember that the support staff should be the first users to access the system. That way they can provide hands-on experience and debugging of the system.

Review Questions

1. How many proxy servers should you install if your company standard is Pentium 16MHz computers and you have 500 clients?

   A. 1

   B. 2

   C. 3

   D. 4

2. Which service will improve performance on your client computers when all clients need to FTP files from a remote location many times per day?

   A. WinSock

   B. Web Proxy

   C. Socks

   D. FTP

3. You have created an array of proxy servers to service your 6000 clients. What is the minimum amount of memory you should install in each array?

A. 32MB

B. 64MB

C. 96MB

D. 128MB

4. You manage a corporate network that also has two branch offices with 56k connections. How should you configure your proxy server to maximize performance of all the computers in the remote offices?

A. Install one proxy server at the corporate office.

B. Install a proxy server at each remote location only.

C. At each remote location, install a proxy server connected directly with the Internet.

D. At each remote office, install a proxy server computer that is chained to the proxy server computer at the central office.

5. You have 400 users and two T1 lines on your network. How should you balance the requests from client computers?

A. Create an array with two proxy servers, and connect one T1 line to each proxy server.

B. Connect both T1 lines to one proxy server.

C. Create a chain of two proxy servers, and connect one T1 line to each server.

D. Create a chain of two proxy servers, and connect both T1 lines to one of the servers.

6. How can you register a domain name?

7. What types of network connections can be used to link to the Internet?

8. What hardware should you use for your current company?

9. What are some of the concerns regarding the selection of an ISP?

10. In what ways does a large network differ from a small network?

APPENDIX

A

Review Answers

Chapter 1

1. Which of the following are functions of a proxy server?

A. Address translation

B. Web page caching

C. Line printer daemon

D. Security

Answer: A, B, and D. A proxy server provides address translation, caching, and security functions. Line printer daemon is a TCP/IP printer service that has nothing to do with the proxy server.

2. What is a proxy server?

A. A device that configures NT Server to talk to Novell servers

B. A system or device that operates between a client application, such as a Web browser, and a real server.

C. A device that connects a T1 to a Frame Relay WAN link

D. A device used to configure EGRP to Windows NT RIP

Answer: B. A proxy server operates between a client application, such as a Web browser, and a real server. It intercepts all requests to the real server to see if it can fulfill the requests itself. If not, it forwards the request to the real server.

3. What are some common reasons that you might want to implement a proxy server?

A. To connect two similar networks together

B. To connect two dissimilar networks together

C. To enhance security to the Internet

D. To connect TCP/IP and IPX networks together

Answer: C. There are an unlimited number of reasons why anyone would use a product. In the case of Microsoft's Proxy Server, some common reasons include enhanced security to the Internet, reduction in Plain Ordinary Telephone System (POTS) phone line expenses at each workstation, integration with Windows NT 4.0, and protocol translation. However, please do assume that these would be the only reasons why an organization would implement this product.

4. What features would you expect to find in Microsoft's Proxy Server?

A. Access authority

B. Event logging

C. Integration

   D. Gateway services

   E. Protocol translation

Answer: Microsoft Proxy Server 2.0 includes all of the above.

5. Explain how shared bandwidth combines with gateway and protocol translation.

Answer: Shared bandwidth allows a single communication line to be shared among many users. Generally, these lines are bigger and cheaper than conventional, single, per-workstation line configurations. Gateway/protocol translation enables a company that is not running TCP/IP to quickly and cheaply gain Internet access.

6. All proxy servers are firewalls.

   A. True

   B. False

Answer: B. Microsoft's Proxy Server 2.0 has many functions and features that give it functionality similar to that of a firewall. However, most proxy servers act more as information relays with restrictions than as secure gateways that function to allow and reject functions by a predetermined criteria. The original Proxy Server 1.0 did not offer integrated firewall protection.

Chapter 2

   1. What is TCP/IP?

      A. A collection of packets sent through the Internet

      B. A collection of packages for use on the Internet

      C. A suite of protocols that provide routing and addressing in WANs, and connectivity to a variety of hosts.

      D. A freeware program

   Answer: C. TCP/IP is just two popular protocols in the Internet Protocol Suite. All of the protocols together make the TCP/IP suite. These protocols allow addressing of hosts and routing.

   2. What are the layers in the DOD four-layer model used by TCP/IP?

      A. Process/Application

      B. Session

      C. Network Access

      D. Internet

      E. Host-to-Host

      F. Transport

   Answer: A, E, D, and C in order from top to bottom. The DOD model was created before the OSI model and is only comprised of four layers: Process/Application, Host-to-Host, Internet, and Network Access.

3. What core TCP/IP protocols are provided with Microsoft TCP/IP?

   A. TCP

   B. UDP

   C. DUP

   D. ICMP

   E. PI

   F. IP

   G. PAR

   H. ARP

   I. CTP

   Answer: A, B, D, F and H. Microsoft includes in its operating system the TCP/IP protocol suite. Included is TCP, UDP, ICMP, IP and ARP.

4. What parameters are required for a TCP/IP host to communicate in a WAN?

   A. IP address

   B. Subnet mask

   C. Zip code

   D. Default gateway

   E. Login name

   Answer: A, B, and D. For a TCP/IP host to communicate in a wide-area network, the minimum configuration for a TCP/IP host is a valid IP address, Subnet mask, and Default gateway.

5. It's Monday morning. Just as you arrive at your desk, your boss calls you into his office, and says he read about TCP/IP in a Microsoft magazine over the weekend. Because he now knows that all Microsoft products are fabulous, he's set on someone implementing MS TCP/IP at all twelve branch office sites. He says that because of your quality work over the past few months, you're his first choice. However, before he names you the project's leader, he wants you to give him a complete explanation of TCP/IP, and how it will meet his networking needs. Can you? Try it.

   Answer: The acronym TCP/IP stands for *Transmission Control Protocol/Internet Protocol.* Essentially, it's a set of two communication protocols that an application can use to package its information for sending across a network, or networks. TCP/IP also refers to an entire collection of protocols, called a *protocol suite.* This collection includes application protocols for performing tasks such as e-mail, file transfer, and terminal emulation.

6. To get a jump on the competition, you need to find some information on a new, highly efficient protocol being developed. Where would you find this information? How would you access it, and through which server? If you have access to the Internet, try this as an exercise on your computer.

   Answer: FTP to DS.INTERNIC.NIC or e-mail to rfc-info@ISI.EDU, including the message: **help: ways_to_get_rfcs.**

7. Your boss tells you she spent lunch at the gym, where she overheard a great way to look up information on the Internet. She tells you that it organizes subjects into a menu system, and allows you to access the information on each topic listed. She's frustrated because she can't remember what its called—can you?

Answer: Gopher organizes topics into a menu system and allows you to access the information on each topic listed.

8. You are the Senior Communication Technician for a small computer store. The sales staff is complaining that they cannot deliver or receive mail on their TCP/IP computers. All other applications on the network seem to work OK. The location of the problem is likely to be on *which layer* of the DOD model?

Answer: The Application/Process layer of the DOD is responsible for sending and receiving mail using the Simple Mail Transfer Protocol.

9. The IS department is planning to implement TCP/IP. Your manager, who knows and understands the OSI reference model, asks you, "What are the layers in the four-layer model used by the DOD for TCP/IP, and how does each layer relate to the OSI reference model?" What do you tell him?

Answer: The four layers of the DOD model and how each relates to the OSI model are shown below:

DOD	**OSI**
Process/Application layer	Application, Presentation, and Session
Host-to-Host or Transport	Transport
Internet	Network
Network Access	Data Link and Physical

10. You are the network administrator for a large accounting office. They have seven offices, all connected. You get a call from a remote office complaining that their workstations cannot connect to the network. After talking with them for a few minutes, it appears that network connectivity is down at all seven offices. What layer of the DOD model is likely at fault?

Answer: The Network Access layer is responsible for network connectivity.

11. You want to collect the TCP/IP frames that are received by your Windows NT Server computer, and then save the data in a file to analyze later. Which utility should you use?

A. NETSTAT.EXE

B. Performance Monitor

C. NBTSTAT.EXE

D. Network Monitor

Answer: D. Network Monitor is used like a sniffer to analyze traffic. Because of the nature of the data, often it is useful to save some of the frames for review. NETSTAT is used to review all inbound/outbound connections to a server; however, it has nothing to do with framing. Performance Monitor measures and counts data statistics, not their content.

12. You need to determine whether the configuration is initialized or if a duplicate IP address is configured on your NT Workstation. Which utility should you use?

   A. ARP.EXE

   B. NBTSTAT.EXE

   C. NETSTAT.EXE

   D. IPCONFIG.EXE

   E. PING.EXE

   Answer: D. IPCONFIG will list the IP address information assigned to each adapter. If a duplicate address has been detected, the address will be disabled. ARP is for resolving IP addresses to MAC hardware addresses. NBTSTAT is used to show NETBIOS over TCP/IP status, such as NetBIOS caching.

13. You have four NT Server computers, and you want to find out which computers send the most traffic to each server. What should you do to find out?

   A. Use Performance Monitor on each server.

   B. Use Network Monitor on each server.

   C. Use NETSTAT.EXE on each server.

   D. Use NBTSTAT.EXE on each server.

   E. Use ROUTE.EXE on each server that is functioning as a router.

   Answer: B. Network Monitor acts as a sniffer to review traffic connections in the instance noted above. Performance Monitor will only show quantity information. NETSTAT is useful for reviewing connections; however, it does not display which information is good and which is bad. NBTSTAT shows the NETBIOS cache, but provides no connection information of any value.

14. You have a network ID of 131.107.0.0 and you need to divide it into multiple subnets. You need 600 host IDs for each subnet, with the largest amount of subnets available. Which subnet mask should you assign?

   A. 255.255.224.0

   B. 255.255.240.0

   C. 255.255.248.0

   D. 255.255.252.0

   Answer: D. First we must examine 252.0 in binary: 11111100.00000000. This tells us that we have 10 bits used for the host ID in the class B network and six bits (+16) used for the network number. This will yield 1022 (1024, less all 0s and all 1s) hosts and 62 (64, less all 0s and all 1s) subnets.

15. You have a network ID of 131.107.0.0 with eight subnets. You need to allow the largest possible number of host IDs per subnet. Which subnet mask should you assign?

    A. 255.255.224.0

    B. 255.255.240.0

    C. 255.255.248.0

    D. 255.255.252.0

    Answer: B. First we must examine 240.0 in binary: 11100000.00000000. This tells us that we have 13 bits used for the host ID in the class B network and three bits (+16) used for the network ID. This will yield 4094 (4096, less all 0s and all 1s) hosts and 14 (16, less all 0s and all 1s) subnets.

16. You have a network ID of 217.170.55.0 and you need to divide it into multiple subnets. You need 25 host IDs for each subnet, with the largest amount of subnets available. Which subnet mask should you assign?

    A. 255.255.255.192

    B. 255.255.255.224

    C. 255.255.255.240

    D. 255.255.255.248

    Answer: B. Because you need 25 hosts, you must reserve five bits for the network ID. That yields 30 IDs (2^5-2). This leaves three bits for subnetting, which is six subnets ($2^3 - 2$). Therefore, the answer is 11100000 or 224.

17. You have a Class A network address with 60 subnets. You need to add 40 new subnets in the next two years and still allow for the largest possible number of host IDs per subnet. Which subnet mask should you assign?

    A. 255240.0.0

    B. 255.248.0.0

    C. 255.252.0.0

    D. 255.254.0.0

    Answer: D. Because you need 100 subnets, you must reserve seven bits for the network ID to equal 126 subnets (2^7-2). The next closest answer is 252, but that is only good for up to 62 subnets.

18. You want to capture and view packets that are received by your Windows NT computer. Which utility should you use?

    A. NETSTAT.EXE

    B. Performance Monitor

C. IPCONFIG.EXE

D. Network Monitor

Answer: D. Network monitor is used to analyze traffic. Because of the nature of the data, often it is useful to save some of the frames for review. NETSTAT will show TCP/IP connections, but not data information. Performance Monitor is used for gathering statistical information; however, it will not show the contents of any data.

19. You have a Class B network, and you plan break it up into seven subnets. One subnet will be connected to the Internet, but you want all computers to have access to the Internet. How should you assign the subnet mask for the networks?

   A. By using a default subnet mask

   B. By creating a custom subnet mask

   C. By assigning a subnet mask of 0.0.0.0

   D. By assigning a subnet mask that has the IP address of the router

   Answer: B. Because you require seven networks, you will need at least a mask of 255.255.240.0 (which gives you 14 subnets). If you used a default mask 255.255.0.0, it would provide 254 subnets, each with 65,534 hosts.

20. You need to come up with a TCP/IP addressing scheme for your company. How many host IDs must you allow for when you define the subnet mask for the network?

   A. One for each subnet

   B. One for each router interface

   C. One for each WAN connection

   D. One for each network adapter installed on each host

   Answer: B and D. Note the key words *host IDs*. Each interface on a router must have an IP address. (The only exception is a Cisco router running without IP.) However, as a default gateway—Ethernet, Token Ring, Serial, and so on—that interface must still be addressed. Also, each PC must have an IP address assigned to it.

21. You are using DHCP on your network. You want all clients from all subnets to access your proxy server by name. You use DHCP to give the WINS address to all clients. What other option must you give to the clients before they will be able to browse across subnets?

   A. Option 28: Broadcast address

   B. Option 47: NetBIOS scope ID

   C. Option 46: WINS/NBT node type

   D. Option 51: Lease time

   Answer: C. In order for the WINS clients to operate with the WINS server, they must first define what type of node they are. For example, they must define whether they are a Broadcast, Peer-to-Peer, Mixed, or Hybrid type.

Chapter 3

1. Explain what CERN compatibility is, where it comes from, and how it applies to Microsoft Proxy Server.

   Answer: CERN compatibility is based on a specification from CERN (Conseil Europeen pour la Recherché Nucleair, or the European Laboratory for Particle Physics) in Switzerland.

2. Explain ISAPI and describe the difference between the Proxy Server ISAPI filter and the ISAPI application.

   Answer: The ISAPI filter provides the benefit of determining which protocol service to issue to the ultimate destination, while allowing monitoring, logging, modification, redirection, and authentication of data from the Internet resource. The ISAPI application is commonly used with Internet applications that involve databases or other data links, and maintains the ability to create dynamic HTML and integrate Web applications.

3. How is a specific application identified on a system through the Internet?

   Answer: To identify an Internet resource, an IP address is used. That IP address, a 32-bit number, describes one, and only one, system on the Internet.

4. Briefly explain how a WinSock Proxy client works and operates with TCP/IP. How about with IPX/SPX?

   Answer: When clients on a network are configured with TCP/IP as a transport protocol, they have the ability to communicate with either local or remote resources. As the client makes resource calls and the WSP client DLL is initialized, a copy of the LAT is delivered to it via the control channel. From this point forward, any new connection attempts will be directed and processed by the WSP DLL. When directed locally, connection requests are passed directly to the WinSock DLLs that are originally installed with the protocol stack. No additional processing or modifications are made to local requests. With IPX, the same process is used; however, all Internet resources are considered remote and therefore only the MSP DLL is used. Finally, the control channel is established via IPX rather than UDP.

5. Explain how Microsoft Proxy Server's caching system works.

   Answer: Microsoft's proxy caching system is comprised of two mechanisms: a passive cache and an active cache. The passive cache is used to record a copy of information retrieved from an Internet resource. Following an algorithm to determine if the object can be cached, data will be either added to the store or simply passed down to the client. Examples of data that cannot be cached include stock market data and other time-specific information. The active cache works on the expectation of data being requested. It bases its caching system on an adjustable TTL, server load, and popularity.

6. Which would you want to cache via Microsoft Proxy Server?

   A. Stock market information

   B. Text and graphics home page data

C. Internet e-mail pages

D. Internet information searches

E. Large FTP data files from beta releases

Answer: B. The only type of information you would want to cache is text and graphic home page data. Stock market information is too volatile, as are e-mail and information searches. Beta files are commonly subject to change and an evaluator will typically only want the latest revision.

7. What are the two types of caches used in Microsoft Proxy Server?

A. Active caching

B. General caching

C. Passive caching

D. Smart caching

E. Advanced caching

Answer: A and C. The two types of caches that Proxy Server implements are active and passive.

8. What are the names of the Windows Sockets Dynamic Link Libraries?

A. WinSock.DLL

B. WSP.DLL

C. Wsock16.DLL

D. WinSock.SYS

E. Wsock32.DLL

Answer: A and E. There are two WinSock Dynamic Link Libraries. WinSock.DLL and Wsock32.DLL are provided as the defaults. WinSock.DLL is used to support 16-bit Windows-based applications and is installed on Windows 3.1, Windows for Workgroups, and Windows 95. Wsock32.DLL is used to support 32-bit Windows-based applications installed on Windows NT and Windows 95.

9. Which operating systems use both a 16-bit and 32-bit WinSock DLL?

A. Windows NT

B. Windows 3.1

C. Windows for Workgroups

D. Windows 95

E. Macintosh

Answer: D. The only system that uses both WinSock DLLs is Windows 95. Windows NT uses only a 32-bit DLL, while Windows 3.1 and Windows for Workgroups use a 16-bit DLL. Macintosh is not supported for WinSock applications.

10. Which of the following are not connectionless-based applications?

   A. RealAudio

   B. Gopher

   C. IRC

   D. NETSHOW

   E. FTP

   Answer: B and E. Both Gopher and FTP are connection-based technologies. You can tell this because they both use TCP. Applications that are not connection-based utilize UDP.

Chapter 4

1. Your company has given you a 386SX-25 system with 12 megabytes of RAM, a 200 megabyte hard drive, and a 14.4k modem. Your boss has read that Microsoft Proxy Server only requires what that operating system has in order to operate. He would like to spend as little as possible on a proxy server for 35 people. Explain why this server is inadequate for the company's needs, what hardware the company should have, and why.

   Answer: As you have probably gathered, a 386 system is obsolete and should be replaced. It has no math co-processor, a 16-bit external channel, and is fairly old. Considering that your boss wants to keep costs low, you should consider acquiring a computer with at least a low-end Pentium (90 MHz) processor. Also, because the Proxy Server software requirement with the service pack is approximately 100 megabytes plus a swap file, the addition of the proxy server would add at least 10 megabytes for the program, 50 megabytes for the basic cache, and 18 megabytes for the 35 users. That is a total basic storage requirement of 178 megabytes. However, to keep with Microsoft's performance suggestion of 100 megabytes for the basic cache, that would require 228 megabytes of storage. So, when all of this is taken into consideration, it would be advisable to purchase nothing less than a gigabyte of hard drive space. If you have used Windows NT with 16 megabytes of RAM, you understand that anything less than 32 megabytes means that the server will constantly page to the hard drive (swapping memory). Finally, considering the fact that you have 35 people, you really should consider an ISDN service or a 56k modem.

2. You have an internal network with Web and FTP servers that do not require security or protection. Currently, all systems on the network use a proxy server. Explain how you can disable the proxy services just for local systems.

   Answer: To disable the Web Proxy service for the local network, simply include the domain in the Exclude box in the Proxy Configuration section of the Web browser. As for FTP services, you may use the one that is built into the Web browser. Or, to use the one that is WinSock-based, select the Disable WSP Client checkbox from the Web Proxy client, then click OK to accept, and restart the system.

3. What is the name of the share for installing Microsoft Proxy Server?

Answer: There is no share for installing Microsoft Proxy Server unless you create one. However, the WinSock support programs are located in the WSP\CLIENTS directory on the Microsoft Proxy Server, which can be accessed by connecting to its network share name, WSPCLNT.

4. What port does HTTP require on a proxy server?

Answer: A proxy server utilizes a port that is used for services. However, unlike typical services such as FTP, which uses port 21, or HTTP, which uses port 80, a proxy server has no default port assignment. The only requirement is that the port specified on the server matches the port used on the client. It is a bad idea to change these items too much as is may make connections to the Internet less manageable at the proxy server.

5. You are going to install Proxy Server for 21 people. How much hard disk storage should your server have available for the proxy cache?

A. 100MB

B. 121MB

C. 110MB

D. 111MB

E. 11MB

Answer: D. The proxy server requires 111MB. That includes 100MB for the basic recommended cache and 0.5MB for each client, rounded up to the nearest megabyte.

6. What is the name of the of the Setup program used to install Microsoft Proxy Server?

A. SETUP

B. INSTALL

C. INSTPRXY

D. CONFIG

E. ADDSERV

Answer: A. This program is located at the root of the Proxy Server CD-ROM.

7. What are the names of the two LAT files?

A. MSPLAT.TXT

B. LOCALLAT.TXT

C. HOSTS.

D. LMHOSTS.

E. SERVICES.

Answer: A and B. The MSPLAT.TXT file is delivered automatically by the server, and the LOCALLAT.TXT file is configured manually.

8. What does LAT stand for?

  A. Local Area Table

  B. Local Address Table

  C. Lite Address Traffic

  D. Long Attribute Type

  E. Logical Address Table

Answer: B.

9. What program is used to remove Microsoft Proxy Server?

  A. SETUP.EXE

  B. REMOVE.EXE

  C. CLEARPXY.EXE

  D. INSTALL.EXE

  E. DELPROXY.COM

Answer: A. The SETUP.EXE utility is used for both setup and removal of Microsoft Proxy Server. Additionally, SETUP.EXE can be used to restore missing or corrupted files and settings.

10. You install Proxy Server on your local network, which has the following configuration:

Internal adapter	192.168.101.165	255.255.255.0
External adapter	172.16.10.2	255.255.255.0
Router	172.16.10.1	255.255.255.0

How should you configure the default gateway on the Proxy Server?

  A. Internal: 172.16.10.1   External: 172.16.10.1

  B. Internal: None   External: 172.16.10.1

  C. Internal: 172.16.10.2   External: 172.16.10.1

  D. Internal: None   External: 192.168.101.165

  E. Internal: Blank   External: Blank

Answer: B. The router is the default gateway for the external network adapter. Since no information regarding the internal adapter is given, you can't configure a gateway. Remember that the gateway and the network adapter must be on the same network. Clearly, we can see that the router's IP address is on the same network as that of the external interface of the proxy server.

11. You need your Proxy Server to access the Internet through RAS, and all users on your local network use the Proxy Server to reach the Internet. Your network configuration is as follows:

Internal adapter: 192.168.101.165 to 255.255.255.0

RAS adapter   172.16.10.3 to 255.255.255.0

What range of IP addresses should you include in your LAT?

A. 172.16.10.0 to 172.16.10 255

B. 172.16.10.3 to 172.16.10.3

C. 192.168.101.0 to 192.168.101.255

D. 192.168.101.0 to 192.168.101.255 and 172.16.10.3 to 172.16.10.3

Answer: C. The IP address range of the LAT should only include those on the internal network. In this case, the internal network adapter is 192.168.101.165 with a mask of 255.255.255.0, which provides us with a network of 192.168.101.0 to 192.168.10.255.

12. You have an NT Server with two NIC cards that you want to install Proxy Server on. The internal network adapter has the IP address of 10.1.1.100 255.255.255.224 and the external adapter has an address of 192.168.10.10 255.255.255.0. Which two addresses must you add to the LAT?

A. 10.1.1.121

B. 10.1.1.100

C. 192.168.10.255

D. 192.168.10.10

Answer: A and B. The Subnet mask of 255.255.255.224 tells us that three bits are used to define the network. In this case, those three bits tell us that there are six (8–2) networks that have the ranges 32–63, 64–91, 92–127, 128–159, 160–191, and 192–223. Clearly, both A and B reside on a common network that is located on the internal side of the proxy server.

13. What services can you use on your network if you have MAC, UNIX, and Windows computers?

A. Only the Web Proxy

B. Only the WinSock Proxy

C. Only Socks Proxy

D. Both Web Proxy and Socks Proxy, but not WinSock Proxy

E. Web Proxy, Socks Proxy, and WinSock Proxy

F. None of the above

Answer: D. Both the Web Proxy and the Socks Proxy servers are platform independent. The WinSock Proxy is only compatible with Windows-based platforms.

14. You proxy server is configured as follows:

Internal adapter	172.16.10.169 255.255.255.192
External adapter	172.16.10.2 255.255.255.0

What IP address range should you include in the LAT?

A. 172.16.10.2

B. 172.16.10.2 to 172.16.100.255

C. 192.168.10.1 to 192.168.10.255

D. 192.168.10.128 to 192.168.10.191

Answer: D. The subnet mask tells us that the ranges will be 64 to 127 and 128 to 191 Therefore, you must include all nodes on that network, which are 192.168.10.1.128 to 192.168.10.191.

15. Your Proxy Server is configured as follows:

Internal adapter	192.168.10.6 255.255.255.0
Internal adapter	192.168.20.3 255.255.255.0
External adapter	172.16.10.3 255.255.255.0

What IP address ranges should you include in the LAT?

A. 192.168.10.0 to 192.168.10. 255 and 192.168.20.0 to 192.168.20.255

B. 192.168.1.0 to 192.168.255.0 and 192.168.20.3 to 192.168.20.3

C. 172.16.10.0 to 172.16.10.255

D. 172.16.10.3 to 172.16.10.3

Answer: A. The internal network range is that of the network portion of the address, with a node range conforming to the mask. In this case, that would be 0 to 255. Since we have multiple internal networks, both must be included in the LAT.

16. Your network has a Proxy Server, but uses an Internet DNS server for name resolution. The DNS server has an IP address of 192.168.10.20. What must you do for clients to be able to use a Web Proxy service to access the Internet?

A. Specify the address of the DNS server on the Proxy Server.

B. Include the DNS server address in the LAT.

C. Specify the DNS server IP address in all client configurations.

D. Make the DNS server the default gateway.

Answer: A. Since the Proxy Server performs all name resolution for clients, you need only specify a DNS at the Proxy Server itself. An easy way to remember this is to think in terms of your clients being all IPX-based such that they can't have a DNS set. Now the only place that a DNS can and should be set is at the proxy server.

17. You want to install Microsoft Proxy Server on a system with two hard drives. Drive C is a FAT file system and is 2.3GB in size. Drive D is an NTFS and is only 300MB. The NT OS is installed on drive C, and during the installation of Proxy Server you want to add a 150MB disk cache on drive C, but drive C is dimmed and drive D is the only one available. What do you need to do to allow the cache to reside on drive C?

    A. Run CHKDSK.

    B. Add another drive.

    C. Convert drive C to NTFS.

    D. Make the FAT partition smaller.

    Answer: C. Only NTFS volumes can be used to store the proxy server cache.

Chapter 5

1. Under Microsoft Windows NT 4.0, FTP management is performed through what?

    A. DOS prompt

    B. Internet Service Manager

    C. Key Manager

    D. Web Manager

    Answer: B. Under Microsoft Windows NT 4.0, FTP management is performed through the Internet Service Manager. As with Windows NT 3.5*x*, you can use any FTP client, including most Web browsers, to connect to the FTP server.

2. The FTP Manager Advanced tab limits access to the FTP server in which two ways?

    A. Login

    B. Source systems

    C. Network utilization

    D. Password

    Answer: B and C. By default, all systems are granted access. You can grant access to all computers with the exclusion of those you add as single computers or a certain group of computers. Also, you can deny access to all computers, with the exception of those you add as single computers or a group of computers. The last way the Advanced sheet allows you to limit access to the FTP server is by setting a maximum network utilization in terms of kilobytes per second.

3. The FTP Manager Messages tab offers which options?

   A. Welcome message (logging on)

   B. Exit message (logging off)

   C. Error Message

   D. Maximum connections message (limit of users logged on)

   Answer: A, B, and D. A new feature, you can now have a message sent to a user when logging on, logging off, or when maximum connections have been reached.

4. Under the FTP Manager Services tab, the maximum connections defaults to?

   A. 500

   B. 20

   C. 200

   D. 1000

   Answer: D. The maximum connections is by default 1000, up from 20 in version 3.5x.

5. Under the FTP Manager Services tab, the default connection timeout is?

   A. 10 minutes

   B. 5 minutes

   C. 15 minutes

   D. 25 minutes

   Answer: C. The default connection timeout value was raised from 10 to 15 minutes in version 4.0.

6. Web pages are constructed in?

   A. HTML

   B. Web

   C. URL

   D. HTTP

   Answer: A. Web pages are constructed in HTML (hypertext markup language), which includes both hypertext and hyperlinks. This is the standard document form Web browsers support.

7. The World Wide Web (WWW) is?

   A. A graphical, easy-to-navigate interface for looking at documents on the Internet

   B. Shareware

   C. Freeware

   D. HTTP documents

   Answer: A. A *de facto* industry standard, Web is an interface for looking at documents on the Internet.

8. Hyperlinks are?

   A. Shortcuts on Web documents to aid in connecting to other pages, downloading files, etc.

   B. Directories in the Web server

   C. Fast Internet connections

   D. FTP servers

   Answer: A. This is an important feature when building or looking at Web pages. This helps locate and connect to other Internet resources quickly and easily.

9. A Uniform Resource Locator (URL) is?

   A. The standard naming convention on the Internet

   B. A HTTP document

   C. A Web server

   D. Shortcuts on Web documents to aid in connecting to other pages

   Answer: A. When you connect to an Internet site, you use the site URL to locate the Web page. URLs are an important feature of the Internet.

10. Web password authentication is done at what three levels?

   A. Allow Anonymous

   B. Basic (Clear Text)

   C. Windows NT Challenge/Response

   D. Disable Anonymous

   Answer: A, B, and C. The anonymous configuration is the most common on the Internet, and is generally used to allow the public to see your Web page. Basic, or clear text, is a simple level of password protection. Windows NT Challenge/Response is a system by which the service will honor requests by clients to send user account information using the Windows NT Challenge/Response authentication protocol.

Chapter 6

1. Explain how logs work. What is regular logging? Verbose? When should they be used?

   Answer: Log files allow an administrator to view how the Proxy Server has been used. For example, suppose that many users were complaining about slow Internet access. While this could be attributed to many factors, including some that are server-related, it is possible to find which certain users are monopolizing the server. In such cases, it may be desirable to either increase bandwidth to meet demand, or separate users to different proxy servers. Furthermore, suppose managers suspect that some employees are spending company time on sites that aren't work-related, or visiting clearly inappropriate sites. A log will provide documentation of who is abusing their Web privileges. In short, the logging options provide audit ability to Internet access.

Regular logging is a subset of verbose logging and includes the more common elements that an administrator would like to work with. While it's limited in some respects, regular logging has the advantage of utilizing less disk space for its reports. Verbose logging provides maximum logging capability, recording of all activities on the server. Although the verbose logging function offers more information, it requires more disk space; and often the additional information is not very useful. The logs should be used as required and as system storage permits.

2. Explain how filtering helps in securing a site. How can it be limiting?

   Answer: The domain filter located in the security section in the shared configuration on any of the Proxy services' Service tab is commonly used to keep users from accessing sites such as pornography, stock market information, or other information that a company may not want their employees viewing. These sites may also contain viruses. For these reasons, some companies take this concept to such an extreme that they want to deny access to all Web sites except those on their "approved" list. Filters can secure a site by ensuring that only trusted sites are accessed, or by keeping those known to be hazardous out of reach. This can also be limiting in that other sites that may be useful could not be access without making an exception to the filter.

3. Will Microsoft Proxy Server 1.0 Integrate with IIS 4.0? Explain.

   Answer: Yes. Microsoft Proxy Server will integrate with all versions of IIS starting with 2.0 and greater. Microsoft Proxy Server requires that you install to a server and not the personal Web services that you would find on a workstation.

4. How do you instruct Proxy Server not to cache certain sites?

   Answer: The cache can be fine-tuned per site by clicking the Advanced button on the main Caching tab. On this tab, you will find a button called Market Cache Filters. Click it, and then click the Add button and type the URL and related information for the site or directory on a site that you do not want to cache. Click the Never Cache option, and select OK.

5. Explain how to change the cache after an installation. How does the cache size differ from caching (passive and active)?

   Answer: The cache size can also be configured from the Caching tab of the Web Proxy service properties. Displayed, the tab page reveals the current total capacity of the cache. Selecting Change Cache Size allows an administrator to adjust the number of reserved megabytes. The cache size is the amount of disk space allocated to be used by the caching process of active and passive caching.

6. Where are the log files stored?

   A. \WINNT\SYSTEM32\PROXYLOGS

   B. \INETPUB\PROXYLOGS

   C. \WINNT\LOGS

   D. In an SQL database file designated during or after installation

   E. Anywhere the administrator designates

Answer: All answers are correct. While the default installation will place the log files in C:\WINNT\SYSTEM32\PROXYLOGS, you may actually designate any location. We apologize for the trick question; however, you should expect something similar to this on the MCSE exam. Try to keep an open mind.

7. Without customization, how can Proxy Server be managed through HTML?

   A. Download PXYHTMG.EXE from www.microsoft.com.

   B. Click Enable Web Publishing.

   C. It is already installed, no changes are required.

   D. By connecting your Web site and /PROXYMGR

   E. It is not supported at this time.

Answer: E. It is not supported at this time.

8. What options can be performed from the Service tab of the WSP Properties page?

   A. None

   B. Change the number of licensed connections.

   C. Enter a Comment for the server.

   D. Check existing user sessions.

Answer: B. You cannot change the number of licensed connections, although you may view them. Also, you cannot check existing user connections from this screen, although you can from the Web Properties page. You can input a description of the service on the Comment line.

9. What types of log files are supported?

   A. Text files

   B. Proprietary encoded

   C. BitMap graphical log

   D. SQL database

   E. Word .DOC format

Answer: A and D. Currently, Microsoft Proxy Server will either place files in a text file or export information directly to an SQL database. Unlike those of many other Microsoft products, Proxy Server log files have no proprietary encoding. Also, there are no functions to create a bitmap log file or Word document. However, the basic text file may be read with Word (but it would not be in .DOC format until converted as such).

10. Of the following, which are the default log name formats?

A. W3*yymmdd*.LOG

B. WS*yymmdd*.LOG

C. WWW.LOG

D. WINSOCK.LOG

E. None of the above

Answer: A and B. Of the above listed names, only A and B are valid names from the automatic chronological listing.

11. What should you do on the Logging tab in the WinSock Proxy Service Properties dialog box when trying to compile a weekly report containing the Internet IP addresses accessed by applications that use the WinSock service?

A. Select the Stop Service if Disk Is Full checkbox.

B. Select the Automatically Open New Log checkbox and specify Weekly.

C. Select the Verbose checkbox.

D. Select the Limit Number Of Old Logs To checkbox and set the value to 7.

Answer: B. One of the basic options of logging to a text file is when to open a new log. These logs can be opened daily, weekly, or monthly.

12. You need to support Microsoft SQL Server with your Proxy Server. The initial inbound port uses port 1433 and then generates an outbound port somewhere between 5000 and 32767. How should you configure the ports on your Proxy Server?

A. In the WinSock Proxy Server service, specify port 0 in the Protocol definitions.

B. In the WinSock Proxy Server service, specify a port range of 5000 to 32767 in the Protocol definitions.

C. In the WinSock Proxy Server service, specify a port range of "any" in the Protocol definitions.

D. Create a protocol entry for the SQL Server and specify a port range of 5000 to 32767.

Answer: B. The WinSock Proxy Server supports a range from 0 to 65535. In the case of this application, you need to specify a port range of 5000 to 32767 in the port definitions.

13. Your users are using the Internet to get weather and sports, and using all the bandwidth so that your Internet connections are starting to get slow. What should you do to stop users from getting sports and weather information?

A. Enable anonymous authentication.

B. Add outbound filters for the sports and weather Web sites.

C. Remove any protocol definitions for the sport and weather Web sites from the WinSock Proxy service.

D. Enable Microsoft Windows NT Challenge/Response authentication.

Answer: C. Some Internet programs require special definitions to be set in the WinSock Proxy service. For example, IRC (Internet Chat) will use its own definition. Removing these non–business-related protocol definitions will eliminate usage.

14. What must you do on the Publishing tab of the Web Proxy Service Properties dialog box if you want to forward all requests from the Internet to your Web service installed on the local server network?

A. Enable Web publishing and select the Discard button.

B. Enable Web publishing and select the Sent to the Local Web Server button.

C. Enable Web publishing and select the Sent to the Local Web Server button and specify the name of the Web server.

D. Enable Web publishing and select the Sent to the Local Web Server button and specify the name of the proxy server.

Answer: B. Unless you are re-routing traffic to an alternate Web site or using the mapping function, you will want to simply send traffic to the local server and make no additional changes.

15. What should you do to the Advanced Cache Policy dialog box to prevent large files from being stored in the cache?

A. Nothing

B. Set a size limit on cached objects.

C. Set a maximum TTL of 512.

D. Set the TTL to 0.

Answer: B. To limit the size of objects that are stored in the cache, you should set a size limit for the maximum-sized object you want to allow.

16. Your clients run only TCP/IP and connect to the Internet by way of the Web Proxy service. How do you find out what sites the users are visiting?

A. Enable Web Proxy logging.

B. Enable auditing for file and object access.

C. Nothing.

D. Look in the cache.

Answer: A. By enabling Web Proxy logging, you are able to track detailed information regarding usage of the service. This usage can include basic (regular) or detailed (verbose) information regarding site access.

Chapter 7

1. Explain how IP routing could effect and compromise security on your network.

Answer: If IP routing is enabled, Internet users have direct access to your network. Although they will have to contend with any security that is in place on your network, hacking into your data will be much easier than if no connection was in place. It is not recommend in any way or for any reason to enable IP forwarding.

2. Describe how implementing a separate domain for your proxy server aids in protecting your network from unauthorized Internet access.

Answer: If you have elected to maintain accessibility to the Internet by any mechanisms including enabling routing, it is best to limit access by creating a new domain that is used specifically with Internet-accessed information. Since Windows NT allows trusts among domains, the domain containing the proxy server can be configured so that it trusts the primary corporate master domain. This means user's accounts can be assigned from the main domain and configured to access the proxy server's domain. Those trying to access your domain will be limited by a single direction trust, which stops access prior to communication to the main domain. Assuming that the proxy server was configured as a PDC, additional servers can be added for e-mail, Web, FTP, and other services, while being managed from the main domain. In this way, Windows NT security will aid Proxy Server in creating a secure environment.

3. How are inbound connections managed from the Internet at the proxy server?

Answer: Inbound connection are not directly controlled by the IIS Manager that is used to configure the proxy server, with the exception of defining which ports are valid or are within a valid range and if Internet publishing is going to be enabled. Typically, configuration is done within the TCP/IP Manager where IP forwarding is disabled and ports are blocked by configuring security in the Advanced section of the IP Address tab.

4. How are outbound connections managed from clients at the proxy server?

Answer: The IIS Manager that is used to configure the proxy server directly controls outbound connections. The two main methods for controlling the connections are assigning users rights to access with various protocols and setting up filters. Assigning a user rights to use Web services, for instances, allows a specified person to access Web pages. Assigning a filter will either block all or grant all requests, with the exception of those items in the exclude list.

5. Is activating Internet Web publishing a proxy server considered a good practice? Explain.

Answer: No. Although secure, Microsoft Proxy Server was not designed or intended for Internet publishing. The main goal of Microsoft Proxy Server is to manage the connections to Internet resources from clients. A preferred solution for Internet publishing is to establish a small network, which can contain any resources that will be published on the Internet. When enabling Web publishing, there are inbound requests (HTTP, FTP, etc.) that are being serviced and the potential for compromising your secured network. Microsoft includes this feature so that the choice of security versus functionality will be at the administrator's discretion.

6. Where do you set protocol permissions?

A. Web Proxy Service Permissions tab

B. WinSock Proxy Service tab

C. Web Service Permissions tab

D. FTP Service Permissions tab

E. Gopher Service Permissions tab

Answer: A and B. Protocol permissions are set from Web and Winsock Proxy services. The Web, FTP, and Gopher services are protocols and do not set or define access from the proxy server. The Web Proxy service provides FTP Read, Gopher, Web, and secure permission options. The Winsock Proxy service provides all other protocols as specified in the protocol list.

7. Where is IP forwarding enabled or disabled?

A. Web Proxy Service Permissions tab

B. WWW Service tab

C. At the client

D. TCP/IP configuration

E. At the router

Answer: D and E. Despite the fact that we did not mention specifically that the router forwards IP information, you should understand that this is, in fact, what a router does. The Routing tab under TCP/IP contains a checkbox to enable IP forwarding. The client, Web service, and Web Proxy do not control IP forwarding in any way.

8. What are the two ways Microsoft Proxy Server secures a network from external users?

A. Disabling IP forwarding

B. Assigning a filter

C. Disabling listening on inbound service ports

D. Setting User Permissions

E. Rejecting User Requests listed in the LAT

Answer: A and C. Microsoft Proxy server does not directly control inbound traffic. However, do not forget that we had mentioned that security is based on disabling IP forwarding and disabling listening on inbound service ports. It is completely up to you to define your own understanding of these components. However, realize that you cannot filter inbound traffic, or assign rights to inbound users (as proxy clients) aside from the anonymous users, and rejecting user requests listed in the LAT denies your network, not the Internet.

9. When filtering a single computer into the exclude list on the Domain Filters tab, how can you use the DNS name rather than IP address?

A. Type the name in the Domain box.

B. Browse the computer list and double-click the computer.

C. Select Learn by Example, type the URL, and click Accept.

D. Click the ellipses button next to the IP address and type the name.

E. Click the Construct LAT button.

Answer: D. Clicking the ellipses button enables an administrator to manually type the DNS name of the server you want to place in the exclude list. That is not to say that this DNS name is excluded from access. Rather, it is not completely granted or denied. There is no Learning by Example function in Microsoft Proxy Server. You cannot browse host names; the browse function only works on NetBIOS names. The Domain box is not used in the method described above, although it would be a close second if it wasn't grayed out. Finally, the LAT is used to determine which systems are local, but not which systems are filtered (by name).

10. What type of trust relationship should be set up between a Proxy Server domain and a main company domain?

A. One-way trust

B. No trust

C. Two-way trust

D. Meshed trust with SSL links

E. None of the above

Answer: A. A one-way trust should be established such that the Proxy Server domain trusts the main company domain. This is to allow users to access resources on the proxy domain, but not vice versa. No trust is completely secure from both the Internet and the private network. However, no users could use it without creating separate identical accounts. That's not good. Do not do it. A two-way trust is also an idea. However, this would allow the Proxy Server domain to communicate back to your private domain, which would be bad. A meshed trusts with SSL links does not exist. A mesh is a network communication pattern where all points connect to all other points. SSL is not applicable to domain trust.

11. You want to be alerted when your proxy server running packet filtering is dropping packets. What should you do?

A. Using the Alerting tab of the Proxy Server Security dialog box, create an alert for Rejected Packets.

B. Using the Alerting tab of the Proxy Server Security dialog box, create an alert for Protocol Violations.

C. Using Microsoft Windows NT Performance Monitor, create an alert on the Packets Received Discarded counter.

D. Using Microsoft Windows NT Performance Monitor, create an alert on the Packets Received Unknown counter.

Answer: A. When testing for dropped packets, you should create an alert for some number of packets that are rejected per second.

12. You enable filtering on your Windows NT Proxy Server and deny access to www.newstoday.com. However, you have one client that needs to get to this site for business purposes. The client is configured for the WinSock Proxy and Web Proxy services. How can the client access this site?

   A. The client can't.

   B. Use the WinSock Proxy Server, then enter the host name.

   C. Use the Web Proxy Server, then enter the host name.

   D. Use the Web Proxy Server, then enter the IP address.

   Answer: A. Since there is a site filter, the only way that the client could access that site is by removing the filter. In a publishing error, Microsoft notes that you must specify that both the domain name and IP address must be used to completely block out a site. In a later publishing, which is available through either Technet or their online knowledge base, they address this issue and note that Microsoft Proxy Server will now block based on either the IP address or the name. The name will resolve to an IP address while the IP address, through reverse lookup, will reveal a domain name. Microsoft Proxy Server 1.0, however, did not offer this function and required both the domain name and the IP address to block a site.

13. Your Proxy Server is configured to allow Anonymous Authentication and Challenge/Response authentication. The Sales department and the Shipping department are both granted access to the WWW protocol in the Permissions tab of the Web Proxy Service Properties dialog box. Which Windows NT groups can access the Internet by using HTTP in the Web Proxy service?

   A. None

   B. All group in the domain

   C. Only the Sales and Shipping departments

   D. Any groups with local logon rights to the domain

   Answer: C. Even though anonymous connections are allowed, if there is no specification in access control for the IUSR_*systemname* account. There will be not authorization to use a protocol in a service.

14. NBTSTAT displays the NetBIOS name cache. How can you keep someone from running this command on your Proxy Server? (Choose two answers.)

   A. Enable packet filtering.

   B. Disable RAS on the external adapter.

C. Enable access control on the WinSock Proxy service.

D. Disable the NetBIOS interface.

E. Remove the workstation service from the external adapter.

Answer: A and D. From the Internet, any user can access your network given proper permissions via NetBIOS utilities. The key issue is resolving names so that users can have this access. To prevent this from occurring and to prevent users even listing NetBIOS resources, you must disable NetBIOS on the external interface and enable packet filtering.

15. Which three of the following events can your Proxy Server alert or notify you of that might affect performance on the local network?

A. When the hard disks are full

B. When packets are rejected by the Proxy Server

C. When the internal network is down

D. When users access restricted Web sites

E. When proxy services are stopped

F. When protocol violations occur

Answer: A, B, and F. The Alerting tab of the Security section of Proxy Server allows alerting when the hard disk is full, when packets are rejected by the Proxy Server, and when protocol violations occur.

Chapter 8

1. Explain how the Event Viewer should be used in system monitoring to identify problems with the proxy server.

Answer: The Event Viewer records system messages as they occur. As such, any problems such as initializing proxy server, IIS, TCP/IP, or dial-up networking will all be listed here. When trying to locate related problems, errors and events that occur on the system will all be found in the Event Viewer.

2. What is the key factor in determining the type of support that an application requires? Is there any mixing of proxy services within a supported application?

Answer: The key factor in determining the type of support that an application requires is whether the application is CERN-compatible or non-CERN-compatible. You may mix applications or even combine them regardless of compatibility. Once support is set up, it becomes transparent to the user and the programs that communicate with each other in an end-to-end configuration.

3. Why would a large company want to maintain an intranet?

   Answer: Maintaining an intranet can provide organizations with a number of benefits. For example, an internal Web can be an effective way to make available HR listings, company information/reports, employee telephone directory information, corporate policies/procedures, listings, technical support, and system file updates. Other benefits include a reduced volume of e-mail, unification of heterogeneous networks, news feeds from the Internet, and sales reports.

4. Explain how Microsoft Proxy Server's user validation for all users differs from validation of specific users.

   Answer: When allowing all users to access a proxy server, you have no control over which users are allowed or not allowed. One the other hand, you may set proxy server so that each user has specific access.

5. Why is caching limited by bandwidth?

   Answer: Caching is effectively limited by bandwidth because you can only cache as much information as can be accessed through the available bandwidth at any given time. For example, once you have 100% utilization of bandwidth, you could not access any additional systems to cache. Effectively, the cache store area would only be able to hold so much data before the remainder of the cache would become useless. Once bandwidth is maximized, cache will have reached its limit. It would be highly advisable to increase bandwidth capacity.

6. As a gateway, which parts of an IPX message does Microsoft Proxy Server not convert?

   A. Data in the message

   B. All addressing

   C. The Request command

   D. The protocol

   Answer: A. Practically all information that is delivered through the IPX gateway is converted, except the data in the message. The only time you will see data converted is when converting from EBCDIC to ASCII, as with mainframes. However, these changes are all made by the terminal program that requests the data—hardly ever by a proxy server. IPX addressing is converted to IP. The request that is made may be converted at the proxy server, and the protocol must be changed to FTP, WWW, Gopher, etc.

7. Which of the following customer complaints should you analyze using the proxy server or related components?

   A. Duplicate IP address error

   B. Proxy Server timeout in the Web browser

   C. Cannot see other systems on the network

   D. Access denied to any FTP site

Answer: B and D. As an administrator, you must know where to check for errors. When the proxy server times out while a Web browser is trying to access it, this indicates that the system is either down or over-taxed with users. When trying to connect to an FTP site and an "Access denied" message appears, you should typically find what the user does not have proper access to or which sites the user has tried accessing that have been filtered out.

8. The caching mechanism of Microsoft Proxy Server benefits an intranet. True or False? Why?

   Answer: True. When accessing TCP/IP-related network services through the Proxy Server, data may be cached as it is with the Internet. This is a very useful function over wide area networks where bandwidth is small. If the proxy server is not used, however, data will not be cached.

9. The IPX gateway on Microsoft Proxy Server is enabled by default. True or False? Why?

   Answer: True. The IPX gateway is enabled by default on Microsoft Proxy Server. The only requirement for the IPX gateway to be enabled is to have the IPX protocol installed and configured on the NT Server.

10. When configured correctly, Windows NT security can be applied to a UNIX system through a proxy server. True or False. Why?

    Answer: True. By segregating the network or limiting the UNIX system to communicate only with the Proxy Server, you may apply the same access as with Windows NT. The key in this configuration is to arrange the setup so that only the Proxy Server can communicate with the UNIX system. At this point, you will have to be validated to access the UNIX system. This also applies to other systems running TCP/IP-based services.

11. You want all your Web Proxy client computers to have access to the sales.com domain, but do not want them to access any other Internet domain. You deny access to all Internet sites through domain filtering, but you need to do one more thing. What is it?

    A. Create a domain filter to grant access to the sales.com domain.

    B. Add sales.com to the list of actively cached sites.

    C. In the Web Proxy service, enable access control.

    D. In the WinSock Proxy service, enable access control.

    Answer: A. If all sites are blocked, you must create a filter that will allow those that you want to access to be available. This is not a caching issue, nor does it have to do with individual user permissions to protocols such as are found in access control.

12. Your clients run IPX and the proxy server runs both IPX and TCP/IP. You want to use the caching features of the Web Proxy service. What must you do on each client computer?

    A. Clients cannot use the caching feature when they are only running IPX.

    B. Install the Proxy Server client, and configure the Web browser so that it does not use the Web Proxy service.

C. Install the Proxy Server client, and configure the Web browser so that it uses the Web Proxy service.

D. Install nothing on the clients, but enable the Web browser to use the Web Proxy service.

Answer: A. Clients running only IPX will use the WinSock Proxy Server for Web access. The WinSock Proxy Server does not provide any caching functions. An easy way to remember this is to think of the interface screen in the IIS Manager where the Web Proxy Server is the only proxy that has a Cache tab.

13. On your network you have Windows for Workgroups, Windows 95, and Windows 3.1 clients. They run IPX to connect to your Netware server. You install a proxy server running IPX, but the Windows for Workgroups and Windows 3.1 users cannot access the proxy server services. What is most likely the problem?

A. You must install TCP/IP on the proxy server so it can communicate with the Windows for Workgroup and Windows 3.1 clients.

B. Microsoft Proxy Server only supports the Microsoft IPX/SPX protocol.

C. Microsoft Proxy Server only supports older Novell VLM clients.

D. Microsoft Proxy Server does not support IPX client software on Windows 3.1 and Windows for Workgroups.

Answer: D. Microsoft Proxy Server does not support IPX clients running Windows 3.1 and Windows for Workgroups. You need to be careful when reviewing a question like this as to the wording of the answer. Many of you may have wanted to answer A. However, TCP/IP would need to be added to the client, not the server. The TCP/IP is a required component of the server. Also, Microsoft Proxy Server does not support the 16-bit IPX client drivers for Windows 95. You must use either the Microsoft or Novell 32-bit drivers.

14. You want your IPX clients to access the Internet by using the WinSock Proxy service. During the setup of Microsoft Proxy Server, you want to specify the Proxy Server computer name in the Client Installation/Configuration dialog box. What must you specify?

A. The computer name of the Proxy Server computer

B. The DNS name of the Proxy Server computer

C. The hardware address of the Proxy Server's internal adapter

D. The IPX internal network number of the Proxy Server computer's internal adapter

Answer: A. Name resolution will not occur on the client until a session is established with the Proxy Server. You cannot use the DNS name and must work with the NetBIOS (computer) name. When working with other proxy services, such as Web Proxy, that use IP only, you must specify the IP address of the proxy server. Do not confuse this with the support that the WinSock Proxy has for HTTP/FTP and its use with IPX. Adapter card information should automatically appear in the MSPCLNT.INI file. If you do not have routers or a Netware Server that provide this information to the Windows NT Server, you will be required to add the information yourself.

15. You want all your IPX clients to use the WinSock Proxy service to access the Internet. What should you do in the Client Installation/Configuration dialog box?

    A. Select the IP Address option button and type the IP address of the internal adapter.

    B. Select the IP Address option button and type the IP address of the default gateway.

    C. Select the IP Address option button and type the IP address of the external adapter.

    D. Select the Computer Name option button and type the NetBIOS name of the Proxy Server.

    E. Select the Manual option button and edit the WSPCFG.INI file on every client computer.

    Answer: D. Name resolution will not occur on the client until a session is established with the Proxy Server. You cannot use the DNS name and must work with the NetBIOS (computer) name. When working with other proxy services, such as Web Proxy, that use IP only, you must specify the IP address of the proxy server. Do not confuse this with the support that the WinSock Proxy has for HTTP/FTP and its use with IPX. Adapter card information should automatically appear in the MSPCLNT.INI file. If you do not have routers or a Netware server that provide this information to the Windows NT server, you will be required to add the information yourself.

Chapter 9

1. Explain how load balancing can be difficult to implement without arrays.

   Answer: Load balancing can be difficult to implement without arrays for many reasons. There are no mechanisms included to directly perform load balancing at the server. This means that all balancing is methodical and somewhat manual. Also, the user base must be analyzed by geographical distribution, utilization of each service, and quantity of users. As such, a number of solutions must be analyzed prior to forming a conclusion that will meet the requirements.

2. Explain how an array can be an effective solution to load balancing and fault tolerance.

   Answer: Arrays were specifically designed to automatically load balance requests between servers. When using the methodical systems for load balancing, it is difficult to determine use, total number of users, and so forth. An array performs this task automatically. Also, if a member of the array is down, requests are sent to other array members, which fill the request.

3. Provide some examples of load balancing for a two-location wide area network, a system where users tend to use one protocol, and a system that is completely mixed.

   Answer: In a two-location scenario, an administrator may want to configure two proxy servers, one at each location. This is dependent on the number of users at each site and their utilization. Systems may be chained to an upstream proxy server. When users tend to use a single protocol, often it is more beneficial for users to utilize multiple proxy servers, each for a specific protocol. For example, having one proxy server for Web Proxy services and another for WinSock may solve this type of configuration problem. In the case of a mixed environment, the load distribution is completely dependent on the network administrator's opinion of what will use the server's resources the most. However, the guidelines as to locale, number of users, types of protocols used, and so on still apply. The strongest characteristics for user needs must be applied. Typically, an array will be implemented in these types of configurations.

4. The type of Name Resolution (WINS versus DNS) used by clients makes no difference when configuring multiple proxy servers. True or false?

    Answer: False. Load balancing multiple proxy servers can depend strongly on the type of network that is implemented. Different options are available to an administrator depending on the resolution type.

5. Which of the following are not issues when implementing multiple proxy servers?

    A. Servers do not communicate.

    B. Cache is different between servers.

    C. Security is different.

    D. Clients are Windows 95–based.

    E. The Proxy Server also contains the DNS service.

    Answer: D and E. Whether a client is using Windows 95, Windows NT, or Windows for Workgroups makes no difference when configuring multiple proxy servers. Also, regardless of where the DNS service is provided, name resolution will remain an independent service from the proxy server or multiple proxy servers.

6. How do proxy servers communicate with each other?

    A. PSIP (Proxy Server Information Protocol)

    B. RIP (Router Information Protocol)

    C. TCP (Transmission Control Protocol)

    D. UDP (User Datagram Protocol)

    E. CARP (Cache Array Routing Protocol)

    Answer: E. Microsoft Proxy Server is delivered as a stand-alone product that does not communicate with other servers unless configured in an upstream/downstream array configuration. While in an array configuration, the Microsoft Proxy Server will use the CARP protocol to allow servers in an array to communicate with each other. You may be able to reach and use answers C and D stating that the proxy server can be set to talk as a server or workstation to another system. However, this is not a proxy-to-proxy communications service, although Microsoft Proxy Server communicates directly using TCP and UDP. RIP is only used on routers, and if your proxy server follows recommendations, no routing is enabled. Finally, PSIP is a fake protocol.

7. Which of the following are problems when working with an array?

    A. Multiple administrators making changes

    B. Number of array members

C. Array members not communicating with each other

D. Proxy server's video can't display all requests

E. None of the above

Answer: A, B, and C. Microsoft Proxy Server may experience problems when multiple administrators are making changes. As an administrator, you may have to accept changes before implementing any of your own. Also, when too many systems are configured in an array, more time is spent searching for information on other systems than if the request was simply sent to the Internet. Finally, if traffic is extremely bad on a network, it is possible that the proxy servers may have difficulty communicating with each, resulting in uneven loads.

8. What options are available when working with arrays?

A. Leave array

B. Join array

C. Synchronize configuration of array members

D. Remove from array

E. None of the above

Answer: A, B, C, and D. When working with arrays, an administrator can join an array (or if one doesn't already exist, create it), remove other servers from the array list, and leave the array itself. Furthermore, the array can be configured to synchronize with other array members.

9. Resolving requests within an array is slower than attempting an upstream Internet connection. True or false? Explain.

Answer: This answer can go either way. If the array contains the information, then the array is 90% faster. However, if the information is not on the array and there are many array members, it is quicker to simply retrieve the information directly. The resolution time on a 20-system array can be quite lengthy.

10. Chaining Microsoft Proxy Server with other proxy servers such as on a UNIX system optimizes the network. True or false? Explain.

Answer: False. Although there may be situations where a UNIX system processes data faster, Microsoft does not recommend this configuration. However, that is not to say that it can't be done. Depending on how brave an administrator feels, the attempt can be made.

11. If you are running three proxy servers in an array, how must you configure the DNS entry for the proxy server array?

A. An MX record must be created for each proxy server.

B. Each computer must have a separate DNS record created.

C. A DNS record that points only to one of the proxy servers must be created.

D. Nothing should be done.

Answer: B. Although an array provides automatic load balancing, you should have an external load balance mechanism for those clients that do not support the automatic load balancing functions. For example, if all systems pointed to a single proxy server in the array, all systems will download the load balancing JavaScript from the server creating a load that is not properly balanced. As with other multiple proxy servers, you should use the round-robin approach for balancing.

12. Your network has grown to 10 departmental LANs. On your main back bone connecting all the departmental LANs together, you have a proxy server that provides Internet access. However, as your LANs have grown, you have noticed a degradation in service to the Internet. What should you do to decrease the amount of network traffic on the back bone LAN?

   A. Disable caching on the proxy server.

   B. Install a proxy server on each departmental LAN.

   C. Install 10 proxy servers on the back bone LAN.

   D. Use on-demand dialing on the proxy server computer.

   Answer: B. By placing a proxy server in each department, a number of requests can be answered by the local cache rather than having to have all of the traffic sent across the back bone. None of the other answers will reduce traffic in this capacity.

13. Your network has grown to 10 departmental LANs. The network uses an array of three proxy server computers located on the back bone LAN to provide Internet access to all the users. How should you configure caching to reduce the network traffic generated between a departmental LAN and the back bone LAN?

   A. Configure the array to use hierarchical caching rather than distributed caching.

   B. Configure the array to use distributed caching instead of hierarchical caching.

   C. Install a second array of three proxy servers.

   D. Install a proxy server on each departmental LAN, and configure them to use the proxy server array on the back bone.

   E. Increase the size of the Web Proxy cache on each proxy server in the array.

   Answer: D. By placing a proxy server in each department, a number of requests could be answered by the local cache rather that having to have the entire amount of traffic set across the back bone. When working with an array, you are already working in a distributed cache environment. Once you install a proxy server in each department, you will have a hierarchical cache design since you will chain the systems together. Installing a second array will not reduce traffic on the back bone nor will increasing the cache of the array.

14. When using the Microsoft Windows NT remote console to remotely administer your proxy server, how do you back up the configuration on your proxy server?

A. Use the Internet Service Manager.

B. Use the HTML-based administration tool.

C. Use the WspProto command-line utility.

D. Use the RemotMsp command-line utility.

Answer: D. The RemotMsp command-line utility is used for remote administration of a proxy server. When used with the SAVE modifier, a backup of the configuration can be made. Note that the IIS Manager can also perform this function, but it has a higher overhead on a WAN and that is why the command-line utility is used. Also, the command-line utility allows for scripting, which can be done through the GUI interface. The HTML-based administration tool does not work with the proxy server, and the WspProto utility is used to control the WinSock Proxy protocols remotely.

15. You have an array of six proxy servers to handle 4,000 clients on your network. However, the Web browsers used on the client computers are incapable of automatically configuring themselves. What is the maximum number of hops that a Web browser will make to retrieve an object from the cache?

A. 2

B. 3

C. 4

D. 5

Answer: A. In the event that clients cannot auto-configure themselves, they will send a request to the proxy server that they are configured to use (hop 1), and it will redirect its request to the proxy server with the object stored in its cache (hop 2).

Chapter 10

1. What are the two type of adapters that can be used with RAS?

Answer: The two types of adapters that may be used with RAS are a modem and an ISDN adapter.

2. Discuss how connecting with RAS differs from using a connection established with PC Anywhere, Timbuktu, Reach Out, etc.

Answer: RAS is designed to allow a client workstation to act as a part of the network as if it were connected directly. PC Anywhere, Timbuktu, Reach Out, and the like are typically designed for remote control of a system that is already on the network.

3. Why is RAS dial-in (server) mode not recommended for use with Proxy Server? What problems might you have when configuring RAS to allow access to the entire network?

   Answer: When using RAS in dial-in (server) mode, the Proxy Server would be sharing its adapter and preventing users from connecting to the Internet (since the line is in use). Also, if configured with multiple adapters where the proxy line to the Internet is not used, the client workstation can only communicate with the proxy server machine. Enabling access to the entire network would enable IP forwarding that compromises NT security. Finally, the additional overhead and potential problems with login credentials may create further problems.

4. Why is PPTP filter typically not used with Microsoft Proxy Server?

   Answer: When PPTP filtering is enabled, no other packets are processed.

5. When Proxy Server is configured in a dialup network, in what ways are users limited in access?

   Answer: In a dialup configuration, users are directly limited by the dialup hours set in the Auto Dial utility. A further limitation is the lack of bandwidth that is typically associated with dialup networking.

6. What is the name of the Auto Dial utility?

   A. AUTOCFG.EXE

   B. DIALER.EXE

   C. WINDIAL.EXE

   D. PRXDIAL.EXE

   E. ADIALCFG.EXE

   Answer: E. The name of the Auto Dial utility is ADIALCFG.EXE.

7. After installing auto dialer, what servers need to be restarted?

   A. WWW service

   B. Browser service

   C. WinSock Proxy service

   D. Web Proxy service

   E. Domain Name service

   Answer: A, C, and D. The WWW, WinSock, and Web Proxy services must all be restarted after the first time auto dialing is configured. You must also restart these services after clearing the entries on the auto dialer.

8. What utility is used to schedule dialing hours of operation?

   A. ADIALCFG.EXE

   B. IISMGR.EXE

C. PRXYTIME.EXE

D. W3DLTM.EXE

E. WINSOCK.DLL

Answer: A, The Auto Dial utility, ADIALCFG.EXE, is used to schedule dialing hours of operations.

9. You want to set up your proxy server by using a dial-up connection to your already existing ISP. You create a Dial-Up Networking phonebook entry for the dial-up account. What else must you do?

A. Configure the Auto Dial utility and enable dialing for the Web Proxy backup route.

B. Include the assigned IP address in the LOCALLAT.TXT file on the client computers.

C. Include the entire dial-up IP address pool from the ISP in the LAT.

D. Configure Auto Dial and specify which phonebook entry and credentials to use to connect to the ISP.

Answer: D. After you have created a Dial-Up Networking phonebook entry for a dialup account, you must specify in the auto dialer to use that phonebook entry and provide a set of credentials (name and password) to access the ISP.

10. The system containing Microsoft Proxy Server cannot service RAS dial-in users. True or False?

Answer: False. Microsoft Proxy Server can service RAS users; however, there are a number of issues involved that may cause problems for RAS dial-in, Proxy Server, or both.

11. PPTP should be installed on the Proxy Server to secure Internet access. True or False?

Answer: False. It is not recommended that you install PPTP on the Proxy Server. Typically, PPTP is used to link wide area networks through the Internet. The problem is that when you're securing the environment with PPTP filtering, all non-PPTP packets are ignored.

12. You want to set up your proxy server by using a dialup connection to your already existing ISP. You need to provide a valid user name and password for the ISP account. What should you do?

A. Configure the Auto Dial in the Proxy Server services by specifying the phonebook entry and the corresponding ISP account credentials.

B. Manually dial in to the ISP by using Dial-Up Networking, and provide a valid user name and password for the ISP account.

C. Configure the Auto Dial in the Proxy Server services by specifying the phonebook entry and the Proxy Server Administrator account and password.

D. No action is necessary, the proxy server will log in to the ISP by using a built-in account.

Answer: A. After you have created a Dial-Up Networking phonebook entry for a dialup account, you must specify in the auto dialer to use that phonebook entry and provide a set of credentials (name and password) to access the ISP.

13. You have a proxy server with one NIC card and a modem with RAS installed. What should you do to minimize the risk of unauthorized access to your Intranet? Choose All That Apply.

    A. Disable IP forwarding.

    B. Disable the WINS client on the dialup adapter.

    C. Add the dialup network adapter's IP address to the LAT.

    D. Install PPTP.

    E. Add a packet filter for DNS lookup.

    Answer: A and B. To secure the internal environment from outside attack, you should disable IP forwarding and the WINS client on the dialup adapter. By disabling IP forwarding, users will not be able to bypass the proxy server from either side. Next, to keep Internet users from seeing any NetBIOS name information, disable the WINS client.

14. You want your proxy server to use on-demand dialing to access the Internet whenever a client request is received. What should you do?

    A. Dial in to your ISP by using Dial-Up Networking and maintain the connection for as long as necessary.

    B. Add the dynamically-assigned IP address to the LOCALLAT.TXT file on each workstation.

    C. Add the dynamically-assigned IP address to the MSPLAT.TXT file on the Proxy Server.

    D. Configure Auto Dial on the Proxy Server services by specifying the phonebook entry and the corresponding ISP account credentials.

    Answer: D. In the Auto Dial utility that ships with Proxy Server, you have the option to configure auto dialing whenever a client request is received. Simply specify the phonebook entry and the corresponding ISP account credentials. You may also select which proxy servers can use the Auto Dial utility.

15. Which Proxy Server service(s) can use on-demand dialing to access the Internet?

    A. Web Proxy

    B. WinSock Proxy

    C. Both Web Proxy and WinSock Proxy, but not Socks Proxy

    D. Web Proxy, WinSock Proxy, and Socks Proxy

    Answer: D. All three proxy services (Web, WinSock, and Socks) can use the on-demand dialing service to access the Internet.

Chapter 11

1. Discuss the five key components that can bottleneck a proxy server.

Answer: The five key components that can bottleneck a proxy server are the CPU, drive, memory, cache, and network. A slow CPU will tend to be unable to keep up with requests at the server itself. This is often the case if too many servers are run from any one unit. If cache memory is too low, the proxy server will download more information than is necessary from the Internet. This means that users will observe the download time rather than just the time associated with requesting the data from the proxy server. If a large cache is used but the drive is too slow, this too may affect performance. Finally, the communications media between nodes may bottleneck the server, depending on its utilization.

2. Explain how Performance Monitor operates as opposed to the Event Viewer.

Answer: Performance Monitor provides an immediate report and state of events as requested by an administrator. For example, if an administrator wanted to know the number of users who connected to the proxy server's FTP, Gopher, or WWW services, they could be viewed through the Performance Monitor graph. The Event Viewer simply reports occurrences that take place on the server. Typically, events are error-based. However, they may be informational. Event Viewer items are listed and stored in a system, application, or security log, depending on the type of occurrence that has taken place.

3. What are the three counter groups that Microsoft Proxy Server provides to integrate with Performance Monitor?

Answer: The three counter groups that Microsoft Proxy Server provides to integrate with Performance Monitor are the Web Proxy Server Cache, the Web Proxy Server, and the WinSock Proxy Server.

4. Describe how Diskperf operates with Performance Monitor. Does it add any overhead to the system?

Answer: The Diskperf command is used to enable and disable the monitor probe for a system's hard drive. While enabled, Performance Monitor can be used to view disk I/O activities. Since the hard drive is being monitored and data is being filtered, there is a slight amount of overhead that may be noticed while using the system.

5. Explain the connections between SNMP and Microsoft Proxy Server.

Answer: SNMP is a network management protocol that can be used in conjunction with third-party monitoring software, such as HP's Openview or IBM's Netview. Through these management utilities an administrator can automate some of the management so there is an automatic review of items reported back from the SNMP's MIB. The MIB is a listing of items that are reported to the SNMP Manager. Before SNMP can be used with Microsoft Proxy, the files must be copied from the CD-ROM, then compiled. Both the proxy services must be running. The SNMP service must be added from the network services and then loaded. Once complete, SNMP activities may take place.

6. Which of the following items could create a bottleneck for the proxy server?

A. Video monitor type

B. Video adapter speed

C. System power supply

D. Hard drive transfer speed

E. None of the above

Answer: D. The only possible bottleneck to a proxy server in the listed items above is the hard drive, and that would only be true if you were using a larger cache and there were delays in transferring data. None of the other items are issues.

7. While using Microsoft Proxy Server, which items can be affected by a slow network?

A. Data transmission rates

B. Number of users that can use the proxy server at a time

C. Access to specific sites

D. Hard drive transfer speed

E. None of the above

Answer: A and B. If the network speed is slow, obviously your will have lower data transmission rates. Your network speed can also define the number of users that can access the server. Although you could continue to add users until the cows come home, you will find that with the low throughput it is not very effective.

8. What items can be affected by too small of a Web Proxy Server cache?

A. Data transmission rates

B. Number of users that can use the proxy server at a time

C. Access to specific sites

D. Hard drive transfer speed

E. None of the above

Answer: A and B. If the cache is too small, users will tend to see lower data transmission rates. Remember that the cache increase affects user data transmissions. Also, since the cache size must be adjusted according to the number of users on your system, too small of a cache could also limit the number of users on a system. The only way specific sites would be limited is if they were cached and then were unavailable. That is stretching for an answer and should not be considered correct. Also, a cache does affect the hard drive transfer speed; however, it is not the Web Proxy Server's cache.

9. Microsoft Proxy Server automatically adjusts itself by fine tuning its internally controlled switches. True or False? Explain.

   Answer: False. In fact, it's a personal gripe of ours that the server does not contain an option to automatically control and optimize resources. The closest Proxy Server comes to optimizing itself is its active cache system. However, that is not truly an internal switch. It would be better if it could have automatically adjusted its run time priority, adjusted the cache as needed, delayed or disabled unnecessary services, cleared memory, and so forth.

10. Enabling SMNP on a unsecured gateway could potentially allow your network routing information to be seen from the Internet. True or False? Explain.

    Answer: True. When traffic is inbound from the Internet, an administrator should always be wary of the problems that traffic may introduce to the network. In this case, SNMP could be a potential problem.

11. You want to build a new proxy server, but you want to keep the configuration changes you made on the old proxy server. How should you do this? Choose all that apply.

    A. Copy the WSPCFG.INI file to the new computer.

    B. Copy the MSPCFG.INI file to the new computer.

    C. On the Service tab of the Web Proxy service Properties dialog box of the current Proxy Server, click the Server Backup command buttons.

    D. On the Service tab of the Web Proxy service Properties dialog box of the new computer, click the Local Address Table command button.

    E. On the Service tab of the Web Proxy service Properties dialog box of the new computer, click the Server Restore command button.

    Answer: C and E. Performing a backup, then copying the backup file to the new server and restoring it will create a duplicate server.

12. When looking at the proxy logs, you notice that 30% of all users are accessing `www.work-related.com`. You want to decrease the network traffic and ensure that Web pages from this site are still cached. What should you do?

    A. Disable caching.

    B. Enable active caching and then select the Fewer Network Accesses Are More Important (Less Pre-Fetching) option button.

    C. Set the cache expiration policy to Updates Are More Important (More Update Checks).

    D. Create a cache filter for the `www.work-related.com` domain and set the Filtering Status option to Always Cache.

    Answer: D. Since you know that 30% of all your traffic is accessing a given site, you should create a filtering option to always cache this site. In this way, the majority of the requests to this site can be answered locally rather than directly from the site itself. This will reduce traffic.

13. You want to check performance on your IDE drive. You open Microsoft Performance Monitor and add the % Disk Time counter from the PhysicalDisk object to examine the time spent reading and writing files to disk. However, no activity is shown for the % Disk Time counter. What must you do to monitor disk activity through the Performance Monitor? Choose all that apply.

   A. Run the Diskperf command.

   B. Restart the Web Proxy service.

   C. Restart the Proxy Server computer.

   D. View the % Disk Time counter from another computer on the network.

   E. Replace the IDE drive with an SCSI.

   Answer: A and C. Before you can monitor disk activity, you must run the Diskperf command and reboot the computer. Note that this command is not automatically enabled since it creates a draw on the resource.

14. In the Web Proxy Service Properties dialog box you select Enable Caching and Use Fewer Network Accesses Are More Important (More Cache Hits), and you also select Enable Active Caching and Use Faster User Response Is More Important (More Pre-Fetching). How does this configuration affect the cache?

   A. The pages have a maximum TTL with the largest percentage of popular cached objects updated.

   B. The pages have a minimum TTL with the smallest percentage of popular cached objects updated.

   C. The pages have a minimum TTL with the largest percentage of popular cached objects updated.

   D. The pages have a maximum TTL with the smallest percentage of popular cached objects updated.

   Answer: A. The setting of More Cache Hits will cause objects in the cache to have the maximum available TTL. This means that a cached object will be available on the proxy server for a longer period of time. The setting of More Pre-Fetching will cause a larger percentage of popular cached objects to be updated.

Chapter 12

1. When researching a client problem, where should you begin? What are the most likely problems the client experiences?

   Answer: When researching a client problem, you should begin by identifying the service that is experiencing the problem, then determining if the problem is originating from the client or the server. Most client problems are related to misconfigurations, incorrect LATs, and problems with third-party stacks.

2. What are some of the sources for information when researching a problem?

Answer: There are a number of places where an administrator can find information. The first place to look is in the product documentation. Other resources include Microsoft TechNet, the Microsoft Network, CompuServe, user groups, Microsoft's Download BBS, and the Internet.

3. Some settings cannot be configured through the IIS Manager. Where can these items be set? How do you set them?

Answer: Items that require advanced configuration may need to have values manually added to the Registry. The most common method is to use the Registry editor (Regedit or Regedt32) to manually type in the settings. There may also be hot fixes and program patches available that accomplish the customization for you.

4. What are the differences between Regedit and Regedt32?

Answer: The Registry can be modified with any number of tools. Regedit and Regedt32 both ship with Windows NT. The primary difference between the two is that Regedit is designed to work with the entire Registry and search all of its items. Regedt32 is used usually with specific keys and only to search for a key, not data or anything else. Regedt32, unlike Regedit, has the ability to assign permissions.

5. Suppose that you recently modified your network, changing the location of the Proxy Server and adding subnetworks. What should you do to the Proxy Server? What about the clients?

Answer: On the Proxy Server, you should update the LAT to reflect your current network environment. There are not many other configuration changes you should make to the Proxy Server; however, if the client setup program refers to the Proxy Server by IP address, you should update the appropriate .INI files as required. Also, you will need to verify that the WINS and DNS servers both have proper identification information for resolving the server's name. Typically, it is a good idea to circulate this information regarding a server to all in an MIS department. The client may or may not require updates. If the Proxy Server is addressed by IP address, you will need to update this information on the client. By default, the proxy client will check with the server for updated configuration information, including the LAT, every six hours. However, to use the system immediately, you will need to click the Update button in the WinSock Proxy client configuration in the Control Panel.

6. Which of the following utilities should be used to check a WinSock client's configuration?

A. CHKWSP16.EXE

B. CHKDSK16.EXE

C. CHKWSP32.EXE

D. CHKPROXY.EXE

E. None of the above

Answer: A and C. CHKWSP16.EXE is used to verify the WinSock Proxy installation on 16-bit operating systems, and CHKWSP32.EXE is used for 32-bit systems.

7. On which platforms does Microsoft Proxy Server support IPX?

A. Windows NT

B. Windows 3.11

C. UNIX

D. DOS

E. Windows 95

Answer: A and E. This is a significant shortcoming of Microsoft Proxy Server. The typical 16-bit audience (Windows for Workgroups) that is commonly working on the NetWare platform is not supported. WinSock Proxy supports IPX only for Windows 95 and Windows NT.

8. It is important to memorize all problems and issues on Microsoft Proxy Server so that you may find problems quickly. True or False?

Answer: False. In this chapter, we listed the errors only to provide insight into Proxy Server's operations. One of the quickest ways to fix faults is to avoid them in the first place by being aware of common problems.

9. Regardless of the LAT configuration, a client should be able to operate with any local WinSock application. True or False?

Answer: False. The table determines which systems are local and which are remote. If the system has the WinSock Proxy client turned off, this does not matter. However, in the case of using the WinSock Proxy client, it does.

10. You need name resolution on your local network, so you install a DNS server. You already have a proxy server that uses a DNS server on the Internet. When trying to resolve a WinSock name on the local network, you receive the error "Host Not Found." The IP address of the destination computer you are trying to resolve is on the LAT. What should you do?

A. Add the host name to the LACLLAT.TXT file on the client computer.

B. Add the host name to the MSPLAT.TXT file on the Proxy Server.

C. Point all clients to the new DNS server.

D. Add the address of the new DNS server to the Proxy Server.

Answer: D. This problem is clearly associated with name resolution. Name resolution is performed by the proxy server. The entry for the DNS must be added at the server.

11. You have installed a proxy server on your network with one NIC card going to your local network and one NIC card going to the Internet. However, you have received an error stating that the user name of your proxy server is already in use. You check all the computers and don't find a duplicate name. What is most likely the problem?

A. The same IP address is assigned to both network adapters.

B. NetBEUI is bound to both network adapters.

C. Each network adapter has a different host name.

D. Both adapters have the same hardware address.

Answer: B. A small bug in multi-homed systems in that they can have problems when a NetBIOS name is bound to more than one network adapter. The first driver to load and have the name bound works fine. However, the second adapter that attempts to bind will receive an error message regarding a duplicate name.

12. You have installed a proxy server, but you did not provide a default gateway address on your external NIC card. What happens when a user tries to request an object from the Internet?

   A. It retrieves it from the Web Proxy cache.

   B. The object is retrieved from the Internet site.

   C. The requested object is retrieved from a host computer on the intranet, regardless of whether the object is in the Web Proxy cache.

   D. The request fails, regardless of whether the object is in the Web Proxy cache.

   Answer: D. When a network adapter does not have a default gateway, the request will fail to be forwarded to its proper destination. Since the resource is on the Internet, there is no way that the request can be filled from the intranet. Also, if the gateway is missing, there is no way that the data could have been in the cache. If no default gateway was specified, but the ISP provides some type of DHCP mechanism, then the gateway would be filled and the object would have been retrieved from the Internet. However, since this is not mentioned and the question refers to the network card rather than the modem, DHCP is very unlikely.

13. Your clients are configured with the WinSock Proxy service, and the Web browsers are configured to use the Web Proxy service. You configure the LOCALLAT.TXT file to contain the IP address 192.168.10.6, which is the IP address of a Web server on the intranet and is not configured in your LAT. When you try to access a site, what happens?

   A. The Web browser uses the Web Proxy service to access the Internet.

   B. The Web browser uses the Web Proxy service to access the intranet.

   C. The Web Browser uses the WinSock Proxy service to access the Internet.

   D. The Web Browser uses the WinSock Proxy service to access the intranet.

   Answer: B. The Web browser will use the Web Proxy service to access the intranet. There are two key give-aways to this question. First, if the Web browser is configured to use the Web Proxy service, the Web Proxy service will be used regardless. Second, if the request is to a private IP address range, such as 192.168.10.x, the Internet will not route the request and the Web Proxy will locate the request internally. If a client is configured not to use the Web Proxy of the local Web server, then the request could be sent directly.

14. You have two internal Web servers, one for Marketing and one for Shipping. All clients use these two Web servers by using the Web Proxy service. DNS is used for name resolution. You switch the IP addresses of the Web servers and now both departments report that the Shipping department is displaying the pages from the Marketing department. What is most likely the problem?

    A. The Web Proxy service is caching Web pages from both Web servers.

    B. The Web Proxy service is caching DNS entries.

    C. The client computers are caching Web pages from both Web servers.

    D. No domain filters are configured.

    Answer: B. The problem with this situation is that the proxy server will cache DNS entries. If you review the Proxy Server counters you will see a share regarding caching DNS entries.

15. Your UNIX computer works fine when using the Web Proxy service, but RealAudio does not work. What is most likely the problem?

    A. The Web Proxy service does not support the RealAudio protocol.

    B. The SERVICES file on the UNIX computer is not configured to use RealAudio.

    C. The Web browser is not configured to use the Proxy Server services for RealAudio.

    D. The client computer has been denied access to the RealAudio protocol in the WinSock Proxy service.

    Answer: A. The Web Proxy service does not support the RealAudio protocol. The RealAudio protocol is only supported under the WinSock Proxy service. UNIX systems do not use the WinSock Proxy service. A UNIX system could only use this protocol under a TCP connection, not its default UDP.

Chapter 13

1. How many proxy servers should you install if your company standard is Pentium 16MHz computers and you have 500 clients?

    A. 1

    B. 2

    C. 3

    D. 4

    Answer: A. One proxy computer should be acceptable from 500 clients (a small environment). Remember that this value is based on the recommendations chart; however, this may change according to users' usage of the Internet.

2. Which service will improve performance on your client computers when all clients need to FTP files from a remote location many times per day?

   A. WinSock

   B. Web Proxy

   C. Socks

   D. FTP

   Answer: B. Due to its caching capabilities, the Web Proxy service will increase performance for files that are sent via FTP multiple times a day. Since none of the other protocols offer caching, they will not improve performance.

3. You have created an array of proxy servers to service your 6000 clients. What is the minimum amount of memory you should install in each array?

   A. 32MB

   B. 64MB

   C. 96MB

   D. 128MB

   Answer: D. The starting memory requirement should be approximately 128MB of RAM. Remember that this value is based on the recommendations chart; however, this may change according to users' usage of the Internet.

4. You manage a corporate network that also has two branch offices with 56k connections. How should you configure your proxy server to maximize performance of all the computers in the remote offices?

   A. Install one proxy server at the corporate office.

   B. Install a proxy server at each remote location only.

   C. At each remote location, install a proxy server connected directly with the Internet.

   D. At each remote office, install a proxy server computer that is chained to the proxy server computer at the central office.

   Answer: D. By installing a proxy server at each of the branch offices, you will benefit from the caching abilities of the Web Proxy. These remote offices should then be chained to the central office. In answer A, there is no benefit from caching across the slow link to the central office, and answers B and C do not provide connectivity for the central office.

5. You have 400 users and two T1 lines on your network. How should you balance the requests from client computers?

   A. Create an array with two proxy servers, and connect one T1 line to each proxy server.

   B. Connect both T1 lines to one proxy server.

   C. Create a chain of two proxy servers, and connect one T1 line to each server.

   D. Create a chain of two proxy servers, and connect both T1 lines to one of the servers.

   Answer: A. By creating an array, you can balance requests between the two T1 lines. By connecting them to two different systems, you will have fault tolerance in case of failure. The problem with answer B is the lack of load balancing and fault tolerance. The problem with answers C and D is that a chain is not a load balancing mechanism. Again, in answer D, you see that there is no fault tolerance.

6. How can you register a domain name?

   Answer: Either request that the ISP register the name or do so yourself directly at RS.INTERNIC.NET. Typically, you should do this yourself to control ownership.

7. What types of network connections can be used to link to the Internet?

   Answer: Virtually any connection technology can be used to connect to the Internet. In this chapter, we discussed dialup modems, ISDN, frame relay, and leased lines.

8. What hardware should you use for your current company?

   Answer: Answers will vary.

9. What are some of the concerns regarding the selection of an ISP?

   Answer: When selecting an ISP, you want to verify that they have an adequate link to the Internet to support your organization in its current and future states. Remember that the fastest link to an Internet resource is only as good as the slowest connection in the channel.

10. In what ways does a large network differ from a small network?

    Answer: Because of the diversity of networks, answers will vary. In short, a small network tends to be of only a single protocol and one type of network. Larger networks are usually established in multiple locations comprised of everything under the sun.

APPENDIX

B

Glossary

Abstract Syntax Representation, Revision #1 (ASN.1)   A description of a data structure that is independent of machine-oriented structures and encodings.

Access Control Entry (ACE)   A configuration component of the Access Control List which is added to designate user or group access to a resource.

Access Control List (ACL)   This list contains security assignments to resources. Access control lists are commonly associated with NTFS-formatted drives.

ACE   *See* Access Control Entry (ACE).

ACL   *See* Access Control List (ACL).

Active Caching   An ability of Microsoft Proxy Server that allows popular sites to be updated in the cache while system utilization is low. *See also* Fresh Data, Stale Data.

Address   In TCP/IP, an IP address is a 32-bit numeric identifier assigned to a node (or user). The address has two parts: one for the network identifier and the other for the node identifier. All nodes on the same network must share the network address and have a unique node address. For networks connected to the Internet, network addresses are assigned by the Internet Activities Board (IAB). Addresses also include IPX addresses—the internal network number and external network number—and the Media Access Control (MAC) address assigned to each network card or device.

Address Resolution Protocol (ARP)   This is the translation protocol that translates IP addresses into hardware addresses.

Advanced Research Projects Agency Network (ARPANET)   A packet-switched network developed in the early 1970s, ARPANET is the "father" of today's Internet. ARPANET was decommissioned in June 1990.

Agents   In the client/server model, the part of the system that performs information preparation and exchange on behalf of a client or server application.

American National Standards Institute (ANSI)   A nonprofit organization responsible for the American Standard Code for Information Interchange (ASCII) code set, as well as numerous other voluntary standards.

Annotation File   A file containing a list of files in a directory on an FTP server. This file is displayed automatically when a browser opens the directory.

Anonymous Logon   A feature in which Internet resources allow accounts to anonymously access a site. Typically, the account is assigned to guest access or to those applied to the IUSR_*systemname* account. Web browsers access these sites without providing a user name or password. FTP clients type **Anonymous** for the user name and enter their e-mail address (which can be any address, even a fictitious one) for their password. Anonymous logon is an option of Internet Information Server (IIS) services.

ANSI *See* American National Standards Institute (ANSI).

API *See* Application Program Interface (API).

Application Layer The layer of the OSI model that interfaces with user mode applications by providing high-level network services based on lower-level network layers. Network file systems like Named Pipes are an example of application layer software. *See also* Named Pipes, Open System Interconnection (OSI).

Application Program Interface (API) A set of routines that an application program uses to request and carry out lower-layer services performed by the operating system.

Archie A program that helps Internet users find files. Participating Internet host computers download a listing of their files to Archie servers, which index these files. Users can then search this index and transfer these files using FTP. Archie functions as an archive search utility, hence its name.

ARP *See* Address Resolution Protocol (ARP).

ARPANET *See* Advanced Research Projects Agency Network (ARPANET).

ASN.I *See* Abstract Syntax Representation, Revision #1 (ASN.1).

Associating The connection of a file name extension to an application. For example, .DOC is associated with Microsoft Word or WordPad. Also known as File Name Extension Mapping.

Asynchronous Data Transmission A type of communication that sends data using flow control rather than a clock to synchronize data between the source and the destination.

Authentication A process in which user access is authorized and verified.

Autonomous System Internet TCP/IP terminology for a collection of gateways (routers) that fall under one administrative entity and cooperate using a common Interior Gateway Protocol (IGP).

Backup Domain Controller (BDC) A server that has been configured to validate user credentials and replicate the master database from the Primary Domain Controller. The server can only be set as a domain controller during initial installation. It is also the database that contains user accounts and assigned rights. *See also* Member Server, Primary Domain Controller (PDC).

Bandwidth In network communications, this is the amount of data that can be sent across a wire in a given time. Each piece of that passes along the wire decreases the amount of available bandwidth.

Bandwidth Control The limiting of data to a maximum speed such that a portion can be reserved for another service (or services) such as FTP, WWW, e-mail, etc.

Basic, Clear-Text Authentication A non-encrypted authentication that is commonly supported by most Web browsers and operating systems. This is most commonly used to access a secure Web site or file transfer area.

Batch Program   An ASCII file that contains one or more Windows NT commands. A batch program's file name typically has a .BAT or .CMD extension. When you type the file name at the command prompt, the commands are processed sequentially.

BDC   *See* Backup Domain Controller (BDC).

Binary   The numbering system used in computer memory and in digital communication. All characters are represented as a series of 1s and 0s. For example, the letter *A* might be represented as 01000001.

Binding   A process that establishes the initial communication channel between the protocol driver and the network adapter card driver.

Bits   In binary data, each unit of data is a bit. Each bit is represented by either 0 or 1, and is stored in memory as an ON or OFF state.

Bits Per Second (BPS)   The number of bits that are transferred between two systems in one second.

Boot Partition   The volume, formatted for either an NTFS, FAT, or HPFS file system, that contains the Windows NT operating system's files. Windows NT automatically creates the correct configuration and checks this information whenever you start your system.

BootP   An early method of assigning IP addresses to a client. While the protocol support is still used on most routers, BootP has been replaced with DHCP.

BPS   *See* Bits Per Second (BPS).

Bridge   A device that connects two segments of a network and sends data to one or the other based on a set of criteria.

Browser   A computer on a Microsoft network that maintains a list of computers and services available on the network. The term browser is also commonly used as a short description of a Web browser, which is an application that is used to navigate and access information on either the Internet or an intranet.

Browsing   The process of requesting the list of computers and services on a network from a browser.

Buffer   A reserved portion of memory in which data is temporarily held pending an opportunity to complete its transfer to or from a storage device or another location in memory.

C2-Compliant   A U.S. government standard that is granted to systems meeting high security requirements.

Cache   A mechanism by which a faster mode is used for commonly accessed data. As applied to Microsoft Proxy Server, a cache stores Web data at the proxy server so that when clients request the data, they are given the cached information, thereby providing them with the information more quickly and saving bandwidth. Web browsers also use caching locally.

Cache Array Routing Protocol (CARP) Microsoft's method for routing requests and resolving data within an array. A hashing algorithm is used to determine a request's path.

Cache Consistency The accuracy of cached material with respect to the source. *See also* Intelligent TTL (Time-To-Live), Object Modification Checking.

CARP *See* Cache Array Routing Protocol (CARP).

Carrier Sense, Multiple Access with Collision Detect (CSMA/CD) Different devices on a network may try to communicate at any one time, so access methods need to be established. Using the CSMA/CD access method, a device first checks that the cable is free from other carriers and then transmits, while continuing to monitor the presence of another carrier. If a collision is detected, the device stops transmitting and tries later. In a CSMA/CD network, all stations have the ability to sense traffic on the network.

CCITT *See* Consultative Committee on International Telegraphy and Telephony (CCITT).

CERN Compatibility A *de facto* industry standard for applications that are proxy server–aware and ready. These applications do not require anything external to operate with a proxy server. CERN-compatible applications include Web browsers, the RealAudio Player, and other applications. The CERN standards are established by the *Conseil Europeén pour la Recherche Nucléaire* (the European Laboratory for Particle Physics), located in Switzerland.

CGI *See* Common Gateway Interface (CGI).

Challenge/Response Authentication *See* Windows NT Challenge/Response Authentication.

Checksum A number that is calculated based on the values of a block of data. Checksums are used in communication to ensure that the correct data is received.

Circuit Switching A type of communication system that establishes a connection, or circuit, between the two devices before communicating and does not disconnect until all data is sent.

Client Any device that attaches to the network server. A workstation is the most common type of client. Clients run client software to provide network access. A piece of software which accesses data on a server can also be called a client.

Client/Server Network This is a server-centric network in which some network resources are stored on a file server while processing power is distributed among workstations and the file server.

Coaxial Cable This is one of the types of cable used in network wiring. Typical coax types include RG-58 and RG-62. The 10Base2 system of Ethernet networking uses coaxial cable. Coaxial cable is usually shielded. The Thicknet system uses a thicker coaxial cable.

Commit Rate A performance counter that identifies the speed that objects or URLs are added to the cache.

Common Gateway Interface (CGI) An interface used by applications or scripts that runs on a Web server when requested by a client.

Communication Protocol   For computers engaged in telecommunications, the protocol (i.e., the settings and standards) must be the same for both devices when receiving and transmitting information. A communications program can be used to ensure that the baud rate, duplex, parity, data bits, and stop bits are correctly set.

Computer + Science Network (CSNET)   A large computer network that is used mostly in the U.S. but that has international connections. CSNET sites include universities, research labs, and some commercial companies. CSNET is now merged with BITNET to form CREN.

Connected Service   Used to describe a stream or a connection-oriented protocol such as TCP or SPX. A connected service offers data integrity checking, packet sequencing, and error correction.

Connection-Oriented   The model of interconnection in which communication precedes through three well-defined phases: connection establishment, data transfer, and connection release. Examples of connection-oriented communication include X.25, Internet TCP, OSI TP4, and registered letters.

Connectionless   The model of interconnection in which communication takes place without first establishing a connection. This is sometimes called datagram. Examples include LANs, Internet IP, OSI, CLNP, UDP, and ordinary postcards.

Connectionless Service   A service which offers no reliability, sequencing, or acknowledgment capabilities. This service is typically used in broadcasting information, such as audio information. Because data is unacknowledged and not sequenced, the service generally offers higher speed as a trade-off. *See also* User Datagram Protocol (UDP).

Consultative Committee on International Telegraphy and Telephony (CCITT)   A committee sponsored by the United Nations that defines network standards, including X.400 and X.500. This committee has been recently renamed to International Telecommunications Union/ Telecommunications Standardization Sector (ITU/TSS).

Control Panel   A Windows utility containing management tools.

Cookie   A piece of information that is delivered by a Web server for multiple reasons. Most implementation use cookies to identify a system. For example, your system can be identified uniquely for security purposes, such as to access a secured Web site. Also, when multiple connections are used to the same site, cookies are used to avoid counting a system twice when calculating connection limits.

CRC   *See* Cyclic Redundancy Checksum (CRC).

Cryptography   The science of encrypting of data such that it can not be decoded by an unauthorized recipient.

CSMA/CD   *See* Carrier Sense, Multiple Access with Collision Detect (CSMA/CD).

CSNET   *See* Computer + Science Network (CSNET).

Cyclic Redundancy Checksum (CRC)   A redundancy check in which the check key is generated by a cyclic algorithm. Also, a system check or error check performed at both the sending and receiving station after a block check character has been accumulated.

Daemon   A utility program that runs on a TCP/IP server. Daemon programs run in the background, performing services such as file transfers, printing, calculations, searching for information, and many other tasks. This is similar to a TSR program in DOS. Daemons are fully supported by UNIX.

DARPA   *See* Defense Advanced Research Projects Agency (DARPA).

Data Frames   These are logical, structured packets in which data can be placed. The Data Link layer packages raw bits from the Physical layer into data frames. The exact format of the frame used by the network depends on the topology.

Data Integrity   The quality of data as it pertains to its ability to remain intact when transmitted from its source. Frequently, data will become corrupt and lose its integrity while being delivered.

Data Link Layer   The OSI layer that is responsible for data transfer across a single physical connection, or a series of bridged connections, between two network entities.

Data Packet   A unit of data being sent over a network. A packet includes a header, addressing information, and the data itself. A packet is treated as a single unit as it is sent from device to device.

Data Source Name (DSN)   A name that specifies a connection to an ODBC data source/SQL database. In Windows NT and 95, the DSN may be configured through the control panel.

Data Transfer Rate   The data transfer rate determines how fast a drive or other peripheral can transfer data with its controller. The data transfer rate is a key measurement in determining drive performance.

Datagram   A packet of information and associated delivery information, such as the destination address, that is routed through a packet-switching network.

Dedicated Line   A transmission medium that is used exclusively between two locations. Dedicated lines are also known as leased lines or private lines. *See also* Leased Line.

Default Gateway   The IP address data is sent when the destination is not on the local network. The default gateway must be on the same network as the system that is sending data to it. This is usually the router interface.

Defense Advanced Research Projects Agency (DARPA)   This is the U.S. government agency that funded the ARPANET.

Device Driver   A piece of software that allows a workstation or server to communicate with a hardware device. For example, disk drivers are used to control disk drives, and network drivers are used to communicate with network boards.

DHCP *See* Dynamic Host Configuration Protocol (DHCP).

DLL *See* Dynamic Linked Library (DLL).

DNS *See* Domain Name System (DNS).

DNS Spoofing The assumption of a DNS name of another system by either corrupting a name-service cache or compromising a domain-name server for a valid domain.

DOD Networking Model DOD is the acronym for Department of Defense, the government agency that provided the original funding for the development of the TCP/IP protocol suite. The DOD networking model is a four-layer conceptual model describing how communications should take place between computer systems. The four layers are Process/Application, Host-to-Host, Internet, and Network Access.

Domain A logical grouping within a network for file servers managed as an integrated whole.

Domain Controller The primary server within a domain and primary storage point for domain-wide security information.

Domain Filtering Controlling access to specific Internet sites by denying or granting permission to access those sites by domain.

Domain Name The name by which a domain is known to the network.

Domain Name System (DNS) The distributed name and address mechanism used on the Internet.

DSN *See* Data Source Name (DSN)

Dumb Terminal A workstation consisting of keyboard and monitor, used to put data into the computer or receive information from the computer. Dumb terminals were originally developed to be connected to computers running a multi-user operating system so that users could communicate directly with them. All processing is done at and by the computer, not the dumb terminal. In contrast, a smart terminal contains processing circuits which can receive data from the host computer and later carry out independent processing operations.

Dynamic Host Configuration Protocol (DHCP) A method of automatically assigning IP addresses to client computers on a network.

Dynamic Linked Library (DLL) A DLL is a shared piece of code that is used by one or more applications. As a shared library, DLLs are used to repeat functions without repeating code. For example, a Windows developer will use the Microsoft DLL to draw a window rather than writing new code to do this.

EGP *See* Exterior Gateway Protocol (EGP).

Encryption   A method used to code data such that it can only be read by authorized systems.

Error Control   An arrangement that combines error detection and error correction.

Error Correction   A method used to correct erroneous data produced during data transmission, transfer, or storage.

Ethernet   The most popular Data Link layer standard for local area networking. Ethernet implements the carrier sense, multiple access with collision detection (CSMA/CD) method of arbitrating multiple computer access to the same network. This standard supports the use of Ethernet over any type of media, including wireless broadcast. Standard Ethernets operate at 10Mbps. Fast Ethernets operate at 100Mbps. *See also* Data Link Layer.

Exterior Gateway Protocol (EGP)   A reachability routing protocol used by gateways in a two-level Internet. EGP is used in the Internet core system.

FDDI   *See* Fiber Distributed Data Interface (FDDI).

Fiber Distributed Data Interface (FDDI)   A network specification that transmits information packets using light produced by a laser or light-emitting diode (LED). FDDI uses fiber-optic cable and equipment to transmit data packets. It has a data rate of up to 100Mbps and allows very long cable distances.

File Name Extension Mapping   The associating of a file name extension to an application. For example, .DOC is associated with Word for Windows or Word Pad.

File Transfer Protocol (FTP)   A TCP/IP protocol that permits the transfer of files between computer systems. Because FTP has been implemented on numerous types of computer systems, file transfers can be done between different computer systems (e.g., a personal computer and a minicomputer).

Filter   A feature that enables data to be processed selectively. As applied to Microsoft Proxy Server, there are packet filters, cache filters, and site filters. These filters are built on the ISAPI module.

Firewall   A system, or systems, that protect a network by maintaining a division where no direct access between two or more networks is established. Typically, these systems have a separate network adapter for each network that they are connected to. Also, information sent through the firewall is subject to filtering.

Frame   This is a data structure that network hardware devices use to transmit data between computers. Frames consist of the addresses of the sending and receiving computers, size information, and a checksum. Frames are envelopes around packets of data that allow them to be addressed to specific computers on a shared media network. *See also* Ethernet, Fiber Distributed Data Interface (FDDI), Token Ring.

Fresh Data   Data retrieved from cache that is confirmed as being current and consistent with the source. *See also* Cache Consistency, Stale Data.

Friendly Name   The host name of a system that is used instead of its IP address. For instance, www.sybex.com is the friendly name for its IP address 206.100.29.83.

FTP   *See* File Transfer Protocol (FTP).

Full-Duplex   A method of transmitting information over an asynchronous communications channel in which signals may be sent in both directions simultaneously. This technique makes the best use of line time but substantially increases the amount of logic required in the primary and secondary stations.

Garbage Collection   This is the removal of obsolete or unutilized objects from the cache.

Gateway   In e-mail systems, this is a system used to send and receive e-mail from a different e-mail system, such as a mainframe or the Internet. Gateways are supported by Message Handling Services (MHS).

Gopher   An Internet tool that organizes topics into a menu system that users can employ to find information. Gopher also transparently connects users with the Internet server on which the information resides.

Gopher Plus   An extended version of Gopher that includes file, author, and document information. Also, information can be displayed as regular text, rich text, and PostScript.

GOSIP   *See* Government OSI Profile (GOSIP).

Government OSI Profile (GOSIP)   A U.S Government procurement specification for Open Systems Interconnection (OSI) protocols. *See also* Open System Interconnection (OSI).

Half-Duplex   A method of transmitting information over a communication channel in which signals may be sent in both directions but only one way at a time. This method is sometimes referred to as local echo.

Handshaking   In network communication, this process is used to verify that a connection has been established correctly. Devices send signals back and forth to establish parameters for communication.

Hardware Address   *See* Media Access Control (MAC) Address.

Header   Information that is located at the beginning of a data packet and that usually defines the source and destination, and sometimes the route.

Hit Rate   The term is usually applied to caching as the number of requests that are filled with cached information out of the total requests sent to the Web Proxy Server.

Home Directory   The root directory of a given service. The home directory contains files relative to that service. For example, the home directory or default directory for the WWW service will contain HTML files. By default, all users have access to this directory and any subdirectories below it.

Home Page   The root Web page of a given Internet resource. *See also* Web Page.

Hop   In routing, a server or router that is counted in a hop count.

Hop Count   The number of routers a message must pass through to reach its destination. A hop count is used to determine the most efficient network route.

Host   An addressable computer system on a TCP/IP network. Examples would include endpoint systems such as workstations, servers, minicomputers, and mainframes and immediate systems such as routers. A host is typically a system that offers resources to network nodes.

Host Name   A TCP/IP command that returns the local workstation's host name used for authentication by TCP/IP utilities. This value is the workstation's computer name by default, but it can be changed by using the Network icon in Control Panel.

Host Table   The HOSTS or LMHOSTS file that contains lists of known IP addresses.

Host-to-Host Layer   The DOD model layer that is equivalent to the Transport layer of the OSI model. *See also* Transport Layer.

HTML   *See* Hypertext Markup Language (HTML).

HTTP   *See* Hypertext Transfer Protocol (HTTP).

HTTPD Server   A system which is identical to a Web server and operates as a daemon-type process. This server uses HTTP for its chief means of communicating with clients. *See also* Daemon, Hypertext Transfer Protocol (HTTP).

Hub   An Ethernet Data Link layer device that connects point-to-point physical layer links, such as twisted pair or fiber-optic cables, into a single, shared media network. *See also* Data Link Layer, Ethernet.

Hyperlink   A link to an Internet resource, such as a Web site or a file. These links are commonly displayed in a color other than text. A hyperlink may also be associated with a picture. Clicking a hyperlink will move a user to a resource or download a given file.

Hypertext   A text-based document that contains entries known as hyperlinks that connect to other documents, files, or Internet resources.

Hypertext Markup Language (HTML)   The standard format used to publish information on the World Wide Web.

Hypertext Transfer Protocol (HTTP)   The communications standard by which Internet resource information is retrieved by clients.

IAB *See* Internet Activities Board (IAB).

ICMP *See* Internet Control Message Protocol (ICMP).

IEEE *See* Institute of Electrical and Electronics Engineers (IEEE).

IETF *See* Internet Engineering Task Force (IETF).

IESG *See* Internet Engineering Steering Group (IESG).

IGP *See* Interior Gateway Protocol (IGP).

IIS *See* Internet Information Server (IIS).

Institute of Electrical and Electronics Engineers (IEEE) A professional American National Standards Institute–accredited body of scientists and engineers based in the United States. IEEE promotes standardization and acts as a consultant to the ANSI on matters relating to electrical and electronic development. The IEEE 802 Standards Committee is the leading official standards organization for LANs.

Integrated Services Digital Network (ISDN) A new network standard that allows high-speed communication over ordinary category 3 or 5 copper cabling. It may someday replace conventional phone systems with high-speed, digital lines. When originally developed, the product did not perform as expected and earned joke acronyms such as It Still Does Nothing and I Still Don't kNow. Today, ISDN is a viable alternative to expensive leased lines and frame relay communications.

Intelligent TTL (Time-to-Live) An algorithm that is used with caching services to extend the useful life for stored objects that are frequently requested. When the object is requested, a new TTL is assigned to the object based on the remaining TTL.

Interactive Applications A program or script that a user can access via a hyperlink. These programs are often written in C, Perl, Java, or as a Windows NT batch file. An example of this is the setup program stored on the Proxy Web Server used to configure WinSock Clients.

Interior Gateway Protocol (IGP) The protocol used to exchange routing information between collaborating routers in the Internet. RIP and OSPF are examples of IGPs.

International Standards Organizations (ISO) A world-wide federation of national standards bodies whose objective is to promote the development of standardization and related activities in over 90 countries, with a view to facilitating international exchange of goods and services.

Internet A global network made up of a large number of individual networks interconnected through the use of TCP/IP protocols. The individual networks comprising the Internet are from colleges, universities, businesses, research organizations, government agencies, individuals, and other bodies. The governing body of this global network is the Internet Activities Board (IAB). When the term *Internet* is used with an uppercase *I*, it refers to the global network. With a lowercase *i*, it simply means a group of interconnected networks.

Internet Activities Board (IAB)   The technical body that oversees the development of the Internet suite of protocols (commonly referred to as TCP/IP). It has two task forces (the IRTF and the IETF), each responsible for investigating a particular area.

Internet Address   A 32-bit value displayed in numbers that specifies a particular network and a particular node on that network.

Internet Control Message Protocol (ICMP)   A protocol at the Internet layer of the DOD model that sends messages between routers and other devices, letting them know about congested routes.

Internet Engineering Steering Group (IESG)   The executive committee of the IETF.

Internet Engineering Task Force (IETF)   One of the task forces of the IAB. The IETF is responsible for solving short-term engineering needs on the Internet. It has over 40 working groups.

Internet Information Server (IIS)   The Microsoft solution to Internet server services. By default, the product delivers WWW, FTP, and gopher services. IIS is included with Windows NT and is the base product from which Microsoft Proxy Server is built.

Internet Layer   The layer in the DOD model that relates to the Network layer of the OSI model. *See also* Network Layer.

Internet Network Information Center (InterNIC)   The organization responsible for DNS name and IP address assignments used on the Internet. They may be contacted at their Web site: rs.internic.net. *See also* Domain Name System (DNS), Internet Protocol (IP) Address.

Internet Protocol (IP)   The Network layer protocol upon which the Internet is based. IP provides a simple connectionless packet exchange. Other protocols, such as UDP or TCP, use IP to perform their connection-oriented or guaranteed delivery services. *See also* Internet, Transmission Control Protocol/Internet Protocol (TCP/IP).

Internet Protocol (IP) Address   A four-byte number that uniquely identifies a computer on an IP internetwork. InterNIC assigns the first bytes of Internet IP addresses and administers them in hierarchies. Huge organizations like the government or top-level Internet service providers (ISP) have Class A addresses. In a Class A address, InterNIC assigns the first byte, and the owning organization assigns the remaining three bytes. Large organizations and most ISPs have Class B addresses. In a Class B address, InterNIC or the higher-level ISP assigns the first two bytes, and the organization assigns the remaining two bytes. Small companies have Class C addresses. In a Class C address, InterNIC or the higher-level ISP assigns the first three bytes, and the organization assigns the remaining byte. Organizations not attached to the Internet can assign IP addresses as they please. *See also* Internet, Internet Protocol (IP).

Internet Relay Chat (IRC)   A standard, text-based, communication protocol that is used in chat rooms on supporting sites. This type of communication is like a room where people talk by typing their messages.

Internet Research Task Force (IRTF)   This is one of the task forces of the IAB. The IRTF is responsible for research and development of the Internet protocol suite.

Internet Server Application Programming Interface (ISAPI) This is the Microsoft Proxy Server application programming interface that establishes a method by which programs can communicate with the proxy server to extend its abilities. ISAPI is also used internally by the proxy server.

Internet Service Providers (ISPs) ISPs are companies that provide organizations and end-users with Internet access. Each ISP purchases bandwidth from a participating telecommunications company or from another ISP that buys bandwidth and then resells it to subscibers.

Internetwork Packet eXchange (IPX) The Network and Transport layer protocol developed by Novell for its NetWare product. IPX is a routable, connection-oriented protocol similar to TCP/IP but much easier to manage and with lower communication overhead. *See also* Internet Protocol (IP).

Internetworking The process of connecting multiple local area networks (LANs) to form a wide area network (WAN). Internetworking between different types of networks is handled by a router.

InterNIC *See* Internet Network Information Center (InterNIC).

Intranet Any private TCP/IP-based network. These networks typically include WWW, FTP, and other services; however, there is no requirement to have any of these services on the network. These networks may be directly connected to the Internet or connected via Proxy Server or a firewall. *See also* Firewall, Proxy.

IP *See* Internet Protocol (IP).

IP Address *See* Internet Protocol (IP) Address.

IP Tunnel A software driver that permits the encapsulation of IPX packets inside of IP packets for transmission over an IP network. This allows NetWare servers to communicate through links that support only TCP/IP, such as those used by UNIX machines.

IPX External Network Number A number that is used to represent an entire network. All servers on the network must use the same external network number.

IPX Internal Network Number A number that uniquely identifies a server to the network. Each server must have a different internal network number.

IPX/SPX *See* Internetwork Packet eXchange (IPX), Sequenced Packet Exchange (SPX).

IRTF *See* Internet Research Task Force (IRTF).

ISAPI *See* Internet Server Application Programming Interface (ISAPI).

ISDN *See* Integrated Services Digital Network (ISDN).

ISO *See* International Standards Organizations (ISO).

IUSR_systemname A default account with anonymous logon privileges for accessing Internet-based services, such as FTP, WWW, and Gopher. This account is created during Microsoft Internet Information Server installation.

LAN *See* Local Area Network (LAN).

LAT *See* Local Address Table (LAT).

Leased Line A line that is leased from a telecommunications company and used in wide area networking. Capacities of these lines vary according to what you order. *See also* Dedicated Line.

Least Recently Used (LRU) This is a term that refers to a process of discarding data that is has not been used as recently as all other cached objects.

Link *See* Hyperlink.

LMHOSTS File A text-based file that is used as a static routing table in Microsoft Windows NT Server to authenticate and register valid IP addresses and associated user-friendly domain names for IP nodes in a local TCP/IP network. Typically, this file is used with NetBIOS names; however, host names may be resolved from it.

Local Address Table (LAT) This is the table of local IP addresses on the private network that is distributed to clients. This table is used to determine if a client is local or not. Often referred to as the LAT, this table is maintained at the Proxy Server and is stored in a text file called MSPLAT.TXT. Clients download this file periodically to C:\MSP\CLIENTS.

Local Area Network (LAN) This is a network that is restricted to a local area—a single building, group of buildings, or even a single room. A LAN often has only one server, but it can have many if desired.

Local Procedure Call (LPC) This is a mechanism that loops remote procedure calls without the presence of a network so that the client and server portion of an application can reside on the same machine. Local procedure calls look like remote procedure calls (RPCs) to the client and server sides of a distributed application.

Log File A file that contains event listings for a service or object being monitored. Output can be either a text file or a database file.

Logging The monitoring of events as they pertain to a service or object. In the case of Microsoft Proxy Server, logs are maintained by packet filtering, the Web Proxy service, the WinSock Proxy service, the Socks Proxy service, and itself. Logs regarding the proxy server's internal operations are established through the event viewer. Logs regarding services are maintained either in a text file or in an ODBC/SQL database.

LPC *See* Local Procedure Call (LPC).

LRU *See* Least Recently Used (LRU).

MAC Address *See* Media Access Control (MAC) Address.

Mailslots A connectionless messaging IPC mechanism that Windows NT uses for browser requests and logon authentication.

MAN *See* Metropolitan Area Network (MAN).

Management Information Base (MIB) The entire set of objects that any service or protocol uses in SNMP. Because different network management services are used for different types of devices or for different network management protocols, each service has its own set of objects.

Map Translating one value into another.

Master Browser The computer on a network that maintains a list of computers and services available on the network and distributes the list to other browsers. The master browser may also promote potential browsers to be browsers. *See also* Browser, Browsing, Potential Browser.

Media Access Control (MAC) Address This is a hardware address burned into the Network Interface cards. It is six bytes long; three of the bytes are given to the manufacture from the IEEE, and three bytes are designated by the manufacturer.

Member Server A server that is joined to a Windows NT domain but is not a domain controller. *See also* Backup Domain Controller (BDC), Primary Domain Controller (PDC).

Message Switching A type of network communication that sends an entire message or a block of data, rather than a simple packet.

Metric Data that is measurable and comparable is some manner in analyzing system information.

Metropolitan Area Network (MAN) A network spanning a single city or metropolitan area. A MAN is larger than a local area network (LAN), which is normally restricted to a single building or neighboring buildings, but smaller than a wide area network (WAN), which can span the entire globe.

MIB *See* Management Information Database (MIB).

MILitary NETwork (MILNET) Originally part of the ARPANET, MILNET was partitioned in 1984 to make it possible for military installations to have reliable network service; the ARPANET continued to be used for research.

MILNET *See* MILitary NETwork (MILNET).

MIME mapping *See* Multipurpose Internet Mail Extension (MIME) mapping.

Modem A device used to convert the digital signals produced by a computer into the analog signals required by analog telephone lines and vice versa. This process of conversion allows computers to communicate across telephone lines.

Multihomed Host A computer connected to more than one physical data link. The data links may or may not be attached to the same network.

Multilink   A capability of RAS to combine multiple data streams into one network connection for the purpose of using more than one modem or ISDN channel in a single connection. This feature is new to Windows NT 4.0.

Multipurpose Internet Mail Extension (MIME) mapping   A method by which browsers are configured to read files that are arranged in multiple formats. We commonly see attached files in e-mail as MIME-encoded attachments.

Name Resolution   The finding of an IP address from a HOST or NetBIOS name.

Named Pipes   This is an inter-process communication mechanism that is implemented as a file system service, allowing programs to be modified to run on it without using a proprietary application programming interface. Named pipes were developed to support more robust client/server communications than those allowed by the simpler NetBIOS.

Negative Caching   The caching of HTTP error conditions related to a URL. When a URL is unavailable, the error response message can be cached and returned to subsequent clients that request the same URL without wasting time with the timeout.

NetBEUI   *See* Network Basic Input/Output System Extended User Interface (NetBEUI).

NetBIOS   A client/server inter-process communication service developed by IBM in the early 1980s. NetBIOS presents a relatively primitive mechanism for communication in client/server applications, but its widespread acceptance and availability across most operating systems makes it a logical choice for simple network applications. Many Windows NT network IPC mechanisms are implemented over NetBIOS.

NetBIOS over TCP/IP (NetBT)   A network service that implements the NetBIOS IPC over the TCP/IP protocol stack. *See also* Network Basic Input/Output System Extended User Interface (NetBEUI), Transmission Control Protocol/Internet Protocol.

Network Address   A unique address that identifies each node or device on the network. The network address is generally hard-coded into the network card on both the workstation and server. Some network cards allow you to change this address, but there is seldom a reason to do so.

Network Basic Input/Output System Extended User Interface (NetBEUI)   The primary local area network transport protocol in Windows NT. It's a simple Network layer transport developed to support NetBIOS installations. NetBEUI is not routable, and so it is not appropriate for larger networks. NetBEUI is the fastest transport protocol available for Windows NT.

Network File System (NFS)   A distributed file system developed by Sun Microsystems which allows a set of computers to cooperatively access each other's files in a transparent manner.

Network Information Center (NIC)   Originally there was only one NIC, located at SRI International and tasked to serve the ARPANET (and later the DDN) community. Today, there are many NICs operated by local, regional, and national networks all over the world. Such centers provide user assistance, document service, training, and much more.

Network Interface Card (NIC) Physical devices that connect computers and other network equipment to the transmission medium used. When installed in a computer's expansion bus slot, an NIC allows the computer to become a workstation on the network.

Network Layer The layer of the OSI model that creates a communication path between two computers via routed packets. Transport protocols implement both the Network layer and the Transport layer of the OSI stack. IP is a Network layer service.

Network News Transfer Protocol (NNTP) A standardized protocol used for reading messages posted in news groups on the Internet.

Network Operating System (NOS) The software that runs on a file server and offers file, print, and other services to client workstations. Windows NT Server 4 is an NOS. Other examples include NetWare, Banyan VINES, and IBM LAN Server.

NFS *See* Network File System (NFS).

NIC *See* Network Information Center (NIC), Network Interface Card (NIC).

NNTP *See* Network News Transfer Protocol (NNTP).

Node In TCP/IP, this is an IP addressable computer system, such as workstations, servers, minicomputers, mainframes, and routers. In IPX networks, the term is usually applied to non-server devices such as workstations and printers.

NOS *See* Network Operating System (NOS).

Object-Cache Scavenger A procedure that reviews the cache for items to be discarded. This includes items that are not very popular, even if the item's TTL has not expired.

Object Modification Checking A caching service feature that checks data integrity against a source. When data is current, it is returned to the cache; otherwise, a new copy is obtained.

Octets A set of eight bits or one byte.

ODBC *See* Open Database Connectivity (ODBC).

Open Database Connectivity (ODBC) A database interchange standard that allows programs to communicate with a database system without being specifically designed for it.

Open Shortest Path First (OSPF) OSPF is a function by which the path with the shortest number of hops is used to establish a connection. In this way, data will arrive at a destination in a shorter amount of time and with less overhead.

Open System Interconnection (OSI) A model defined by the ISO to conceptually organize the process of communication between computers in terms of seven layers, called protocol stacks. The seven layers of the OSI model help you to understand how communication across various protocols takes place.

OSI *See* Open System Interconnection (OSI).

OSPF *See* Open Shortest Path First (OSPF).

Packet The basic division of data sent over a network. Each packet contains a set amount of data along with a header, which contains information about the type of packet and the network address to which it is being sent. The size and format of packets depends on the protocol and frame types used.

Packet Internet Groper (PING) A packet used to test how easily destinations can be reached by sending them an ICMP echo request and waiting for a reply. The term is used as a verb: "Ping host A to see if it is up."

Packet Switching A type of data transmission in which data is divided into packets, each of which has a destination address. Each packet is then routed across a network in an optimal fashion. An addressed packet may travel a different route than packets related to it. Packet sequence numbers are used at the destination node to reassemble related packets.

Packets A unit of information transmitted as a whole from one device to another on a network.

Passive Caching A common type of caching in which requested Internet data is stored. When clients request the same information, the data is pulled from the cache. This is often referred to as on-demand caching. Note that not all data is cached and that it must meet certain criteria before being stored.

Password Authentication *See* Authentication.

PDC *See* Primary Domain Controller (PDC).

Peer-to-Peer Communication A networked computer that shares resources with other computers and also accesses the shared resources of other computers.

Peer-to-Peer Network A local area network in which network resources are shared among workstations without a file server.

Peer Web Services A scaled-down version of IIS designed for Windows NT Workstation. These services allow personal material to be published. The services include WWW, FTP, and Gopher.

Physical Layer The cables, connectors, and connection ports of a network. These are the passive physical components required to create a network.

Ping *See* Packet Internet Groper (PING).

Point-to-Point Protocol (PPP) The predecessor to SLIP, PPP is the standard communications for Windows dial-up networking. PPP operates via analog modems and standard telephone lines. PPP implementations can vary from vendor to vendor. This protocol allows the sending of IP packets on a dial-up (serial) connection. It supports compression and IP address negotiation.

Point-to-Point Tunneling Protocol (PPTP) A protocol designed to allow wide area connections via the Internet. PPTP provides full security and multiple protocol encapsulation.

Policies The rules that are set by a company and implemented by an administrator. Policies include use of Internet services, expiration of passwords, etc.

Polling The process by which a computer periodically asks each terminal or device on a LAN if it has a message to send and then allows each to send data in turn. On a multipoint connection or a point-to-point connection, polling is the process whereby data stations are invited, one at a time, to transmit data.

Port A designated number that defines an application in the TCP/IP communications process. For example, the port number for WWW is 80.

Potential Browser A computer on a network that may maintain a list of other computers and services on the network if requested to do so by a master browser.

PPP *See* Point-to-Point Protocol (PPP).

PPTP *See* Point-to-Point Tunneling Protocol (PPTP).

Presentation Layer That layer of the OSI model that converts and translates (if necessary) information between the Session and Application layers.

Primary Domain Controller (PDC) The domain server that contains the master copy of the security, computer, and user accounts databases and that can authenticate workstations. The primary domain controller can replicate its databases to one or more backup domain controllers and is usually also the master browser for the domain. *See also* Backup Domain Controller (BDC), Member Server.

Process/Application Layer The upper layer in the DOD model that refers to the Application, Presentation, and Session layers of the OSI model.

Program File A file that has can be run or that can be used to start an application. Typically, these files have an extension of .EXE, .PIF, .COM, .CMD, or .BAT.

Protocol A model for accomplishing a given task. In computers, there are many types of protocols; however, most protocols pertain to communication.

Protocol Suite A collection of protocols that are associated with a particular communication model and that implement a particular communication model (such as the DOD networking model or the OSI reference model).

Proxy An intermediary device that indirectly connects two systems.

Proxy Client A system that uses a proxy server or host to gain access to a service or object that can not be reached directly (logically or physically).

Proxy Host The intermediary system that acts as a relay between clients and servers. Communications to servers is established from the proxy host (or server) on the behalf of the client.

Proxy ISAPI Application   A dynamic linked library (DLL) that serves as an active, in-process device for extending Web server functionality. The Proxy ISAPI application provides client authentication, domain filtering, cache searching for requested objects, retrieval of requested objects from the Internet as necessary, updating cached data, and so on.

Proxy ISAPI Filter   A dynamic linked library (DLL) that is called by Microsoft Proxy Server (or a Web server). The Proxy ISAPI filter determines if a client-initiated HTTP request is to be treated as a proxy request. If so, it is handled by the Web Proxy service and forwarded to the Proxy ISAPI application. Otherwise, the request is forwarded as a standard HTTP request.

PSTN   *See* Public Switched Telephone Network (PSTN).

Public Switched Telephone Network (PSTN)   A global network of interconnected digital and analog communication links originally designed to support voice communication between any two points in the world. PSTN was quickly adapted to handle digital data traffic when the computer revolution occurred. In addition to its traditional voice support role, the PSTN now functions as the Physical layer of the Internet by providing dial-up services and leased lines for private and public use.

RARP   *See* Reverse Address Resolution Protocol (RARP).

RAS   *See* Remote Access Service (RAS).

RealAudio   A protocol designed for streaming audio. This protocol operates on UDP and is supported by Microsoft Proxy Server. The RealAudio Player operates as a stand-alone application or it can be integrated into a Web browser.

Registry   Windows NT combined configuration database.

Remote Access Service (RAS)   An add-on service to Windows NT that allows remote client computers (RAS clients) to establish a link that places their system on the network. RAS supports operating systems including MS-DOS, Microsoft Windows, or Windows NT. RAS is also used for its PPP abilities to dial into an Internet Service Provider.

Remote Administration   Administering a system from another computer.

Remote Procedure Call (RPC)   A message-passing facility that allows a distributed application to call services that are available on various computers in a network.

Request for Comments (RFCs)   The set of standards defining the Internet protocols as determined by the Internet Engineering Task Force and available in the public domain on the Internet. RFCs define the functions and services provided by each of the many Internet protocols. Compliance with RFC standards guarantees cross-vendor compatibility.

Retrieve Rate   The speed that data is pulled from the cache.

Reverse Address Resolution Protocol (RARP)   The TCP/IP protocol that allows a computer with a Physical layer address (such as an Ethernet address) but not an IP address to request a numeric IP address from another computer on the network.

RFCs *See* Request for Comments (RFCs).

RIP *See* Router Information Protocol (RIP).

Router One definition is a device that connects two dissimilar networks and allows packets to be transmitted and received between them. A router can also be a connection between two networks that specifies message paths and may perform other functions, such as data compression.

Router Information Protocol (RIP) A distance vector routing protocol used on many TCP/IP internetworks and IPX networks. The distance vector algorithm uses a "fewest hops" routing calculation method.

RPC *See* Remote Procedure Call (RPC).

Script A set of commands that are compiled into a file. Script files include CGI-based scripts, Windows NT batch files, and so on. *See also* Common Gateway Interface.

Secure Sockets Layer (SSL) A secure data communication protocol that offers data encryption and decryption.

Sequenced Packet Exchange (SPX) The connection-based transport protocol developed for use in Novell networks. SPX is comparable to the Transmission Control Protocol (TCP) used in TCP/IP. *See also* Connected Service, Internetwork Packet Exchange (IPX).

Serial A method of communication that transfers data across a medium one bit at a time, usually adding stop, start, and check bits to ensure a quality transfer.

Serial Line Internet Protocol (SLIP) A protocol that permits the sending of IP packets on a dial-up (serial) connection. SLIP does not support compression or IP address negotiation by itself.

Server Message Block (SMB) Protocol The communications system that is used between two Windows NT–based systems. This is equivalent to Novell NetWare's Network Core Protocol.

Service A program that adds functionality to a system. Under Windows NT, services include DNS, WINS, DHCP, etc. As applied to IIS, services include WWW, Gopher, and FTP. As applied to Microsoft Proxy Server, these services include Socks Proxy, Packet Filtering, Web Proxy, and WinSock Proxy.

Session Layer The layer of the OSI model dedicated to maintaining a bidirectional communication connection between two computers. The Session layer uses the services of the Transport layer to provide this service.

Simple Mail Transport Protocol (SMTP) This is the Internet electronic mail protocol. SMTP is defined in RFC 821, with an associated message format description in RFC 822.

Simple Network Management Protocol (SNMP) A management protocol used on many networks, particularly TCP/IP. It defines the type, format, and retrieval of node management information. *See also* Management Information Database (MIB).

Simplex   Data transmission in one direction only.

SLIP   *See* Serial Line Interface Protocol (SLIP).

SMTP   *See* Simple Mail Transfer Protocol (SMTP).

SNMP   *See* Simple Network Management Protocol (SNMP).

Socket   A designated communications channel used by TCP/IP applications. Sockets are logical data structures created by using a combination of device IP addresses and reserved TCP/UDP port numbers.

Socks   A standard by which clients communicate via TCP/IP. This is the basis for other developed standards such as WinSocks. UNIX and Macintosh clients both utilize Socks. As applied to Microsoft Proxy Server, it supports version 4.3a of Socks.

SPX   *See* Sequenced Packet Exchange (SPX).

SSL   *See* Secure Sockets Layer (SSL).

Stale Data   Data stored in the cache whose TTL has expired or that no longer matches its source.

Standard Proxy Protocol   Another way to refer to the standard CERN protocol that defines proxy connectivity for proxy-aware applications. *See also* CERN-Proxy Protocol.

Start Bit   A bit that is sent as part of a serial communication stream to signal the beginning of a byte or packet.

Static Page   An HTML page that is not dynamic and is prepared in advance of a request. No special actions are required with these pages. *See also* Interactive Applications.

Stop Bit   A bit that is sent as part of a serial communication stream to signal the end of a byte or packet.

Subnet Mask   Under TCP/IP, 32-bit values that allow the recipient of IP packets to distinguish the network ID portion of the IP address from the host ID.

Switched Line   A communications link (such as the public telephone network) for which the physical path may vary with each use.

Synchronous   Pertaining to two or more processes that depend upon the occurrence of a specific event, such as a common timing signal.

Tag File   A file that typically contains information about files on a Gopher server in addition to the file name that you are accessing, the host name of the system that contains the data, and the port number of the service.

TCP   *See* Transmission Control Protocol (TCP).

TCP/IP *See* Transmission Control Protocol/Internet Protocol (TCP/IP).

Telnet A TCP/IP terminal emulation protocol that permits a node, called the Telnet client, to log into a remote node, called the Telnet server. The client simply acts as a dumb terminal, displaying output from the server. The processing is done at the server.

Terminal Emulation The process of emulating a terminal, or allowing a PC to act as a terminal for a mainframe or UNIX system.

Time-to-Live (TTL) A designation that defines the expiration of a piece of information. As applied to Microsoft Proxy Server, cached items are assigned a TTL value to ensure freshness. TTL originates from a field in a TCP/IP header that notifies receiving stations if data is still valid or should be discarded.

TLP *See* Transport Layer Protocol (TLP).

Token Passing *See* Token Ring.

Token Ring The second most popular Data Link layer standard for local area networking. Token Ring implements the token passing method of arbitrating multiple-computer access to the same network. Token Ring operates at either 4MB or 16MB. FDDI is similar to Token Ring and operates at 100Mbps. *See also* Data Link Layer.

Topology The wiring and configuration that comprises a network. Examples of topologies are star, ring, bus, mesh, and point-to-point. Commonly, the wiring type is used to designate the topology, such as Ethernet, Token Ring, or Arc Net.

Transmission Control Protocol (TCP) The connection-based transport protocol from the TCP/IP suite.

Transmission Control Protocol/Internet Protocol (TCP/IP) A protocol suite that is a standard for Internet communications. Many operating systems, including Windows, UNIX, and Mac, support this protocol.

Transport Layer The OSI model layer responsible for the guaranteed serial delivery of packets between two computers over an internetwork. TCP is the Transport layer protocol for the TCP/IP transport protocol.

Transport Layer Protocol (TLP) Implements guaranteed packet delivery using the Internet Protocol (IP).

Transport Protocol A service that delivers discrete packets of information between any two computers in a network. Higher level connection-oriented services are built on transport protocols.

TTL *See* Time-to-Live (TTL).

UDP *See* User Datagram Protocol (UDP).

UNC *See* Universal Naming Convention (UNC).

Uniform Resource Locator (URL) A standard addressing convention that is used to uniquely locate any object on the Internet. Information includes the location of a host system, directory, or file on the Internet. A URL specifies the protocol used to read a resource, such as Gopher, HTTP, and so on. An example of a URL is `http://www.sybex.com`.

Universal Naming Convention (UNC) A multivendor, multiplatform convention for identifying shared resources on a network.

UNIX A multitasking operating system, created by AT&T's Bell Labs, that is used on a wide variety of computers, including Internet servers.

URL *See* Uniform Resource Locator (URL).

Usenet The most popular newsgroup hierarchy on the Internet.

UseNet A massive, distributed database of news feeds and special interest groups maintained on the Internet and accessible through most Web browsers.

User Datagram Protocol (UDP) A non-guaranteed network packet protocol implemented on IP that is far faster than TCP because it doesn't have flow-control overhead. UDP can be implemented as a reliable transport when some higher-level protocol (such as NetBIOS) exists to make sure that required data eventually will be retransmitted in local area environments.

VDOLive Player An application that provides stream-oriented service for continuous video imaging. VDOLive Player can be configured to either integrate with a Web browser such as Internet Explorer or operate on its own.

Virtual Directory The Windows NT IIS counterpart to a symbolic directory in UNIX. These directories appear to clients as subdirectories of a home directory; however, they are not. The WWW, Gopher, and FTP services of IIS offer this ability. Note that a virtual directory may be located on a different system.

Volatile Objects Objects that change or are changed frequently. An example is stock market data displayed on a Web page.

WAN *See* Wide Area Network (WAN).

Web Browser An application such as Netscape Navigator or Internet Explorer that is used to read HTML documents published on a Web server. The document is displayed in graphical format. Web browsers also contain the ability to anonymously transfer files (FTP Read) and in many cases offer additional services such as an e-mail client.

Web Page A document published on a Web server. A Web page is the primary interface that we access to view a site's information, retrieve files, spawn sounds, etc. When viewing a URL, it can be said that you are viewing that site's Web page. The root Web page is often referred to as a home page.

Web Proxy Service   This service provides a means for Microsoft Proxy Server to act as a proxy host.

Web Server   A host system that publishes Web pages. Microsoft's version of a Web server is include with Internet Information Server (IIS). Typically, a Web server offers HTTP, FTP, and Gopher protocols.

Wide Area Network (WAN)   A network that extends across multiple locations. Each location typically has a local area network (LAN) and the LANs are connected together to form a WAN. WANs are typically used for enterprise networking.

Windows Internet Name Service (WINS) Server   A network service for Microsoft networks that provides Windows computers with Internet numbers for specified NetBIOS names, facilitating browsing and intercommunication over TCP/IP networks.

Windows NT Challenge/Response Authentication   An authentication method developed by Microsoft to provide secure access to clients. This type of authentication encodes a user name and password such that they can't be read by decoding packet information.

Windows Sockets (WinSock)   A standardized set of procedures and program calls that are used by an application to communicate via TCP/IP. Windows Sockets are often referred to as WinSock. WinSock is an extension of UNIX Socks and is native to Windows. *See also* Socket.

WINS Server   *See* Windows Internet Name Service (WINS) Server.

WinSock   *See* Windows Sockets (WinSock).

WinSock Proxy Service   The proxy server responsible for servicing Internet requests from WinSock-compatible applications.

World Wide Web (WWW)   A term used for the collection of computers on the Internet running HTTP (Hypertext Transfer Protocol) servers. The WWW allows for text and graphics to have hyperlinks, which connect users to other servers. Using a Web browser, a user can cross-link from one server to another at the click of a button.

WWW   *See* World Wide Web (WWW).

Index

NOTE: Page numbers in *italics* refer to figures or tables; page numbers in **bold** refer to significant discussions of the topic.

O

S

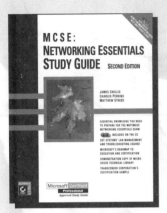
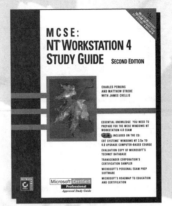

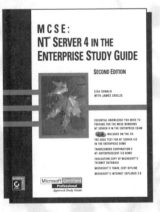
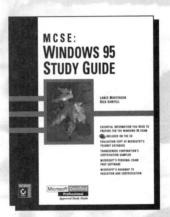

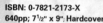

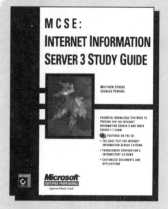
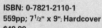
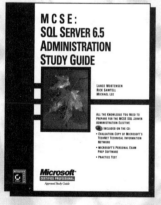

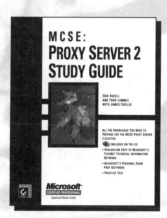

Exam Objectives for 70-088: Implementing and Supporting Microsoft® Proxy Server 2.0